Freedom's Coming

Freedom's Coming

Religious Culture and the Shaping
of the South from the Civil War
through the Civil Rights Era

PAUL HARVEY

The University of North Carolina Press

Chapel Hill and London

© 2005 The University of North Carolina Press
All rights reserved
Manufactured in the United States of America

Designed by April Leidig-Higgins
Set in Minion by Copperline Book Services, Inc.

The paper in this book meets the guidelines for
permanence and durability of the Committee on
Production Guidelines for Book Longevity of the
Council on Library Resources.

Library of Congress Cataloging-in-Publication Data
Harvey, Paul, 1961–
Freedom's coming: religious culture and the shaping
of the South from the Civil War through the civil
rights era / Paul Harvey.
p. cm. Includes bibliographical references and index.
ISBN 0-8078-2901-3 (cloth: alk. paper)
1. Southern States—Church history.   2. Southern
States—Race relations—History.   3. Protestant
churches—Southern States—History.   4. Race
relations—Religious aspects—Christianity—
History.   I. Title.
BR535.H38   2005
277.5'082—dc22   2004013687

09 08 07 06 05   5 4 3 2 1

Publication of this work was aided by a generous
grant from the Z. Smith Reynolds Foundation.

for Leon F. Litwack
and Samuel S. Hill
"tell about the South"

Contents

Illustrations

Acknowledgments

As this book shows, "freedom's coming" has many meanings. Having worked on the subject of religion and race in the South for nearly twenty years now, perhaps "freedom's coming" is, for me, the long-awaited end of this book project. Yet, I wouldn't trade anything for the journey, which has taken me across the country in search of treasure troves in libraries and archives, introduced me to a generous cast of people in and out of academia and religious communities, and inspired me to think deeply about questions at the heart of American history.

I have been blessed with generosity from people, granting agencies, librarians and archivists, and institutions too numerous to mention. Early in the project, a grant from the Louisville Institute got me started, and assistance from the University of Colorado's Committee on Research and Creative Works provided funding for research travel. Subsequent research grants from the American Academy of Religion Research Grant Program, the Women's Studies Research Grant Program at Duke University, the "Behind the Veil" Project Research Grant also at Duke, and the Gilder Lehrman Institute of American History provided the resources for extensive research trips to libraries and archives stretching from New Orleans to New York. Very late into the project, after I turned in the original manuscript, research funds from the Institute for Oral History at Baylor University and the University of Wisconsin Friends of the Library Fellowship provided for supplementary archival time that enriched the last two chapters of the book. A year's leave provided by the National Endowment for the Humanities in 1999–2000 provided me the intellectual space for writing most of the first draft of the manuscript. In the spring of 2001, a semester's support at the Virginia Foundation for the Humanities in Charlottesville afforded me intellectual companionship (as well as evenings of fried chicken and cheap pinot noir and listening to Billie Holiday and Brahms) for which I will ever be grateful—and for that, I am ever in the debt of Roberta Culbertson and Nancy Damon of the foundation, and my fellow fellows and treasured friends Anne Jones, Ralph Luker, Jahan Ramazani, Lauren Winner, and Grace Elizabeth Hale.

Over and over, librarians and archivists directed me to sources I would have missed or passed over too easily. I wish especially to thank Elizabeth Dunn of the Special Collections Library at Duke; the wonderful staff of the Southern Historical Collection in Chapel Hill; Harold Hunter of the Pentecostal Holiness Church Archives in Oklahoma City; Glenn Gohr of the Assemblies of God Archives in Springfield, Missouri; Bill Sumner of the Southern Baptist Historical Library and Archives in Nashville; Rebecca Hankins of the Amistad Research Center in New Orleans; and Laurie Williams of the interlibrary loan department at the University of Colorado in Colorado Springs.

Friends and colleagues gave extravagantly of their time to read portions or all of this manuscript. Several of them gave it ruthless and needed critiques and improved the work immeasurably as a result. Beth Schweiger of the University of Arkansas worked over my writing with her famously active red pen, and Colleen McDannell of the University of Utah raised probing questions and numerous useful suggestions. My good friend and co-editor of two other books, Philip Goff of the Center for the Study of Religion and American Culture at IUPUI, has been a steady source of help, as well as college hoops analysis, since our days together in the Young Scholars in American Religion program. David Chappell of the University of Arkansas has been a valued intellectual colleague and sparring partner over the material in Chapter 5. I also received help, support, advice, research notes, admonitions, laughter, crash pads, wine recommendations, and, of course, restaurant tips and baseball tickets from numerous other friends and colleagues along the way, including Donald G. Mathews, Glenda Gilmore, Jane Dailey, Fitzhugh Brundage, Clarence Walker, Waldo Martin, Andrew Manis, Barry Hankins, Will Glass, Randy Sparks, Xiaojian Zhao, Cita Cook, Randall Stephens, Tracy Fessenden, Anthea Butler, David Morgan, Yvonne Chireau, Joel Martin, Daniel Stowell, Karen Kossie, Greg Wills, Julia Walsh, Barbara Savage, Wayne Flynt, Charles Reagan Wilson, Ted Ownby, Larissa Smith, Pat Sullivan, Houston Roberson, Sarah Gardner, Emma Lapsansky, Julie Greene, Stephanie Paulsell, Sariya Jarasviroj, Sue Ann Marasco, and my valued colleagues in the History Department at CU–Colorado Springs, including Harlow Sheidley, Chris Hill, Rick Wunderli, Rob Sackett, Christina Jimenez, Jan Myers, and Judy Price.

The University of North Carolina Press has been a most supportive friend of three of my projects now. For that, thanks go especially to Elaine Maisner, who took in this prodigal son project and offered expert counsel throughout.

I have dedicated this work to two teacher-scholars who profoundly have influenced me both personally and professionally. As for Susan Nishida, freedom's coming is surely the end of this book project as well, for she has lived with it for nearly a decade, even while reminding me of the constant sacrament of praise and what it means to see it again for the first time.

Paul Harvey
July 2004

Abbreviations

AMA	American Missionary Association
AME	African Methodist Episcopal Church
AMEZ	African Methodist Episcopal Zion Church
ARIS	American Religious Identification Survey
ASWPL	Association of Southern Women for the Prevention of Lynching
CIC	Commission on Interracial Cooperation
CIO	Congress of Industrial Organizations
CLC	Christian Life Commission
CME	Colored Methodist Episcopal Church
COFO	Council of Federated Organizations
COGIC	Church of God in Christ
CORE	Congress of Racial Equality
FSC	Fellowship of Southern Churchmen
FOR	Fellowship of Reconciliation

MEC	Methodist Episcopal Church (alternately, Northern Methodists)
MECS	Methodist Episcopal Church, South (alternately, Southern Methodists)
NAACP	National Association for the Advancement of Colored People
NBC	National Baptist Convention
NCC	National Council of Churches
PCUS	Presbyterian Church of the United States (alternately, Southern Presbyterians)
PHC	Pentecostal Holiness Church
SBC	Southern Baptist Convention (alternately, Southern Baptists)
SCHW	Southern Conference for Human Welfare
SCLC	Southern Christian Leadership Conference
SIM	Student Interracial Ministry Program
SNCC	Student Non-Violent Coordinating Committee
SRC	Southern Regional Council
STFU	Southern Tenant Farmers Union
WCTU	Woman's Christian Temperance Union
WMU	Woman's Missionary Union of the Southern Baptist Convention
UCW	United Church Women (renamed Church Women United in 1971)

Freedom's Coming

I, myself, being a Deep South white, reared in a religious home and the Methodist church realize the deep ties of common songs, common prayer, common symbols that bind our two
races together on a religio-mystical level, even as another brutally mythic idea, the concept of
White Supremacy, tears our two people apart. — Lillian Smith to Martin Luther King Jr., 1956

We discussed that crap and it never did really soak in. Not as much as they thought it was
soaking in. — Money Alan Kirby, black Arkansan

Introduction

Freedom and Its Coming

In the early 1960s, freedom riders seeking to desegregate public transportation
took up this playful riff from a popular 1950s tune:

> Freedom, freedom, freedom's coming, and it won't be long
> Freedom, freedom, freedom's coming, and it won't be long.

But freedom would come only through constant struggle and suffering, as expressed in this song from some of the most difficult days in the civil rights
movement in Mississippi:

> They say that freedom is a constant struggle,
> They say that freedom is a constant struggle,
> Oh Lord, we've struggled so long,
> We must be free, we must be free.

Ultimately, freedom would come in what activists envisioned as the beloved
community—a utopian religious vision that inspired devotion and sacrifice
and, inevitably, created disappointment and disillusion.

From the Civil War through the civil rights movement, white and black evangelical Protestants in the South understood the history of their times as part of
sacred (albeit sometimes competing and contradictory) narratives about God's

intents and purposes in history. What did freedom mean, and what would it look like when it came? Was it coming in the sense of "having already come"? Was it *coming* in the immediate present, as portrayed in the freedom songs of the 1950s and 1960s? Or was it *coming* in a future, millennial sense? Generations of southern believers vividly expressed their struggles for spiritual freedom in song, sermon, tale, and dance. Meanwhile, many black and a few white Christians fought for freedom through social justice, another constant struggle from the Civil War through the civil rights movement.

The relationship and interaction of three key terms—"theological racism," "racial interchange," and "Christian interracialism"—best synthesize the fundamental argument of this book. *Freedom's Coming* traces how the theologically grounded Christian racism that was pervasive among white southerners eventually faltered, giving way to the more inclusive visions espoused in the black freedom struggle. Racial interchange in cultural expressions helped to undermine the oppressive hierarchies of the Jim Crow South. So did the constant struggle of black and white prophets who formed a southern evangelical counterculture of Christian interracialism. Ultimately, freedom's coming was based upon the joint and parallel efforts of generations of black and white southerners who envisioned and struggled toward the beloved community.

"Theological racism" refers here to the conscious use of religious doctrine and practice to create and enforce social hierarchies that privileged southerners of European descent, who were legally classified and socially privileged as white, while degrading southerners of African descent, who were legally categorized and socially stigmatized as black. White supremacy was a deep-rooted, interlocking system of power that enveloped white southerners in an imagined community, encompassing and stretching beyond the social conflicts that divided them. In everyday speech, folklore, self-published tracts and pamphlets, Sunday school lessons, sermons, and high-toned theological exegeses, white southern theologians preached that God ordained the division of the races and the sexes and, therefore, that God sanctioned the inequality between white and black and between men and women. This Christian mythic grounding for ideas of whiteness and blackness was powerful. But it was also unstable, subject to constant argument and revision. The biblical passages about God's providence in slavery and segregation were open to multiple readings, even among biblical literalists. In the twentieth century, this theology of race was radically overturned in part through a reimagination of the same Christian thought that was part of its creation. By the 1960s, segregationists defended Jim Crow more on emotional ("our way of life"), practical ("tradition"), and constitutional ("states rights") than theological grounds. In doing so, they lost the battle to spiritually inspired activists who deconstructed Jim Crow.

White and black Christians organized into racially defined denominations, baptized their converted in separate pools, and buried their dead in segregated cemeteries. Yet within southern culture existed strata of white and black religious experience seen rarely in the institutional churches—the reigning triumvirate of Baptist, Methodist, and Presbyterian—but evident in the interstices of community life. In religious expression, the racial interchange to be explored in this work threatened to undermine the hierarchies under which people were obligated to live. "Racial interchange" refers to the exchange of southern religious cultures between white and black believers in expressive culture, seen especially in music, in the formation of new religious traditions, and in lived experience. In those liminal moments, the bars of race sometimes lowered, if only temporarily. When they did come down, they opened up possibilities for cultural interchange that fed into the "shared traditions" outlined by historian and anthropologist Charles Joyner. Like Huck and Jim on the raft, black and white southerners, Joyner argues, "continued to swap recipes and cultural styles, songs and stories, accents and attitudes. Folk culture simply refused to abide any color line, however rigidly it may have been drawn."[1] White and black believers drew from common evangelical beliefs and attitudes, formed interracial congregations, and swapped oratorical and musical styles and forms. On occasion, they fell into moments of religious transcendence, before moving back into the world where color delimited everything.

This common evangelical sharing eventually, if unintentionally, created openings for "Christian interracialism," or self-consciously political efforts to undermine the system of southern racial hierarchy. In the years leading up to the civil rights movement, a few white and many more black believers struggled toward mutual respect, desegregation, and a politics (if not altogether a culture) of interracialism. Courageous black believers who formed the rank and file of the civil rights movement exposed the frail social and political underpinnings for segregation, and buried some of the folklore of blackness as inferiority that had enslaved so many Americans for so many centuries. While religious institutions were resistant to change, many religious folk, black and white, devoted themselves to a southern social revolution precisely because they perceived God was there.

Freedom's Coming focuses on the theology, the lived experience, the expressive cultures, and the political/civil struggles of white and black Christians in the South. The first portion of the book analyzes the connection between religious and political organizing among both black and white evangelicals from the 1860s to the 1950s. Chapter 1 traces the manner in which black and white Christians repositioned themselves through Reconstruction and into the era of southern apartheid. Chapter 2 follows to the mid-twentieth century the fortunes of southern Populists, progressives, liberals, and social radicals—those who carried on the constant struggle for freedom in the public and political world through treacherous times. The middle section of *Freedom's Coming*, Chapter 3, addresses the overarching theme of racial interchange by focusing on moments of cultural exchange in the sacred sphere: worship styles, religious beliefs, folk practices, and the creation of new religious and musical traditions. The final section, Chapters 4 and 5, considers the relationship among evangelical Protestantism, the black freedom struggle of the 1950s and 1960s, and the growth of the southern religious right through the twentieth century.

Religion in the post–Civil War and twentieth-century American South was both priestly and prophetic. If southern formal theology generally sanctified the regnant hierarchies, evangelical belief and practice also subtly undermined the dominant tradition. In one sense, the seeds of subversion were embedded in the passionate individualism, exuberant expressive forms, and profound faith of believers in the region. *Freedom's Coming* captures southern Protestant religious expressive cultures in their complexity, tragic pain, obstinate literalism, creative explosiveness, and reconciling possibilities. If the Freedom Summer of 1964 was "God's long summer," as memorably described by theologian and historian Charles Marsh, the era from the Civil War through the civil rights movement might be described as God's long century, for it was in the South during this time that American Christianity may be seen at its most tragic and its most triumphant.

Prayer is best 'ting, for it got us out of slavery. —ex-slave from Oklahoma

We act toward them as brethren, but never shall we again let them rule us as masters.
—Arthur Waddell, black missionary in South Carolina

Let Negroes and Chinamen and Indians suffer the superior race of white men to whom Providence has given this country, to control it. —*New Orleans Advocate*, 1879

Chapter One

Redemption

*Religion, Race, and Reconstruction
in the South, 1861–1900*

The granddaughter of an enslaved woman recounted the stories she heard about the last days of the Confederacy, when the overseer said to her grandmother's family, "Now you must pray because the South is losing. They always had family prayers and then prayed aloud and she said they knew what was going on. They knew if the North won they would have a little more freedom.... But she said her mother and father said now we must pray out loud for the South to win but in our hearts we must pray that the North will win." The familiar subversive delight of "puttin' on Ole Massa" was rehearsed one last time. Late in the Civil War, as freedom's coming drew nigh, enslaved Christians more openly and frequently sent up their prayers for deliverance from bondage.[1]

Shortly after the Civil War, Prince Murrell, a black Baptist minister from Tuscaloosa, Alabama, attended a freedmen's convention in the Gulf Coast city of Mobile. As a slave, Murrell had been mentored by his owner, Basil Manly Sr., who helped to found the Southern Baptist Convention (SBC) in 1845 and served as president of the University of Alabama. While in Mobile, Murrell received a ministerial ordination from some white northern clergymen who were in attendance.

Afterward, Basil Manly's son Charles protested the "uncandid and unfair proceeding as well as unscriptural and disorderly way of pronouncing a sort of *quasi ordination*" for the freedman Murrell. Black Tuscaloosans, in turn, organized their own congregation and called Murrell as their pastor. His congregants held no "hard feelings against [their] former owners," Murrell reported, but they also recognized that white southern churches would not "have anything to do with any northern churches. They say that religion is the same as it was before the war. They will have nothing to do with any colored churches that think they ought to have the same rights to serve God in their own way." Similarly, in South Carolina white believers still demanded the old "slavish custom" of black worshippers sitting in the balcony or standing outdoors during services. Christian freedpeople could not abide such gestures of submission. "We act toward them as brethren," the black missionary Arthur Waddell pronounced, "but never shall we again let them rule us as masters." For Murrell, Waddell, and the nearly four million recently enslaved people in the South, freedom's coming in 1865 was at once legal, psychological, and spiritual.[2]

White fears of black religious independence waxed along with conflict over the relative political and economic power of former masters and the freedpeople. Basil Manly Sr. had pastored biracial churches in South Carolina in the 1830s. Within the severely circumscribed limits available to him, he attempted to deal fairly with slave members of his church. For example, he licensed black men to preach and allowed black members to conduct disciplinary actions in church courts. During the war, he wondered if God was "chastizing our guilty people" because of their failure to evangelize the servants with sufficient vigor. After Appomattox, the Manly patriarch impressed on former slaves the "dignity of labor," evidently oblivious to the painful irony such messages held for the former bondspeople. Manly's black congregants "seemed to enjoy and be affected" by his preaching, he ruminated, yet "the idea seems never to have entered them, that all which they see of power or attainment is the result of labor—labor such as they themselves can perform." Meanwhile, Basil Manly Jr. adopted a far less paternalistic posture than his father in July of 1866 as he armed himself to protect his property against any marauding freedmen: "I loaded all my shooting irons—be ready, if that was necessary: which I did not really anticipate any difficulty: but I had determined to shoot without delay, if there was any violence attempted about my place." Basil Manly Jr.'s bitterness toward the freedpeople left him shaken. "I should be satisfied—to live and raise my child in a 'white man's country'—and if I get a chance to do so, I may accept it," he wrote to his brother Charles in 1868. White southern believers like the Manlys recognized that they were "unexpectedly in the midst of one of the greatest social changes which the history of the world presents."[3]

For white southern Christians, the term "redemption" infused deeply religious meanings into often deadly political struggles. Redemption was simultaneously freedom's coming for the body's soul and for the body politic. The region's sins and impurities, signified by the staining presence of "Black Republican" rule, had been washed by the blood. The image took on even more tangible power by the sheer amount of blood that was shed in reimposing white supremacist rule. White clergymen such as the Methodist Simon Peter Richardson were perfectly capable of taking the business of Redemption in their own hands. When asked what to do about black soldiers foraging in the countryside, he told a group of whites to "bushwhack them." He learned later that the group "made a few shots at the negroes, and that kept them at close quarters." There was nothing wrong in what white southerners had done, he wrote in 1900, and there was "no justifiable reason why they ought not to do it again." The Ku Klux Klan "seemed to be the only remedy to keep the negroes in check, and to enable the farmers to make a living for themselves and the negroes." Suspicious of democracy in politics and ecclesiology, he decried the "constant tendency" in Methodist congregations "to throw off the governmental restraints of the Church."[4]

For northern missionaries in the South such as John Emory Bryant, a white Methodist and Republican Party activist, freedom's coming beckoned as an opportunity to bring the light of Christian civilization to a benighted land. Intending to educate the freedpeople and defend their rights in the new southern regime, the Maine native moved to Georgia after the war. Despite years of disappointment and difficulty, he remained certain in 1878 that God had called him to the "work of political evangelization in the South, and also in the North." Explaining this to his long-suffering wife, from whom he was frequently parted, he said, "The evidence is so strong that I can not doubt it. As I have often said, if He has called me to this work, He will take care of me, if I obey Him." His endeavors for Republicanism and education, moreover, had shed "much light upon the subject of holiness," and, he said, "[I] think I understand where I am spiritually."[5]

White and black Christians in the post–Civil War South struggled over what constituted the terms of freedom's coming. The work of figures such as ex-slaves Prince Murrell and Arthur Waddell, white ex-masters and ministers such as Basil Manly Sr. and his sons, and northern missionaries, including the Methodist John Emory Bryant, shaped southern religious institutions for a century to come. In the end, none of their visions triumphed completely or failed totally. Yet some of their prayers apparently were more equal than others. Northern hopes very nearly failed, for white southern denominations resisted ecclesiastical re-incorporation while newfound black southern religious institutions steered free of white control, northern or southern. African Americans established independent religious institutions yet were painfully aware that the Promised Land was nowhere in sight. Ultimately, a white southern conservative vision prevailed, and it provided a powerful theological imprimatur for American apartheid.[6]

African American Religious Organizing in the Post–Civil War South

Black believers saw in the war the fulfillment of prayers for emancipation, education, and the right to worship freely in churches of their own directing. Quasi-independent African American churches existed in the antebellum era, but white authorities monitored them closely. In black communities after the war, independent churches and denominational organizations sprung up quickly, including thousands of small local congregations and major national organizations such as the African Methodist Episcopal Church (AME) and the National Baptist Convention (NBC). Only a decade after the war, hardly any black parishioners still worshipped in the historically white southern churches.

Through the last part of the nineteenth century, black church membership grew rapidly. By the 1906 religious census, the National Baptist Convention claimed more than two million communicants, or over 61 percent of black churchgoers. The African Methodist Episcopal Church numbered some 500,000, the African Methodist Episcopal Zion Church (AMEZ) about 185,000, the Colored Methodist Episcopal (CME) sect approximately 173,000, and the Methodist Episcopal Church (MEC) about 60,000 black adherents. Catholics claimed around 38,000 African American worshippers, while the Presbyterians and Congregationalists together counted some 30,000. Altogether, church membership among African Americans rose from 2.6 million to 3.6 million from 1890 to 1906.[7]

More important than tallying up these rather uncertain (likely inflated) and self-reported numbers, however, is understanding the critical role church life and key clergymen played for the freedpeople in the first generation after emancipation. Independent African American churches organized in part as a response to the refusal of whites to grant black Christians equality in church. But most important, African American churches and denominations represented the initiative of freedpeople in carving out separate cultural spaces. "The emancipation of the colored people made the colored churches and ministry a necessity, both by virtue of the prejudice existing against us and of our essential manhood before the laws of the land," explained one black Baptist clergyman.[8]

Black and white missionaries in the post–Civil War South, including the white Republican activist John Emory Bryant and the black Methodist stalwart Henry McNeal Turner, pursued the work of "political evangelization," the securing of religious and political rights for the former bondspeople. Turner was a legendary evangelist for the venerable African Methodist Episcopal Church. Officially organized in 1816, the AME anchored the embattled free black community in the North. White southern authorities banned the black denomination from the South in 1822 following its suspected role in the abortive Denmark Vesey slave revolt. Thereafter, the church could make no headway in the South until the providential turn in human history in 1861.

Remembered later for his caustic editorials advocating black American emigration to Africa and denouncing the American flag (which in the 1880s he castigated as a "rag of contempt" and the Constitution a "cheat, a libel, . . . to be spit upon by every negro in the land"), Turner helped to establish the African Methodist Episcopal Church in the South. Born free in 1834 in South Carolina (which he later dubbed "that pestiferous state of my nativity"), raised by an extended family of women, and by 1848 an avid Methodist, Turner learned early on the importance of black self-reliance and respectability. In the 1850s, Turner moved to Georgia, the state where he would make his name and career. There, biracial crowds eagerly gathered to hear his powerful preaching, although some incredulous whites pronounced him a *"white man galvanized."*[9]

Following service as a Union army chaplain, Turner established himself as a prominent AME churchman, missionary, legislator, newspaper editor, and rhetorical firebrand. The AME and its sister competitor, the African Methodist Episcopal Zion Church, sent missionaries to evangelize what they perceived to be waiting masses of freedpeople who needed the leadership of the venerable black ecclesiastical bodies. Turner and his fellows envisioned their religious work as essential to securing full citizenship rights for the freedpeople. Civil rights, church organization, and racial uplift would go hand in hand. Turner expressed this sentiment when defending the continued use of the word "African" in the AME denominational title. "The curse of the colored race in this country, where white is God and black is the devil," he insisted, was in "the disposition to run away" from blackness. "In trying to be something beside themselves," he said, black Americans would "never amount to anything." Turner advocated a different course: "honor black, dignify it with virtues, and pay as much respect to it as nature and nature's God does." Or more succinctly: "respect black."[10]

Turner also served as a delegate to the postwar constitutional convention in Georgia. In his brief term in the reconstructed state legislature, he placated whites by taking conciliatory positions on key symbolic issues. " 'Anything to please the white folks,' has been my motto," was his own sardonic self-assessment. But his efforts at winning over potential adversaries failed. White opponents forcibly and illegally removed Turner (and other black lawmakers) from the 1868 legislative session. By 1871, the Peach State had been redeemed from Black Republican rule, one that whites perceived as contrary to the will of God. The derogatory terms "Radical" and "Black Republican" stuck in spite of the fact that Reconstruction governments, including the Georgia legislature from which Turner was removed, were largely made up of white officeholders.[11]

With his political career forcibly terminated, Turner settled into three more decades of ceaseless work for the AME in the South and, later, South Africa. He traveled constantly, edited the official denominational hymnal, and eventually was elected bishop. He fought internecine battles with northern bishops over the degree of education necessary for ministerial ordination and the place of women in the church; in both cases, Turner argued for democratizing church polity by extending opportunities to those historically excluded from leadership positions. When southern-style racism swept the country in the 1890s, Turner blasted American hypocrisy. As editor of the *Voice of Missions* in the last two decades of his life, Turner articulated what later would be called black theology. He organized African conferences of the AME while struggling to overcome the cultural gulf separating American and African AME leaders. Turner died in 1915, memorably eulogized by his fellow Georgian W. E. B. Du Bois as "a man of tremendous force and indomitable courage. . . . In a sense Turner was the last of his clan: mighty men, physically and mentally, men who started at the bottom and hammered their way to the top by sheer brute strength."[12]

Turner's career was indeed remarkable; yet throughout the South dozens of black ministers and missionaries forged equally significant lives in political evangelization, including the Georgia Baptist William Jefferson White. The son of a white planter and a mother who was probably of mixed Native American and African American ancestry, the ambitious young Georgian could pass as white but self-identified as black. In the 1850s, he worked as a carpenter and cabinetmaker, thus securing the artisanal economic base that underwrote his independence into the era of black freedom. As a stalwart of Augusta's free black community, an educational leader, newspaper editor, and political spokesman, White labored for freed African Americans. At the first meeting of the Georgia Equal Rights and Education Association (held at Augusta's historic black Springfield Baptist Church in early 1866), White's eloquent address drew the attention of General Oliver O. Howard, director of the federal Freedmen's Bureau.

White also helped to found schools for freedpeople in the growing southeastern Georgia town, including Augusta Baptist Institute. Upon taking over the institute in 1867, Charles H. Corey, a white Canadian-born Baptist missionary, confronted bitterness, prejudice, and poor facilities. The KKK dispatched unmistakable "warnings" against his efforts to establish a black theological institution. "Bad passions" were "still rampant" then, he recalled; it was a time "when hate prevailed, and not love." White Christians would "almost turn pale with fear when I asked them to sell me a piece of land"; few locals would sell or lease a building if it would be used as a black school. "Times were critical," White remembered, "and in some respects, dangerous, for whites engaged in teaching colored people." Seeking political cover and surer sources of funding, black Augustans cultivated local white benefactors. During these years, the institute trained some talented students who would leave a significant mark on black Georgia, including Emmanuel K. Love (later pastor of Georgia's largest black Baptist church and a founder of the National Baptist Convention). But the school languished in Augusta, compelling its 1879 move to the rapidly growing and more centrally located city of Atlanta. Atlanta Baptist Institute eventually took the permanent name of Morehouse College, honoring the white northern Baptist educator Henry Morehouse. The college served as a base for the twentieth-century educator John Hope and trained Martin Luther King Jr., Julian Bond, and other civil rights leaders. Like so many other stories from this era, William Jefferson's White's efforts created key institutions for the future of black America.[13]

In 1880, White began publishing the *Georgia Baptist*. With its masthead reading "Great Elevator, Educator, and Defender of the People," the *Georgia Baptist* was one of the most widely distributed black newspapers in the late-nineteenth-century South. The Republican Party activist and pastor of Harmony Baptist Church in Augusta aggressively defended black rights amidst the growing racial turmoil. "The dark clouds of internal discord have gathered in some localities," he wrote after witnessing the racial pogrom in Wilmington, North Carolina, in 1898, "and the murderous lyncher, though walking around with the blood of his brother almost dripping from his fingers, goes unpunished. The deadly firearm, the deadly hemp, and well-lit torch have all been called into service by irresponsible and irrepressible mobs; many lives have paid the penalty and the appetite of blood thirsty lynchers is unsatisfied." His hopes that the "tide turns with the closing of the year and the Tillmanish brutality has seen its best days" were not realized. After White publicly denounced a local lynching and defended its victim, his life was threatened. His black friends took up sentry posts outside the paper's offices. Seeking to spare his life and career in Augusta, White publicly recanted the earlier angry editorial. Privately, he was profoundly disturbed by the turn of events. "We seem to be standing on a volcano," he wrote to his son.[14]

White lent vocal support to streetcar boycotts that sprang up in a number of southern cities in the early twentieth century in response to the newly enacted segregation laws on public transportation systems. "The colored people of Augusta are keeping off the street cars because of the revival of Jim Crowism on them, and some of the white papers of the city are howling about it," he exclaimed. "They howl if colored people ride on the cars and howl if they stay off of them. What in the name of high heaven do the white people want the colored people to do?" In 1906, White joined W. E. B. Du Bois, John Hope, and other race men to establish the Georgia Equal Rights League. The brutal Atlanta riot of that year again mocked their hopes for a reprieve from racism. "Negroes like [W. J.] White ought to be made to leave the South," the local white newspaper opined. "The place for them is, either where there are no Jim Crow laws or where it is too hot for street cars. Augusta has no room for such incendiary negroes, and we should waste no time letting them know it." By the time of his death in 1913, White's Reconstruction-era hopes of equal rights for all were a distant memory.[15]

Denominations such as Turner's AME Church and White's Baptists proselytized vigorously for the ecclesiastical allegiance of the freedpeople. The battles among various Methodist groupings are particularly instructive in illustrating the nexus of race and religion in the postwar South. In 1865, the Reverend James Lynch organized the first officially recognized African Methodist Episcopal congregation in the postwar South, in Savannah. Born in Baltimore in 1839, the son of a slave mother purchased out of bondage by his father, Lynch was educated in New Hampshire. During the last two years of the war he preached in South Carolina and Georgia. As Lynch later told a throng of freedmen in Augusta, his convictions impelled him to "unite my destiny with that of my people[,] to live with them, suffer, sorrow, rejoice, and die with them."

As editor of the *Christian Recorder*, the influential and widely read organ of the AME, he wrote aggressively about the racial politics of Reconstruction. Yet Lynch feared that the African Methodists as a denomination lacked adequate resources for the immense task of evangelizing and educating the freedpeople. Bishop Gilbert Haven, a politically radical Northern Methodist bishop, recruited him to organize for the MEC (or Northern Methodists) in the South. Bishop Haven would soon be notorious for his endorsement of interracial marriage (or "miscegenation," a word invented by a Democratic critic of Abraham Lincoln during the Civil War to vilify sexual relations—and, by implication, any other social relation—between white and black people) as one answer to the race problem. Haven's commitment to racial desegregation in Methodist conferences won over Lynch. Beginning in 1867, Lynch served as a presiding elder for the MEC in Natchez, Mississippi, and pursued a political career in the state senate while editing the *Colored Citizen's Monthly*. Lynch scorned the claims of the Methodist Episcopal Church, South (MECS), to be above politics: "Never was a church more partisan," he wrote of the Southern Methodists. In league with Democratic politicians, they would "with intelligence and skill contest every inch of ground with us." Lynch excoriated the "vilest democrat negroes in the state" who cooperated with white Southern Methodists. He also fought with his former colleagues in the African Methodist Episcopal Church, whom he saw endorsing "every slander breathed against the M. E. Church or its functionaries." Lynch wondered whether in the "terrible whirlwind of political excitement of which we are the subjects," the church might starve "for the bread which I would give were I devoted with singleness to ministry. My political relations & labor increase the borders of the church for as I go *I preach*, but it does take from my ability to spiritualize and discipline." Lynch later served as a delegate to the Republican National Convention and the General Conference of the Methodist Church before his untimely death from pneumonia in 1872.[16]

The politics of racial ecclesiology played out in particularly complicated ways in the various Methodist denominations, with divisions not only between whites and blacks but within white and black religious communities. Still, southern church membership eventually settled in a pattern familiar in nearly every religious organization: virtually complete racial separation. Theological racism certainly played a part in this, but so did sentiments of black self-determination from black Baptists and Methodists. James W. Hood, leader of the AMEZ Conference in North Carolina, argued in 1874 that circumstances had "made the African church a necessity." The color line in religion was not one of hate or "dread of contact, but a line sanctioned by custom till it has the force of law." Through this providence, he concluded, God had "raised up an effective colored ministry" who would not be employed without congregations of their own people.[17]

Once persuaded that racial separation was inevitable, white Southern Methodists supervised the formation of yet another black denomination in 1870, the Colored Methodist Episcopal Church. Two Southern Methodist bishops, Robert Paine and Holland McTyeire, presided over the CME's founding General Conference. The nonpolitical status of the CME denomination, written into its founding constitution, was a condition of the church receiving and holding property from Southern Methodists for the benefit of black members. The CME leaders, Southern Methodists assured white southern believers, guarded religious assemblies "from that complication with political parties and demagogues that has been so damaging to the spiritual interests of the colored people of the South."[18]

Isaac Lane and Lucius Holsey were two of the CME's best-known early organizers. Both Lane and Holsey, who were praised by whites for their "respectful attitude" and "manifest desire to improve [their] people in knowledge and religion," initially trusted that cooperation with paternalistic whites would best aid black advancement. The two assumed that accommodating sympathetic white allies would improve the status of the freedpeople. The CME fought simultaneously against competition from the Northern Methodists and the AME in a three-way battle for the souls of the freedpeople. AME missionaries, Lane bitterly remembered, "constantly referred to us as a Southern Church, a rebel Church, and the like, and those names were very distasteful to our people." Northern Methodists were also contemptuous of the early CME. As a Northern Methodist in New

Orleans said to one CME minister who had come to see about some church property, Southern Methodists did not "recognize the negro as a man . . . and I believe that if they had no colored members and possessed this property they would as soon thought of ordaining a mule as a colored man to put in it."[19]

Born in Georgia of a white slaveholding father and slave mother, Lucius Holsey maintained a close relationship with white Methodists through most of his life, especially with his mentor and examiner, the Southern Methodist bishop George F. Pierce. After the war, he farmed cotton and in 1868 began pastoring in Methodist churches. He saw "no reasons for any feelings of hate or revenge" and thought it imperative that whites and blacks cooperate closely. Holsey struggled through the 1870s to provide for his family while presiding over a church that was, in his words, "scarcely organized at all." He remained loyal to the CME, as he explained, "not because I thought it the best church in itself, not because I thought it purer and better than other such organizations, but because I thought it to be the most fitted religious power to meet the peculiar conditions that exist in the Southern States." It was clear to him that "the white ministry was the only standard of excellence by which the colored ministers could be inspired to reach a higher plane of fitness." In 1898, he declared slavery to be "providential," with the Negro receiving an "upward propulsion that he could not have obtained in his native land."[20]

The advent of legally mandated segregation and a surge in racist violence shattered Holsey's vision of paternalistic white-black cooperation for mutual progress. By the early twentieth century, the CME bishop perceived that black success inflamed white hatred—precisely the opposite of the view preached from thousands of pulpits across the South. Holsey forecast that the conflict of races would only end in "total defeat," for "good breeding, politeness, kindness, self-respect and all the virtues may be added and retained by a black man . . . but these, instead of helping him to live in the esteem of his white neighbor, actually put him in a precarious condition, and endanger his life and property." As he awoke from his dream of biracial cooperative amity, Holsey advocated total race segregation and even emigration to Africa, moving to an ideological place close to that of his onetime bitter foe Henry McNeal Turner. When even the most accommodationist strategy had failed miserably, then what would temper white hatred or aid black advancement? These were the painful questions asked by figures as divergent as William Jefferson White, Henry McNeal Turner, and Lucius Holsey during the resurgence of white supremacy in the late nineteenth century.[21]

Whether from principle or from pragmatism, some white and black believers rejected the general practice of racial separation in church life. The history of Methodism in New Orleans presents a striking example. The Crescent City was unique in the way that French Creoles, free blacks, ex-slaves, and white southern members of the MEC moved in complicated alliances with and against one another. Their history was set against a backdrop of Louisiana radical politics, labor violence, and ethno-religious conflict between Catholics and Protestants. Yet Methodist and Catholic parishioners in New Orleans developed a tradition of interracial religious organization almost to the end of the nineteenth century, far after most southern churches were completely separated by race. A major exception to the usual pattern of ecclesiastical separation, these believers in New Orleans demonstrated support for racially integrated church organizations as important symbols for a society not divided by race. In doing so, they encountered difficulties that ultimately were insurmountable.

As was typical of congregations everywhere in America, churches in the historic Louisiana city diverged by class and color. Despite such divisions, politically radical and racially desegregated Methodism found a home in New Orleans. The Methodist Episcopal Church, with a membership of about 3,000 white and black parishioners in New Orleans, became a middle ground for whites seeking respite from the Confederate religion of the MECs and African Americans who objected to the racialist emphasis of the AME. "We shall need the good will and kindly aid of the whites—ku-klux, white leaguers and bull-dozers excepted—to enable us to carry on the work of education so auspiciously begun as well as to compass our political aspirations," a black MEC minister explained. AME members might boast of "race pride, self-assertion, freedom, manhood, and patriotism," he said, but in fact their actions were "but another form of demanding, asserting and upholding color-caste and the COLOR-LINE."[22]

The official organ of the Louisiana Conference of the Methodist Episcopal Church, the *Southwestern Christian Advocate*, was an outspoken proponent of racial equality. Its editor, Joseph Hartzell, was a native of Illinois who came to New Orleans in 1869. He pastored the Ames Methodist Episcopal Church, whose parishioners included Governor Henry Clay Warmoth and other notable Republicans. His church faced the opposition of wealthy locals who were yet "*bitter rebels* politically," as well as those who feared Hartzell's congregation would "force *Negro* equality on them." Black Methodists later eulogized Hartzell as one who "slept in our cabins, shared with us our scant meal and wept over our departed dead."[23]

Hartzell hired A. E. P. Albert as the assistant editor of the *Southwestern Christian Advocate*. Aristides Elphonso Peter Albert was born in St. Charles Parish, thirty-five miles from New Orleans, where he grew up as a French-speaking Catholic slave. After the war, he converted to Methodism. In the 1880s, he was named presiding elder of the Louisiana Conference and editor of its paper. Albert made his position unmistakably clear: any people who would "submit patiently" to segregationism were "unworthy to be free men." He decried the "pretentious hypocrisy practiced by many of the so-called Christian people of the South." They would be "held responsible before God . . . for the shedding of innocent blood." Emphasizing the necessity of protecting political rights, Albert entertained the possibility of using violence in self-defense.[24]

In the 1870s, the Methodist Episcopal Church granted the right of individual conferences in the denomination to segregate themselves racially. In the Louisiana Conference, however, black and white Methodist ministers jointly led worship services and conference meetings, trusting that such interaction would prove "necessarily powerful among the people whom we serve as pastors." They advised preachers not to "stoop in order to conciliate prejudice," lest they "finally crawl out of the country defeated."

Over time, however, even Methodist churches in the New Orleans area gradually succumbed to de facto racial separation in individual church conferences. After placing great hope in the MEC as a beacon of Christian interracialism and opponent of theological racism, A. E. P. Albert expressed frustration at the powerlessness of African American believers to gain the appointment of a black bishop or shape any major decision at the denominational level. He urged his fellow ministers to "contend for equality; show backbone, grit and grace, but let us stay together and fight it out." In the 1890s, just prior to the ominous *Plessy v. Ferguson* decision ratifying the constitutionality of racial segregation in public transportation, Albert formed alliances with Creole Catholics in civil rights organizations, political activism that landed him in trouble with increasingly conservative white Methodists. When Joseph C. Hartzell resisted the racial segregation of Methodist conferences, national leaders removed him from his post at the *Southwestern Christian Advocate*. They replaced him with Marshall Taylor, a black Kentuckian who defended newly racially separated Methodist districts and endorsed the turn away from politics in the black religious community. By the early twentieth century, the Louisiana Conference of the MEC was defined simply as "the colored work in the state of Louisiana." Similar attempts elsewhere to create a biracial Methodist polity in the South met the same fate. For these black and white Methodists, theological racism among whites combined with the rise of black religious institutions left unfulfilled the vision of Christian interracialism.[25]

In the antebellum era, pious slaveholders boasted of their Christian care for "their Negroes." The enslaved Christians never accepted this paternalism in the same way it had been offered by whites. Yet they never altogether rejected it either, for it brought them tangible gains—some partly independent churches, unsanctioned literacy courses, and white mentors and protectors to whom they could appeal.

While such cooperation was real and significant, it was primarily the drive and initiative of freedpeople that resulted in independent black church organization after the war. In Charleston, a missionary attending a black Congregational church service watched as 200 members raised a subscription of more than $400 to erect their own building. "Are these the low people who in freedom were to relapse into barbarism? Things do not look like it here," she commented sharply. Throughout the South, freedpeople purchased lots, built churches, and paid for ministers. In rural communities, household production accounted for what little discretionary income most freedpeople could afford. Resources scrabbled together by raising chicks, selling garden produce, and borrowing to purchase stock animals provided the assets necessary for the acquisition of land and building materials for churches. The support offered to black Sabbath schools (including firewood, food, and small sums of cash) were precisely the types of monetary assets most readily generated within this household economy. By such means, freedpeople funded many of the Sabbath schools that provided education for up to two-thirds of the black pupils reported to be in school in the South between 1866 and 1870.[26]

Baptist churches drew by far the greatest number of freedpeople. The independent structure of Baptist church governance allowed for entrepreneurial spirits to attract strong local followings. Long-established congregations such as the First African Baptist Church of Savannah spun off scores of satellite congregations. Savannah's First African appointed apprenticed preachers to evangelize among the freedpeople in the Georgia low country. These emissaries supplied about a dozen "praise houses" (or "pray's houses") with ministerial leadership who reported back to the mother church. W. J. Campbell, minister of the Savannah congregation during Reconstruction, was the visual representation of the same traditions of independence that low-country workers had carved out toiling in the rice and cotton fields. "The people around the coast would hail his coming among them as a priest," a colleague recalled of Campbell's work.[27]

Throughout the South, urban black congregations sprang up to serve the spiritual, social, and political needs of the freedpeople. Richmond's historic First African Baptist Church originated in an old building donated to slave members of a white congregation in 1841. The Reverend Robert Ryland, a white pastor ministering to enslaved people, led the daytime services of the fledgling congregation. After the war, Ryland's congregants at First African occupied the building in which Virginia delegates had voted for secession. In 1866, the church acquired the deed to the property. Recognizing that his members preferred black leadership, Ryland resigned in 1867. He was replaced by his protégé, James Henry Holmes, a former slave who had worked in Richmond's tobacco warehouses. Holmes pastored the church until 1901. Along the way, although his relatively apolitical leadership angered critics, he turned First African in Richmond into one of the largest congregations in America.[28]

Throughout much of the South, most especially in urban areas, black-led congregations (usually Baptist or Methodist) were the strongest religious institutions. White mission congregations, often Congregationalist, Episcopalian, or Presbyterian, were significantly smaller. The Tennessee cotton center of Memphis boasted twelve congregations by the 1870s: six Baptist, four AME, and one AMEZ and CME each. In Memphis, class and color stratification also defined the texture of religious life, with the color line between lighter and darker-skinned congregants well understood and informally enforced. Light skin, according to Memphis oral tradition, was a virtual prerequisite for those aspiring to become bishops in the CME. Collins Chapel (CME) in Memphis gained a reputation as the "most refined and quiet large congregation in the city," its pews filled with strivers who dissociated themselves from slave folkways and religious customs.[29]

Political leadership for freedpeople came mostly from the ranks of men who had been free people of color, such as William Jefferson White and Henry McNeal Turner. They were generally literate and skilled in artisanal or professional trades. Religious leadership, by contrast, was open to anyone with charisma and perseverance. This opened the doors for figures such as the Reverend Morris Henderson, a Virginian originally brought to Memphis as a carriage driver and ordained at age forty-seven in 1864. Starting out with a small group that met in a brush arbor, Morris Henderson boasted the largest congregation in Memphis by 1870, with over 2,500 members and active women's societies that raised most of the $5,000 needed for a church lot and eventually the $44,000 for a substantial building. Sensing that political activity was futile, good mainly for incurring the wrath of whites, Henderson eventually closed his church to political meetings (as did many of his clerical peers). After Reconstruction, many churches sacrificed political activism in favor of cultivating their own growth and prosperity as major community institutions.[30]

In Atlanta, the freedpeople organized eight churches after the war and fourteen more by 1880. The First Colored Baptist Church in Atlanta, commonly called Friendship Baptist, originated in 1868 with twenty-five members who met in a boxcar on the west side of the city. By 1882, the congregation had grown to 1,500 members, who met in a handsome wooden structure valued at $35,000. In the 1890s, E. R. Carter, a well-known minister and temperance activist, presided over the church's 2,500 constituents and $60,000 worth of property. Its basement became the first home of Spelman College, a center for the higher education of black women. Another of Atlanta's major black congregations, the Wheat Street Baptist Church, was founded in 1870 in response to the needs of ex-slaves. A two-week-long revival in 1878 brought in new converts and complaints from whites that washerwomen had "gone crazy with the prospect of getting religion" and with "fetish follies." But Wheat Street Baptist combined religious fervor with political exercises even after Reconstruction. Black Republican Party officials met there in 1880 to plan strategy after their victory within the state party organization. And the following year, those same washerwomen supposedly obsessed with fetish follies were organizing to block license fees imposed on them in an attempt to break a citywide strike of black domestic workers. The development of "institutional churches," including congregations such as Friendship Baptist and Wheat Street Baptist that tended to the multiple needs of urban African Americans, was perfected in the early twentieth century by the Reverend Henry Hugh Proctor of Atlanta's First Congregational Church, a major figure in black social life discussed further in Chapter 2.[31]

Reconstructing White Southern Christianity

Defeat, emancipation, and Reconstruction stunned white southern evangelicals, compelling them to reassess their deepest assumptions. Their ruminations on the meaning of the war abounded with the theology of chastisement. In this view, God sent the war to test the faithfulness of the chosen people and rebuke the shortcomings of piety in the region. One Confederate soldier trusted that a "God who rules the destiny of things and is a God of wisdom and justice will never suffer a determined and Christian people to be overcome by a cruel Tyrant." By the end of the conflict, another equally faithful southern soldier feared that "the subjugation of the South" would "make an infidel" of him. He could not "see how a just God can allow people who have battled so heroically for their rights to be overthrown." Christian Confederates across the region pondered the same quandary. One Methodist paper put it this way:

> Some have been very confident and speak with assurance. . . . They *know* that God brought it about, employed all the wicked and demoniacal agencies which manipulated its inception, which blew the spark to aflame and which now carries it on with hellish hate, for the accomplishment of His great purposes. They ask God to give us victory when they are doubtful whether it be God's will to grant it to us or not; they pray for peace, though they admit we are not sufficiently humbled for our sins; when they doubt whether God's wrath is yet satisfied or not; they pray for a speedy deliverance of our people from the hand of the oppressor, when they doubt whether God's time has yet come to effect it. Now who does not see there is no *faith* in these prayers. . . . Reader, search and see, if this calamity still settles down upon the land, because of the dereliction or unfaithfulness of God's people.[32]

As Confederate fortunes declined, repeated invocations of chastisement barely held together the tattered theology of the faithful. Clergymen assured southern believers that they remained the chosen people, especially in times of travail. Perhaps it was God's purpose to "withhold success from his most faithful servants," a group of Virginia Baptists surmised. Norvell Winsboro Wilson was a Baptist minister in Chapel Hill, North Carolina. In May of 1862, on a day designated by Jefferson Davis for "humiliation and prayer," Wilson tried to "feel the danger to which we are exposed as a nation. But we are all more or less hardened under the influence of war." Later, he described the "overcast" political horizon of the Confederacy's waning days, "with portentous darkness, and the atmosphere surcharged with blood-red war—There is a dark pall enshrouding the infant nation—and yet God hath not forsaken, but chastens us in love." He found the Yankees he met to be the "most Godless of men—blasphemous and vulgar—they have neither morals nor manners." Christian Confederates such as Wilson trusted that God would turn their afflictions into "sources of humility, patience, resignation, and submission to Divine will." Southern Christians would "come out of the furnace doubly purified for the good work and fight," a Mississippi woman fervently hoped, "for to the people of the Confederacy is given the sublime mission of maintaining the supremacy of our Father in Heaven."[33]

The outcome of the Civil War and the advent of Reconstruction raised difficult theological questions. If God had sanctioned white caretaking of Negroes in bondage as the divine plan for southern Christian civilization, then what was God's will in a world without slavery? If the South was the moral exemplar of obedience, how could God allow a marauding army to destroy slavery and pillage the land? "There is such a change in every thing, and such a revolution since we were given over into the hands of the Enemy. I have not been really cheerful in many months," a churchgoing woman in Tennessee penned in her diary. "To think of the desolations of Zion, the Church of Christ languishes. I never saw such a state of things in all my life." At her church, many members had died or lost faith, "nearly all of the rest worldly minded," meetings "broken up because iniquity abounds." She felt "stript" but hoped it was "all for my good to make us seek our rest and happiness in God alone."[34]

Those who had been devoted to mission work among the slaves puzzled over God's workings in the new order. Charles Colcock Jones, educated at Princeton as a rising star in the Presbyterian Church, was uneasy about the slaveholding planter's life he inherited. After engaging in a long internal struggle, he sublimated his antislavery views and spent three decades preaching to slaves while occupying a major pulpit in Savannah as one of the South's foremost advocates of Christian paternalism toward the lower orders. Jones's wife, Mary, however, spurned the earnest regard for the souls of the enslaved people that was her husband's trademark. She never suffered doubts about the peculiar institution and was glad to be rid of Negro servants after her husband's death in 1863. "I shall cease my anxieties for the [black] race," she wrote to her children at the close of the war. "My life long I have been laboring and caring for them . . . and this is their return. . . . I am thoroughly disgusted with the whole race. . . . My heart sickens at a prospect of dwelling with them." After the war, Mary sold the family's plantation and settled in New Orleans. Embittered white southerners such as Mary Jones interpreted freedom's coming as emancipation from their burden of caring for an inferior people.[35]

These "afflictions" and "chastisements" so frequently mentioned in postwar white southern writings included the trial of dealing with former servants who were no longer playing the roles that God theoretically had assigned them. Whites who had convinced themselves of the faithfulness and docility of their Negroes faced the postwar South with bitterness and contempt for their former slaves. Laura Comer was married to a cotton planter in Alabama but resided in a wealthy and established Savannah neighborhood during the war. Comer was the niece of Henry Ward Beecher, pastor of a fashionable congregation in Brooklyn, New York. Writing inland to her husband from their Savannah home, Comer complained constantly of troubles with her servants: "O, God, with my Heavenly Father; enlighten the dark minds of the servants and give them obedient hearts, I beseech Thee—for in them how great is the darkness!" Truly it was a "terrible task" to "govern these semi-barbarous, half-enlightened beings." She sought divine light on her torment. "Is it to humble us?" she asked. If so, it had been "truly effectual." She found solace in church, attending both the Episcopal communion and a Baptist congregation: "I love all pious people, who are pressing on, through life to God." After the war, her burdens only deepened. The "discipline of *severe* trials and disappointments" through which she passed induced "*excruciating* mental and bodily pain." She tried to calm herself with reminders "*that we are to be perfected through suffering.*" She sickened at the thought of spending "the precious days of my life, following after and watching negroes. It is a terrible life." During Reconstruction, she pondered the dark possibility that sin "*so grieved Thy Holy Spirit*" that God had turned away from the nation. Finally, she sold the plantation and returned to New York.[36]

Through the next several decades, white southern Christian women filled their diaries and letters with their frustrations in dealing with black domestic servants, in a manner much as their predecessors had done with house slaves. Dolly Lunt Burge, a Georgia farmer's wife, never felt entirely comfortable with slavery, sensing that it was sometimes abused. Yet she knew also that the "purest and holiest" of men had owned slaves, including the Bible's venerated patriarchs, and that nothing in the scriptures specifically forbade it. In the language common to many a plantation mistress, she complained, "I have never ceased to work, but many a Northern housekeeper has a much easier time than a Southern matron with her hundred negroes." When the young Methodist Magnolia Wynn LeGuin experienced trouble with one "saucy" and "impudent" servant, she wrote of how "unsettled and *nettled*" it made her. Burdened with a growing farm family in Georgia and a modest income, she prayed for help "under such provocation to keep calm—preserve me gently in my commands when darkies are insolent. Oh, how agitated I have become over the impudence of the negroes this morning. . . . Lord, help me to be right in Thy sight when the negroes are provoking me. . . . I feel so bad, so hurt and tears spring to my eyes."[37]

White southern Christians sought counsel where they could find it. For some, conventional religion had failed to answer their difficult questions or assuage the personal agonies wrought by the war and the revolutionary politics of Reconstruction. Some found refuge in spiritualism and other heterodox religious movements. Ella Gertrude Clanton Thomas struggled with the theological implications of emancipation. A resident of Augusta, Thomas raised ten children through financially pinched and personally tumultuous times but still managed an active public career as a schoolteacher, temperance activist, and leader of the Daughters of the Confederacy. As she reflected on the huge financial loss her family faced after the war, she recognized "how intimately my faith in revelations and my faith in the institution of slavery had been woven together—true I had seen the evil of the latter but if the *Bible* was right then slavery *must be*—Slavery was done away with and my faith in God's Holy Book was terribly shaken." She spent months away from any church, unsure any longer of who or what represented divine truth. Although a Methodist, Thomas dabbled in unorthodox practices and beliefs, including Swedenborgianism and spiritualism. She occasionally sought contact with her father in the afterlife.[38]

Religion, politics, and personal life also intertwined for Sara Chilton, an upper-class white woman in Jackson, Mississippi. Her son Charles was killed while defending the ballot box from potential black voters during the violent election season of 1875; in her view, he was a martyr to the cause of Redemption. "I have endured great sorrows in my life, but this seems to me the heaviest of them all," she confided to a friend in New Orleans. She comforted herself with spiritualism, becoming a "*writing medium*" and receiving communications from her deceased husband. She knew of the "odium attached to these things by nearly every one," given spiritualism's reputation for frauds and hoaxes. Yet she found it a great solace, despite worrying about her inexperience and ineptitude as a medium. In one spirit communication, her father assured her that he had seen Sara's children with Jesus. "This thing of being a medium is governed by certain laws," she explained, those of science and not of the miraculous. The spirit world could only be contacted in a place of absolute peace and quiet, with no servants or children; it was "governed by laws of affinity and repulsion and further than this one has no power spirits come at their own will they do not come at the call of just any person." She communicated with the spirits infrequently for fear of embarrassing her church. Chilton's story suggests that the theology of chastening could only go so far. To bear up under so much suffering, even the orthodox required more direct communication from the spirits.[39]

Since the antebellum era, white southern believers generally had maintained the useful fiction of separating the pure realm of the church from the impure world of politics. This theological tradition continued into the Civil War. Southern Methodist bishops, for example, deplored the "too extensive influence of the war spirit" among their preachers and opposed the conscription of clergymen. Bishops enjoined on their congregations submission to governmental powers and deprecated "any intermeddling of churches or ministers *as such* with political affairs." At the same time, they warned that Northern Methodist calls for reunion would necessitate turning over church property and interests to those who would "absorb or exterminate us." Southern believers, they feared, would be compelled to confess guilt over slavery and the war and become "political hucksters instead of Gospel ministers."[40]

Despite the hardships of the postwar era, Southern Methodism gradually recovered and prospered. Membership in the MECS reached 535,000 from 1867 to 1870 despite the virtually entire removal of nearly 200,000 black congregants from its rolls. By 1885, the MECS numbered some 860,000 parishioners. Under the leadership of Holland N. McTyeire, bishops democratized their church polity, lengthened pastoral terms from two to four years, and made provisions for lay representation in the conferences and courts of the MECS. Although outstripped in numbers by the Baptists, Southern Methodists drew a considerable following from the growing middle class of landowners, shopkeepers, and town professionals.[41]

Unlike the Methodists, whose southern and northern branches reunited in 1939, and the Presbyterians, who did the same in 1983, the Southern Baptist Convention remained a regionally separate denomination from its origin in 1845 through the twentieth century. With the creation of a home missionary agency in the 1880s and a Sunday school publication board in the 1890s, the SBC grew exponentially through most of the twentieth century, eventually becoming the largest Protestant denomination in the United States. As a church, the Southern Baptist Convention was probably the most broadly representative of the white South, drawing in everybody from sharecroppers to school superintendents, lumber camp workers to lawyers, millworkers to mill owners. The Southern Baptists perfectly symbolized the relation of the white South to the rest of the country. They were not quite in, and not quite of, the world of the American middle class, uncertain whether they really wanted to be part of that world.[42]

Like the Southern Baptists and Methodists, members of the Presbyterian Church of the United States (the PCUS, or Southern Presbyterians) insisted they were not guilty of any "schism" and rejected entreaties to reunite with northern coreligionists. Cleric and conservative social theorist Benjamin Morgan Palmer headed a Southern Presbyterian committee established in 1870 to respond to northern offers of reunion. The Southern Presbyterians could not "form these relations ... with a political church," Palmer insisted, without "endorsing the very error which drove us into ecclesiastical exile." Presbyterian polemicist Robert Lewis Dabney added that such relations with the Northern Presbyterians would compel "ecclesiastical amalgamation with negroes, accepting negro presbyters to rule white churches and judge white ladies," both of which entailed a "direct step towards that final perdition of Southern society, domestic amalgamation." Fusion with Northern Presbyterians, he added, "would mean our betrayal of our righteous testimony against the rationalistic and skeptical features of modern Abolitionism." American Presbyterians thereafter remained divided into regionally separate organizations until their reunion in 1983.[43]

The Southern Presbyterians best articulated the doctrine they referred to as the "spirituality of the church." In this view, the church prescribed duty as obedience to God while the state enforced it as "the safeguard of order." Slavery itself, for example, was a matter for the state. The church's obligation was to preach obedience and duty within the given social order. But the Southern Presbyterian position on slavery and segregation was more complicated and political than that. The nationally known Presbyterian theologian in Charleston, James Henley Thornwell, argued that by a "gracious Providence," Africans were brought to American shores and thereby redeemed from "barbarism and sin." The peculiar institution was thus a "link in the wondrous chain of Providence, through which many sons and daughters have been made heirs of the heavenly inheritance." As the PCUS General Assembly declared in 1864, the "long-continued agitation of our adversaries have wrought within us a deeper conviction of the divine appointment of domestic servitude, and have led to a clearer comprehension of the duties we owe to the African race." The institution certainly could not yield to "the dictates of fanaticism and to the menaces of military power." Presbyterian theologians thus spiritualized the most contentiously political of American social institutions.[44]

Among white Christians of the South, too, could be found many neutrals, Unionists, and men who saw military service as contrary to their Christian mis-

sion. The Methodist minister George Richard Browder might have been devoted to the righteousness of the southern cause "against the mad schemes of an
abolition fanaticism," yet he worried that "the public mind is so absorbed in war
& its parties that people hardly find time to think of anything else." Much as he
yearned to devote himself to scriptural study, Browder could not resist consuming the "exciting intelligence" about the war in the newspapers. Despite his southern sympathies, he refused to "sin against my convictions of right," those being
that he should not "gird on carnal weapons & go forth to stain my hands in the
blood of battle, then return to minister at God's altar." A friend finally found him
a substitute, allowing him to pay an exemption and escape army service. Fulfilling his perceived scriptural duties, he preached to his servants. They did not,
he noted succinctly, seem to relish "close plain preaching on that scripture that
requires obedience to masters." Despite his convictions against violence, his conscience was untroubled after he tied up a slave and threatened to whip him severely for insulting his wife. At war's end, he was "resolved to submit without
murmuring to the Providence of God" but believed that the North would yet
"be scourged, for unnecessary cruelties and oppression to the Southern people."
White southerners had been "freed from a grievous burden & a crushing responsibility for escape from which they will someday be thankful." Believers such
as Browder suggest the tenuousness of the connection between piety, wartime
patriotism, and army service. For them, serving the Confederate state was not
necessarily equivalent to obeying God.[45]

White southern Unionists welcomed the aggressive proselytization of the MEC,
as well as the subsidies provided by the federal government for church construction. John Caldwell's career illustrates the difficult path faced by those who labored in groups that rejected the white supremacist religion of the mainstream
southern denominations. Once a firm supporter of slavery and the Confederate
state, the former MECS preacher in Georgia "received new light and life from
above, and during that night of agony and penitence formed a resolution which
has continued unchangeable . . . that was, to speak plainly to the consciences of
the people on a long forbidden topic—the evils of slavery." He did so even at the
risk of "social ostracism and perhaps the risk of [his] life." Caldwell persevered
despite charges that he was one of the "*paid instruments*" of Radicalism—a religious scalawag. Exiled by the Southern Methodist hierarchy to the remote southern Georgia countryside, where he faced threats to his life, Caldwell became
convinced that the "Northern Church was Providentially called to the South chiefly
for the benefit of millions of poor people who were in need of schools and
churches for their enlightenment and salvation." In February of 1866, Caldwell
further affirmed his "loyalty to the National Government and hearty approval
of the antislavery doctrine." For the next six "long years of turmoil and strife," he

fought for "reconstruction, both civil and religious." He accepted a nomination to the state constitutional convention in Georgia, hoping to secure legal protections for his controversial religious work, and also served in the state legislature and as a district judge. A victim of the widespread calumny directed at scalawag ministers, he and others who had joined the MEC were "held up before the public as a set of politico-ecclesiastical propagandists; as malignants, bent on mischief, provoking the ex-slaves to hate, and take revenge on, their former masters; as disturbers of the peace and harmony of the churches." Caldwell narrowly escaped the Klan assassins who hunted him in Columbus, Georgia. His brothers in northern Georgia also preached for the MEC. They allied themselves with federal military authorities to gain financial support for their educational work and encouraged the rise of Union Leagues, or fraternal groupings of men who swore allegiance to the Union and the Republican Party.[46]

Northern Methodist missionaries such as John Emory Bryant and William George Matton endured even greater hostility for their alliances. A native of Maine and a devoted Methodist and Republican, Bryant worked with southern MEC leaders such as John Caldwell and Erasmus Q. Fuller, the controversial editor of the *Atlanta Methodist Advocate*. "Our politics and religion agree admirably, and in harmony they lead to the elevation of all races," Fuller believed. Hatred for Bryant only worsened when he helped to form the Georgia Equal Rights and Educational Association and affiliated himself with Republican newspapers such as the *Loyal Georgian*. Always at the center of fights among the increasingly factionalized Georgia Republicans, Bryant remained active in the Union League and in educational efforts for southern whites through the 1880s.[47]

The New York Methodist George Matton came to Virginia and North Carolina in 1867 to minister for churchgoers loyal to the MEC and the federal government. Although sent to serve whites, he soon was preaching to blacks who had been driven out of Southern Methodist churches and told to go to the Yankees —"excellent advice," he noted ironically, which many of them took. Matton cooperated with the Freedmen's Bureau in setting up a school that was "looked upon with much disfavor, by some of the old Proslavery citizens, and their anger was stirred against me; and one of them declared with much contempt that he would not touch that miserable yankee preacher with a ten foot pole." Pressing on, Matton conducted services in which white and black congregants attended together, sitting on separate sides of an aisle frequently crowded with penitent souls. Hostile whites made Matton a pariah. In Lincolnton, North Carolina, women lifted their skirts to avoid brushing against his wife, and white ruffians broke up camp meetings attended by biracial crowds. Such was the "Ku Klux influence," Matton later remembered, that juries routinely acquitted those accused of violence against northern missionaries. Southern Methodists constantly attacked Yankee "political preachers." These were, as Matton sardonically noted, the same divines who had assured their parishioners that fighting for the Confederacy was a religious duty. In such a setting, it was hardly surprising that white believers sympathetic to the Union struggled to recruit members for their churches. "I beilve that we are full brouthers as Loyl men to the united states," wrote one southern Unionist and MEC adherent to Matton. "I say to you that the Rebs. tuck all most every thing from me that I had on the account of my being a unon man and because my Sons and Sons in Law all went to the fedrel army an fought for the Government." These southern Unionists found no place for themselves in postwar southern religious organizations, as white and black denominations organized under the banners of white supremacy and black independence. As they discovered of spirituality in the postwar South, religion often became politics by other means.[48]

Immediately after emancipation, white southern Christians assumed that religious services would follow the same course as before: white leadership of biracial churches with segregated seating, preferably with blacks in a balcony and whites in the main auditorium. For southern whites, this arrangement in the religious community symbolized the proper spiritual and political hierarchy. Black withdrawal from southern biracial congregations compelled a rethinking of this illusory construction. The ex-slaves, reported one white Virginian, were impatient "of even the *appearance* of control—and counsel has that appearance *to them*—by their former masters."[49]

Whatever their initial reservations, white Christians eventually accepted the withdrawal of most black members from their churches as necessary and even beneficial. "Disguise it as we may," a North Carolinian explained to his colleagues just after the war, "our colored brethren are disposed to independent action—they want preachers and churches of their own." By 1880, in fact, many whites had concluded that "the races can be grouped into separate organizations, and they will be safer and happier so." At the centennial anniversary of one of the oldest southern black churches, First African Baptist of Savannah, the white divine Henry Holcombe Tucker reminded the celebrating congregation that the "providence of God has made us two; and what God has put asunder let not man join together. . . . If God himself has drawn the color line, it is vain as well as wicked for us to try to efface it." By that time, the theological racism of the white southern tradition justified separation as practiced in church life and codified in law in the coming decades. The biracial worship patterns of antebellum churches were becoming a distant memory, and Christian interracialism a virtual impossibility in the context of southern apartheid.[50]

The debates of Southern Presbyterians over the best response to emancipation illustrate the quandaries faced by many white southern ecclesiastical bodies after the war. John Lafayette Girardeau, formerly pastor of a black congregation in Charleston, directed the efforts of the PCUS toward the freedpeople. Without such efforts, he feared, freed slaves would lapse into a "condition of baptized heathenism." Girardeau initially argued against an "organic separation between the two races ecclesiastically," a move he likened to "casting loose a towboat from a great steamship in the middle of a stormy ocean." Later, he considered the policy of retaining black members to be "*theoretically*" the better one while acknowledging that "practically, separation *now* seems a necessity," for black members wanted it. Meanwhile, Robert Lewis Dabney objected vociferously to any black participation in the PCUS, as he believed freed slaves were "almost universally banded to make themselves the eager tools of the remorseless enemies of my country, to assail my vital rights, and to threaten the very existence of civil society and the church, at once." The mere consideration of blacks for the PCUS ministry, he argued, would serve as the "pretext for a partial and odious lowering of our standard." Dabney's view won the day. His persuasive orations, as one correspondent expressed it, had countered the "sickly religious sentiment, which would have wrought immense damage if it had not been held in check by an infinitely wise and gracious Providence."[51]

The difficulties faced by the smaller and more formal denominations, especially the Presbyterians and Episcopalians, appear clearly in the effort to build one denominational institution for black Presbyterians. C. A. Stillman, a pastor in Tuscaloosa in the 1870s, called for the establishment of an institute to train black Presbyterian clergymen. His plan resulted in the founding of Stillman Institute in 1876. In its early years, the school attracted only a few dozen students.

In 1896, seeking to invigorate Presbyterian evangelization and education among black southerners, Oscar Bickley Wilson began ministering to students at Stillman. The white missionary hoped to "make common cause" with his students and "exemplify for them the dignity of manual labor." His idealism met resistance on all sides. "So far from ever showing the least gratitude or appreciation for my aid," he wrote of his students, "they do not even do me the courtesy of asking me to help them in any way—any of those ways which are supposed to mean appreciation, or honor!" He felt "peculiar" walking through black neighborhoods as he experienced the constant gaze and disapproval of whites: "Oh! These iron-bound prejudices of ours! And the fears that come into our hearts!" When he went into one white home and asked to see the cook, the woman was "surprised and *shocked*." Nevertheless, he "conversed with her [the cook] and accomplished my mission." He visited one sympathetic ally in town, who had been "shamefully persecuted" for ministering to Negroes. "We are accustomed to flatter ourselves that we are the most orthodox people on earth," he scoffed, "pre-serving as no other people do, the purity of the infant church, in its unworldly character—and yet for the sin of *humanity* (!) to a wretched Negro this man was refused admission into one of our orthodox churches!" He talked with a white church member who would not consent to "'mix up with the niggers,' she evidently thinks the Negroes are a 'bad lot.' . . . she was set in her ways, and has no negro-philism in her constitution." Some white parishioners who heard Wilson suggesting a biracial communion service "paid their respects to [him] by saying 'Wilson ought to be tarred and feathered.'" The apathy of the PCUS toward the cause was "criminal and disgraceful," he fumed. Despite the obstacles, Wilson managed to recruit Theron Rice to head a Sunday school for black children in Atlanta. Rice later became an influential Presbyterian educator.

At the time of Wilson's death in 1900, Stillman's enrollment consisted of fifty students who were taught by three white instructors. Black Presbyterians remained relatively few in comparison to the Baptists and Methodists. "All we desire," Wilson's successor wrote, "[is to] remind our Christian people that racial differences are not barriers to the gospel, and that Colored Evangelization should be based upon the same plans of support as foreign missionary effort anywhere among any ignorant and backward race." By the early twentieth century, this view represented the dominant thinking of missionaries of both sections toward black southern Christians. It was a far cry from the more hopeful rhetoric of the post–Civil War era, when white and black missionaries from both North and South envisioned leading the freedpeople into full citizenship rights.[52]

Missionaries, Freedpeople, and White Southerners

After the Civil War, missionaries in the South—both black and white—preached their gospel of uplift to the freedpeople. In their own eyes, they were fulfilling a providential role, bringing spiritual and social salvation to a people abandoned in slavery, backwardness, and barbarism. At the same time, their work in political and spiritual evangelization embroiled them in myriad difficulties. By the end of the nineteenth century, they were frustrated by white supremacist resistance even as they grew more accepting of white southern governance over black subjects. Freedom's coming, as they perceived it, would be channeled through the work of educational institutions that would train a talented tenth.

In April of 1866, Lydia Schofield, a Presbyterian missionary to the freedpeople, attended a service where, following the prevalent custom, whites and blacks sat in separate sections of the pews. The preacher predictably lingered on the torments awaiting the eternally damned. "It seemed dreadful to me," wrote Schofield, "this misrepresenting of Him whose name is *Love*, and I thought perhaps the idol of Slavery had stood between him and the Infinite One, so that he had never been *near enough* to realize and feel that God is our Father and all they who do his will shall enter the kingdom of heaven." Schofield urged her missionary subjects in the Sea Islands to "give up the curses of slavery & almost the worst thing was filth and breaking up of family ties—you must *prove* yourselves worthy of freedom, you are free men & women, responsible for every one of your acts." She reminded them of how both enemies and friends would judge the results of emancipation from their behavior: "*education* is the only thing that can raise you to a position worthy of that freedom for which *our* soldiers, & *you*, God bless you, have fought for."[53]

The public reports of missionaries such as Schofield were imbued by hopes of educating a rising and appreciative class of freedpeople. This reflected both genuine desire and belief, as well as the expected rhetoric of fund-raising. Privately, the evangelists and educators more often ruminated on the supposed character defects of the Negro race. As one missionary despaired, "It is one thing to sit in one's office or drawing room and weave fine spun theories in regard to the negro character, but it is quite another to come into actual contact with him." Such views only further convinced northern evangelical leaders to pursue their vision of changing the whole fabric of southern society. "We begin at the foundations of society, and hope to impart to schools, homes, and people an elevating and Christian power," explained one publicist. The "real difficulty" resided in the "ignorance and degradation of the blacks and the prejudices and hatreds of the whites—in other words it is in the *minds and hearts* of men." Transforming those hearts and minds through the talismanic powers of true education and proper religion was the dream of these cultural missionaries.[54]

Just after the commencement of the war, the American Missionary Association (AMA) dispatched teachers to Fortress Monroe, Virginia. This "Gideon's Band" provided evangelical teaching that at times dovetailed all too conveniently with the plans of businessmen who hoped to indoctrinate a disciplined class of free workers in a revitalized cotton plantation economy. By 1866, the nondenominational missionary organization employed over 350 workers in southern schools and churches. In 1868, there were 532 laborers in the southern field. Through the latter part of the nineteenth century, the AMA also hired nearly 500 black teachers and missionaries, about half of them from the South.

In many locales, missionary teachers found blacks already operating schools and the residents making clear their preference for black instructors. During the post–Civil War years, AMA workers taught over 21,000 pupils in daytime and evening schools and 16,000 in Sabbath schools, in over sixteen states and 200 distinct fields of work. Over time, its missionary philosophy shifted from an emphasis on primary school fundamentals to normal school and higher education —that is, training those who would be teachers at the lower levels. During its initial efforts from 1861 to 1869, the AMA expended over four million dollars more than its next closest ecclesiastical competitor, the Freedmen's Aid Society of the Methodist Episcopal Church. Indeed, the northern Congregationalists spent more money than the Freedmen's Bureau itself during that government agency's tenure from 1865 to 1869. Congregational minister John Alvord fostered cooperative efforts between the Freedmen's Bureau (for which he served as superintendent of schools) and the Congregationalists. He set up the first meeting between bureau director Oliver O. Howard and missionary secretary George Whipple. As late as 1890, northern Congregationalists were still training about one-third of black normal school students in the region. More than any single benevolent or governmental agency, AMA schools were responsible for creating the ranks of a black schoolteacher corps in the postwar South.[55]

The AMA's policy of spreading Congregationalism in the South largely failed, even as its educational efforts bore much fruit in the form of long-lived institutions of higher education. Congregationalists eschewed the mass evangelism of the Baptists and Methodists. As a result, few of their churches in the South were self-supporting. The AMA's true legacy resides in its colleges, including Straight University in New Orleans, Louisiana; Fisk University in Nashville, Tennessee; Howard University in Washington, D.C.; Atlanta University in Atlanta, Georgia; Hampton Institute in Hampton, Virginia; Talladega College in rural Alabama; and Tougaloo College near Jackson, Mississippi. Its colleges spanned a spectrum of educational philosophy. Atlanta and Fisk represented a more traditional academic liberal arts approach, at that time referred to as classical education. Hampton, Talladega, and Tougaloo supported programs of industrial education. Atlanta University and Fisk educated and employed scholars such as W. E. B. Du Bois, while Hampton Institute was the alma mater and model for Booker T. Washington, founder in 1881 of the industrial education mecca of Tuskegee Institute in Alabama.[56]

By the 1870s, missionary educators became convinced that their efforts should look toward the training of a "*race of young ministers.*" Other denominational missionary societies, including the Freedmen's Aid Society of the Methodist Episcopal Church, reached the same conclusions. Northern Methodist missionaries outlined the project of their denominational schools:

Our schools have rendered essential aid in the work of restoring social order, of bringing about friendly relations between the employers and laborers, in promoting habits of cleanliness, industry, economy, purity, and morality, rendering more emphatic the grand distinction between right and wrong, false-hood and truth, enforcing fidelity to contracts, portraying the terrible consequences of intemperance, licentiousness, profanity, lying, and stealing, teaching them to respect the rights of others, while they are prompt to claim protection for themselves. . . . The schools have met a great want which no military or political organization could supply, and without which it will be impossible for peace and harmony to be restored.[57]

The $60,000 expended in the first year of the society's existence, its organizers proclaimed, showed that the heart of Methodism was in "the cause of crushed, yet rising humanity." Echoing nearly every missionary group of the era, Methodist leaders felt assured that the freedpeoples' "passionate desire for education" was unmistakable evidence that God was "preparing them by his Spirit for the freedom to which he has led them by his providence." Ministerial training was crucial, for illiterate preachers would have no way of restraining hearers from "fanaticism and superstition, nor instruct them in the doctrines of the Church."[58]

Northern Methodist missionaries were startled by the backwardness and resistance of the South to change. A. S. Lakin worked around Huntsville, Alabama, where he perceived a "general apathy and indifference in regard to Religious Matters" combined with "prejudice of the masses against all northern men." The southern membership eventually ordered him out of the local church, and he was forced to close his freedmen's school. Methodist missionaries also faced the hostility commonly experienced in the postwar South by the allies of black education. At an 1873 meeting, an unnamed correspondent ("we dare not mention names") left this account: "Bands of armed and masked men are prowling around nights, whipping some, and murdering others. Politicians, at a public meeting, have threatened our schools, and being isolated from every human protection, we are in great fear and peril. I have devoted the nights to watching, for the protection of life, and to guarding our buildings against fire." Another missionary despaired that the "enemies of the freedmen and our Church are trying to starve these teachers, and they have well-nigh done it." The white South was "more implacable and determined in its spirit now than ever," a Methodist near Augusta, Georgia, wrote to John Emory Bryant, "and every northern man in the South is practically considered a spy operating clandestinely to thwart their plans to regain political supremacy." He had helped to form Augusta Institute for educating black ministers and served on its board of trustees. Yet the institute was "almost totally ignored by professing Christians of the South on ground that it is founded by northern men and that the education of the colored race is wrong in principle."[59]

By the 1870s, however, many northern missionaries were increasingly sympathetic to their southern counterparts. The work of "redeeming the colored race in earnest," one Northern Methodist suggested, could only begin when a large army of men "thoroughly educated, well drilled in theological truths" ascended to the black pulpits. Only then would "inherited heathen and superstitious notions" be erased from the minds of the freedpeople. The answer for the race problem would come through "using the three great forces, *self-interest, education, and religion.*" Such statements signaled an increasing acceptance of paternalism in missionary work and an acquiescence to white southern control over "the Negro." Bishop T. U. Dudley of the Protestant Episcopal Church of Kentucky warned in 1885 that "separated from us, their neighbors and their friends," Negroes would "retrograde toward the barbarism whence they are sprung, and then, alas, we might be compelled to wage relentless war against them for our own preservation." A white Methodist bishop in Mississippi who supported education for freedpeople suggested that in the ideal school, "carefully selected" portions of the Bible would define the curriculum and black pupils would be taught that "race integrity is obedience to God's own creation and appointment, and that race intercourse, kindly and cordial, is not race equality." To be sure, these sentiments were not universal. The American Baptist Free Mission Society, for example, entrusted the management of funds and labors to its black subjects, hoping to "thus work through them rather than for them." Or as these egalitarian Baptists also expressed it, "What slaveholders found it most necessary to withhold, we consider most necessary to give." This neo-abolitionist society passed from the scene in the 1870s. Most northern missionaries increasingly focused on training the talented tenth, withdrawing from the more broad-based vision of religious uplift and political citizenship they had originally entertained. Their dreams of biracial cooperation and Christian interracialism succumbed to the theological racism that swept the South, and the rest of the country, in the late nineteenth century.[60]

The Gospel According to Radicalism

After the Civil War, black churches imparted the powerful message that freedpeople were equal citizens under the law. To white Redemptionists, this was subversive preaching, especially given the connection of black churchmen to the Republican Party. One black minister and Union League organizer in Virginia, reading of the assassination of a fellow Union Leaguer three weeks back, determined to return to that location and "give them a dose of my radical Republican pills and neutralize the corrosive acidity of their negro hate." Even whites who frequently expressed exasperation at the supposed superstitions of ignorant ex-slaves acknowledged that they were organized into leagues that were "opened by prayer, for the preachers are generally there, and they are counseled as they love their immortal souls to vote no other than the straight republican ticket." In many local congregations, allegiance to the party of Lincoln was de rigueur. At a church service in Virginia shortly before one Reconstruction election, a student of southern political life described prayers being "offered up as fervently for the Republican candidate as if the very existence of the blacks depended upon the election." Mississippi black Baptists during Reconstruction prayed for their defender, the Republican Party, and resolved to defeat candidates who were "opposed to us having equal rights before the law." In 1872, they warned that a Democratic victory would mean a "fast retreating step back again to the land of whips for our own backs, to labor unrequited, to all the laws forbidding the peaceful and happy enjoyment of our rights as American citizens." In some congregations, casting a Democratic ballot could spell excommunication. Parishioners in a Baptist congregation just outside Little Rock threatened their pastor just after his heretical vote became known. Following this election, congregants declared the pulpit vacant. In other locales, congregational leaders held trials after ballots were cast, demanding that Democratic sinners confess their transgression before being readmitted into good fellowship. "The voting of a Democratic ticket by a colored man was an evil, and should be shunned," asserted one black Republican.[61]

At an AME church in North Carolina, the presiding minister expressed his yearning to see freedmen "up to the court house putting their votes in the ballot box." Throughout the South, black men followed that advice. More than 230 black clergymen held local, state, or national office during Reconstruction. Ministers such as Henry McNeal Turner, Ulysses Houston, James Simms, and William Jefferson White in Georgia; Jesse Boulden and Henry Jacobs in Mississippi; Isaac Brockenton in South Carolina; and numerous others looked after the rights of the freedpeople in church and state. The first African American to win a seat in the U.S. Senate, Hiram Revels of Mississippi, was an AME cleric. The postwar constitutional convention in Georgia included nine ministers of the AME. The same held true for Mississippi, where six of the sixteen black men at the 1868 constitutional convention were clergymen, as were some 40 percent of the black men who served as organizers for the Union Leagues. A white newspaper in Jackson, Mississippi, complained that these divines were undercover agents who, "while pretending to teach the gospel," would amass "their flocks together under the pretense of religious service, and then administer to their deluded victims the unlawful, irreverent, irreligious, and blasphemous oaths of the Loyal League." In Augusta, Georgia, black churches served as meeting places for laboring men who mixed religious sentiments and working-class politics. Some eighty black laborers in the growing town sent this account of their proceedings to a northern missionary ally: "Was meet at the time apointed the meting Was open by Reading the 78 Chapter of Psalm, and singing o god our help in ages past our help for years to come by the Rev. Charles R. Edwards and pray by Rev. John Megee after witch Rev. Charles R. Edwards stated the call of the Meting one month ago fore to unit[e] the laboring men in the country into associations."[62]

The consultations during Reconstruction between government officials, including the Freedmen's Bureau, and black clergymen suggested the remarkable changes wrought by emancipation. In January of 1865, African American ministers from Savannah and the Georgia low country advised Union war officers on assisting the refugees set free by Sherman's march. Longtime Baptist pastor Garrison Frazier counseled William Tecumseh Sherman and Secretary of War Edwin Stanton that "the way we can best take care of ourselves is to have land and turn it and till it by our own labor . . . and we can soon maintain ourselves and have something to spare." Frazier suggested as well the decided preference to "live by ourselves" rather than "scattered among the whites," over the objections of the Methodist James B. Lynch, who took the view that ex-slaves and southern whites "should not be separated." Sherman set aside for black war refugees lands in the Georgia and South Carolina low country and the Sea Islands, a decision soon transformed in the prevailing folklore ("forty acres and a mule") as a governmental promise to provide land for the freedpeople. Ulysses L. Houston, one of those who had met with Sherman, was another influential Baptist clergyman in the area. Brought to Savannah as a house servant, he learned to read with white sailors while working in the city's hospital and earned extra income by hiring out his time. From 1861 to 1880, he pastored the Third African Baptist Church and served twice as president of the black Baptist convention in Georgia. Houston also helped to plan a village for the freedpeople on Skidaway Island.[63]

Throughout the South, black religious leaders followed Houston's lead, actively shaping African American life under freedom. James Simms, too, pursued an active career as a minister-missionary and politician. Born a slave in Savannah, he purchased his freedom in 1857 with money raised from working as a masterbuilder. During Reconstruction, he worked with the Freedmen's Bureau and the American Baptist Home Mission Society, served as a Union League organizer, and later won election to the Georgia House of Representatives. During that time he became the only black district judge in the state. His political success left him vulnerable to Klan attacks, which eventually chased him from the lowcountry region into Atlanta. As Simms later explained, socially conscious black clergymen of that time "had to leave their flock and legitimate field of labor to enter the arena of politics to secure right and justice for their people . . . notwithstanding the white citizens among whom they lived and served, and the late owners, [who] constantly spoke disparagingly of the ministers who served in these positions." At one meeting concerning black suffrage, Simms subverted the attempts by white ministers to "manage every thing their own way." He said that "it was the first time he ever had such an opportunity of speaking to white men, and should improve it to tell them *some plain truths. . . .* For once, at least, they heard the unvarnished truth." Simms also testified before Congress on behalf of the freedpeople and edited the Savannah-based *Freedmen's Standard.* His ministerial colleague Thomas Allen, a politician in Jasper County, reminded his congregants that the Yankees had freed them and that "they ought to vote with them; to go with the party always. They voted just as I voted."[64]

Many religio-political leaders of the freedpeople emerged from the class of free blacks or relatively educated ex-slaves. They often lived in urban areas and were self-sufficient in artisanal trades. William H. Heard's career serves as a good example. Born in 1850 and sold twice as a slave when young, Heard rose to a leadership position in the AME during Reconstruction. In 1867, Heard saw William Jefferson White, the Augusta educator and publisher. White was the first well-educated black man Heard had personally witnessed in a public forum. "He very much influenced me," Heard later reminisced, "and I determined from that night to be a MAN, and to fill an important place in life's arena." That night, Democrats tarred White's horse; the next morning he took care of his animal and went on his way, "always outspoken for Orthodox Religion and for the Republican Party." Inspired by such heroism, Heard worked for the party of Lincoln. Democratic candidate Wade Hampton's posse of election supporters, the infamous "Red Shirts," nearly assassinated Heard during the violent 1876 election season in South Carolina, when Heard was trying to protect black voters. While serving as an AME bishop, Heard brought suit before the Interstate Commerce Commission against railroad segregation.[65]

In many cases, well-educated black clerics took places of importance in local and state governments. James Walker Hood of the AMEZ served as the assistant to North Carolina's first postwar superintendent of public education, the Congregationalist missionary Samuel Stanford Ashley. These examples could be multiplied many times over. Elsewhere, scores of ministers took up the radical gospel. In North Carolina, the Reverend A. A. Ellsworth of New Bern anonymously edited a paper called the *Radical.* Several clergymen went as delegates to the state's constitutional convention in 1868. In Arkansas, a Freedmen's Bureau official discovered (to his dismay) black ministers "teaching the people that they should, *of right,* own every foot of soil." Such politically active clergymen, southern white religious leaders claimed, would be satisfied with nothing less than "the Gospel according to Radicalism," a complaint testifying to the widespread influence of black religious activists. John Paris, a white Methodist, recounted how ex-slaves once had enjoyed their religious privileges along with whites in a Christian community, before scheming northerners educated the freedmen in the "science of party politics." Once organized into Union Leagues, the freedmen, in Paris's view, were duped into turning away from the white mentors "who had been laboring for their religious ideal." Black members of Paris's congregation, for example, met one Sunday and formed a Union League society. The following week, only twenty of his black parishioners convened to hear Paris preach. A political organizer, Paris believed, had convinced "these simple minded people" not to attend "upon the religious instructions and ministration of the Southern Ministers of the gospel." White divines such as Paris had been "blamed against them as enemies of the colored race."[66]

While white churchmen emphasized their paternal regard for black believers and assistance to the organization of black churches, Christian freedpeople circulated their own harrowing accounts of harassment, terrorism, and savagery. "God wasn't pleased with the treatment given us by some of the whites and he sent a people down to protect us," a black Georgian later reminisced. "I was always shown, by a voice, by a sign, that He was working for us," as seen in the governor's provision for a militia to protect black citizens. The frequent reports of "hellish, and incarnate brutalities" served as a reminder of this bitter struggle. Traveling on a coach car in South Carolina in the mid-1870s, the president of a black Methodist college was "assaulted, insulted, and called radical sons of bitches by the South Carolina Chivalry of red-shirt notoriety and rifle-club fame. They demanded that he should discontinue to teach those niggers in that school, or they would break it up." The assailants sought to force the college president to "take a drink of Hampton whisky" (referring to the ringleader of Redemptionist forces in South Carolina, Wade Hampton). The Klan in Texas perpetrated some "turrible things" during Reconstruction days, an ex-slave recollected. Her response: "But I just built a wall of the Lord 'round me so they couldn't get at me." Another ex-slave in Arkansas remembered how white gunmen "used to come 'round and bother the church services looking for this one and that one." When the Klan heard "the least thing nigger preacher say," another former bondsperson recounted, "they whoop him. They whooped several." As a result, black clergymen had to be "might particular what they said in the preachin" to the freedpeople. One ex-slave most succinctly expressed the view of black Christians about freedom's coming after the Civil War and the turmoil of Reconstruction: "That was about equalization after freedom. That was the cause of that." Contending religious visions of equalization after freedom—about the terms of freedom's coming—shaped the evolving political struggle in the South through the end of the nineteenth century.[67]

"A Christian Triumph":
Redemption and the Rise of Jim Crow

James Mallory, a white farmer and Methodist in Alabama, watched freedom's coming with trepidation. As he perceived it, men quarreled over political doings rather than tending to the state of their souls, and ex-slaves did not "seem to desire change where it is plain it is not to their advantage, they do not reason or calculate." During a season of revivals in August 1868, he observed that freedpeople "continued their religious exercises night and day, the wildest excitement continues, screams, yells, and distressing cries rend the air for hours." Although hardly a diehard Confederate, Mallory was elated at the advent of Redemption, marking the end of the remarkable period of biracial democracy in some southern states from 1867 to the mid-1870s. In 1874, Mallory's own congregation held a "thanksgiving for good bread crops and deliverance from our cursed rulers."[68]

The term "Redemption," used by historians to describe the end of Reconstruction in the mid-1870s, assumed an especially powerful meaning for white southern believers. Redemption signified individual salvation, as well as the deliverance of society from "cursed rulers." Submission to the North in politics, they feared, would mandate what some called "Yankee faith"—theological liberalism and racial egalitarianism. Lincoln's secretary of state, William Seward, had upheld a "higher law than the Federal constitution, in politics," wrote one appalled Alabama Baptist. Likewise, northern zealots maintained a "higher law than the inspired Constitution [the Bible] in religion." This southerner interpreted the events of Reconstruction as part of God's plan for allowing the "twin sisters" of "liberalism and fanaticism" to run their ruinous course. Thus chastened, southern piety would emerge strengthened.[69]

For some white Christians, the end of slavery and the coming of Reconstruction was an order of Providence. Even if burdensome, it had to be accepted. For others, however, it was a call to arms. Virginia Baptist ministers after the war deemed it their "duty as patriots and Christians to accept the order of Providence." Yet these same Virginians, including the editor of the state Baptist periodical, the *Religious Herald*, condemned Yankees who had

> waged against us a lawless war, which, instead of being regulated by the rules of warfare, . . . has been conducted in a spirit of savage, or rather, draconian cruelty and devastation. Not satisfied with the unbridled spoilations, robberies and thefts, which we have suffered; or with the midnight screams of naked females escaping from their burning houses; or with our incarcerated ministers, separated from the people of their charge, and doomed to lose their health and strength in filthy prisons; not satisfied that we have accepted the

issues of the war, and declared our allegiance to the existing government, or with the impoverished and ruined condition to which we have been reduced ... not satisfied with all this their unsatiated and insatiable malice (what else can we call it) is still ever pouring upon us its bitter and dirty streams of vituperation and abuse.[70]

As would be the case a century later during the civil rights movement, white Democratic politicians during Reconstruction employed an evangelical language of sin and redemption combined with measures of political organization and extralegal violence. A Tennessee Confederate veteran chose the following as his tombstone epitaph: "Belonged to the Ku Klux Klan, a deacon in the Baptist Church and a Master Mason for forty years." A Georgia Baptist minister named E. T. Winkler defended groups such as the Ku Klux Klan as the necessary response to the anarchies of Black Republicanism: "In a state of society where there is no law, and where men must form temporary organizations for the redress of intolerable grievances and the maintenance of social order, justice itself is perverted by attacks on these organizations." The Enforcement Acts of 1871, which took action against groups that blocked the exercise of civil rights, symbolized the oppression of the white South. Winkler offered no such justifications for "temporary organizations" (such as Union Leagues) that defended the embattled citizenship rights of the freedpeople.[71]

When some African American men exercised rights of political citizenship, it appeared to white conservatives as an overturning of a divinely ordered hierarchy. Their polemic against "the gospel according to Radicalism" proceeded from many of the same assumptions regarding natural hierarchy that had guided the proslavery argument. The specter of "negro domination" (the defaming slogan aimed at Reconstruction governments, which were in fact predominantly white) exhibited how the South would be "oppressed in every way in which a robbing, revengeful, blood-thirsty, unprincipled Party can oppress us," wrote a white Redemptionist. Clerics such as the gentlemanly South Carolinian Richard Furman, who had opposed secession while defending slavery, advised Christians to "reverently acknowledge the hand of God in the great events which have transpired and calmly to acquiesce in the orderings of his Providence." Few white believers in his state followed the advice. Interpreting the war's conclusion, a religious Redeemer in South Carolina granted that "God *has brought it about*" but disputed the necessity of loyalty to the reconstructed governments, a notion of "such daring and insulting blasphemy, that thousands here feel like abandoning a religion which gave birth to such atrocities." Bemoaning the conquering of a government ordained by Providence, a white Alabamian expressed the most common sentiments of the religious Redeemers: "I hope to submit like a Christian to the dealings of my creator," he wrote to a friend, "but I wish to have nothing to do with those who have ruined our country, stolen our property, burned our villages, and murdered our people."[72]

Southern Redemptionists battled to restore a white supremacist order and claimed, without any consciousness of hypocrisy, that their churches were undefiled by the politics that disgraced northern and black religious organizations. White southern Christians viewed their Redemptionist activity as essentially religious, an extension of the cosmic struggle between order and disorder, civilization and barbarism, white and black. With minds embittered by the "teachings of religious fanatics and political scoundrels," a New Orleans churchman ominously warned, "hoards of armed negroes assemble, and threaten to rape the women, murder the men, and burn the homes of a community." The *Wilmington Daily Journal* indicted black political clergymen for carrying the "Radical platform concealed among the leaves of the Holy Bible." North Carolina Presbyterians protested in "*the name of the Church of God, against ministers who turn politicians being regarded as representatives of the clergy* in any sense whatever." White churchmen attributed political meetings among the freedpeople to the "cunning of Satan, as represented by his agents in the Gorilla convention." One South Carolinian condemned black ministers for delivering "political harangues" that "engender[ed] strife and bitter hatred" while advising his own ministerial troops to be "vigilant and active" in their state electoral contests. "I consider that minister recreant to his duty he owes to his country," he wrote in 1867, "who does not feel and *manifest* an interest in political affairs in the present crisis." Given the stakes, southern conservatives celebrated the often violent restoration of Democratic governments as a "Christian triumph"; it was clear to them that "duty to the Democracy" was "paramount to duty to God and the church."[73]

On October 26, 1876, white Democrats in South Carolina declared a day of prayer and fasting in preparation for Wade Hampton's campaign. The Democratic hero's supporters led prayers, sang hymns, and preached sermons along the campaign trail. Those who joined in the crusade, including some white Republicans who had given up on their candidate, were praised for coming over to the "Lord's side." The Reverend James H. Elliot of St. Paul's Episcopal Church in Charleston read a sermon promising that God would "be jealous for His land, and pity His people . . . [and] remove far off from you the northern army." The workings of political Redemption thus fulfilled the theology of chastisement. With their due repentance, God's people emerged triumphant. After the "long night" of Radical rule, a South Carolina Baptist leader remarked after Hampton's victory, "we now met in the sunshine of the recent wonderful political changes which had been wrought by the hand of God." The North's policy, a Methodist editor reminisced in 1880, had been to "visit upon us all the results of the war to the bitterest extremity, deny us equal rights before the law, consume our effects, and absorb us religiously." Redemption had brought a marked change, for "conciliation, brotherly love, and the preservation, of all our institutions, liberties, and forms of law" would be the "one great purpose of all our people." Rather than offering "wild theories of a maudlin, bloated philanthropy," northerners finally were comprehending the race question according to God's law. "Not a Negro at the polls," the *New Orleans Advocate* crowed in 1879: "Let Negroes and Chinamen and Indians suffer the superior race of white men to whom Providence has given this country, to control it."[74]

"Race Pride and the Christian Spirit": Blackness and the Theology of American Apartheid

Freedom's coming for black Christians, so memorably dramatic in 1865, held far less promise by 1895. The bright hopes of the Reconstruction era for "equalization after freedom" dimmed in the harsh reality of the segregated southern order constructed in the late nineteenth and early twentieth centuries. Freedom, it became clear, would come only through a constant struggle. "With strategic ingenuity which I cannot commend," as a black Methodist clergyman put it in 1888, white southern conservatives had moved the struggle for "Southern rights" from the "field of blood to the forum of political polemics. They saw that they could gain under the forms of law and in defiance of it all for which the South had contended in open revolt, save and except for slavery." In doing so, they won the battle to control the political and economic order of the postwar South.[75]

Traveling to a religious conference in Jacksonville, Florida, in the 1880s, Daniel Alexander Payne was assured that he would encounter no trouble. On the train, however, the conductor ordered the elderly AME bishop to move to the Jim Crow car. Payne responded, "I'll not dishonor my manhood by going into that car," and demanded that he be left off the train rather than switch to the inferior seat. The conductor ejected him five miles from his destination. This paragon of propriety walked the rest of the way, carrying his baggage. Jacksonville's black Methodists responded with an "indignation meeting." Because legal cases had been filed, Payne determined to let the "heavenly court" judge his situation. Payne's experience set a gloomy forecast. Indeed, he escaped rather lightly compared to the thousands who were cheated, beaten, and murdered during this violent era.[76]

Colloquially termed "Jim Crow," southern segregation might also be designated by the word that later described the racial caste system of South Africa — "apartheid." As statutes in southern states enforced the segregation and disfranchisement of black citizens, white southern theologians gave divine sanction to the hard fight that imperfectly secured the Jim Crow order. In the process, they entertained notions of scientific racism that historically had been anathema to the theologically orthodox.

This theological transition may be seen in comparing the great antebellum Southern Presbyterian divine James Henley Thornwell with his successors in the postbellum era. In 1850, Thornwell's famous sermon "The Christian Doctrine of Slavery" expressed the proslavery sentiments of southern clergymen at their intellectual peak. The Charleston Presbyterian emphatically rejected the newly emerging school of scientific racist thought of the Negro as a "beast," derived from some animal genesis previous to Adam. On the contrary, he insisted, all were descended in common from Adam's loins and lay prostrate before God's throne of judgment. "We are not ashamed to call him [the Negro] our *brother*," he told the elite crowd gathered for the dedication of a sanctuary built especially for ministering to slaves. Inequality was inevitable in a world cursed by sin, he said, but even curses could be transformed into blessings. For example, the earth's very sterility induced men to industry and labor, producing good out of Adam's original sin. As the Book of Romans assured believers, all things worked together for good. This was also the case even with imperfect social institutions such as slavery, assuming that humans cheerfully and obediently fulfilled their social duties according to their place and station in life. Only hopelessly naive philanthropists could demand perfect equality and justice in a fallen world.[77]

Thornwell died in 1862, before he could witness God's verdict on the fate of slavery in the United States. After the Civil War, Presbyterian divines such as Benjamin Morgan Palmer updated religious theories derived from Old Testament passages to meet the new conditions of the postemancipation South. Palmer's colleague Robert Lewis Dabney's arguments against black membership in the PCUS had won him over, especially Dabney's insistence in 1874 that black separation came from the "most controlling sentiment known to the human heart — *the instinct of race*." Into the 1880s, Palmer reminded his Presbyterian subjects that God had "divided the human race into several distinct groups, for the sake of keeping them apart," and that God confused human speech and scattered Noah's ancestors in order to restrain man's wickedness in the future. Attempts during Reconstruction to force groups together that God intended to keep separate arose from an "infidel humanitarianism" akin to the "usurpation and insurrection of the first Nimrod," the descendant of Ham who broke Divine commandments and compelled God to destroy the Tower of Babel. Since that time, Palmer concluded, all attempts to restore the unity of mankind had been "providentially and signally rebuked."[78]

Scientists, historians, and early anthropologists joined religious thinkers such as Palmer and Dabney in undermining any surviving notions of racial or spiritual equality. The late nineteenth century witnessed the apogee of polygenesis and scientific racism, seen in full-length expositions such as *Anthropology for the People: A Refutation of the Theory of the Adamic Origin of All Races.* Published in 1891 by William Campbell under the pseudonym "Caucasian," this work straddled the nineteenth-century world of close biblical exegesis and the twentieth-century reliance on science. These two perspectives produced truly miscegenated offspring, including a mytho-scientific racism that blended folklore, Darwinian science, and biblical exegesis. "Caucasian" attacked the notion that all the world's races sprang from Adam's loins, substituting for that a religio-scientific mythology that led to an especially virulent form of white supremacist thought:

> From this theory, that God made the yellow and the black races inferior, physically, mentally and morally, we infer that he designed them for a subordinate and dependent position; that to impose upon them the duties, obligations and civilization of the superior race and give them the same mental and moral training, is to do violence to their nature and must result in evil; that the Creator, having made different races, intended that blood purity should be preserved, and for this purpose implanted the instinctive mutual and universal repulsiveness of races; that political and social equality is unnatural and repugnant to the best human instincts, and that miscegenation, or admixture of races, is not only an enormous sin against God, but a degrading bestiality which can result only in unmitigated evil and final destruction.

In Caucasian's view, nonwhite peoples were not descendants of Adam and therefore not "brothers in any proper sense of the term, but inferior creations." Polygeny —the theory of the separate origin of the human races—was thus the "only theory reconcilable with Scripture." The biblical flood was a consequence of the union of the Adamite (white) and pre-Adamite (nonwhite) races, the "only union we can conceive of that is reasonable and sufficient to account for the corruption of the world and the consequent judgment." In other words, sexual unions between white and nonwhite peoples in the ancient world compelled God to wash the world away and start over again. Noah preached against miscegenation, but the people persisted in making "unholy alliances that ended in their destruction." God intended that the Adamic (white) race "be kept free from admixture with any inferior blood." The pre-Adamite races belonged to the "*genus homo*" in a "zoological sense," but the "mode of their creation concludes them only in the highest order of animals, and subjects them to the dominion of the Adamite." Nonwhites were not adapted to the spiritual religion of the New Testament: "whenever the Christian influence of the superior race is withdrawn, they go back to feticism [fetishism] and idolatry, which are natural to them."[79]

The fear of race mixing, particularly between white women and black men, the symbol of virginal purity encountering the black beast rapist, was a pernicious and brutally effective justification for segregation and racial violence. The pervasive specter haunted southern folklore. By its very nature, tangible proof was irrelevant. Race purity was at stake. Nowhere was the violence enforcing white supremacy more gruesomely displayed than in the horrific acts by which white men claimed to preserve the honor of the race—that is, in lynching black men. Well over 4,000 lynchings (4,786 by one count) occurred in the United States from 1880 to 1950. Black men made up the majority of the victims. Any reality behind the incendiary allegations of the defilement of the white woman usually was of secondary concern to the perpetrators. The mere mention or rumor often sufficed as a call to light the homemade torches and loop the rope knots. Some of the best-known incidents of racial violence from 1880 to 1950 were what one historian has called "spectacle lynchings." These purposeful and solemn rituals witnessed dozens, hundreds, or even thousands engaged in acts of purification (hence the frequency with which lynching victims were burned, and the invocations pronounced at such events by clergymen). The injustices perpetrated within the legal system simply added to the violence meted out to black Americans outside the legal system. In either case, there was no respite, no safe space, no real means of recourse.[80]

For centuries, Anglo-Americans had identified blackness with impurity and found biblical sanction for this connection. This helped to justify slavery and had devastating consequences within the post–Civil War South. Prayer services preceded a lynching of two men in North Carolina in 1889. When Methodist bishop Warren Candler explained that vigilante violence destabilized the social order, a Methodist layman responded that the Bible supported it. In the late 1890s, Anthony Crawford, secretary of an AME church in Abbeville, South Carolina, got into a dispute over cotton prices and was thrown in jail. After his release, a white mob hunted him down and then tortured him in preparation for his lynching. Sitting in his jail cell, "Crawford was heard to say, while spitting blood where they had kicked out his teeth, 'I thought I was a good citizen.'"[81]

Against the onslaught of such deeply rooted myths and religiously sanctioned degradation and violence, black Christians stood little chance of mounting an effective theological defense. Nevertheless, they tried. Black clergymen repeated their defenses of the race, pleas for justice, and eschatological hopes for the future. Attempting to fathom what could be God's purpose in subjecting them to slavery and segregation, some turned to the same theology of "chastisement" that had once been the province of white theologians. "In modern times the idea of God has been very largely determined by what is known as racial consciousness, and racial necessity," wrote an AME minister. There would be no brotherhood among men "until we have a common Father, a common heritage, a God . . . whose radiances dispel the malignant and diabolical nightmare of racial superiority and strikes down bigotry, dictatorship, arrogance in church and in state." African American thinkers of the Jim Crow era puzzled over the theological status of the white man, who was both a Christian brother and a tireless oppressor. "No man or race of men is Christian when of them it is indisputably known that they oppress the weak, despoil the ignorant, victimize the unoffending, and impiously murder their fellow men both in body and in spirit," concluded one minister. It would be up to black churchmen, another cleric argued, to point out how the emerging southern segregationist order "menaces our Christianity and cripples civilization."[82]

In the later nineteenth century, a small but significant set of educated African American theologians encountered the romantic and racialist ideas of their era. Many of them responded by trying to write the black man *into* the reigning mythologies and categories. As one black Methodist proclaimed, "It is race pride and the Christian spirit to which we must trust and which will find their way when they are once thoroughly awakened to the task to which we are calling them." It was biblically prophesied that the destiny of black Americans was to bring civilization back to their home continent. According to George Wilson Brent, an AME minister, biblical stories provided evidence of the black man's indispensable role in furthering human history. "Africa, our fatherland, the home of the Hamitic race," he proclaimed, was the "only country on earth whose past, present, and future so concerned the Lord." Even the son of Ham himself, Canaan, was blessed, for he "invested and built up a country and settled a nation bearing his name, whose glory . . . remains today the typical ensign of the Christian's hope, concerning Africa's future glory prophecy says 'Ethiopia shall soon stretch forth her hand to God.'" Brent dated the origin of the white man to *after* Noah's flood, meaning that the black man could claim the more ancient pedigree than the white man, no matter what the current state of power relations.[83]

Many black theologians produced race histories that explained the origins and destiny of the Negro people to African American readers. Even when diverging on specific points, these race writers collectively disputed the racist notions of inferiority inherent in the Western idea of blackness. Whether to invert the standard biblical mythologies (as did George Wilson Brent), or to put on display entirely new mythological constructs, or to insist that blackness and whiteness were simply not scriptural categories because "of one blood hath God made all nations," African American religious thinkers responded vigorously to the creation of blackness as a synonym for inferiority and shame. Few white Americans listened. "Neither character, the accumulation of property, the fostering of the Church, the schools and a better and higher standard of the home" would ensure respect for the race, a black Methodist editor observed in the early twentieth century. He had lost his "confidence in the justice, humanity, and fair play" of the white South. "Our people are restless, more so now, than I have ever known them," another black clergyman informed a white newspaper editor.[84]

In the twentieth century, however, southern religious progressives and radicals gradually awakened to the radical injustice perpetuated in the Bible Belt. They knew that freedom would come only through a constant struggle.

It was a thin but tough community of folk. —Randolph Taylor, Presbyterian minister

Our time had come, and it went past, and we did what we could. And you needed these more radical fellows. —Charles Jones, Presbyterian minister

Chapter Two

Freedom's Struggles

*Southern Religious Populism, Progressivism,
and Radicalism, 1890–1955*

"Will the churches of the South," a progressive southern Congregational minister asked in 1945, "whose denominational roots are revolutionary and whose Holy Book is not a stick of candy but a stick of dynamite, . . . bring to the farm and factory worker a good wage, a decent house, a free assembly, a brotherhood enfolding all races?" This cleric articulated the challenge that motivated a generation of southern evangelical Populists, progressives, and radicals. For them, the "spirituality of the church" was irrelevant at best, a heresy at worst. They instead pursued the sanctification of politics, envisioning religious ideas as central to achieving a more just order for ordinary southerners, white and black. In the process, they moved far beyond the initial assumptions of early-twentieth-century progressivism and into radical thought and action in the struggles of the mid-twentieth century for social justice. They learned that freedom's coming required a constant struggle of political action in this world.[1]

From the 1890s through World War II, black and white religious leaders engaged in extensive efforts to uplift their people. Like their northern counterparts, white southern progressives of the early twentieth century championed

Russell Lee, "Negro boys and girls humming spiritual at UCPAPWA (United Cannery, Agricultural, Packing, and Allied Workers of America) meeting, Bristow, Oklahoma. The union meeting has become a main social gathering in these sections and has taken on some of the spirit of the old time revival. Spirituals vie with the union songs for popularity." February 1940, Library of Congress, Prints and Photographs Division, LC-USF34-035154-D.

uplift and democracy while sanctioning hierarchies of race and culture, including pseudoscientific defenses of white supremacy. They argued for progressive political reforms and sought to implement coercive measures of social control. They pursued uplift and social improvement while limiting local participation and control. Their efforts met with mixed success. The rural South proved resistant to progressivism, a movement that ultimately depended upon industrialization and urbanization. The dependence of southern progressives on schemes of modern racial control (such as urban segregation) doomed efforts to address issues of social justice. Black progressives, for their part, operated within the tight constraints of a system that denied their humanity and citizenship and thus fatally crippled what alliances could be made with white progressives. Recognizing these limitations, social radicals and reformers tried to harness democratic means to advance social justice in the South. In doing so, they, too, confronted the uncomfortable truth that the use of democratic means might well lead to undemocratic ends. They learned this lesson most painfully in the local support for segregated schools and anger at federal power used to enforce civil rights over local custom in the 1950s and 1960s.

The religious radicals of the next generation following Populism and progressivism—including men and women such as Howard "Buck" Kester, Myles Horton, Modjeska Simkins, Ella Baker, Gordon Blaine Hancock, Lillian Smith, Nelle Morton, Charles Jones, Virginia Durr, Glenn Smiley, Septima Clark, and Jo Ann Gibson Robinson—saw through the progressive prism of uplift ideology. Fueled by deeply religious visions, they envisioned an interracial democracy. Their influence was limited in the best of circumstances, more so when anticommunist crusades made suspect all questioning of southern traditions. Historians have noted how little impact racial progressivism and radicalism made on the seemingly solid South. Yet an undercurrent of dissent persisted as southern religious radicals poked at comfortable evangelical assumptions and challenged the established order. As two veteran southern progressives later reminisced, their "thin but tough community of folk" had a "sense of religious community" that kept them "going in periods of defeat."[2]

"The Christian Religion in Concentrated Form": Southern Evangelical Populism

Social reformist and radical impulses in white southern religion sprang organically from the Farmers' Alliance and Populist movements of the late nineteenth century. Southern Populists preached a rural social gospel, meshing the language of evangelical pietism and agrarian protest to organize God-fearing farmers living in difficult times. Alliance men and women understood that religion should engage moral, not merely partisan, issues. For them, the pressing questions of the day were fundamentally moral rather than political. Continued national obeisance to the gold standard, for example, was not just a matter of monetary policy, for it portended "abject slavery to your children and their posterity."[3]

Fervent evangelicalism and social gospel eschatology filled Farmers' Alliance literature. Sam Adams, a farmer-activist in Alabama, advised his fellow believers that "those Christians who believe in the freedom of the mind, soul, and body, will have to take hold of the politics of this country, or we will be enslaved by the rule of a class of men who have no regard for the souls of men." Just as a man could not "love Christ and serve Hell," so could no man "live with Christ in glory who votes with Satan for wickedness." To the extent there was a "movement culture" of Populism, it was tied integrally to the evangelical culture of the region, as political gatherings were imbued with the passion of religious revivals and camp meetings. Evangelical churches provided key personnel to the Populists. One of them was Richard M. Humphrey, a white Baptist minister who headed the Colored Farmers' Alliance and led black farm workers in the early 1890s in striking against "starvation wages" (a move that drew the condemnation of many whites in the Farmers' Alliance). Another was John B. Rayner, a black Baptist minister and Republican activist who stumped through eastern Texas in 1894 on behalf of the Populist-Republican fusion ticket. Despite a barrage of criticism from the southern denominational establishment, rural religious agitators felt that "instead of the Alliance leading a preacher away from his high calling of God it will lead him to it; he becomes more intimate with his flock, knows more of their needs, learns more of their cases, their joys and their sorrows."[4]

Discontented farmers understood contemporary issues through the restorationist and millennialist language that was a deep part of their religious world. While large landholding or urban professional churchmen distrusted the agrarian radicalism of small landholding farmers and tenants, some denominations, especially restorationist groups such as the Disciples of Christ, were heavily represented in local farmers' alliances. The restorationist/Populist coalition included Free Will Baptists, the Methodist Protestant Church, the Disciples of Christ, Quakers, some Baptists, and others. Though generally smaller in terms of regionwide numbers in comparison to the dominant Baptists and Methodists, these groups held significant strength in areas that also attracted considerable Populist sympathies—in parts of Texas, Oklahoma, the Arkansas hill country, Missouri, western North Carolina, and the up-country regions of the Deep South. Democratically organized religious groupings such as the Methodist Protestant Church (a branch of Methodism that was congregational in church governance, in contrast to the Episcopalian hierarchy of Methodism) sought to restore Jeffersonian democracy in both church and state. These congregational Methodists and allied groups criticized established denominational and political machines alike. Churchgoers linked evangelical and political democracy, seeing in them a means of restoring a primitivist purity to Christianity and agrarian virtue to American culture.

Scottish common-sense moral philosophy, a pervasive nineteenth-century intellectual tradition, provided the theology and political framework of the restorationist groups and the evangelical Populists. As the moral governor of the universe, went this reasoning, God ordered both the natural and social worlds in ways that men could perceive through their common sense. All men could comprehend natural law; likewise, all men should prosper under a moral economic system. The philosophy of evangelical Populism also revived Jeffersonian democratic ideals: economic independence on a personal level, freedom of the individual conscience in voting and religion, strict economy in government, and suspicion of centralized government and urban life. Losing political and religious independence, the evangelical Populists argued, would "eventually poison the whole of Christian civilization in America." It would spell the loss of "American manhood and liberty" and subject the people to "political tyranny . . . and religious Romanism." Populist thought also incorporated well-defined views on woman's role in the household and the place of black southerners—perhaps equal, but certainly separate.[5]

The southern Farmers' Alliance drew deeply from the evangelical values of the exercise of individual autonomy and conscience, patriotic millennialism, and social Christianity. To this mix, Populist Party supporters added political action. Evangelical churches provided networks in which Populist ideas could circulate, the true believers who threw themselves into the movement, and the cultural logic that bound together political reform with the broadest understanding of God's kingdom on earth. Rural church people responded with enthusiastic participation. J. M. Mewborne, a Disciples of Christ elder in eastern North Carolina, served as state president of the Farmers' Alliance and later stood for office on the Populist Party ticket. While stumping for the farmer's movement, Mewborne protested his denomination's plan for a more centralized system of collecting missionary dues, a scheme that he feared would enrich an organizational machine in religious life alarmingly akin to that already present in the political and economic world. By the early 1890s, prominent clergymen grew alarmed over the way that politicized pietism had co-opted church people. In return, southern religious Populists denounced the centralized machinery of money, one they believed had distorted the Christian denominations. The moral applied equally to the realms of politics and religion. As one Christian Populist put it, "We are taking the first steps toward the absolute monarchy, Popery . . . if machine methods are the best we submit; but we still know that we are not the free men our fathers were."[6]

Tar Heel Baptists sympathetic to Populism published the *North Carolina Baptist*. It competed with the standard denominational weekly, the *Biblical Recorder*, a paper Populist dissenters alleged was tied into the "bossism" of the state church hierarchy. All three editors of the new journal—G. M. Duke, Lunsford Lloyd, and the Reverend John Ammons—served as Alliance organizers in western North Carolina. J. F. Click, a Baptist Populist, demanded justice for producers who were being robbed by the plutocracy. The Bible provided inspiring examples of God sending "prophets, holy men and women to warn nations, cities, and individuals of danger to come. . . . So it is in our day . . . if we do not correct the evils of our government and bring about a reign of justice where men will more nearly do unto others as they would wish to be done by." The established Christian churches once again had taken the side of slavery and not liberty, wrote North Carolina Alliance president Cyrus Thomson. The venerable doctrine of the spirituality of the church, he charged, deflected attention from social conditions that defied the divine principles of God's moral governance.

The premier Populist supporter in North Carolina was Thomas Dixon Jr. The former Shakespearean actor and social gospel orator also was a popular writer best remembered for his notorious novel *The Clansman*. In the hands of pioneering film director D. W. Griffith, Dixon's works metamorphosed into the 1915 cinematic masterpiece of racist propaganda *The Birth of a Nation*. Even as Dixon's father remained loyal to the doctrines of the Democratic Party and the spirituality of the church, Thomas Dixon Jr. praised Populism as the "Christian religion in concentrated form." The *North Carolina Baptist*, the *Progressive Farmer*, and the *Caucasian* all printed Dixon's weekly sermons. The Alliance, in Dixon's estimation, found its true form in the "religious nature of the millions of undermasses who compose its rank and file."[7]

The Georgia Populist leader Tom Watson wrote acidly of Joseph Brown, a wealthy Baptist, former scalawag, and sometime governor of the state: "Joe Brown is a millionaire. Of course. He is a convict lessee. Of course. He is a rigidly correct member of the church. Of course." Established denominational leaders felt the sting of such attacks. Firing back, they lambasted preachers who had been "drawn into the political whirlpool," thus becoming "champions on the hustings of considerable notoriety." A conservative Alabama minister despaired that "politics and money-making" were the "absorbing topics among the preachers —it is so common, indeed, that one seldom hears them discuss anything else." In North Carolina, Democratic Party officials enlisted the Presbyterian and Baptist progressives Alexander McKelway and Josiah Bailey, Methodist educator John C. Kilgo, and even Primitive Baptist elder E. P. Gold to speak out against Populism. Bailey later became a major voice for the disfranchisement of illiterate poor whites and blacks. Such a measure, he hoped, would deny votes to Populist candidates while also supporting his larger cause of compelling education for poorer whites.[8]

African American farmers also voted Populist, and black ministers contributed considerably to the Colored Farmers' Alliance. Thomas Watson, later to become the race-baiting newspaper editor and governor of Georgia, suggested in the 1890s that southern folk could pursue their common economic interest without threatening social equality between the races. At the same time, white supremacist rhetoric also contributed to Populism's demise. It was, after all, the Populists who threatened to split the white vote and thus cede states to Black Republicans and "Fusionists," as Democrats delighted in pointing out. Picking up the hoary but still useful theme of Redemption, the Reverend N. M. Jurney of Trinity College (later Duke University) opened a Democratic rally this way: "Let us feel this day the vibrations of our coming redemption from all wicked rule, and the supremacy of that race destined not only to rule this country but to carry the Gospel to all nations and maintain Civil and Religious Liberty throughout the world."

In tandem with the political establishment, white religious elites insisted that "the white people of the South mean to rule, and they will rule."[9]

The central themes of southern evangelical individualism, including the spirituality of the church and white supremacy, eventually tamed the Populist critique of the demise of Jeffersonian democracy in church and state. Southern rural reformers themselves often failed to overcome their distrust of collective cooperative solutions, and their theological racism hindered biracial cooperative efforts such as those tentatively formed through the Colored Farmers' Alliance. Yet the extent to which Populist enthusiasms entered white southern church life in the 1890s showed how evangelical piety, transplanted into Populist camp-meeting fervor, could disturb the conservative social order of the region. Unlike Populism, the more urban movement of twentieth-century southern progressivism enjoyed considerable support among the established religious leaders.

"The Right-Minded Members of That Race": Southern Religious Progressivism

Southern denominational leaders in the early twentieth century personified the rise of a middle-class urban evangelicalism among congregants who were still predominantly rural. The growth of commercial enterprise, as the southern religious progressives understood it, was essential to the rebuilding of the region's economy and its churches. Religious organizations would have to recruit the growing white southern middle class in supporting benevolent endeavors organized by professionalized denominational workers. "Scientific management is the slogan of every organization except the church," a progressive Southern Baptist lamented. The southern religious progressives aimed to make it such.[10]

Southern progressive reformers usually came from towns, were middle class, and viewed the world through the language of Protestant missions. They pursued a variety of sometimes conflicting goals: prohibition of alcohol, programs for public health, assimilation of immigrants, education of poor whites and mountaineers, support for institutions of public higher education, industrial development, revitalization of country life, and disfranchisement of the "lower orders" of both races. As a biology professor and president at Wake Forest College in Winston-Salem, North Carolina, William Louis Poteat was a classic early-twentieth-century southern religious progressive, one who represents both the democratic as well as the more disturbing sides of the movement. A devout evangelical and teetotaler, Poteat was also a far-seeing educator who built his institution while fending off threats from the reactionaries who would stifle freedom of thought in the region. As a Christian and a scientist who taught Darwin's ideas on evolution in his classroom, he led battles for improved education and social reform under the aegis of paternalistic white elites coaxing the region to a better future. At the same time, Poteat supported eugenics as part of a program to improve the human race.[11]

During the Progressive Era, the social gospel found some hardy exponents in the South. Charles Spurgeon Gardner, a professor of religion and sociology at Southern Baptist Theological Seminary in Louisville, was a prototypical social gospeler rather than a minister with a generalized espousal of social Christianity, as was the case with many of his peers. Writing much like a progressive muckraker, he depicted American society as an "organized system of greed—a mad, selfish, unscrupulous struggle for gain, operation with but little restraint of conscience through great impersonal, 'soulless' corporations." He thought "the extension of the dominion of the Kingdom of God over these corporations" was "one of the great religious tasks of our time." The state's regulatory powers could act as the hand of God, replacing the now failing invisible hand of the classical economists. "The more definitely the goal of social evolution is worked out by the students of social science," he asserted, "and the more adequately the concept of the Kingdom of God is grasped by the students of the gospel, the more nearly they will be found to correspond." A surprising number of socially aware professors such as Gardner mentored several generations of students who later assumed positions of regional religious leadership—a fact that rankled conservatives in all denominations. Gardner's students in Louisville wrote to Southern Baptist Theological Seminary president E. Y. Mullins, a noted theologian and successful executive administrator at the growing school, that more emphasis on religious sociology would compel preachers to "become familiar with those burning social questions which are uppermost in the world consciousness of the present day."[12]

Social reformers and social gospelers were active but isolated and frustrated in the post-Reconstruction South. Suspicion of state activism, evident in the antebellum era, heightened even further because of the exercise of federal power during Reconstruction. Republican libertarianism, with its opposition to centralized power and resistance to large outside forces, clashed with notions of coercive state intervention necessary to achieve the progressives' aims. Historian William Link has argued that southern progressives needed a single "language of discontent" to supply the "ideational glue" for the differing approaches of scientific experts, social humanitarians, religious idealists, and political reformers. Prohibition was the glue, the one program that enjoyed nearly universal support in the secular and religious progressive coalition. It came with a price: prohibition ultimately divided black and white communities further, as temperance campaigners dipped deeply into the fetid waters of theological racism.[13]

The ethics and self-discipline that came out of evangelical individualism iron-ically fed into one of the largest efforts in American history to deploy state power to control individual behavior, the Prohibition movement. This move did not come without a fight. Rather than seeking solutions through public pol-icy, nineteenth-century evangelical temperance reformers preferred the "con-stant, persistent, and never ceasing business of preaching repentance" to those who sinned. In 1914, Southern Presbyterians resolved initially to "do all properly within our power" to secure a Prohibition amendment. Opponents responded that the resolution was a "deliverance upon a political question" and hence was "contrary to the historical position of our Church on the right of the Church to make political deliverances." Evangelicals also harbored lingering doubts about the enforceability of prohibition measures. Josiah Bailey of the Baptist *Biblical Recorder* warned that imposition of state prohibition would impose "a China-like centralization" and a "practical constabulary occupation of the country." He advocated local option as the best synthesis of evangelical reform with demo-cratic means of limited government.[14]

In the early twentieth century, temperance advocates embraced public pol-icy as the means to effect righteous reform. The *Methodist Advance*, a progres-sive paper in North Carolina, intoned that besides the gospel of salvation, the "preaching and practicing of Temperance" was the "most important matter to engage the attention of all people. Either it is right to make sell and drink the in-toxicating beverages which have since the days of Noah brought curses upon the sons of men and misery and woe to the daughters of all lands, or else it is wrong." The reformers gradually saw some limited results, including local option and alcohol-free zones around schools and churches. Prohibition at the state and na-tional level caught the eye of the progressive evangelicals. Because prohibition could be defined outside the realm of the merely political, it was safe grounds for arousing religious sentiment on a public policy question.[15]

Progressive evangelical women forcefully advocated more direct governmen-tal intervention on public policy issues such as the regulation of alcohol. With-out the Woman's Christian Temperance Union (WCTU), even in its diluted form in the South, prohibition probably would have failed. The WCTU pushed tem-perance education in Sunday schools and agitated for denominations to ad-vance the cause. Ignoring the implorings of fearful clergymen, the WCTU spear-headed a church-based prohibition drive in Alabama beginning in 1882. In 1904, men from the Anti-Saloon League (ASL) took over leadership of the state move-ment. W. B. Crumpton, head of the Anti-Saloon League in Alabama, used his state Baptist denominational newspaper to press for federal legislation banning the transport of liquor across state lines. The strength of women in mobilizing voters empowered organizations such as the ASL. The crusade against alcohol thus transformed evangelical women into a political force. After local option initially passed in Alabama, opponents enlisted schoolteachers as lobbyists to argue that restricting sales of alcohol would deny to the state treasury monies from the liquor tax, which funded state public education. Undeterred, the WCTU sent a sizable delegation to Montgomery on December 31, 1908, for the first of several statewide legislative showdowns. Critics fumed that the "calm dignity of the women of Alabama had given place to that which bordered on fanaticism." Nevertheless, Alabama's Protestants succeeded in winning statewide prohibition several years before passage of the Eighteenth Amendment to the U.S. Constitution.[16]

Social and theological racism also heightened the fight against alcohol. In the late nineteenth century, the battle against alcohol initially seemed to unite the "better classes" in southern cities, white and black, against a common enemy. The black AMEZ paper of North Carolina, the *Star of Zion*, editorialized in 1886 that the "white people of the South have learned more of the ability of the Negro through the Prohibition agitation than from any other question which has been discussed since the war. We gladly welcome it." White interracialists such as Joseph Hartzell in New Orleans hoped that the temperance momentum would mean that "all hearts and races shall flow together." But, as with Populism, hopes of biracial cooperation in southern progressivism faltered. Prohibition eventually provided political reformers and white supremacists another justification to disfranchise black men. "The more righteous the white people of this State grow against . . . the liquor traffic," fumed the New Orleans black Methodist A. E. P. Albert, "the more they hate the Negro." Whites blamed the failure of early prohibition campaigns on black resistance to temperance candidates who failed to espouse racial equality. White progressives feared marginalized black men living outside the constraints of conventional society as "the most difficult sociological problem any people ever had," a problem that "the Liquor Traffic only tended to complicate." In communities with saloons, wrote the Atlanta Baptist leader John E. White, race war had become a "perilously possible occurrence." The danger lurked especially among the "lower levels of both races," where the "inflammable fringes hang loose."[17]

Charlotte, North Carolina, provided an ideal social and institutional home for black southern progressivism, but it also exemplified progressivism at its most class-driven and racially divisive. The African Methodist Episcopal Zion Church established its publishing house there in 1894. The growing southern city was home to a proud, if embattled, black middle class, with a number of well-established churches and black social clubs and institutions. Mary Lynch, a professor at Livingstone College (the flagship educational center for the AMEZ) nearby in Salisbury, headed the state Colored Woman's Christian Temperance Union. Congregations such as Clinton African Methodist Episcopal Zion Chapel, 7th

Street Presbyterian Church, and other pillars of the African American religious establishment led the fight against the sale of alcohol. Yet prohibition in Charlotte split black churches along class lines, and controversy tore apart major churches of the AMEZ denomination in North Carolina. "The building of a new church is essential with us now," wrote one AMEZ church leader and temperance supporter, "to rid our youth of fogey ideas, sentiments, etc., and to bring them up to *proper moral sentiments* and religious belief." Black Christian supporters of temperance and other progressive reforms accused church members of not "exerting enough influence with regard to temperance and Christian piety generally." Black progressives in the Charlotte AMEZ formed their own congregation, Grace Church. Critics of the breakaway group alleged in return that the new church provided an exclusive club for the light-skinned, akin to the black fraternal orders that segregated by skin color and tone. A similar dispute wracked black Baptists in Charlotte. In 1886, controversies over alcohol policy broke out between the pastor of the First Baptist Colored Church and his congregation. The pastor supported banning alcohol, but a group of churchwomen who had been summoned to a prohibitionist meeting warned the minister that "they would do him like another was done, cease paying him," if he insisted on enforced abstinence.[18]

The early years of temperance brought together white and black progressives. In its first efforts in the 1880s, the Charlotte Anti-Saloon League had built a tentative biracial coalition of white and black evangelicals pitted against common enemies. Two decades later, however, white progressives pursued very different political strategies. At that point, when white ministers in Charlotte circulated a petition for municipal prohibition, the Anti-Saloon League ignored black religious progressives. Rather, the campaign's leadership resorted to the inflammatory image of the sexually depraved and drunken Negro to arouse sentiment for restrictions on the sale and consumption of alcohol. Ultimately, then, prohibition was a divider, not a uniter. The rhetoric about uplift, which black progressives initially seized upon as an avenue of biracial cooperation, proved to be a chimera.

Progressive southern reformers learned significant lessons from the Prohibitionist crusade. The message about moral decline pushed by WCTU and Anti-Saloon League activists fed into any number of campaigns to preserve families (which were the "bulwark of good government, the source of our truest and noblest earthly happiness"), condemn divorce and card-playing (the latter being the source for "every rank and vile weed of infidelity" and "every species of evil association"), and castigate the theater (that "vestibule of the brothel"). Progressives looked to governmental action to meet their moral objectives, including limitations on child labor and support for universal primary education. They referred to this as building the kingdom of God on earth, while secular progressives moved to the call of science and rationalism. Both groups converged on issues such as prohibition and child labor. Allied reformers in women's suffrage, child labor, education, and health adopted the techniques perfected in social purity crusades—mobilizing public opinion, using muckraking journalism, manipulating public opinion about a single issue, and applying pressure expertly in the political system.[19]

The movement against child labor provides one example, albeit one less successful than the national campaign for Prohibition. Missionaries of middle-class morality recognized the wide chasm separating them from their subjects. Child labor crusaders, for example, faced the reality that working-class families needed income-earning children. Realizing this, mill owners set a "family wage" that factored in the labor of working-class white children. The labor of black children in the region, of course, was simply assumed; it never reached the status of being an issue for white progressives. Southern cotton mills alone, by contemporary estimates, employed no fewer than 60,000 children under fourteen. Mill owners set aside for children certain positions, particularly those requiring quick and repetitive manual dexterity. Children also labored in other southern industries, but the young white cotton mill worker symbolized the broader regional problem.

Alexander McKelway was a leading figure of the white progressive South and a spokesman for the crusade against the abuse of laboring children. He was also an apologist for southern racism, including the Wilmington massacre (mislabeled "riot") of 1898. In this sense, McKelway serves as another prototypical southern religious progressive. McKelway graduated from Hampden-Sydney College in 1886 and Union Theological Seminary in Richmond in 1891. From 1892 to 1897, he pastored a Presbyterian church in Fayetteville, North Carolina, then resigned to become editor of the *Presbyterian Standard* in Charlotte. In 1904, he became the Southern Secretary for the National Child Labor Commission, a position that consumed the remainder of his working life. McKelway focused his concern on white youngsters, the labor of black children being a question of no particular importance. Child labor, he feared, would result in the "race degeneracy" of the "purest American stock on the continent." By insisting that Christians should be "concerned only with the individual and not with society as a whole," religious leaders by default were condemning the church to defeat. While socially awakened believers attended church, the "exploiters of their fellowmen sit with comfortable conscience in their pews and reckon up their gains." McKelway insisted that the "pulpit must awake to the fact that it has to preach social justice if it is not to lose its remaining power for this generation. It must make the anti-social man as uncomfortable as it has made the atheist or the libertine. And this will cause a gradual change in the constituency of the Church."[20]

McKelway and his colleagues in the child labor movement enjoyed some limited successes. After two decades of agitation, Alabama progressives succeeded in garnering support for a law prohibiting employment of those under the age of fourteen and limiting children over that age to no more than forty-eight-hour work weeks. Like most other southern states, however, enforcement was lax. Reformers remained frustrated at the resistance of state legislatures and at what they believed was the short-sightedness of southern working-class families who persisted in putting their children into factory work.[21]

Black progressives carried on a program similar in its multiple emphases to that of the white progressives, with whom they sometimes were allied and other times fought. They stumped for prohibition and public education and against illiteracy and disease. Within their churches, moreover, they promoted "intelligent worship," their term for the assimilation of Afro-southern religious practices into the American Protestant mainstream.

Perhaps the best-known black southern man of the cloth identified with progressivism and reform was Henry Hugh Proctor of Atlanta. He grew up eleven miles from Pulaski, Tennessee, site of the first Ku Klux Klan. "The Ku Klux remain a grim reality," he later wrote, "but the same spirit of true americanism that overthrew them then will reassert itself and rid our democracy of this irresponsible group of self-appointed regulators." His parents were poor but valued education, and Proctor attended a school that doubled as a church. He experienced religious conversion as a "wakening up," where he discovered his "supreme desire" for education. Despite financial difficulties, he made his way to Fisk University in Tennessee. Established by Congregationalists in 1866, the school best known for its famous Fisk Jubilee Singers drew black intellectual talent from across the country to Nashville. Proctor attended school there with both W. E. B. Du Bois and Margaret Murray, who later married Booker T. Washington. Reflecting on the debate that dominated black public intellectual life around the turn of the century, Proctor later concluded that there was no need to choose ideological sides between the philosophe and activist Du Bois and the practical accommodationist Washington; both philosophies, he believed, were required for black advancement. In his own politics, however, the pragmatic clergyman Proctor adopted the Washingtonian strategy of forging strategic alliances with white elites and eliciting white financial support for black institutions.[22]

Seeking to serve the body, mind, and spirit of his congregants, Proctor took the pulpit at First Congregational in Atlanta in 1894. The church historically had been pastored by white clerics who oversaw biracial congregations. By Proctor's tenure, however, the congregation was all black. Proctor immediately doubled the church membership to 400 and launched groups such as a local chapter of the Christian Endeavor Society (a huge nationwide organization of Christian youth), a Working Men's Club, and others. He hoped to make religious institutions as enticing as the local dives. He sought to "hitch up the religion of the South," which was "sentimental rather than practical, individual rather than social," to solving the great problems of the age. "The spirit of cooperation, not only between the various wings of the race but also between white and black," he wrote in his autobiography, was the "chief contribution the First Church of Atlanta made to social betterment during the quarter of a century of my pastorate."

The Atlanta riot of September 1906, the single worst racist pogrom of the era, tested Proctor's intention of mediating between racial communities. In those three days of mayhem in the New South City, white mobs attacked blacks on the streets, in streetcars, and in their neighborhoods and homes, killing over twenty and injuring hundreds. Impromptu black militias fought back, driving white mobs from neighborhoods. Their actions suggested that self-defense might be more efficacious in defending black interests than would biracial "cooperation" among the "best people" of the city, but Proctor remained faithful to his idea of biracial amity engineered by white elites and black spokesmen. "Some among my own people felt that I was giving away their case by seeking cooperation with the whites," he said of his role at that time, while "others thought that because I had openly denounced the conditions productive of riots that I had therefore produced the riot." After the brutal melee, he served on a local "Committee on Church Cooperation," where he tried to dispel the "continuous rumors of approaching 'Race Riots' which creep like poisonous reptiles through the community." Normally circumspect, he nevertheless condemned the white preacher as the "most cowardly character in the whole Southern situation. . . . If he would only speak out he could turn the tide." There was little to cheer in this regard. Proctor's white allies on prohibition or child labor turned their backs on the race issue. Alexander McKelway, for example, described the riot as a "thunderstorm" that had "cleared the atmosphere." A "long era of peace between the races has begun," he cheerfully forecast, with the "altered demeanor" of the Negro noticeable especially in the decline of "'bumptiousness.'" For Proctor, the idea that blacks could rely on uplift through cooperation with paternalistic elites and progressive reformers such as McKelway, supposedly the "best friends of the Negro," proved to be a delusion.[23]

The same might be said for the increasingly conservative black denominational leaders, most of whom repeated the prevailing clichés of the common interest uniting the better class of whites and blacks. "The negro church pledges itself to teach cleanliness and sobriety," an AMEZ bishop proclaimed before a gathering of white Southern Methodists, "and asks that you meet us a little way by providing for those of our people who are daily in your employ such places of abode as will conduce to their health and happiness." This bishop traded in the common currency of sacrificing rights of the franchise and unionization in exchange for white protection and jobs in the industrializing New South order. In Birmingham, Methodist minister Oscar Adams, editor of Alabama's largest black weekly, cultivated a close relationship with coal mine operators. The mine owners vetted ministers in company-sponsored camp churches to ensure they were sound on the "labor question"—that is, anti-union. One black miner complained that the preachers were "nothing more than stool-pigeons for the coal companies," paid off to spout the "doctrine of union hatred." Coal operators, he said, "would rather pay fat salaries to these ministers than to recognize that labor has any rights to a decent pay for a day's work." Joining Adams was P. Colfax Rameau, a minister and editor of the *Workmen's Chronicle*, who tried to dissuade black laborers from joining the United Mine Workers. The African American working class in the Birmingham area responded by ignoring the established churches or attending those pastored by itinerants who were miners themselves and often sympathetic to unionization. Such uneducated and emotional preachers, Rameau charged, were not "prepared to lead [their] people intelligently."[24]

Southern progressivism dovetailed with the coming of state-sanctioned (as opposed to merely customary) segregation and disfranchisement and an upsurge of racist violence directed mostly against black men. Respectable black clergymen of the Progressive Era were hardly exempt from this visceral hatred. Gordon Blaine Hancock was uplift personified. A graduate of Benedict College in South Carolina (where he learned that "an education puts no man or woman above work"), he pastored a church near Columbia. He led meetings of the black state convention, was a principal of a Baptist high school, and served as a statistician for the National Baptist Convention. After moving near Greenville in 1917, he urged rural blacks to band together to improve their condition. The rumor soon spread that he was "out to turn niggers against white folks," and the Ku Klux Klan set out to "discipline" him. His standing in the community afforded him no real protection. Hancock left the state to attend Colgate University. Later, he came back to teach at Virginia Union University in Richmond and became a leading southern black moderate in the Southern Regional Council (SRC).[25]

If an outstanding figure such as Hancock was vulnerable, so were other black southerners with far less visibility. After purchasing some land in a white-dominated county in Florida and farming it successfully, black Baptist minister S. C. Garner received threatening letters ordering him to leave. He decided to stay. More hostile letters arrived, but he held his ground. A local sheriff assured him that "he would be safe as any law abiding citizen of that community." Five days later he "was found by the buzzards with his body riddled with bullets." A Methodist minister stumbled across him and laid him to rest.[26]

Black religious progressives struggled to comprehend this deepening racial divide and increasing violence. Their theology of hope and uplift offered them precious little intellectual space in which to grapple with the devastating effects of segregation, disfranchisement, legal repression, and extralegal violence. The black progressives organized conferences, sponsored protest resolutions, petitioned governors and legislatures, pleaded for the "thinking element" of both races to stand together against racially based disfranchisement, formed alliances with elite white churchmen and politicians on prohibition and other issues, and thundered from their pulpits against oppression—all to little or no avail. The white pulpit, as some of them came to understand, more often justified rather than condemned white supremacist rule.

As northern academics and social reformers came south to investigate lynchings, they connected the relative prevalence of Baptist and Methodist churches in a given area with the incidence of the grossest forms of racial violence. The correlation was chilling, giving substance to the NAACP's Walter White's charge that lynching was fed by "a relentlessly vitriolic and ignorant ministry." Arthur Raper, in researching his classic study *Tragedy of Lynching*, found that white pastors shared the view that "lynching, though unfortunate, was inevitable." Timid white parsons feared they would divide churches by calling for the prosecution of perpetrators in their midst; bolder white clerics were immobilized in the face of "an almost fierce resistance to anything that resembled recognition of Negro equality," as Joseph Martin Dawson, a pastor in Waco, Texas, early in the twentieth century, put it. He witnessed the notorious mass carnivalesque lynching of Jesse Washington in 1916 and felt "entirely helpless because five thousand monsters participated and who was I, a lone individual, to do anything about it." When he introduced a resolution at a pastor's association denouncing the act, he later recalled, "to my utter surprise, when they discovered they had burned an innocent man, they found the guilty, the only comment I heard around town ... was 'Well, it's fine. At last, they got the right Nigger.' " Meanwhile, most black churches were too small and financially dependent to take a public stand. The average congregation numbered about eighty members and worshipped in modest structures, often built with financial assistance from local white planters. A cautious middling class of farmers, launderers, and small business owners who feared challenging the status quo peopled the larger black churches.[27]

Even when allied with black progressives, many white southern Christians seized on segregation and disfranchisement as God's plan to preserve racial peace through white rule. The Richmond *Christian Advocate*, a major Southern Methodist outlet, announced that white southerners lived "in the midst of a race but a short remove from barbarians of the lowest type. Only fear of their superior neighbors and the certainty of swift retribution hold down the savage passions of these sons and grandsons of the Voodoo African." After the 1898 constitutional convention in North Carolina that effectively disfranchised black men, the Baptist *Biblical Recorder* exulted, "The battle for the supremacy of the white race now leads, as we all hoped and prayed, for the supremacy of the right-minded members of that race." This view presaged the dominant racial politics of southern progressivism.[28]

A few white southerners kept watch over the corpse of paternalism. George Washington Cable attempted to rally what he optimistically, if euphemistically, termed the "silent South." The New Orleans Presbyterian organized an "Open Letter Club" that was to produce essays and discussions of regional problems. His efforts elicited praise from AME bishops and national figures such as labor economist Richard Ely and *Outlook* editor Lyman Abbott. But Cable's South mostly remained deafeningly silent. Even mild expressions of racial paternalism met with hostile responses. Methodist bishop Atticus Haygood, the well-regarded president of Emory College, was a victim of the rising hostility among whites to any rational discussion of the "Negro problem." In his 1881 work *Our Brother in Black: His Freedom and His Future*, Haygood suggested that southern whites had an obligation to help uplift blacks who had been degraded in slavery. The following year, Haygood accepted a post as the southern field representative of the Slater Fund, a philanthropic venture designed to support the construction of black schools in the South. Soon after the publication of *Our Brother in Black*, fellow Southern Methodists condemned the book as an "inflammatory" example of "Yankee fanaticism." His form of racial paternalism, once a staple of southern religious rhetoric, now seemed the worst form of "negrophilism." Haygood's rapid physical wasting and financial embarrassments in the 1890s seemed to symbolize the decline of his brand of home-grown southern paternal liberalism.[29]

In responding to Atticus Haygood's condemnation of savage mobs, Walter Hines Page, the well-known North Carolina newspaper editor, pointed out that the "community accepted and acquiesced in the mob's work." In the early twentieth century, other progressive ministers found out firsthand about the tyranny of the southern majority. In 1902, Andrew Sledd, a Virginia Methodist who taught at Emory College, depicted the savagery of southern violence for a national audience in the *Atlantic Monthly*. He described his experience when a train conductor stopped a car that Sledd was on so that the riders could witness the lynching and burning of Sam Hose (an event that also elicited one of W. E. B. Du Bois's most searing essays). Sledd lambasted the "wild and diabolical carnival of blood" that came from as "brutal a mob as ever disgraced the face of the earth." Sledd also defended the capacity of the Negro to rise if given a fair chance and envisioned a more just regime than the emerging Jim Crow order. White public opinion in Georgia (and within the Emory administration) soon aligned against the suspect theology professor. After being burned in effigy, threatened in the press, and hounded on the street, Sledd resigned his Emory position (although he was able to return in 1914, and thereafter he influenced a younger rising generation of progressive Southern Methodist ministers). In another case, the Reverend Whitely Langston of a Methodist church in Statesboro, Georgia, published the names of church members who took part in the torture and execution of two black men suspected of murder. They refused to repent, and other members left the congregation in protest against Langston's action. No one in this mob was indicted.[30]

Some southern divines took up the mantle of protectionist paternalism originally adopted by George Washington Cable and Atticus Haygood. In Mississippi, Bishop Charles B. Galloway, leader of the state's Methodists and a vigorous proponent for the memorialization of the Confederacy, attacked the new state constitution for imposing a permanent state of segregation and disfranchisement on the state's majority black population. Until his death in 1909, a passing mourned by Jackson's black community, Galloway remained a forceful critic of the worst practices of southern racism. "There is no disguising the fact," he said in the 1890s, that there was a "great unrest and growing discontent among the negroes of the South. They feel friendless and almost helpless." He noted with disgust the "lynchings that disgrace our civilization, the persistent efforts to deprive the negro of the rights of citizenship, the advocacy by some politicians of limiting the school advantages provided for them, and the widening gulf of separation between the younger generation of both races." Galloway's colleague, the Episcopalian and Lost Cause paternalist Reverend Theodore DuBose Bratton, was a founding member of the Mississippi Council on Interracial Cooperation. He defended the rights of the black citizen: "that, as justice is the right of life, he be accorded it; that, as a citizen, he be granted the rights of citizenship —the equal right of life, liberty and the pursuit of happiness; that laws governing citizenship be applied with equal justice to Negroes and to Whites."[31]

In addition to figures such as Galloway and Bratton, William J. Northen of Georgia and Edgar Gardner Murphy of Montgomery represented the active if ineffectual paternalist elite who fought against "southern outrages." Northen was one of the biggest planters in Hancock County, Georgia. He served as governor of the state in the early 1890s and periodically as president of the Southern Baptist Convention. He blamed southern "lawlessness" on the southern elite's failure to educate the masses properly in their social roles. In 1907, he outlined for a national audience the white conservative view on race: paternal regional elites would protect the defenseless and childlike Negro, who would in return show his appreciation by loyalty, docility, and hard work. After the bloody Atlanta riot, Northen called for the organization of "Christian Leagues" to promote cooperation among the best men of both races. Few of his ministerial colleagues, even those of a reformist and progressive bent, supported him. Even church members who were in Northen's own Gospel Businessmen's Association shied away from the well-meaning planter's antilynching efforts, while some black leaders implicitly endorsed the use of violence in self-defense. In a state gubernatorial campaign, his demagogic opponent Hoke Smith assailed the efforts of "negrophiles" such as Northen. The progressive crusader Alexander McKelway, Northen's ally on many other issues, felt that the melee in Atlanta had "impressed" southern blacks "with the truth that the individual criminal who lays his hand upon a white woman is a menace to the mass." By 1911, nearly bereft of allies, the defeated patrician reformer Northen castigated lawless whites and ignorant Negroes equally for the failure to live peaceably.[32]

Such was the fate of many of the white racial paternalists and progressives. White voices of moderation idealized a time of relative racial harmony in an older South, one supposedly undisturbed by the rising influence of lower-class whites or impudent Negroes. Men and women such as Northen upheld the imagined tradition of a Christian South over what southern journalist Wilbur J. Cash later termed the "savage ideal." What they failed to account for was the very modernity of racial violence, its synergy with the same forces—railroads, better roads, more extensive media—so praised by advocates for the New South. A "progressive" South could more effectively enforce apartheid, both through the legal system and through an economic order that provided circumscribed opportunities for poorer whites while repressing the subordinated class of black rural laborers.

Like Northen, southern social gospelers did not ignore race relations, but neither could they reach a consensus on handling what they called the "Negro problem," and they increasingly just turned away from it in favor of uplifting poor whites. Edgar Gardner Murphy was one such social gospeler. He graduated from the University of the South in 1889 and then studied at New York's General Theological Seminary. Murphy's mother had moved to south Texas to help the young Episcopalian recuperate from his lung problems. Murphy eventually returned to San Antonio, where he articulated a social gospel theology for his troubled region.[33]

Murphy was a theological modernist, racial conservative, and economic progressive. His mentors at the University of the South, including William Porcher DuBose, taught him a progressive theology that borrowed heavily from German thinkers who were normally distrusted in the conservative South. They stressed social hierarchy and stability, including segregation in the social and religious world. Murphy thus rejected both the evangelical and economic individualism common to his era. To be fully human and Christian, Murphy argued, meant to live in community: "In matters social, political, and industrial, there can be at last no full and perfect rescue of the individual except in company with other men. Together must the many and the one be saved." Against an overweening emphasis on property rights, Murphy preached a philosophy of organicism, one valuing order over freedom.

In the early twentieth century, Murphy, now well-positioned in Alabama's state capitol, made his name first as an exponent of enforceable child labor laws. Like most southern progressives, however, he feared that federal efforts might break the gathering momentum in individual states for reasonable restrictions on child labor. Upon taking supervision of an Episcopalian parish in Montgomery, Murphy established the Church of the Good Shepherd, an African American congregation, as a means of addressing immediate social needs, and promoted annual sessions on the study of southern social issues. Late in his life, Murphy devoted his energies to the Southern Education Board. It was white illiteracy and ignorance, he had concluded, that accounted for the region's most intractable problems. By freeing himself of ministerial encumbrances, Murphy felt able in a way that a burdened parish pastor never could to be "closely and practically identified with the struggle for specific legislation without prejudice." Murphy's 1909 book *The Basis of Ascendancy* suggested how superior and inferior races could live together in community. Through democratic imperialism, the superior race could guide lesser peoples in constructing a better and more harmonious world. After the disfranchisement of the ignorant classes, both white and black, then the welfare of all could be entrusted to a privileged and progressive elite.[34]

Following Murphy's early lead, a variety of paternalistic white racial reformers and progressives carried forward the elite reform agenda. They sought to discuss social problems openly without upsetting the delicate racial truce in the region. Willis D. Weatherford was from a rural evangelical background. After taking a Ph.D. at Vanderbilt in classical studies and theology, he spent several decades working for racial "understanding" within the system of segregation. "It is not the negro that is on trial before the world," he said, "but it is we, the white men of the South." In 1910, he supervised the production of *Negro Life in the South*, a significant Progressive Era study in race relations widely used as a college text. Weatherford helped to organize the Southern Sociological Congress of 1912, attended by 700 ministers, educators, representatives from the Federal Council of Churches, and other reformers. Delegates to the congress called for action on a variety of endemic southern problems: racial conflict, political corruption, illiteracy, child labor, convict leasing, and diseases such as tuberculosis in urban areas and hookworm in the countryside. Weatherford was also a member of the Commission on Interracial Cooperation (CIC), founded by Will Alexander, the minister at his own Nashville Methodist Church, in response to the racial crisis after World War I.[35]

White southern progressive Christianity such as that personified by Weatherford ultimately was mugged by reality, shaken down by its own inability to measure fully the social evil that it wished to ameliorate. "Dr. Weatherford was a sweet man, good and well intentioned, beloved and respected," a student in later years commented, "but he was an obstacle to change, not an inspiration for it." Many evangelical progressives, moreover, were attracted to disturbing panaceas such as eugenics, ultimately imparting an air of elitism to what they had seen as a progressive vision of democratic Christianity. Conservative religious leaders in the region resisted the nostrums of social Christianity and defended the doctrine of the spirituality of the church. Christians could not be so "absorbed in a Christless social service," a bishop proclaimed to the 1914 General Conference of the MECS, or press the church into "all sorts of pretentious programmes of 'social betterment,' 'improved environment,' and the like. They conjure her to rely upon eugenics rather than upon regeneration by the Holy Spirit for the making of a new and nobler race."[36]

In the interwar years, the thin but tough community of liberals, Christian socialists, and radicals revolted against the limitations of Progressive Era notions of reform and uplift. They mounted a significant challenge to southern evangelical thought and practice and explored avenues toward Christian interracialism. The work of churchgoing women paved their way.

Women's Missionary Societies and Progressive Social Reform

In one common understanding of religion and gender politics, Protestant women have moved from the radical left wing (such as abolitionism and women's rights in the nineteenth century), to the progressive mainstream (as in the settlement house and other Progressive Era ventures), to the antiprogressive right wing (as in contemporary fundamentalist groups). The history of white and black southern women's religion and social concern, however, suggests a different interpretation. Southern religious women—saints, subordinates, and subversives—kept southern garb firmly in place while also raising and distributing remarkable sums of money, running complex organizations, and poking holes in the region's dominant racial and gendered mythologies. Before making their mark in missionary societies and in advancing social justice, first they had to campaign for basic rights within their own denominations, vote in church business meetings, and exercise some control over the expenditure of funds. For well-educated women such as future Daughters of the Confederacy leader Ella Gertrude Clanton Thomas, the experience could be trying. When the Southern Baptist Convention meeting in 1885 refused to admit two women (including the wife of the governor of Arkansas), Thomas wrote that "it taught the women of the church that they were yet in a state of bondage." Thomas had rallied from personally difficult days after the war ("for a time I doubted God") and organized one of the first groups to erect a monument to the Confederacy. She led the Ladies Missionary Association of her own Methodist church, served as secretary and vice president of the WCTU in Augusta, and eventually campaigned for women's suffrage. Thomas's colleague Nellie Nugent Somerville of Greenville, Mississippi, developed religious arguments for suffrage. Divine Providence, she insisted, had "opened the domain of moral leadership to the Christian women of this nation," who would unite moral and political power.[37]

Women like Thomas were the driving force behind prohibition, and the preachers knew it. Despite being a relative latecomer to the region, the WCTU received a favorable reception in southern communities already full of teetotaling evangelicals. It also confronted controversy over women in the pulpit, whether for preaching or for leading reform movements. After accepting an invitation to address a WCTU meeting in Georgia, one woman withdrew her name rather than risk violating the "observed customs" of her "fellow churchmen" by speaking in public from the pulpit. Over time, women grew bolder. The head of the Georgia WCTU hoped that national president Frances Willard would visit the state, for her very presence seemed to inspire feats of activism. "The last meeting of our Union was the first we have ever had without having gentlemen present," she wrote to a correspondent, "and I find that they act as a 'check' upon us. For we have never done as much talking and acting as we then did—rather than waiting for them to do it all. But I think now, it will be better not to have them at every meeting—as the ladies are afraid to talk before them." It was a "southernly" custom to wait for men "to take the lead. And the men *ought* to take the lead," she added, "and we hope they will be aroused to a sense of their duty and take the whole lead of carrying out this movement. . . . But as the cause for the present is in our hands we must do more of the work that is waiting for us."[38]

Many prominent southern clergymen wanted no part of a WCTU that encouraged women in ministerial roles. Powerful Georgia Methodist bishop Warren Akin Candler proudly labeled the Methodist Episcopal Church, South as "the best temperance organization in the land." Nevertheless, he discouraged WCTU efforts among Methodists in his state because of his disapproval of women such as Frances Willard. "I am unwilling to imperil the harmony of our church by following the leadership of revolutionary woman suffragists and 'reformers,'" he announced. The woman question was but a "Trojan horse" that would destroy the "peace, unity, and power" of Southern Methodism. Like his Methodist friends, the Southern Baptist minister J. B. Hawthorne welcomed the activities of the WCTU until the body endorsed female preaching. Hawthorne summarized southern evangelical male views on godly gender roles:

> God would have women erect her throne in the home. There, away from the vulgar gaze and applause of the world, the true woman wields a mightier scepter than any of her notoriety-loving sisters, who are wont to thrust themselves into every arena of public debate, and into all manner of noisy and unnatural competitions with men. The woman who builds a home in which every influence is pure, gentle, sweet and elevating; a home in which Christ is a constant test; a home whose brightness lingers upon a husband's face through all the business and cares of the day, and to which sons and daughters return with songs of gladness, moves in a broader sphere, and does a thousand times more for the betterment of the world's condition, than any woman who spends her life in courting public attention, making political-stump speeches and delivering lectures.

Hawthorne expressed a skepticism that ran deep in southern evangelical culture about women who would "revolutionize the social system" through agitation in progressive movements.[39]

Allied with the "whiskey rings" they otherwise so bitterly fought, conservative churchmen inveighed against woman suffrage. Their theology assumed the subordination of Negroes and of women in church and society as the will of God. "In the economy of the divine creation man and woman have each his or her distinct sphere," a group of ministers in Nashville explained. An antisuffrage tract distributed around Raleigh, North Carolina, asked simply, "How can you repudiate St. Paul as an inspired writer and as a biblical authority without knocking the entire structure of the Christian Faith?" Bishop Candler intoned that the "whole basis of the woman's suffrage movement" was "unscriptural." Conservative evangelicals also opposed most efforts to extend the franchise; they distrusted an excess of democracy in church or state. The best course for the South, one Methodist clergymen argued, would be to "diminish suffrage instead of increasing it. Take the ballot out of the hands of thousands who now vote as they are told, and hired to do." He wondered, "What sort of state of things should we have down South if all the negro women were put to voting?"[40]

Still, whatever their qualms about activist women, evangelical men needed women's moral suasion and political lobbying in Prohibition campaigns. The leadership of women in progressive reforms persuaded many churchmen that women were needed in the public sphere for the creation of a godly society. Churchwomen, especially Episcopalians and Presbyterians, took up the suffrage cause. In her close study of Galveston, Texas, Elizabeth Hayes Turner has shown how WCTU members typically came from the more evangelical churches, Methodist and Baptist in particular, and "tended to confine their activism to those organizations where Christianity provided the organizing principle." Suffrage supporters more often attended churches with a history and theology of community activism and social service, such as Episcopalian and Presbyterian. The Virginia Episcopalian Lucy Randolph Mason, one of the foremost suffrage advocates in her state, found in the movement a "deep strain of spirituality and altruism, which gives it a peculiar moral significance."[41]

Protestant women of the early twentieth century allied themselves with progressive social reformers. They worked to change divorce laws, restrict child labor, beautify cities, criminalize prostitution, close down saloons and red-light districts, improve public education, and mount public health crusades. Southern churchwomen embraced social gospel reform with an enthusiasm rare among their male counterparts. Analyzing the rise of women's associations in southern churches of the late nineteenth and early twentieth centuries, historian Anne Scott has written that the "struggle of church women to attain some autonomy of action as they pursued their missionary objectives had an ironical side. By opposing what might easily have been interpreted as the natural right of women members ... church men created the very thing they feared. In the face of condescension and opposition, women began to reassess their position and one group after another began demanding an expansion of their rights within the churches. ... These campaigns came to mirror, in language and spirit, the secular drive of women's suffrage." This was true among both black and white southern churchwomen. Behind the scenes, black women often instigated and prodded along white women's tentative gestures at interracial cooperation. A comparison of black and white Baptist and Methodist women's missionary societies illuminates the parallel struggles they faced, as well as the very different situations in which they operated. In both cases, women's missionary societies provided a venue for ventures of biracial cooperation and, on occasion, egalitarian Christian interracialism.[42]

Black women in the Jim Crow era vigorously pursued the work of evangelization and moral uplift, raising significant sums for benevolent endeavors and filling more pews in church than black men. Black Baptist women organized themselves under the dynamic direction of Nannie H. Burroughs, once little known by historians but now resurrected by the work of historian Evelyn Brooks Higginbotham. In 1900, Burroughs proposed her idea for a Woman's Convention, Auxiliary to the National Baptist Convention, the largest black church organization in the country. She met the predictable resistance from convention churchmen with a determined rhetoric of "righteous discontent" and "burning zeal." By 1909, Burroughs's Woman's Convention had raised nearly $63,000 and owned the only educational institution run by black women in the country. African American women believed "with a conviction that cannot soon be uprooted," she announced in 1903, "that the masses of our sisters must hear the gospel of industry and heed its blessed principles before they can be morally saved." Racial segregation, she added, could be fought not only in political protests but also through "soap and water, hoes, spades, shovels and paint."[43]

Burroughs also lent her eloquent public voice to protesting racial proscriptions. In 1903, she noted how faithfully black southerners had followed every prescription for individual and collective success, even while the "powers that be" were "combining against us." She lashed out at the complicity of the "good white people" in racial oppression and warned that God might be "preparing to smite this merciless nation" because of its sins. "The mob is now setting fire to Negro tenements, but that fire is going to spread, and it will reach the mansions before many years," she told one audience in 1908. The "peculiar silence" of the so-called friends of the Negro had "emboldened our enemies, until they attack us with impunity." Burroughs urged cooperation with the NAACP, the Southern Sociological Congress, and other organizations working for improvement in race relations. She excoriated Negro caricatures in popular culture and history texts and implored black families and schools to teach their children to "give their lives to redeem the race."[44]

In the early twentieth century, Burroughs belonged to a network of black female reformers that included women such as Mary McLeod Bethune in Florida; Lucy Laney and Florence Hunt of Georgia; Nettie L. Napier and M. L. Crosthwait of Tennessee; Jennie Moton and Margaret Murray Washington of Alabama; Maggie Lena Walker in Virginia; and Charlotte Hawkins Brown in North Carolina. In Atlanta, a group of black women led by Lugenia Hope (wife of the president of Morehouse College, John Hope) formed a professional settlement house organization in 1908. The self-interest of the middle classes, they understood, was tied up with the fate of the lower orders. Tuberculosis, for example, respected no class boundary. Hope divided her adopted city of Atlanta into sixteen districts, each with a Neighborhood Union known and endorsed by locals. At first, the middle-class interests of leaders dominated the settlement work. Gradually, the departments expanded to include an entire panoply of social, spiritual, intellectual, and physical needs. Worried about the lack of play facilities for black children, Hope started Gate City Free Kindergarten Association following her attendance at a conference on the welfare of black children. By

1917, Hope's Neighborhood Union cared for 3,000 youngsters. The union also conducted extensive investigations of social problems and pressured for better salaries for teachers, paved streets, reduction of exorbitant rents, and the removal of foul privies. Other churches joined in this religious progressivism. Atlanta's Bethel AME Church offered an employment bureau for domestics and employers, Wheat Street Baptist Church opened a home for elderly women and a school for black laborers, while Friendship Baptist Church built a house to care for the indigent and elderly. Black churchwomen thus made the goals of "institutional churches" a reality.[45]

White women's missionary societies followed a similar path from missions work to social concerns. The history of the Woman's Missionary Union (WMU) in the region's largest denomination, the Southern Baptist Convention, exemplifies this story of women's associations in the South. Women in the Southern Baptist Convention approached the public arena slowly and cautiously. They came from a conservative denomination with tight strictures on gender roles and fewer women of wealth who could direct independent organizations. Ironically, it was precisely this background of an insular and conservative denomination that allowed Southern Baptist women to maintain a separate and independent organization that survived through the twentieth century.

Protestant men ritually praised the moral influence of the true evangelical woman. In reality, as women well knew, informal or domestic influence rarely equaled formal power. The well-publicized leadership of abolitionist women in the early feminist movement personified white Southern Baptist fears of blurring the carefully delimited racial and gender boundaries. "Owing to the fact that the question of Woman's Rights in other fields has been pushed to such an offensive extent in more northern latitudes," a Mississippi Baptist association noted, "our people have been bitterly opposed to our women being brought forward in any cause." Beyond that, the preponderance of rural churches and the tenuous urban civic life of the nineteenth-century South simply made it difficult for members of organizations to gather at all, particularly for women who could not travel alone without scandal.[46]

In the late nineteenth century, some Southern Baptist churchwomen chafed at quietist prescriptions for female piety. "The gospel is the Magna Charta of human liberty. It will eventually sweep away all despotism," a Texas woman proclaimed in 1881. Missionary society organizers in local churches and state Baptist organizations assured skeptics that they would not pursue separate fields of work. That would be "out of harmony with the clinging tendril nature of the refined Southern woman," they explained. Rather, as was true for many other southern denominational groups, white and black, they designed their woman's auxiliary to enlist support for larger denominational mission work.[47]

Meeting in Richmond, Virginia, in 1888, a group of actively pious white Southern Baptist women organized the Woman's Missionary Union, Auxiliary to the Southern Baptist Convention. They disclaimed "all intention of independent action," seeking instead to stimulate "the missionary spirit and the grace of giving, among the women and children of the churches." Annie Armstrong, a native of Baltimore who headed the WMU from its founding until 1906, dismissed as "absurd" any charge that her organization would push for "*women's rights.*" Still, the WMU allowed for a twentieth-century southern evangelical womanhood, one resembling neither the nineteenth-century "true woman," twentieth-century feminist activism, nor contemporary fundamentalism. Their work in enlisting individual churches in missions projects, WMU advocates pointed out, simply encouraged the development of a missionary conscience, not "speaking from the rostrums, Women's Rights, dynamite, [or] Nihlism." Denominational leaders happily announced that "these noble Christian women are gladly cooperating with our Boards, and . . . manifest no disposition to . . . usurp authority."[48]

Behind the scenes, the indefatigable Armstrong brushed off resistance to her ideas. As she once impatiently put it, "I have heard so much about the 'woman's sphere,' and her going beyond proper bounds, that I think I am beginning to feel on this point as the children do when they are told 'children should be seen and not heard.'" Much of women's work, she said, was "hidden work, as are the springs which feed the watercourses of mighty rivers." To those who scoffed at what "sentiment" might accomplish, she answered, "It is woman's sentiment which has in the last forty years changed the codes of many states, and revolutionized the thoughts of the nation, on the subject of temperance. The creation of sentiment is as womanly as powerful." Armstrong tried to mold the WMU in her own image, to energize volunteers who would devote themselves to raising money for missions. Much to her consternation, the organization gradually followed the imperatives of professional philanthropy, including the employment of a full-time staff. The growth of the SBC into a twentieth-century benevolent machine owes much to the fund-raising techniques devised by WMU leaders.[49]

WMU leaders also formulated social responses to the gospel in a region suspicious of the social gospel. During Fannie E. S. Heck's years leading the WMU, for example, she also served as vice president of the Southern Sociological Congress. Engaging in a whirlwind of charitable, reformist, and missionary society activities in North Carolina, she participated in ecumenical conferences and supervised the publication of the WMU's periodical, *Our Mission Field*, later known as *Royal Service*. At her urging, Southern Baptist women expressed approval of state legislative efforts to limit women's working hours and supported educational programs, child labor restrictions, and racial uplift. Suggesting measures to meet the needs of the "unlovely people about us"—factory children, cotton mill workers, mountain women, and Negroes—the South Carolina WMU advocated measures to alleviate "poverty, ignorance, disease, and crime." These southern evangelical women endorsed "child labor and temperance legislation, welfare work, prison reforms, social service centers, every activity of this kind" as a way to "make the world ready for His coming." Prominent women sat on public boards and commissions that investigated child labor abuses, pushed for prohibition, condemned convict leasing and penal brutality, and fostered tentative efforts at interracial cooperation. This form of women's religious progressivism peaked in the 1910s, when the national WMU set as its agenda support for "those forces in our country which make for righteousness: patriotism working toward universal and permanent peace, prohibition, Sabbath observance, the sacredness of the home, the effort toward a more general re-establishment of the family altar, and the crusade against poverty, disease, illiteracy, vice, and crime." Southern Baptist women extended their work to settlement houses, child labor law advocacy, and other staples of the progressive movement.[50]

Later in the twentieth century, when the social gospel had fallen into disrepute elsewhere, Southern Baptist women heard frequent social gospel addresses. In the 1930s and 1940s, WMU president Olive Martin deliberately scheduled early feminist theologians (whom she lightly referred to as "heretics") such as Georgia Harkeness into public speaking engagements at Southern Baptist women's meetings. Challenging southern social customs with another sort of heresy, she also invited several black women to the podium. The speakers tapped into the developing moderate conscience of the region. Through this quiet practice of biracial cooperation, many white southern women gradually learned that racial injustice was more endemic and systemic, less amenable to individual acts of Christian kindness, than evangelicalism historically had preached.[51]

Annie Armstrong tested the boundaries of regional restrictions on biracial ventures in religious work. Armstrong aided Nannie Burroughs in forming the Woman's Convention, Auxiliary to the National Baptist Convention, and worked with Richard Boyd, founder and manager of the National Baptist Publishing Board, to supply Sunday school literature to black churches. "You have no idea of how . . . thankful I am that God is allowing us this opportunity to help to elevate the colored woman as well as to assist the work in Africa," she wrote a denominational colleague. "It will prove to the colored people that we are anxious to help them." Despite Armstrong's penchant for paternalistic language, which normally riled Nannie Burroughs, the two women maintained a good working relationship. Indeed, if Burroughs had drawn the line at paternalistic rhetoric, it would have been virtually impossible to work with any white agencies at all. Burroughs later appreciated Armstrong as a "trail blazer in Christian cooperation between white and Negro Baptist women of the south."[52]

Over time, such delicate efforts took hold. In the 1930s and 1940s, Burroughs and other black women worked with Una Roberts Lawrence, a WMU leader and appointee to the Committee on Farm Security in the New Deal. Lawrence and Burroughs collaborated on the *Worker*, a quarterly publication that promoted contacts between white and black Baptist women. "I am very glad to receive another letter from you," Burroughs wrote to Lawrence in 1934. "It shows you are beginning to think colored." While she would "never be bitter" in discussing the real problems of the region, Burroughs also insisted that she would "have to speak the truth in kindness." Burroughs retained primary editorship of the journal, while Lawrence contributed numerous articles and editorial suggestions. Lawrence and Burroughs agreed that "race and color will be forgotten and only the fact that we are women working together will be remembered." In 1947, Burroughs appeared on the cover of the WMU's periodical, *Royal Service*, which only a year before had pronounced the demands of blacks "frightening, difficult, dangerous, revolutionary and unreasonable." The WMU integrated its training school in Louisville in 1952 and two years later endorsed the Supreme Court's decision *Brown v. Board of Education*. Locally, WMU workers affiliated themselves with groups such as United Church Women (UCW, as discussed in Chapter 4). They usually did so unofficially rather than risk the reputation of the missionary society by associating it with even slightly controversial causes.[53]

Southern Methodist women also moved from home missionary societies into social gospel action. Will Alexander, head of the Commission on Interracial Cooperation, found Southern Methodist women to be the "most progressive and constructive religious group" in the white South: "Out of all the vast expensive machinery of religion in the South, the women, in their simple and largely non-ecclesiastical groups, have been most effective in changing racial patterns." Because their work "had never been recognized officially by the church," a group of "plain, middle class women" had been set "free to do the kinds of things they wanted to do," Alexander concluded.[54]

From a few thousand members at its origins in the 1880s, the Southern Methodist woman's home missionary society grew to some 60,000 participants by 1910 and more than 300,000 members at the time of Methodist sectional reunion in 1939. In the early twentieth century, women fought for laity rights in the MECS. Seeking voting privileges in ecclesiastical bodies, they sent up dozens of petitions from regional and state conferences to the church's massive quadrennial General Conference. Southern Methodist bishops at first summarily dismissed their ideas: "We have reason to believe that the demand for this kind of equality is not in harmony with the general sentiment of our women who, in the main, look upon their relation to the work of the Church in the light of duties to be performed rather than of rights to be claimed. We believe, furthermore, that the spirit of this movement is against the view which our people have held and still hold in regard to woman's place in the Church and in society." Proponents of laity rights lost several more times before the measure finally passed in 1918.[55]

While agitating for laity rights, Southern Methodist women joined their Southern Baptist sisters in advocating measures of social progressivism. Lucinda Helm, an early leader of Southern Methodist women, perceived the "apathy of presiding elders and pastors" as the major barrier to overcome. The independent publication of the Woman's Home Mission Society she began editing in 1892, *Our Homes*, opened a forum for social gospel ideas to Southern Methodist female readers who were convinced that "we must know causes before we can deal with conditions, for the source often explains results." Bertha Newell, a Kentuckian and graduate of the University of Chicago, defended an activist state as "God's ministry of organization, through which He must work." Helm and Newell urged Southern Methodist women into the realm of social action. Their successors furthered that legacy, in part through cooperative endeavors with black women of the denomination with the closest ties to white Methodists, the Colored Methodist Episcopal Church.[56]

Belle Bennett, a patrician Kentuckian, served as president of the Home Mission Society from 1896 to 1910 and the Woman's Missionary Council from 1910 to 1922. In 1892, she founded Scarritt Bible and Training School College. Scarritt trained generations of white Southern Methodist women who worked on home and foreign missions projects, as well as in civil rights and social justice struggles. As an early biographer wrote of her, Bennett had been "shown that a closer knowledge of the problems of human society and technical instruction in helping to relieve or reconstruct social conditions was of prime importance to the women who were to lead in religious work." Well-enforced laws, Bennett pointed out, would "do more to change and ameliorate their condition" than all the "philanthropic institutions that we could establish in a half a century." Bennett helped to found more than forty settlement houses sponsored by MECS organizations: Wesley Community houses for whites and Bethlehem houses in urban black districts staffed by women from CME churches. Bennett also endorsed the social gospel call to stand for "equal rights and complete justice for all men in all stations of life." She sponsored black speakers such as W. E. B. Du Bois at Methodist gatherings, where she refused to allow segregated seating, and vowed to use tongue, pen, and the ballot box to "arouse and develop a public sentiment" against the "barbarous crime of lynching."[57]

Women such as Bertha Newell, Belle Bennett, and Lucinda Helm pioneered efforts in biracial alliances in the apartheid-era South. Black Methodist women employed socially conscious white Methodists as their allies, resource providers, and protectors. Another early proponent of biracial cooperation was Lily Hammond, wife of the white president of Paine College in Augusta. Originally viewing the "Negro problem" as a field of missions endeavor, Hammond later published *In Black and White*, a work articulating her understanding about the social effects of race prejudice. "The truth is, we know nothing about what Negroes were made for or what they are capable of," she told her white readership. Mary DeBardeleben, daughter of an Alabama Methodist minister and Hammond's colleague and successor, organized a string of southern settlement houses in Augusta, Nashville, and elsewhere. DeBardeleben's Methodist theology taught her that just as sinners with free will could progress to God, humans could perfect their societies and understand that "underneath the outer differences we *are one*." She came to an "appreciation of what was good and true and beautiful in the Negro race and to a sense of shame and humility for having been so blind and dumb as not to understand more readily." Many other southern evangelical women followed in the path established by these white Baptist and Methodist women, encouraged by black churchwomen who prodded along these understandings. The optimistic Wesleyan theology of the human soul's progress away from sin and into holiness also influenced future Southern Methodist women who joined the freedom struggle of the mid-twentieth century.[58]

Southern Evangelical Liberalism and Radicalism in the Mid-Twentieth Century

The southern labor activist and writer Katherine Du Pre Lumpkin's lyrical autobiography, *The Making of a Southerner*, recounts her background in an upper-class Episcopalian family steeped in the heritage of her father's service in the Confederacy. After attending a women's college in Georgia, Lumpkin went to graduate school at Columbia University, worked with the YWCA, and authored important studies of child labor and other southern social problems. During her early years with the YWCA, it was considered revolutionary for a black woman to deliver an address at a meeting. Yet after her initial experience, as she reminisced, "I found the heavens had not fallen, nor the earth parted asunder to swallow us up in this unheard of transgression. Indeed I found I could breathe freely again, eat heartily, even laugh again." The "tabernacle of our sacred racial beliefs," formerly "untouchable," had now been breached: "But I had touched it. I had reached out my hand for an instance and let my finger-tips brush it. I had done it, and nothing, not the slightest thing had happened."[59]

The religious radicals of the next generation tore at the curtain partitioning the tabernacle of sacred racial beliefs. Moving beyond the progressives' pieties about uplift, their "thin but tough community of folk" outstripped the cautious defensiveness that marked the public stance of their religious institutions.

Early efforts at biracial understanding—the kind of work spearheaded by kindly white figures such as Willis D. Weatherford—drew from a carefully delimited, painfully respectable model of civility, a courteously negotiated set of rules for segregation. Sickened by the violent Red Summer of 1919, Will W. Alexander, a minister in Nashville, organized the Commission on Interracial Cooperation. As a Missouri farm boy and the son of devout Methodists, Alexander came into close contact with numerous preachers; he remembered them mostly for being gluttonous at the table and intellectually dull. Nevertheless, Alexander was ordained into the ministry almost a decade before he earned his theological degree at Vanderbilt in 1912. In seminary, he "never heard the race question referred to. . . . In those days in the South you just didn't admit that there was a race problem and therefore you didn't talk about it." Taking over the pulpit of a church in Nashville during World War I, Alexander ministered to unemployed men and black children. Startled by the depth of the human misery all around him, he realized his helplessness as a minister and constantly warred with church authorities who, as he later said, "wanted me to love the Lord but . . . didn't want me to love any Negro children." Alexander used the opportunity provided by the war to leave the ministry and work on projects of reconciliation, including teaching basic literacy skills in training camps for American soldiers. Initially supported by the YMCA, Alexander realized that "we would eventually have to take stands on matters that were probably not acceptable to many people in the community." The YMCA itself, he found, was "another one of those institutions that had to build itself rather than build a better world."[60]

Alexander persuaded philanthropists in Atlanta and elsewhere to fund the Commission on Interracial Cooperation. The group formed separate white and black committees in hundreds of individual counties that investigated particular incidents and proposed local solutions to racial conflicts. Separate and equal was the CIC's formula, both in terms of the social philosophy it endorsed and in how the organization itself operated. Under Alexander's able leadership, the CIC publicized egregious instances of southern hate crimes. Walter White of the NAACP frequently called on Alexander's resources to investigate lynchings, beatings, and economic fraud perpetrated on sharecroppers. Through the efforts of the CIC and other groups, the tide slowly, if unevenly, turned. CIC member Quincey Ewing, a Mississippi Episcopalian, even advocated federal intervention (since Reconstruction a white southern bête noire) when local and state authorities failed to enforce proper legal form. In another case, the CIC member Reverend P. T. Holloway of Midway Methodist Church in Liberty County, Georgia, denounced the lynchings of two men in Wayne County, Georgia, in 1922. CIC pressure helped to gain the indictments of twenty-two men and the convictions of four for these murders. In the 1930s, state women's CIC committees gathered over 40,000 signatures demanding that southern sheriffs restrain mob violence.[61]

The limitations of this kind of white southern reform have been well documented in works such as John Egerton's magisterial chronicle *Speak Now Against the Day*. Most whites in the CIC looked upon the organization as an "instrument of fairness and conciliation vital to the maintenance of 'separate but equal' segregation." Willis D. Weatherford and his fellow racial paternalists, including industrialist John Eagan and Atlanta Baptist pastor M. Ashby Jones, dominated the CIC's board. Their presence hemmed in Will Alexander, who was impatient to denounce segregation as a system rather than merely to ameliorate its worst effects. As early as 1926, Alexander publicly had opposed segregation, nearly costing him his CIC post. Subsequently, he worked behind the scenes. The CIC thus "developed a curious image of liberal activism within the bounds of cautious and proper respectability." Some black observers held a less charitable view. They saw biracial "cooperation" among so-called moderates as smoothing over, rather than challenging, an intolerable oppression. As the black progressive and Atlanta Neighborhood Union organizer Lugenia Burns Hope admonished, while CIC personnel imposed their own views on the black southern leadership, the "forces of darkness" managed to agree on what was "'best for the Negroes.'"[62]

When Alexander accepted a position in the Roosevelt administration, the CIC collapsed. Alexander later condemned segregation in a 1944 issue of *Harper's* magazine. He had traveled a long way from his boyhood on a Missouri farm and his well-meaning efforts at charity in the Nashville neighborhood where he first pastored. His leadership of the CIC provided a limited but crucial precedent for future efforts. Members of a later generation expanded on this work considerably, even as they criticized its timidity. "The very fact that the first interracial work in the South began in Georgia has proved recently to be a deterrent to progress," Lillian Smith noted in 1957. "The old-timers are dogmatic; they stirred up a lot of dust in their day; all right, they say, that is the only way you can stir up dust, paw the ground the way we did. You can't move them. Some are dead now but their ghosts are still around. I appreciate what they did and what those still around are doing. But we need a fresh approach. Something younger, more vital, more risky, full of fun and ardor." Alexander himself sensed this. Later in his life, he chaired the race relations board of the Federal Council of Churches and guided the drafting of its report that called for a "desegregated church in a desegregated society," a first for the organization.[63]

From the Great Depression to *Brown v. Board*, progressive southern Christians pursued interracial justice. Starting where Will Alexander and his cohorts left off, they moved beyond mere goodwill statements and official denominational resolutions. Writing about the rise of southern liberalism, historian John Egerton explains,

> More often than not, the institutional church, white and black, did prove to be an obstruction to the prophetic voices that arose within it, rather than a stage for them. Many a Southern activist was led by his or her religious faith and teachings into a deepening personal commitment to social reform, only to find that the church was more interested in preserving its traditions and privileges than in reforming itself or the larger society. The church, like the university, may have been a wellspring for the intellectual and philosophical stimulation out of which some reform movements came—but when the institutions themselves shrank from joining the fray, it was often their sons and daughters, acting in new alliances or as individuals, who moved the dialogue and the action to a higher plane.[64]

Clarence Jordan, founder of Koinonia Farm, the important communal experiment in southwest Georgia, exemplifies Egerton's analysis. Trained in the 1930s at Southern Baptist Theological Seminary, Jordan intended to pursue a standard career trajectory up the denominational bureaucracy. In Louisville, however, he encountered professors who shocked students with progressive ideas, propelling him on a different path. His determination deepened as he encountered the intensifying poverty in the Depression-era rural South. Jordan brought a progressive gospel and progressive farming to the desiccated theologies and worn-out lands in the rural southern countryside. Like the young Tom Watson, he realized that white and black poor farmers were in the same ditch, facing common problems only worsened by political demagoguery. Jordan's initiative resulted in the formation of Koinonia Farm, near Americus, Georgia. Opened in 1942, the experiment in Christian communal living and progressive farming stood as an embattled but unmistakable witness to radical southern Christianity. One of Koinonia's earliest residents, a former missionary to Burma and progressive Southern Baptist named Jasper Martin England, explained its purpose as "making a witness in the dirt as real farmers, not as professionals or as ministers going in to tell people how to live on a farm in Georgia. . . . It had to be worked out as dirt farmers if we expected people to take seriously what we were about." England left Koinonia after two years, by which point locals already were enraged that members were taking black children to school and encouraging interracial dialogue.

Koinonia experienced problems normal to communalist experiments, worsened by controversies incited by its audacious rebuke to regional economic and theological orthodoxy. In the late 1950s, local authorities and vigilantes tried to drive Jordan out of Sumter County, eventually fraying the small community. Jordan's dream of communal sharing conflicted with his equally treasured vision of whites and blacks working together peaceably. Local black farmers needed economic opportunity and stability and could ill afford to dump their meager resources into a community pot, a reality that Jordan understood. Nationally, church groups assumed that the farm served as a base for civil rights activities, despite Jordan's insistence that Koinonia was primarily an experiment in Christian communalism and involved in politics as part of this larger radical witness. In the early 1960s, Koinonia harbored Charles Sherrod and other civil rights activists. Yet Jordan shied away from the civil rights movement's philosophy of active nonviolent resistance. He hewed instead to a Quaker-like faith in nonresistance and a progressive farmer's belief in economic independence. Jordan's *Cotton-Patch Gospels*, his version of biblical stories told in a southern vernacular, inspired a new generation of southern Christian Populists.[65]

While Jordan patiently toiled away in rural Georgia, other Christian labor radicals and interracialists pursued their own visions of social and economic justice. After hearing Jordan speak at her college, a self-described "good Baptist girl" named Helen Lewis realized that there was "no turning back," no way she could "not make those connections" between religious faith and the call to action against injustice. Born in 1924 in a small Georgia town, Lewis was raised by her father, a mail carrier and one of the few whites in the area to hold down a respectable job. Though baptized as a young girl, Lewis later came to see evangelical conversion as a "puberty ceremony more than anything else." As a college student, she explored issues of oppression through her stint in the Baptist Student Union and the YWCA. But at a student convention meeting, when she described the plight of sharecroppers, her boldness angered the local Baptist constituency. Those "good Christian farmers," she discovered, quickly formed nasty red-hunting and race-baiting posses. "Asking for that kind of Christianity was dangerous," she concluded. Later she organized for the Congress of Industrial Organizations (CIO), worked with the Tennessee Valley Authority, and documented the environmental devastation caused by strip mining in the southern mountains.[66]

Other southern social gospelers condemned dangerous conditions in the Bessemer steel mills, proposed public supervision of industrial machinery, exposed abuses in convict leasing, and joined in crusades against child labor. Pastors such as A. C. Davidson of Southside Baptist Church in Birmingham cited Christian economists such as Richard Ely on the critical need for labor organizing. Davidson and others attempted to recruit institutional churches to provide social services for working-class people. At its 1938 meeting, the Southern Baptist Convention recognized the "right of labor to organize and engage in collective bargaining to the end that labor may have a fair and living wage, such as will provide not only for the necessities of life, but for recreation, pleasure and culture."[67]

Despite the intense hostility to union inroads in southern industry, the CIO and other labor groups benefited from southern religious activists who promoted working-class organizing. None was more significant than Lucy Randolph Mason, an elite Virginian who committed herself to liberate working southerners, white and black, from "poverty, ignorance, and insecurity." Mason was heir to a family of Episcopalian ministers and lay leaders. Her father was an Episcopalian clergyman, and her mother a part of the Virginia prison reform movement. Both her parents were centrally located in the lively world of social Christianity in Richmond, home to a remarkable constellation of religious progressives from the "better classes" of Virginia society. This group included Samuel Chiles Mitchell, head of progressive education forces; Robert H. Pitt, editor of the Baptist *Religious Herald* and critic of corporate power and the social oppression of labor; Lila Hardaway Valentine, leader of Virginia's women's suffrage movement and otherwise involved in nearly every progressive crusade of the era; Walter Russell Bowie, Episcopalian editor of the *Southern Churchman* and advocate of what he called a "reverent Modernism"; James Cannon, controversial Methodist Prohibitionist and modernist; and Douglas Southall Freeman, the tireless history professor, Robert E. Lee biographer, and star-attraction Men's Sunday School class teacher. Richmond's Protestants were proud that the "Fundamentalist-Modernist row" missed their city. The city's religious leaders were not about to let the public civility treasured by the Bourbon and urban elite be disturbed by backwoods cranks or ill-educated preacher boys.[68]

As a pious young woman, the Richmonder Lucy Randolph Mason learned that personal goodness hardly sufficed for social justice. Reading Walter Rauschenbusch and other theologians of the social gospel convinced her that being a true Christian mandated action for social reform. She became involved in women's suffrage, a movement that seemed to her a "divine discontent." She worked for the Richmond YWCA as its industrial and then general secretary (1920s), then moved on to the National Consumers League in New York. "I have spent my life working religion out in social action," she wrote of her decision to join the labor struggle. "Church people ought to do something to bring about the Kingdom of God on earth. That's why I am in the labor movement." She was a close ally of Myles Horton and Highlander Folk School, a place she turned to repeatedly even after Highlander broke with the CIO in 1949.[69]

As a public relations representative for the CIO in Atlanta during the Depression, Mason organized for the Textile Workers' Organizing Union. On Labor Day in 1937, she asked southern clergymen to "speak clearly and courageously on behalf of the rights of workers to organize and bargain collectively through Representatives of their own choosing," and not be dissuaded by bogus allegations of communism. In her travels, she frequently encountered ministers who were "hopeless to try to educate . . . too old to learn." Others were too "scared and ineffectual" even to articulate the social creeds passed by their own denominations. In Staunton, Virginia, Mason talked with sympathetic Protestant ministers, including some who had left their ministerial association because of its segregationist policies. Mason also visited black unionists and was moved when she witnessed them opening one meeting with lined-out variations on the Lord's Prayer.[70]

Mason discerned a disturbing nexus between anti-union propaganda and evangelical revivalists who were funded by manufacturers and trade groups. In the months before a union election at a mill near Rome, Georgia, for example, workers began receiving free subscriptions to the *Militant Truth*. Edited by Sherman Patterson, the industry-sponsored propaganda sheet spewed the antiunion and race-baiting spiel to textile workers who were being courted by union organizers. The CIO, the tabloid blared, was anti-Christian, antisegregation, antisouthern. The house journal of the textile industry manufacturer's association, the *Textile Bulletin*, picked up on the popular theology of racial segregation, quoting Leviticus 19:19 ("Thou shalt not let thy cattle gender with a diverse kind. Thou shalt not sow thy field with a mingled seed") to prove that God forbade the races from amalgamating. And race mixing was, of course, the ultimate goal of the CIO. Such rhetoric had a chilling effect on labor. The issue of ending segregation within southern CIO unions was difficult and trying for activists who wished to uphold principles of equality without alienating the very working-class men and women they hoped to band together.[71]

In the 1940s, the CIO conducted a South-wide campaign to unionize laborers in a region still characterized by low wages, long hours, and few collective bargaining rights. A steel worker from Oklahoma named John Gates Ramsey became the Presbyterian Church's liaison during Operation Dixie. He and Lucy Randolph Mason facilitated luncheon meetings between clergy and labor leaders, pulled together a religion-labor fellowship in Birmingham, and produced pamphlets informing readers of the support they had garnered from denominational leaders. In 1951, Mason and Ramsey published *The Churches and Brotherhood*, updating a former pamphlet titled *The Church and the Labor Unions*. By that time, advocates of working peoples' rights had secured supportive statements from many denominations.

Southern labor leaders and their religious allies faced difficult obstacles and met more failure than success. Massive actions such as the general strike among textile workers in 1934 and the postwar Operation Dixie campaign both faltered. Employer resistance, race-baiting, suspicion from millworkers concerned about protecting their race-privileged jobs, and unfavorable labor laws hindered the efforts. Explaining why she did not want to join the United Textile Workers Association's strike effort in 1934, a female millworker responded, "I, like thousands of others did not strike with the union, because we knew we would [lose] our jobs like thousands of others have done before us. Even though we might have had faith in the union we simply couldn't afford to quit because we live right up to every penny we make. . . . It is true that every textile worker in the South would walk out of the mill today if they were not afraid of starvation. I don't believe that God intended people to suffer as we have suffered." Such statements evoke both the hopes and the limitations of southern unionization. Despite the setbacks, the woman known as "Miss Lucy of the CIO" kept alive her faith in labor and in God through decades of frustrating toil.[72]

Women, the Social Gospel, and Civil Rights

In addition to Lucy Randolph Mason, many other southern evangelical women in the generation before the civil rights movement awoke to Katherine Lumpkin's epiphany about the "tabernacle of our sacred racial beliefs." In the 1920s, black and white Methodist women established the Women's Committee of the Commission on Interracial Cooperation. Brought together by Will Alexander and women in the MECS, white and black southern women met at a YWCA in Memphis. At the 1921 gathering, according to Alexander, the black women "boxed the compass pretty well for these white women about what it meant to be a Negro woman and Negro wife and have a Negro family in the South." The black North Carolina educator Charlotte Hawkins Brown recounted for the delegates the humiliations she experienced on board the train to Memphis. And, at one point, as black women entered the hall, Belle Bennett led a group of white women in singing "Blest Be the Tie that Binds," an emotional moment for many present. The conference led to the formation of the Women's General Committee of the CIC, with seven white and seven black members. Through the 1920s and 1930s, women's biracial cooperation in Christian groups took root, as black women gradually revealed for white southern churchwomen a bit of truth about life behind the veil.[73]

When the CIC waned in influence, Methodist women made up most of the membership of the Association of Southern Women for the Prevention of Lynching (ASWPL). Headed by Jesse Daniel Ames, the group engineered localized responses to the social disorder of lynching without advocating any broadly inclusive program of equal rights. Ames succeeded in highlighting lynching on the national agenda while refusing to back federal antilynching legislation. Yet Ames's

organization provided an entrée for many white women to dissociate themselves from the rhetorical patina of chivalry that had covered up southern racist
violence.[74]

If Ames's organization ultimately confined itself to one-issue politics, other
white southern Methodist women pressed further. Louise Young and Thelma
Stevens charted such a path for white southern Christians struggling to move
beyond Jim Crow and white moderate maternalism. Young grew up near Memphis, was educated at an Episcopal school for girls, and later earned a BA at Vanderbilt and did graduate work at the University of Wisconsin and Bryn Mawr.
From 1925 to 1957, she chaired the Department of Sociology and Social Work at
Scarritt College for Christian Workers in Nashville, the school for young women
established by Belle Harris Bennett. During those years, Young directed the
Methodist Woman's Missionary Council, was an early member of the ASWPL,
and served on the board of directors of the Nashville Bethlehem House and the
national board of the YWCA. Her male counterparts in Southern Methodism,
she remembered, primarily pursued statistical growth in church membership,
whereas women "were after it in terms of social work almost totally. Social work
and teaching."[75]

Teaching in Augusta from 1919 to 1922 at Paine College, a school for black Methodists supported primarily with white money, Young was "literally living in a
Negro world." She worked closely with Charles Johnson, an African American
sociologist at Fisk. There was "very little color between us," she later reminisced.
Young also mediated the sometimes tense relationship between Jesse Daniel Ames,
a forthright "organization person" (in Young's words), and Will Alexander, who
"was really a persuader." Through her association with the Tennessee Council for
Human Relations, she befriended Eleanor Roosevelt. For a time, Young taught
at Highlander Folk School in Tennessee, the remarkable experiment in training
for social change run by Myles Horton. Eventually she retreated from that work,
fearing that the school's reputation for radicalism might embroil Scarritt in
controversy.[76]

Young's protégé at Scarritt, Thelma Stevens, was a native of Mississippi who
devoted her life to issues of racial justice. In 1919, as a young schoolteacher in the
Magnolia State, Stevens rode with students on a chartered bus to witness a public lynching spectacle. As she determined afterward, "If the Lord would let me
live long enough, . . . I would do something to bring a little bit of relief from fear
and a little human dignity to black people in Mississippi." After graduating from
Scarritt College, Stevens succeeded Young as director of the Bethlehem Center
in Augusta. In the 1920s, believing that the church was too "isolated from life,"
she conceived of her work in Augusta as community development, not settlement

house charity. She sought to transcend the customary missionary society "for the Negroes" model, realizing that, in their dealings with black Methodist women, whites "weren't working on a horizontal level."[77]

In 1938, Stevens attended the founding meeting of the Southern Conference for Human Welfare (SCHW), where a sizable crowd of southern New Dealers, liberals, and radicals collectively envisioned revolutionizing the South. As head of the newly created Methodist Bureau of Christian Social Relations, Stevens put together the first truly interracial Methodist conference, held at Paine College in Augusta. Stevens pressed for actual implementation of the idealistic credos periodically issued by ecclesiastical bodies and usually ignored by local churches. For example, fully knowing the southern resistance that would be provoked, she argued successfully for passage of the Methodist Charter of Racial Policies. As she explained her philosophy in 1945, "The new day calls for a new way of life where the Negro, the Mexican, the Jew, or the Japanese-American can secure and keep a job commensurate with his skill without fear or hurt. The Christian Church is in a position to lead the way to creating a conscience that means justice for all."[78]

Through the mid-twentieth century, the Mississippi native Thelma Stevens contributed one of the most significant voices for racial integration in any major American denomination. The Woman's Division of the Methodist Church, headed by Stevens, did not depend on approval from bishops and superintendents or contributions from General Conferences. Stevens took advantage of this opening and helped to secure the desegregation of the leading educational institution for Methodist women, Scarritt College, in 1952. Meanwhile, Stevens's Bureau of Christian Social Relations trained local leaders to run workshops in addressing local crises. In Clinton, Tennessee, members of the Woman's Society of Christian Service of a local congregation reached out to black Methodists after whites in the town attacked blacks seeking to desegregate schools. In other locales embroiled in school desegregation and civil rights struggles—Nashville, Danville (Virginia), and Shelbyville (Kentucky)—Methodist women held integrated prayer group meetings and formed alliances with black Methodist groups. Stevens befriended James Lawson, a young black Methodist who transmitted the Gandhian ideas of active resistance through nonviolent civil disobedience to Nashville student leaders. Methodist women's groups endorsed nonviolent civil disobedience as "an opportunity for Christian witness." In the 1960s, Stevens implored Methodist women to support voter registration for African American citizens. "Clear forthright leadership of Christian women," she insisted, would "open doors to thousands of eligible Negro citizens" who had been deprived of their constitutional rights.[79]

Dorothy Tilly joined Stevens and other Methodist activists in sparking reform. Born in Hampton, Georgia, Tilly was the daughter of a Methodist minister and junior college president. While her mother avoided public involvement in racial issues (not wishing to sink her husband's career), she also introduced the young Dorothy to ugly realities, once taking her to the servant's entrance of a luxury hotel in Atlanta to show her children eating out of garbage pails in the back. As a young adult, Tilly directed summer conferences at Paine College and was a charter member of Jesse Ames's ASWPL. In 1944, she was named to head the Southern Regional Council, the successor to Will Alexander's CIC. Two years later, she visited the site of a racial massacre in Columbia, Tennessee, where she collected and publicized information about the appalling resurgence of violent racism that greeted African Americans returning from World War II.

Tilly secured her national reputation in 1948 as the only white southern woman to serve on the presidential commission that produced "To Secure These Rights," a critically important endorsement of desegregation as national policy. The following year, she created the Fellowship of the Concerned. Tilly used the meetings of this biracial coalition of church people interested in civil rights to confront white southerners with the "injustices, discriminations and hurts of the past so that our present and future may be better." Taking a page from the strategy of southern antilynching groups, she extracted pledges from sheriffs and police chiefs that extralegal violence would be prosecuted. She also enlisted white women to monitor southern trials, intending to compel fairer treatment of poor and black defendants. "Justice would not only have to be blind, she would have to have a clothespin on her nose to stand what goes on in some of our courts all over the nation," Tilly said of the judicial system. The Fellowship of the Concerned also worked with the SRC's voter education project and supported the Mississippi Freedom Summer of 1964.[80]

For these efforts, Tilly was denounced in newspapers and subjected to frequent harassment. One columnist castigated her as a "parasite who while living upon funds furnished by the Methodist Church had rendered much of her service to the cause of Socialism and Communism." Describing what Methodist women were doing to "allay the tensions of the South," Tilly wrote in a private letter to a church editor: "Since my conversations with you the tensions have grown greater. The women are still meeting and working but are giving no publicity to what they are doing. They are very bravely trying to work in spite of opposition so great that it might affect their husband's business—and in some instances, it has already affected their standing in the community." Answering criticism that she should concentrate on church work, Tilly replied, "If the church needs saving, it is not worth saving."[81]

Southern churches spawned a number of remarkable women who, like Tilly, became stalwarts of the white progressive religious South. Few were better known than Alabama native Virginia Foster Durr. She grew up believing that wealth was "ordained by God," was "in the blood." Her father pastored Birmingham's South Highland Presbyterian Church, a congregation she remembered as being "full of fine, upstanding, moneyed citizens. It was one of the leading churches in the city, and very fundamentalist." The church later ousted Durr's father from this pulpit because of his nonliteralist views on biblical interpretation. In her youth, Durr briefly visited the mourner's bench at a revival led by the fundamentalist Bob Jones (founder of Bob Jones University in Greenville, South Carolina, a stronghold of racist theology). She concealed her actions from her parents, realizing "they would think it was common—to be sung over and prayed over. . . . It was just ordinary, common people who did that kind of thing." Durr had few contacts with African Americans until she attended Wellesley College, where her views began to evolve. Durr later became one of the foremost "inside agitators" of the white South. In Washington (where her husband, Clifford Durr, was a liberal lawyer with the New Deal), Virginia befriended Eleanor Roosevelt and participated in reformist groups such as the Southern Conference for Human Welfare, where she met black leaders such as Mary McLeod Bethune.

Durr found a true spiritual home in her long affinity with the southern freedom struggle. She spearheaded a national effort to repeal poll taxes, a primary means employed to disfranchise black and poor white citizens. In the early 1950s, she led a delegation from United Church Women to meet James O. Eastland, Mississippi's powerbroker, racist senator, convict lessor, and Methodist layman. Eastland's sister was a member of the Woman's Society of Christian Service in a Mississippi Methodist church. This mattered little when the delegation queried the senator about racial injustice, inciting Eastland to a memorably incoherent rant about race-mixing. Upon moving back to Montgomery, Durr discovered two UCW organizations divided by race. She resolved to integrate the two. The white women met with Coretta Scott King and other prominent black Montgomerians to "pray and sing and hold hands and have a cup of tea afterward." When a local newspaperman published their names, harassing phone calls soon followed. Some of the white women's husbands forced them to stop the gatherings. "I thought that was the lowest point of the whole civil rights struggle when these lovely churchwomen were repudiated by their own husbands," an angered Durr later recounted. A friend of Rosa Parks and other Montgomery-area activists, Durr supported the bus boycott initiated by blacks in Alabama's capitol city. She assisted Parks and others in training with Myles Horton at Highlander Folk School (an event Mrs. Parks herself considered a turning point in her life).[82]

Few white southerners identified their life so closely with the cause of redeeming the region as Lillian Smith, or had as complicated a relationship with a region and religion they loved and hated. Smith was the daughter of Methodists and for three years in the 1920s was a missionary in China. Together with her partner, Paula Snelling, Smith ran experimental summer camps in the hills of northern Georgia. In her controversial essays and novels, Smith explored the Freudian underpinnings of racial hatred and sexual repression in the South. She kept in close touch with southern progressive leaders and served as a mentor to young women (especially Jane Stembridge of the Student Non-Violent Coordinating Committee [SNCC]) on the front lines of civil rights. Southern moderates of her own generation quarreled with her, sometimes viciously. She and Ralph McGill of the *Atlanta Constitution* attacked each other with particular venom. Smith lambasted what she saw as McGill's tepid moderation; McGill shot back with nasty asides on Smith's relative solitude and reputed sexual orientation. When black civil rights organizing arose in the 1950s, Smith wrote to Martin Luther King Jr. that "only through persuasion, love, goodwill, and firm nonviolent resistance can the change take place in our South. . . . In our South, the whites, too, share the profoundly religious symbols you are using and respond to them on a deep level of their hearts and minds. Their imaginations are stirred: the waters are troubled." After the Montgomery bus boycott, Smith accepted an invitation to speak at the Institute of Nonviolence and Social Change in early December 1956. Stricken with cancer, Smith sent her speech, "The Right Way Is Not a Moderate Way," to be read in absentia. Eschewing the dominant rhetoric of the day, which vapidly condemned "extremists on both sides," Smith saw that "moderation" would accomplish nothing. The critical question was "what kind of extremist" one would choose to be. She believed that there were many "white Christians in the South who know segregation is wrong. They want to do right. But they are not free to do right. Every day they do what they know in their hearts is contrary to Christian belief."[83]

Through their lives and careers, women such as the social gospelers Belle Bennett and Lucinda Helm, Methodist activists such as Jessie Daniel Ames and Dorothy Tilly, labor organizers such as Lucy Randolph Mason and Anne Lewis, religious liberals such as Virginia Durr and Thelma Stevens, and social critics such as Lillian Smith sanctified secular notions of justice. Moving from tentative forays at paternalistic uplift, into ventures of Progressive Era biracial cooperation, and then into deep commitments to Christian interracialism, they tilled the ground for the freedom struggle to come. And when it came later in the twentieth century, their daughters embraced Christian interracialism in the beloved community.

Southern Activism in the War Years and After

In 1947, at an Apostolic Faith Church of God in Washington, D.C., the longtime independent Pentecostal minister Smallwood Williams held a celebratory wake for Mississippi's recently deceased Theodore Bilbo. Over 2,000 worshippers turned out at Smallwood's congregation to give the odious former senator his proper burial. "I know his white ministers preached the funeral, but it is not properly preached until a colored minister preaches it," Williams triumphantly intoned. "We are the people who suffered under the racial blasphemy of Bilbo. I prophesied on watch-meeting night January 1, 1947, that he would not be here another year. The ending of the infamous career and death of Mr. Bilbo is a merciful act of God. It is an answer to the prayers of the oppressed. . . . Just as God dramatically removed Mr. Bilbo from the political scene, he is able to erase Bilbo-ism, and all that Bilbo stood for, from our country and from the face of the earth." Because of their faith in the imminence of Christ's return, Pentecostals developed a reputation (usually well deserved) for political quietism. For these black Pentecostals, however, services mixed secular and spiritual salvation. At the close of the sermon, twenty-seven came to the altar for the experience of the Holy Ghost. For them, as for civil rights believers in freedom services over the next two decades, the religious became the political, indeed *was* the political, as the altar call became a ceremony of claiming citizenship rights.[84]

In many ways, the 1940s were the de facto takeoff point of the modern civil rights movement. Activism from a younger generation of African Americans merged with larger developments in American society, the incipient Cold War, and a liberal intellectual embrace of equality. Wartime agencies such as the Fair Employment Practices Commission achieved modest gains. Civil rights forces also won significant victories in the courts, including the Texas case of *Smith v. Allwright*, the 1944 court case that (in theory) outlawed the white primary.

The war against Hitler's vision for Aryan domination invigorated black activists at home. Often this was through personal experience in the military. At other times it involved a simple recognition of the way the war had shaken the South. The Reverend Elbert Williams, founder of an NAACP branch in Brownsville, Texas, launched a voter registration campaign in his south Texas town in 1940. The Reverend James Arthur Parsons, who pastored four black churches in the north Mississippi hamlet of Tupelo, declared his candidacy for Congress in 1942. He ran for the seat held by longtime Mississippi congressman John Rankin. Both Williams, who was murdered, and Parsons, forcibly told by whites to drop his candidacy, paid a price for their daring.[85]

Despite such intimidation, other black ministers revived civil rights organizations such as the NAACP, which had been repressed and in some places virtually extinguished in the 1920s. Ralph Mark Gilbert, pastor of Savannah's historic First African Baptist Church, convened Georgia's first statewide meeting of the four existing state NAACP branches in the late 1930s. Gilbert traversed Georgia, creating or reviving more than fifty NAACP branches statewide and preparing the ground for significant black political activism. In South Carolina, Modjeska Simkins teamed with James Hinton in mobilizing voters in Greenville. Hinton was a Baptist cleric and a district manager for a black-owned life insurance company. He served as director of the NAACP State Conference of Branches; Simkins was his assistant. In response, Klan groups listed the names of the newly registered black voters in the local press and ransacked the homes of some African Americans who had signed up. "Whites who speak out for equality of opportunity, they are good citizens and heroes," Hinton commented acidly, "but a NEGRO, when he speaks for equality of opportunity, or ending of segregation, he is impudent." The Reverend I. DeQuincey Newman also joined the struggle in South Carolina. He helped to form the first NAACP branch in Orangeburg, where he was a Methodist cleric, and organized the first local unit of the Progressive Democratic Party, an entering wedge for the NAACP as well as a challenge to the dominant white supremacist Democratic establishment.[86]

In Mississippi, the Reverend William Albert Bender was one of the first to test *Smith v. Allwright*. Bender enlisted two students from Tougaloo College in Jackson, Mississippi, where he was a chaplain, to drive him to the polls a few miles from their campus. Physically prevented from casting a ballot, he filed a complaint with U.S. Attorney General Tom Clark. Shortly after this incident, local whites burned a cross at the college. The racist demagogue Theodore Bilbo won the primary, as expected, but sixty-eight blacks (including Bender) challenged the legality of the election. Before the judicial controversy was settled, Bilbo died. His successor, Judge John Stennis, was more patrician than his crude predecessor but stoutly defended Mississippi's segregationist way of life through the 1960s. Bender was part of a generation of black professionals and civil servants who were relatively immune from white economic retaliation. In Mississippi, however, this group did not often include ministers, who generally proved hesitant to open their church doors to civil rights meetings.[87]

Building from the legacy of missionary societies and progressive reform groups, black women of evangelical background moved into civil rights organizing. Ella Baker, a key transitional figure in this narrative, grew up in North Carolina. From 1918 to 1927, she attended Shaw University, a black Baptist school in Raleigh established during Reconstruction under the auspices of the northern American Baptist Home Mission Society. Like most schools of its type, Shaw accepted black students from junior high through postgraduate level. It subsisted on the meager income provided by its low tuition, contributions from black churches, the work of its students, and the support of white missionary societies. Shaw prided itself on providing a Christian education to sober young men and women who would become preachers, teachers, progressive farmers, and tradesmen. The school enforced rigid behavior codes that grated on the instinctively rebellious Baker. She led a student protest at Shaw against dress codes for girls and the obsequious practice of the college choir entertaining white visitors by singing spirituals. While chafing at such restrictions and humiliations, Baker also learned that "your relationship to human beings was far more important than your relationship to the amount of money you made," a lesson she carried through a lifetime of ceaseless itinerant preaching and organizing for justice.[88]

Baker then moved to New York City, where she imbibed the free flow of ideas from intellectuals, activists, street-corner orators, and black nationalists who vied for followers on the streets of Harlem. In 1941, she became an assistant field secretary for the NAACP and spent the better part of the next two decades on the road. Along the way, she stored up organizing wisdom that she later imparted to younger men and women in the civil rights movement. Her tense relationship with other men in the NAACP reinforced her growing suspicion of larger organizations, a wariness that extended to the Southern Christian Leadership Conference (SCLC). In 1960, Baker's alma mater in Raleigh, Shaw University, hosted the organizing meeting of the Student Non-Violent Coordinating Committee. Baker presided as a spiritual mentor and practical adviser to the students, who met originally to form a youth auxiliary wing of SCLC. Baker advised the students not to be tamed and patronized by their elders. SNCC, she believed, could become the kind of committed organizing cell that would not rely on media statements from charismatic leaders. Baker remained a trenchant critic of the institutional church's complacency and cowardice. Still, she used organized religious institutions as points of organizing and educating, for her own upbringing and education taught her about the church's central role in black southern communities. As she later expressed it, "I became active in things largely because my mother was active in religion."[89]

In retrospect, progress in overturning southern apartheid appears inevitable, just a matter of time. These presumptions appear so clearly only from a safe distance. One year after VE day, nineteen recorded lynchings, the highest level since the dark period of violence just after the First World War, suggested very different conclusions about the war's meaning for victory at home.[90]

World War II intensified the conflict over freedom's coming fought during Reconstruction, quelled by the ascendancy of white supremacy, but reignited by the New Deal and the promise of the Four Freedoms. The international conflict provided ammunition both for progressivism and for racist reaction. There was more than one good war, and church people fought on all sides. Progressives deployed the rhetoric of democracy, freedom, and self-determination but had ample reason to fear a repeat of the racist clampdown following World War I. The growing power of conservatives in Congress since Roosevelt's failed campaign to oust southern Democratic critics in 1938, the rollback of New Deal measures during the war, and the simple coercion involved in the war effort could feed forces of reaction. White southern religious institutions, moreover, were ready instruments of reactionary politics, while black churches often appeared cowed, their ministers too complacent or complicit to challenge received customs.

In 1938, the Southern Conference for Human Welfare brought together a motley roster of moderate liberals, progressives, and radicals who were interested in harnessing evangelical ideals of equality before God to progressive causes such as elimination of the poll tax, antilynching legislation, and a redistribution of economic and political power in the South. Its leadership included whites such as the Tennessee rural radical Aubrey Williams, minister and labor organizer James Dombrowski, and university president Frank Porter Graham. African American participants such as the noted educator Benjamin Mays and Eleanor Roosevelt's emissary to the black community, Mary McLeod Bethune, also were there. The fiery up-and-coming law enforcer Eugene "Bull" Connor of Birmingham, Alabama, was not invited but showed up anyway, determined to re-establish segregated seating at a meeting where Eleanor Roosevelt deliberately set her chair in the middle aisle separating white and black delegates. Five years later, 500 southern progressives (including many members of the Fellowship of Southern Churchmen [FSC]) attended a SCHW conference in Raleigh on the theme of "Christianity, Democracy, and the Healing of the South." The delegates heard speakers ranging from the black minister Mordecai Johnson to southern laypeople such as Lillian Smith. The Christian socialist Howard Kester exulted that the gathering "affirmed our conviction that in the South is a body of men and women whose religious faith transcends both denominational and racial lines and who are concerned to bring . . . the redemptive and healing influence of this faith."[91]

The white participants in the SCHW represented a generation of southern liberals and radicals typified by James Dombrowski. After studying with Harry F. Ward at Union Theological Seminary in the 1930s, the native of Tampa, Florida, practiced his version of the gospel by jumping into working-class struggles during the Depression. He hitchhiked to the North Carolina piedmont to join in textile strikes, and in the 1930s he helped to found Highlander Folk School and the FSC. In the early 1940s, sensing an enormous "opportunity for progress on the race issue," Dombrowski and his SCHW colleague and co-chair Clark Foreman led a conference in Nashville addressed by Franklin and Eleanor Roosevelt. Five hundred delegates attended, one-third of whom were black and the majority of whom were affiliated with organized labor. The war made possible this inspirational meeting for reshaping the southern racial order. Because its membership included some individuals suspected of being (and some who actually were)

Communist Party members or sympathizers, the SCHW did not survive the Cold War. Other groups took up its causes, including the Southern Conference Educational Fund (itself a direct spinoff of the SCHW) and the Southern Regional Council. In 1949, the SRC declared its official break from segregation, even though it had started originally to resurrect the CIC's notion of reforming and ameliorating apartheid. Momentum for change seemed to be building—but so was sentiment for massive resistance.[92]

As black activists pushed for reform in local areas, some white evangelical leaders also questioned the southern system of theological racism. Just after World War II, the state convention of Baptists in North Carolina declared that "segregation of believers holding the same tenets of faith because of color or social status into racial or class churches" was a "denial of the New Testament affirmation of the equality of all believers." In urban areas of the Upper South, ministerial associations and religious leaders followed the lead of denominational organizations and social groups such as the SRC. In the election year of 1948, the Presbyterian minister and social activist Aubrey Williams convened an interracial gathering of ministers, writers, educators, and other social leaders in Charlottesville, Virginia. There the group called upon churches and professional associations to integrate their memberships. It was a high point for this brand of moderate southern liberalism. "We cannot face both ways," wrote Thomas C. Allen, director of the Department of Interracial Cooperation of the Virginia Council of Churches. Christians could not believe in a "master race" while espousing "the democratic principle of equality," nor could they "achieve this new attitude without the dynamic of the Christian Gospel which recognizes the wrongs of the old ways, which leads us to love our neighbors and even our enemies." His committee gained more employment opportunities for black men returning from wartime service.[93]

From the 1930s to the 1950s, Will Alexander, Lucy Randolph Mason, and others who came of age in the early twentieth century were joined by a new generation of religious progressives, iconoclasts, and radicals. Like their predecessors, they drew inspiration from religious faith while breaking from the largely conservative institutions that nurtured them. Many were affiliated with churches in university towns and other settings, where they enjoyed a bit more freedom than normal in more provincial locations. One of them was Charles Jones, a Presbyterian cleric in North Carolina beginning in the 1940s. Many who lived in the university town during these years remembered Jones's central role in goading Chapel Hill residents to take seriously the gospel many of them professed. A complex person, Jones was averse to institutional traditions. Describing Jones as the "most profane preacher I've ever met in my life," a Chapel Hill editor recalled that "some of our people have conferred sainthood on him, other people feared him, some of our people hated him." Black North Carolinians admired him. "He could explain what segregation felt like, from the inside. He'd say suppose you had a shoe that didn't fit and it hurts your heel," remembered one resident. At one meeting in the 1960s, black ministers in the area told their youth to be wary of involvement in civil rights. By contrast, Jones encouraged them to "go ahead and do it. And they cheered because they had heard this behave yourselves, do like we've been doing for 100 years. And so they followed his advice." Black minister and author Henry H. Mitchell also looked up to the Presbyterian heretic, who ate at the same table with his domestic servants: "He insisted his children should not grow up seeing or being involved in any arbitrary discrimination." Jones was one of those people "who from their first breath was always on the right side of things, no matter what ever happens and no matter what they come out of, what their background is, where they were born, whether they got money or they ain't, that are just always on the right side of the right thing," recalled another contemporary.[94]

Chapel Hill in those years, Jones later remembered, was very open, "so long as it wasn't made public" and there was no "fuss." He befriended and was a minister to a number of influential state leaders, including the president of the University of North Carolina, Frank Porter Graham. Jones saw Graham, a carefully circumspect voice of moderation on race, as a southern professional tied down by institutional responsibilities. But Graham was also loyal to his church, even when his controversial pastor's actions landed the university president in embarrassing spots. Jones also grew close to Howard Odum, noted sociologist of the South who once inscribed a book, "To Charles Jones, in the long and gradual fight for equality." In 1941, Jones brought to town the nationally known black minister and humanist Howard Thurman and attempted to host debates with known radicals. After the war, however, when he invited in the left-leaning presidential candidate and former vice president Henry Wallace, Jones found a much cooler reception to controversial speakers. The same Cold War that provided some momentum in the early civil rights struggle also hindered the efforts of the southern left, who were simultaneously red-baited and race-baited.[95]

In 1947, along with other fellow idealists and pacifists (including two white Methodist ministers from North Carolina), the black political radical Bayard Rustin embarked on the Journey of Reconciliation. This interracial bus trip through the Upper South foreshadowed the later Freedom Rides. The participants sought to make a test case of a 1946 Supreme Court decision banning segregation in interstate travel. They expected a peaceful entrance into Chapel Hill, but local hooligans attacked them on their arrival. The group refused to leave their vehicle unless the police turned up a warrant for the riders' arrest. When local cab drivers told the policemen they would "get those niggers off," Jones sped away with some of the riders. The cab drivers tailed him and waited outside his home with rocks and sticks, threatening arson. Jones repeatedly but ineffectually called the police for protection. Later he drove some of the activists to Greensboro and secreted others in houses around town. The local newspaper subsequently attacked Jones, implying he was "possibly communist oriented . . . [or] at least a radical," as Jones put it. Jones's church secretary, Nelle Morton, recounted how "all night long taxis buzzed around my home frightening a white student couple then living with me who took to the woods back of my home." When the Journey of Reconciliation riders eventually served their punishment on road gangs, Jones and other members of the Fellowship of Southern Churchmen saw to their welfare. Bayard Rustin, later a key adviser to civil rights groups, expressed his appreciation to the Chapel Hill supporters: "When I think of the ease with which certain types of progress can be made in New York as compared with the more serious problems that southern Christians and liberals face, I always feel that I should take off my hat to those of you who continue in the struggle."[96]

Jones's theological and social heresies drew the ire of conservative Presbyterians in North Carolina. His church officers insisted that the only reason Jones had been singled out was because he "practice[d] Christ in the field of race relations," including admitting African Americans to worship services and allowing the NAACP to meet there. As early as 1944, a church member complained that the number of Chapel Hill Presbyterians was declining because pastor Jones preached "social equality among the races. . . . We need a *pastor*, not a fanatic on the Negro question. He has them in his home (for meals), [then] says he doesn't visit congregation because he is too busy. . . . I like Negroes, but why neglect your own flock for them." In 1952, the Judicial Commission of Orange Presbytery, which had been authorized to investigate charges that his church had departed from traditional order, reported disapprovingly that Jones's congregation was "not interested in denominationalism in general, nor Presbyterianism as such, but rather in the practical application of Christianity in terms of an active demonstration of Christian brotherhood." Even before Jones's tenure, the theology of the congregational leaders was "generally uninformed respecting the theological position of our Church," wrote the Presbytery committee. When Jones saw his opponents' determination to oust him, he stepped down from that pulpit and pursued an alternative experiment in interracial worship, the Community Church of Chapel Hill. He remained a controversial figure in local politics thereafter by debating segregationists over the justice of the *Brown* decision and participating in Chapel Hill sit-ins in the early 1960s.[97]

Jones put his own actions and position in modest perspective. Southern religious progressivism, he later acknowledged, was "insight but little action." Churches would "issue their papers and so forth, but there was no implementation for it. It was sort of like the Creed. If you repeat the Creed, you're okay." Reminiscing on his days as a southern religious progressive, he remarked, "Our time had come, and it went past, and we did what we could. And you needed these more radical fellows." This epitaph serves as an elegant summary of the career of the white southern religious progressives of his generation.[98]

The most significant cadre of the white southern religious progressives shared common experiences in the southern backcountry and mountains, unburdened by some of the myths and traditions of the Old South. They commonly broke from racist dogmas through work with the YMCA and YWCA, as well as graduate training at institutions such as Vanderbilt and Union Theological Seminary in New York. The life of Howard "Buck" Kester illuminates the dreams and limitations of white religious radicalism in the years leading up to the civil rights movement.

The lifelong peripatetic southern Christian socialist spent a remarkable, if ultimately disappointing, career in ministering and agitating. Kester grew up in West Virginia in the 1910s, where he witnessed the bitter lives of coal miners and millworkers. His father, a Disciples of Christ churchgoer, was involved for a short time with the Klan but grew disillusioned by its violent vigilantism. After attending Lynchburg College, Kester matriculated at Princeton University, which turned out to be too theologically conservative for his tastes. He finally found academic satisfaction at Vanderbilt, where he joined an interracial group that met at Fisk University and affiliated himself with the Fellowship of Reconciliation (FOR). This group of Quaker- and Anabaptist-influenced radicals came out of World War I advocating nonresistance as a philosophical underpinning to pacifism. Kester later broke with the FOR after he accepted armed protection during his investigations of union activity among southern sharecroppers. As he saw it, the ethereal pacifism of his former colleagues was meager fare for the starved and defenseless workers and sharecroppers he had suffered with in some of Tennessee's poorest counties.[99]

At Vanderbilt, Kester fell under the influence of Alva Taylor, who joined the faculty in 1928. "When science gives the technique and the Church gives the social passion," Taylor had written, "we will possess the power to make the world over into the Kingdom of God." Until he was forced out by the university chancellor in 1936, Taylor taught a generation of southern social radicals, including Kester, labor organizer Ward Rodgers, the poet and preacher Don West, and Claude Williams, a Tennessee sharecropper's son who preached in Presbyterian churches, served as a labor organizer—and, secretively, joined the Communist Party, compelling Kester to bar Williams from the FSC. Alva Taylor provided Kester with a link to a renewed and radicalized social gospel, one less tame than its predecessor.[100]

Following college and his service in the YMCA, where he worked out some of his ideas about the social gospel, Kester attended Union Theological Seminary in New York in the early 1930s. Moving from Christian progressive liberal to social radical, Kester absorbed the lessons of his mentors, including the seminal religious thinker Reinhold Niebuhr. Kester formed friendships with fellow southern-born radicals and pacifists, including James Dombrowski. He also befriended the 1932 socialist presidential candidate Norman Thomas. Kester sought to move beyond the goodwill fellowship efforts of the YMCA and CIC. The black educator Ira De Augustine Reid praised one interracial conference attended by Kester for avoiding the "shadow-boxing that is usually so typical of meetings of this sort. Both sides attempted to see their weaknesses and find a common ground and identity of interest whereupon they might meet. . . . The Fellowship of Reconciliation appears to be in a position to advance this program far better than anyone else." Kester followed it up with another gathering of southern radicals, black and white, at Shaw University.[101]

In the mid-1930s, Walter White, the executive secretary of the NAACP, asked Kester to investigate the notorious lynching of Claude Neal in northern Florida. It was a harrowing experience for the young social gospel idealist. Whites in town spoke to him freely until his cover was exposed, forcing him to flee for his life. Fearing reprisals, the president of Florida A & M, the black state college in Tallahassee, refused to cooperate. Avoiding the usual clichés about lower-class mobs, Kester analyzed lynching as a mechanism of economic control. White distributed Kester's searing report across the country as part of a campaign for passage of a federal antilynching law. Kester's language prefigured Wilbur J. Cash's famous passages about the "savage ideal" in *The Mind of the South*, published seven years later.

Increasingly influenced by Niebuhrian realism, with its goal of a "rough approximation of justice," Kester left behind his youthful YMCA-influenced social gospel idealism, as well as the doctrinaire pacifism common to religious radicals of the era. Both paled beside the squalor and terror that he experienced firsthand while living among southern working people, detailed in his memorable exposé *Revolt among the Sharecroppers*. Kester's involvement with the Southern Tenant Farmers Union (STFU) and southern labor leader Henry L. Mitchell stemmed from his investigation of tenant farmers organizing in the Arkansas Delta. Kester recounted the violence that hounded STFU members, including the bullets that rang through the house of its black president and former disciple of Marcus Garvey, the Reverend E. B. McKinney. Kester and others taught local sharecroppers about relevant provisions of the Agricultural Adjustment Administration. In theory, the New Deal measure required a fair distribution of allotment payments between landowners and their tenants and sharecroppers. Of course, actual possession of the government payments, as Kester and the farmers well knew, was nine-tenths of the law. At one confrontation, gunmen hired by a plantation owner broke up a tenant farmers' meeting held at a black church near Tyronza, Arkansas. Planters terrorized other rural radicals, including one who was to be sent down to the county farm for hard time before being rescued at his court hearing by an angry group of sharecroppers.

Black organizer and preacher E. B. McKinney and white seminarian Ward Rogers treated the fledgling union like a congregation. "My people are emotional, and a *Group Conscious* People," wrote one black unionist, "and 98% of them can be reached in the churches." Such thinking fit with Kester's own upbringing and socioreligious emphases; he described the ministers on the STFU's executive council as "social revolutionaries with a religious drive." Yet his work with the sharecroppers convinced him that pressure and the right to self-defense trumped persuasion and goodwill in achieving any Niebuhrian "rough approximation of justice." In *Revolt among the Sharecroppers*, the young religious radical Kester took aim at the CIC, deriding the "Atlanta school" for "attempting to show that the rich man with his vast benevolence and paternalism is the Negro's best friend, conveniently forgetting that if the poor white man is the Negro's worst enemy it is the members of the so-called 'best families' who force these equally exploited groups to struggle against each other."[102]

While traveling through Mississippi through the 1930s, Reinhold Niebuhr, Kester's mentor at Union Seminary in New York, observed the Delta Cooperative Farm, an experimental venture that modeled alternatives to the oppressive southern economics of tenantry and sharecropping. Local clergymen, Niebuhr quickly discovered, disdained common farmers and resisted any religious and social experimentation. "The organized church as such does not serve them," he observed, for the church was

> as middle class in the [S]outh as anywhere else. In the countryside it serves the planters and the merchants of the village. The sharecroppers are served by lay preachers, who develop spontaneously without religious training. Their theological notions are crude but their close relations to their people drives them into socially significant actions which the more intelligent church leaders might well envy.... Lay preachers have been in the forefront of the movement for the organization of both agrarian and industrial laborers in the South.... They express the religious protest against social injustice in terms reminiscent of the classical examples of this protest. They know their bible.

In a somewhat strained effort to merge his mystic spirituality with his Jeffersonian ideal for southern farming life, Kester invented a ritual called "Ceremony for the Land," which Niebuhr witnessed among Delta Farm participants. In later years, Kester formed a rather quixotic group called "Friends of the Soil," which briefly kept alive his version of radical religious agrarianism.[103]

In 1934, Kester, James Dombrowski, and a group of southern religious radicals formed the FSC. Originally named the Younger Churchmen of the South, the group included several graduates of Niebuhr's theology of progressive social action. The Fellowship was by design a "confederation of interested people rather than an organization," not a new denomination or sect. Its members hoped to infuse a new spirit into the prevailing religious organizations. "The group itself can be a demonstration center of Christian Fellowship," wrote one FSC member. "Our members must spearhead radical Christianity within their churches and denominations." The Fellowship drew special strength from a number of churches in the university corridor of North Carolina—Watts Street Baptist Church in Durham, Pullen Memorial Baptist Church in Raleigh, University Baptist in Chapel Hill, and Second Presbyterian in Chapel Hill—as well as other progressive congregations scattered through the region. In "We Affirm," the FSC's original manifesto, Kester proclaimed, "We seek to identify ourselves with the emerging minority of prophetic Christians who are trying to discover and give practical expression to the historic redemptive mission of our religion.... We thus commit ourselves to the task of creating [the kingdom], by the power of God and in the brotherhood of man, liberated from poverty, ignorance and insecurity, healed from the wounds of hatred, exploitation, and strife, laboring together in love and peace." Kester's pamphlet tied together the "redemption of the individual and of society" as "one and inseparable." As he explained to a Fisk University faculty member, "my mind has been drawn increasingly toward the necessity of instilling a deep and powerful religious motivation of a revolutionary nature among those individuals and organizations which offer some hope for the future. I am extremely anxious to see the Fellowship of Southern Churchmen act as such an instrument and to express its faith in creative terms in whatever areas of life are open to them." FSC members acknowledged the "wide-spread poverty, class-conflict, racial bitterness, general unemployment, and the overt and covert warfare, together with the consequent spiritual disintegration, moral confusion, and overwhelming sense of futility and despair throughout the world today."[104]

Published irregularly from the mid-1940s to the early 1950s, the FSC's journal, *Prophetic Religion*, provided an outlet for socially conscious ministers and laypeople. Because the church had "too often denied in practice the Divine command to champion the cause of justice and to redeem men and women from exploitation and insecurity," wrote two FSC members in 1946, the periodical sought to awaken fellow believers to the mandate of progressive action in the South. Too many preachers, one FSC member pointed out, felt constrained from considering broader themes of social justice. They resorted instead to hackneyed harangues against alcohol and Sunday baseball. "Is it any wonder, therefore," asked a *Prophetic Religion* article, "that like hundreds of other southern clergymen, this average pastor, with his emphasis on petty ethics and hair-splitting metaphysics, and with his financial dependence upon 'Christian' employers, will oppose the labor organizer?" Such comments ran headlong into the reality of the number of ministers who lost positions because of participating in the fledgling Religion and Labor Fellowship, six alone in the area of Lynchburg, Virginia.[105]

As the guiding spirit of the FSC, Kester merged personal spiritual growth with social concern. It was difficult for him to straddle these religious and philosophical worlds. Kester felt that "those of us who today pledge ourselves to work for a more Christian South will also become dried cisterns unless we flood our minds and hearts continually in study and in prayer, with God's Word." This formula exasperated those who prized action over contemplation. Kester's tilt away from pacifism in the 1930s had alienated his original support group, the Fellowship of Reconciliation, while his adoption of a mystic spirituality and move away from hardcore political organizing frustrated H. L. Mitchell and other comrades from his days in the Southern Tenant Farmers Union.[106]

Taking up residence near Asheville, North Carolina, in the 1940s, Howard Kester removed himself from the main scene of labor and civil rights struggles. The FSC floundered as Kester wavered in his commitments. Kester, the mystic radical, increasingly mystified those around him. The group asked Charles Jones, the unorthodox Presbyterian minister in Chapel Hill, to become its new chairman. Moving its base from Black Mountain (a small town just outside Asheville, near a Presbyterian meeting ground and college) to Chapel Hill, the FSC expanded beyond its original base of supporters thanks to the effective duo of Nelle Morton and Charles Jones. Morton grew up in Kingsport, Tennessee, a model city that was part of the Tennessee Valley Authority project of the New Deal. Later in her life she became a pioneering feminist theologian, serving on the faculty of Drew University and teaching one of the first courses in American seminaries on women and religion. Prior to her academic career, she worked in church and youth camps for Presbyterians. Whereas Kester had worked as a prophetic loner, Morton was a group organizer par excellence. During her tenure as executive secretary of the FSC, the group conducted summer work camps and other ventures. All of them brought together black and white young people in experiments of working and living together, including one project in which an interracial team shepherded cattle being delivered to war-ravaged regions of Europe. Morton hoped these ventures would encourage younger people to socialize in nonsegregated environments, preparing the way for an integrated society.[107]

FSC projects that challenged segregation had mixed results, and frequently engendered controversy. While the YMCA and other youth camps long had mixed black and white volunteers, after World War II such ventures drew un-welcome attention. At Gammon Theological Seminary in Atlanta, one project brought students together to live communally and interracially at the Bethle-hem Center while working for local industries. Some students had difficulty finding jobs. The situation worsened when policemen broke up a recreational dance that intermingled some young women from the Atlanta YWCA with an in-terracial group of campers. Those in attendance were fined for disturbing the peace; an Atlanta newspaper publicized the event in predictably lurid terms. At another work project in North Carolina devoted to helping the Tyrrell County Credit Union, angry locals drove out participants upon learning of the arrival of some young white women from Virginia who had come to visit the North Car-olina campers, a group that included some young black men.[108]

From a "lonely beginning group," as one participant described it, the FSC be-came a "tremendous security blanket" for workers in interracial projects before 1954, giving voice to the growing number of sympathetic southern believers com-mitted to justice over southern tradition. "Due to the changed and changing sit-uation in the region during the past twenty years," Kester wrote in 1952, "there are a great many Southerners who can and should be harnessed to liberal and pro-gressive movements such as the Fellowship." With his typically eclectic crazy-quilt of ideas, he worried that the *Brown* decision had "crystallized the fears of a pseudo-democratic majority," but he kept faith that the "feudal character" of the South would yield "stubbornly, hesitatingly, and slowly when at all to the ideas of Jesus, Jefferson and Einstein." He insisted, "We will keep hammering away . in the church, at the church, with the church," for those who had been "schooled in the fires of southern life know that many things must needs come before we move on toward a large measure of democracy and a greater kinship with the mind of Christ."[109]

In the 1950s, as the civil rights revolution gathered strength, the FSC collapsed. Kester's inability to persuade potential supporters (especially liberal founda-tions) to commit resources to the struggling progressive southern Christians hastened its decline. As he complained, "Our religious approach seems to get us nowhere with the foundations." Kester's conflicts with other FSC members, more-over, exacerbated internal divisions about the disparate aims of the organiza-tion. Beyond that, Kester was a loner and "there was just no place for loners any more," Nelle Morton remembered sadly. By 1955, many in the FSC came to real-ize that their time had come and gone. The failure of fund-raising activities and the consequent deterioration of the organization's camp facility at Swannanoa, North Carolina, deepened their problems. Purchased with private philanthropic funds in the late 1940s, the Swannanoa campgrounds interested FSC members who recognized the advantage of managing their own place for meetings and projects. Kester envisioned a "seminary in the cornfield," where members could discuss theological tenets while tending crops and working on camp improvements. But the facility required constant efforts at fund-raising, Kester's weakest skill. White reformists in the SRC and civil rights organizations such as the SCLC proved more attractive to those funding direct action for racial justice. A pragmatic remembrance of the FSC came from Everett Tilson, a Vanderbilt professor and author of an important text dismantling biblical prosegregation arguments, *Segregation and the Bible*. Concerned that historians would overplay white liberalism, Tilson pointed out that if left up to the "fellowship of upper-middle class professionals" (as he referred to the FSC) and "other white organizations of this sort, there would be no civil rights movement. . . . It took a black light really to bring the blacks together."[110]

The FSC brought together scattered and often iconoclastic individuals interested in awakening a prophetic white southern Christianity. "It may have been that people were unhappy because we weren't out organizing on various issues like the Southern Tenant Farmers Union had done," one participant later recalled, "but there was as sure as hell a need for somebody like Buck [Kester] to be traveling around to young pastors like me who had their necks way out and to organize support structures for us." The Fellowship, recalled another participant, "helped to lay the . . . christian basis of the civil rights movement in the South. This wasn't just some hot head IWW idea or the early reincarnation of Tom Watson before he became a bigot and a senator. These had biblical roots and that was the great strength physically in Buck." The Fellowship meant "that a few lonely individuals over the South were trying to come to terms with some new light that had struck somewhere and needed somebody to cozy up to. They just needed somebody to know that I'm not the only one that's thinking like this, trying to make something out of it, and that's all it really was." Nelle Morton remembered her time in the group as the "only work that I have been in that's been as deeply satisfying, because I mean you felt you could put everything you have in this, because this is the way it ought to be." The FSC "just saved me," she said; "I just couldn't believe that there were that many people who felt about things like I did." Polite public biracial meetings sponsored by the FSC and others, she remembered, soon became private gatherings in each other's homes. In this sense, public biracial cooperation broke down private racial separations and fostered Christian interracialism. In the 1960s, she observed the sit-in movements with satisfaction, knowing they were possible in part because "we had an intercollegiate, interracial, ecumenical council in Greensboro, Raleigh, and other university centers . . . quietly challenging segregation in churches, public meetings, and eating places, letting people know that desegregation could happen and without fanfare."[111]

Kester's daring challenge to southern mores in the 1930s made him something of a legend, but his inability to work successfully with others frustrated supporters and potential allies. Early in their working days, Myles Horton broke with Kester. The two shared a similar background and goals. Both trained for the ministry but ended up in freelance social careers. Born in 1905 in the hill country of East Tennessee, Horton attended Cumberland Presbyterian College prior to training at Union Seminary in New York. Like Kester, he spent time as a state secretary for the student YMCA, hitchhiking around the country in the late 1920s and visiting communal experiments. Struggling to synthesize his experiences and beliefs, he found comfort when his mother showed him the "difference between the preachers and the churches, and Christian values." Horton later reminisced, "She showed me how to avoid mistaking the church for religion. From Jesus and the prophets I had learned about the importance of loving people, the importance of being a revolutionary, standing up and saying that this system is unjust. Jesus to me was a person who had the vision to project a society in which people would be equally respected, in which property would be shared . . . he was a person who said you have to love your enemies, you have to love the people who despise you." By the late 1920s, Horton had lost interest in organized religion, setting him apart from Kester and other contemporaries. Horton was more attracted to grassroots organizing and local self-help ventures.[112]

Following his years at Union Theological Seminary, Horton was mentored in Chicago by Jane Addams and other pioneers of the settlement house movement. Horton incorporated the innovations of Addams, as well as lessons drawn from his experience in the folk schools of Denmark (where he spent a year in residence). Deliberately rejecting the usual nostrums of paternalistic uplift or missionary proselytization, his work respected existing cultures. Reflecting on the legacy of religious missionary work and philanthropy in the southern mountains, he saw the persistent poverty that defied all the money spent and well-meaning effort exerted. The old approaches were flawed; he dedicated his life to finding new ways to effect social justice. In the early 1930s, after securing assistance from Sherwood Eddy and Norman Thomas, Horton established Highlander Folk School. Horton also enlisted the aid of James Dombrowski, a southern labor organizer and seminary-trained clergyman, and for a short time worked with Don West, an eccentric poet and religious radical.

Highlander's role, in Horton's words, was to "multiply leadership for radical change," to train people who could then take their skills to various battles. He sought to adapt quickly to changing circumstances by using small, flexible, and democratically run programs. For example, Horton recruited black beauticians to attend workshops at Highlander, ostensibly to help with their trade but more importantly to develop contacts in the black community. Horton's first efforts in labor were in mobilizing southern tobacco workers. During those efforts, folk singer Pete Seeger introduced a new version of an old spiritual, "We Shall Overcome," a song brought to Highlander and championed by Zilphia Johnson, a southern labor organizer who became Horton's wife. Myles Horton also developed the concept of citizenship schools and attempted an early model of this idea at Highlander. Later, Septima Clark, Dorothy Cotton, and Andrew Young ran citizenship institutes in the Sea Islands and at a camp near Dorchester, Georgia, teaching adults whose formal education was minimal but whose native leadership skills were substantial.[113]

Horton scorned the usual southern evangelical sentiment that "changing hearts" was a prerequisite for real social change, insisting that the only way to learn democracy was to practice democracy. He witnessed this lesson firsthand in teaching white workers and labor leaders to organize cooperatively with black laborers. When the civil rights movement came along, he recalled, "these white people who were struggling with their souls got those souls right in a hurry," without the benefit of a "long drawn-out attitudinal change. . . . They got changed because black people said they were not going to take it any longer. Blacks started moving, and they saved not only their own souls but some of ours as well."[114]

Horton shied away from involvement with the FSC and resisted the idea of using revivals for union organizing, even as Kester and allies in the STFU were doing precisely that. "That's the last thing I wanted, a revival," Horton said. While the Protestant Church in the South was "one of the most potent cultural factors" and ignored only at one's peril, it was akin to civil religion for most people, Horton sensed, joined for social reasons not unlike membership in the Democratic Party or the Rotarians. He felt vindicated when he saw the extent of evangelical opposition to the black freedom struggle. Even when the most sympathetic congregations "preached the right thing," he pointed out, "they wouldn't practice it; wouldn't back you up when you're on a picket line, they were against it because they were against violence."[115]

Howard Kester was essentially a spiritual mystic, whereas Myles Horton was a grassroots activist. Kester was a social radical but over the years developed an increasingly Agrarian bent. "I don't think Buck had an analysis," Horton said of his old comrade. "When I knew him, Buck was like a saint. He never made the kind of an analysis that would include working with other people or taking social movements into consideration, taking other people's problems into consideration; he did what he thought was the right thing to do. . . . He never learned to work with other people." The FSC itself, Horton scolded, "once it lost its radicalism, it hadn't served any purpose. It was just another reformist good-will fellowship sort of thing." As Horton sensed the cresting of momentum for civil rights, he established workshops at Highlander to train people in the methods of nonviolent civil disobedience. Meanwhile, following his last years leading the FSC, Kester moved to Illinois in the 1950s to teach at a small college. "He became very bitter," Horton remembered. "He was the person that inspired me and he was our leader, but he was . . . unable to function."[116]

For all the frustrations they experienced, and even if progressive religious southerners sometimes had "insight but little action," as Charles Jones wryly put it, individually committed Christians still prepared the ground for the southern freedom struggle. Randolph Taylor, a Presbyterian minister and SCLC member, remembered white southern Christians sympathetic to transforming their region as a "thin but tough community of folk," whose job was not just to lance the boil "but to see to the healing that's involved. It's painful, but it's a very important discipline."[117]

After World War II, the South was poised for and fearful of change. Progressive and reactionary forces alike understood that they were entering a new era. Progressive Christians seized new opportunities. In 1947, Sarah Mitchell Parsons, an Atlanta housewife, heard the Progressive Party presidential candidate Henry Wallace speak at the black Wheat Street Baptist Church, the only place where supporters could hold an integrated meeting. From that point forward she threw herself into the civil rights struggle: "Once I started looking more closely at the world around me," she said, "I could never go back." Lillian Smith believed that if ministers would "speak out bravely, quietly, persuasively," they could "give direction to the feelings of millions of white southerners who don't know what to do or where to turn." Southern churches burdened with guilt about segregation, she hoped, could "take on a new spiritual life." Meanwhile, reactionary forces knew that the southern way of life was under attack, and they would not give up without a fight. "Many of our laymen feel that the best way to quiet these preachers down is by getting the lay members of our church informed as to what is involved in the issue," wrote one segregationist.[118]

Few on either side, however, could have anticipated the sheer dramatic power of the black freedom struggle in the coming two decades, theater for which the years from the 1890s to *Brown v. Board* had served as prologue.

God and Negroes and Jesus and sin and salvation are baled up together in southern children's minds and in many an old textile magnate's also.—Lillian Smith, *Killers of the Dream*, 1949

Negro entered into white man as profoundly as white man entered into Negro—subtly influencing every gesture, every word, every emotion and idea, every attitude.
—W. J. Cash, *The Mind of the South*, 1941

We're two brothers children and I believe God sees fit to have that miracle work. He sees fit to have that miracle work until some of the children could be black and some white. . . . And I know right now you might not accept it but I'm your first cousin . . . and everybody will love their cousins.—Josephine Dickey, Summerton, South Carolina

Chapter Three

The Color of Skin Was Almost Forgotten for the Time Being

Racial Interchange in Southern Religious Expressive Cultures

July 10, 1895: A general merchandise store owner in Darlington, South Carolina, sorted through his impressions of going to see "the Negro Girl Preacher" visiting his town. That evening, E. B. Ingram recorded in his diary, there was a "crowded house white and [colored] about 300 mourners don't know what to say." The following week, he "went to hear the Mulattoe 12 year old girl Preach to night don't know what to think. Big crowd white & [colored] white ladies and all sorts." There was at least "good behaviour there to night," in marked contrast to the frequent times when young men made sport of solemnities in church. Whites and blacks sat across from each other when a "colored girl preacher" came to North Carolina and exhorted in the African Methodist Episcopal Zion church in New Bern. In Selma, Alabama, AME pastor and bishop Winfield Henry Mixon led a camp meeting in 1903, where, as he noted laconically, there was a "great crowd, many white friends out." In May of that year, AME bishop W. J. Gaines also visited town, lecturing to a "very good crowd, white and colored."[1]

Marion Wolcott, "Traveling Preacher Talking to Two Negroes, One Whose Wife is Sick and Needs Help." Belle Glace, Florida, January 1939, Library of Congress, Prints and Photographs Division, Reproduction LC-USF34-050927-D.

Russell Lee, "Group of People Assembled Under Tree to Listen to Revival Rally on Saturday Afternoon, Tahlequah, Oklahoma." July 1939, Library of Congress, Prints and Photographs Division, Reproduction LC-USF33-012335-M1.

Gordon Parks, "Washington, D.C.: A Young Deacon Doubling on the Guitar at the Church of God in Christ." November 1942, Library of Congress, Prints and Photographs Division, Reproduction LC-USW3-010254-C.

Traveling evangelists, itinerant songsters, faith healers, and other religious novelties attracted biracial crowds in the segregated South. At one meeting in Louisville, Kentucky, in 1888, faith healer Maria Woodworth-Etter recounted, "God came in such wonderful power it was not long till they seemed to forget the color. The altar was filled with seekers, white people on one side and colored on the other." Ignoring the scorn of local whites, she felt "no desire to drive [black attendants] away, but felt glad to have the privilege of leading them to Christ." A black sister visiting one Etter meeting reportedly broke up the house

Marion Wolcott, "Itinerant Preacher Spreading 'religion' to Farmers Outside Warehouse While Tobacco Auction Sales Are Going on, Durham, North Carolina." November 1939[?], Library of Congress, Prints and Photographs Division, LC-USF33-030740-M5.

with a spontaneous prayer that "took hold of God in such a way as to shake every member of the congregation and came near raising them all on their feet." Independent Spiritualist congregations, which practiced an amalgam of Pentecostalism and Catholicism in the unique religious milieu of New Orleans, sometimes had biracial congregations. Leafy Anderson, the female founder of one such Spiritualist sect, led a church that was described as a "shrine of hundreds of men and women of both races."[2]

Within a rigidly circumscribed context of legal apartheid and extralegal degradation and terror, what was the meaning of racial interchange in religious gatherings? And how much could cultural expression reinforce or undermine the racial order? Through the era of segregation, white and black southerners gathered to celebrate, observe, question, and mock their common evangelical heritage. Christians, spiritual seekers, curiosity hounds, socializers, and village atheists attended special community occasions, including events such as the visit of the child evangelist who drew E. B. Ingram's curiosity, as well as town-wide revivals and river baptisms. Seen rarely in the institutional churches, this racial interchange instead found its way into the interstices of southern religious culture. In contrast to the biracial work in the public sphere narrated in Chapter 2, racial interchange in religious expression involved cultural interaction in more private spaces of religious experience. And yet those examples of racial interchange eventually informed public life as well, and in some cases provided avenues to interracialism.

Blacks and whites shared social evangelical customs—impassioned sermons, folk songs and gospel hymns, revival services, baptisms, foodways, and folk-ways. Growing up in North Carolina, an African American woman named Ruth Johnson remembered that "when revival time come, you know the week of preach-ing and whatnot, we sit in the back of the church . . . to listen to the revival, preaching and they [whites] would come in our church and listen. We had sep-arate buildings but we interact just the same." Amy Jones witnessed immersions at a big pond behind the white folks' church: "And it would be people—you could look all through them woods and as far as you could see, wasn't nothing but peoples all the way around that. And it wasn't only blacks, it was black and white. Because they love to hear him preach. Yeah. And it was really, really great . . . there would be a lot of white people in our baptizing just to hear Reverend Cheers preach." Corresponding with the African American sociologist Charles Johnson at Fisk University, Lillian Smith described the small camps she super-vised in northern Georgia and western North Carolina in the 1950s. Few in the respectable southern establishment would believe that the "little rural (Holy Roller) church at the foot of my mountain is unsegregated. It is officially a white church. But they invite the Negro Baptists—over in the valley—to come very often to their church; and they go to the Negro church. I mean by 'they': the en-tire congregation. Both Baptist rural groups (white and Negro) use my swim-ming pool for their baptisms. Last summer, the white group invited the Negro group to witness the baptism service. There were white and colored rural Bap-tists roaming all around my place."[3]

Perhaps white and black southerners worshipped in the same place or used similar cultural forms—but how much could that really mean? It might simply have reinforced the white supremacist regime. In antebellum churches, white divines provided the standard rationalizations for power—submission, obedi-ence, contentment with one's lot in life—to masters and a captive audience. Slaves knew the drill: the insufferably pious white man pretended to preach, and they pretended to listen. The Catholic Church in the South, concentrated pri-marily around New Orleans, was officially not segregated, but that made little difference to black parishioners racially demarcated in a separate parish school system and humiliated at Mass. Herman James grew up a Catholic near New Iberia, Louisiana, where the back three rows of the Catholic church were re-served for black parishioners. If enough whites showed up at any given service, even those seats had to be sacrificed. "It was a way of life at that time. I was at a young age not knowing any better," James recalled, and yet "you couldn't help but feel inferior . . . you couldn't help but have a certain degree of hatred."[4]

While race is fictive, racism as a social practice is real—hence the ambiguity plaguing both scholars and society about the use of race as a concept. Even if socially constructed rather than essentially *real*, the concept of race nevertheless defined and fatally disfigured human aspirations and social interactions. Blacks who grew up with Jim Crow remembered both the power of the system and its limitations. The folklore of segregation, one survivor reminisced, was gained by absorbing "the language of signs and expressions and all that[;] there are some places you don't go and things you don't do and things you don't say." One learned to be careful that "you would not act in a way that would not make white persons feel that you didn't know they were white." Race took on meaning in the performance of everyday life—in the most minute gestures of social interaction, as well as the largest issues of politics and economics. Yet while black people put up with segregation, an Arkansas native added, Jim Crow never "did get down into the core of the black thinking to where they really [were] brainwashed. Some of our folks let it rub off on them but the vast majority of folks and we went on to church conventions, lodges, and so forth . . . we discussed that crap and it never did really soak in. Not as much as they thought it was soaking in." People would "go along with it, tolerate it," he said; they were "astute enough to play along with it and work for change and change did come."[5]

Still, whites and blacks in the South often approached God together, whether in the stilted and tense settings of the biracial antebellum churches, or more informally. In the late nineteenth century, entertainment seekers from both South and North flocked to hear John Jasper, an "old-time" black exhorter in Virginia known regionally for his florid funeral orations, preach his famous sermon "De Sun Do Move." Yet at least some of these cultural tourists recognized a spiritual movement in themselves that penetrated their ironic bemusement. Jasper's white contemporary in the Virginia Baptist ministry, William E. Hatcher, eulogized the orator in *John Jasper: Unmatched Negro Philosopher*, a genuine albeit hopelessly condescending effort to give the folk preacher his due. Jasper's sermons, wrote Hatcher, "had the ring of the old gospel preaching so common in the South. He had caught his manner of preaching from the white preachers and they too had been his only theological teachers. . . . Wherever he went, the Anglo-Saxon waived all racial prejudices and drank the truth in as it poured in crystal streams from his lips." Whites who heard these funeral sermons were "stirred to the depths of their souls and their emotion showed in the weeping." If considerably exaggerated, this show of emotion is not entirely imagined. Even minstrel shows in northern cities, with their vicious parodies of the slave Sambo on the plantation and the dandyish Zip Coon character, sometimes moved white audiences to tears. Jasper, too, was simultaneously a figure of parody and some empathy.[6]

There were obvious differences, including class distinctions, within the social world of southern evangelicalism, yet a regional style remained evident. In national publications such as *Harper's* and *Lippincott's* and regional venues such as

Southern Workman and the *South Atlantic Quarterly*, observers portrayed southern believers variously as exotically primitive, pathetically backward, folkishly quaint, or heroically resistant to the homogenizing trends of corporate capitalist America. For them, southern religion was emotion. It was too overwrought, anti-intellectual, and devoted to personal experience over formalized understandings of faith. In short, it was too "negro."

"Substantially the two races have the same religion," noted Orra Langhorne, a Republican activist and cultural anthropologist for Hampton Institute's important postwar journal, the *Southern Workman*. Solomon Conser, a Methodist cleric in Reconstruction-era Virginia, described the "extravagant devotions" of freedpeople, how they fell "into trances and cataleptic fits and professed to see visions of angels and demons." Such "spasmodic excesses," he commented acidly, punctuated worship services among white and black believers. Frances Goodrich, a teacher at a Presbyterian mountain mission school in the 1890s, described a service in which one woman started to "tremble" and go into a "fit. Her hat went off and she gave a great shout and sank down again grabbing at my hat as she went. I eluded her grasp and held her down. . . . At last she sank on my shoulder and told me how she loved me. My feelings may be imagined." Another churchgoer remembered white Methodists from the early twentieth century who would dance "and their hair would get down and almost pop and crack. They'd dance and run the benches just like Pentecostals do now. I've seen them jump from one bench to another." In the 1930s, an ex-slave witnessed "both white and colored people responding to preaching in much the same way as in his early life," with exhorters appealing "to the emotions of their flock." In such ways, southerners expressed spiritual freedoms that they were denied in the larger public sphere.[7]

References both explicit and cryptic hint at the meaning of this biracial southern evangelical culture. In her life story scrawled out in the 1920s, Elizabeth Johnson Harris, a black resident of Augusta, Georgia, recounted the aid from white and black residents after the Civil War that built her beloved home church, the Rock of Ages Colored Methodist Episcopal Chapel: "I was young, but proud to be a member of the Church by true conversion and always proud to fill my seat in Church at every opportunity." Her faithfulness earned her the appellation "little pastor." When the Chicago-based mass revivalist Dwight Moody came to her town, white and black Augustans gathered together to hear the nationally renowned Christian crusader. He was, according to Johnson, "perfectly free and friendly as a man of God, with both white and colored. He extended a free invitation to one and all, to these services. The audience was sometimes mixed, the crowds were great, and the Holy Spirit seemed to be in such control over the house that the color of skin was almost forgotten for the time being." Harris devoted her life to cultivating God's kingdom on her postage stamp of soil in Georgia. Accordingly, she seized on any indication of evangelical cooperation and said little about racial conflicts. Yet her account suggests that biracial religious gatherings on occasion provided communal spaces for worship, spectating, and entertainment.[8]

A twentieth-century example of racial exchange comes from Eli Evans's narrative of growing up Jewish in Durham, North Carolina. Evans felt himself an outsider—white but not really white—and identified with black styles of expressive culture. His friends "didn't seem to see any distinction; black and white Christianity was all mixed up in their minds." Evans saw it differently. As a teenage boy, he "did what most other white boys did on the weekends"; he went to rural black churches to see the "holy rollers shake and chant" and bathed in the "'Oh tell it . . . tell it' magic of hypnotic stimulation between preacher and congregation, each driving the other on to mounting excess of singsong sermonizing and jump-up conversions and twitching moments of 'cain't-stand-it-no-more' spiritual release and liberation. For us white boys clustered way in the back where we had to stand to see anything, it was more like going to a performance than to a religious service. It was a special experience for me to immerse myself in a kind of Christianity without fear." For once, he could rest assured that none of his chums would be "swept away and go down front to be saved, and leave me as the only unwashed outsider at the service." Later, he joined in "moaning and crying out the 'praise de Lawd' accents of the panting sermons." If white fundamentalist churches, in Evans's young eyes, "churned up resurrection and retribution," black churches "conveyed a sense of gentleness and consolation." Evans implicitly respected the African American folk liturgy, but even his rowdy friends came back for more. In their fascination, and even in their mockery, they paid tribute to the passionate theater of southern religious performance.[9]

Spiritual Expression in the Postwar South

Southern denominationalists, white and black, recognized that their constituency drew as much from vernacular forms of ecstatic worship, visionary beliefs, and supernatural healing and harming as from standard evangelical orthodoxy. For these religious reformers, uplifting their people represented both a cultural crusade and a political imperative. Proper public behavior, a signifier of uplift, would lead to recognition, political rights, and regional progress—or so they (naively) hoped. But these missionaries of bourgeois spirituality worked in a region where bivocational ministers in small churches exhorted passionately and expected emotional, bodily, and auditory responses in return. Southern pastors and church members alike, complained a northern Baptist missionary in the

1880s, were "as tenacious of their rights and prerogatives as the most intelligent churches in the land."[10]

Black and white believers alike stitched together strands of evangelical theology and biblical texts with pervasive understandings of personal visions, dreams, and vivid supernatural encounters. A black Baptist worker in the 1880s told of how he met with "some strange customs and teaching not warranted by the word of God" in his mission travels. "These I deal with gently," he said, "but earnestly and pointedly." His congregations had not learned "to bring the movements of the world and the doings of the day into the churches." In a strikingly similar fashion, churchmen depicted plain-folk whites in the region as descended from "sturdy" stock but degraded and indolent. Progressive southern citizens faced a huge trial, wrote the prominent Atlanta minister John E. White, with the mass of "undrilled, undeveloped, uninstructed, raw recruits of civilization, who do not know the rules of the march and who easily riot among themselves." In 1917, a clergyman in North Carolina explained to a correspondent the obstacles pastors encountered in teaching their congregations a modernized religious ethic: "Nearly all of us are driven by the force of circumstances to be a bit more conservative than it is in our hearts of hearts to be. I am frank to say to you that I have found it out of the question to move people in the mass at all, unless you go with a slowness that sometimes seems painful; and I have settled down to the conviction that it is better to lead people slowly than not at all."[11]

Religious leaders in black and white churches encouraged the practices of respectable churches and vilified customs such as vision quests, dreams, ecstatic conversion experiences and testimonies, spiritual dancing, ring shouts, and songlike sermonizing. A black clergyman in Savannah angered congregants because, "instead of teaching dreams and visions," he emphasized the necessity of an "intelligent Christian experience." Because of his refusal to countenance folk tradition, he had been "cast out as an evil" by those who clung to faith in "dreams, visions, and root-work superstition." A Mississippi black Baptist association discouraged "the practice of moaning, shouting, and jumping in churches," insisting that the "true church must fight against barbarism, superstition, conjuration." Black progressive educator Lucy Laney sought to stamp out the custom of "Egypt walking" as "sacrilegious" and "unbecoming." Likely a variation of the ring shout that others (such as folklorist Lydia Parrish) were attempting to record on the Sea Islands, the practice of Egypt walking smacked of the slave past. Advocates of racial uplift condemned it vociferously. These efforts were not without effect. One missionary in the late nineteenth century recounted a baptismal service where, when a few ex-slaves raised a shout, "they were sternly and promptly suppressed" by a female worship leader. She acknowledged that "such emotional demonstrations doubtless still occur in the remote rural regions among what the Africans call 'old issue black folks.'" A white minister who would not permit shouting found approval for his "powerful good sermon," with one elderly congregant commenting in response, "It most killed me to hold in them shouts." Such exertions at self-control demonstrated the gradual internalization of public respectability.[12]

Yet ordinary white and black believers still found outlets for cherished forms of religious expressive culture derived from earlier days of evangelicalism in the South. The North Carolina journalist Walter Hines Page described the change in religious styles he observed from the Civil War to the early twentieth century. He remembered religious meetings in 1866 in which "mourners" (those seeking salvation) would dash through congregations, fall into trances, and be carried off by ushers. To find similar anachronisms in the early twentieth century, he added, "one must now go to remote regions where the religious habits of the whites are of a similar kind." In the churches of coastal South Carolina, as a respected black minister described it, there was as much "dignity, decorum and quietness . . . as one will find in the average white assembly." The solemn demeanor in these congregations was preserved precisely because black worshippers found other venues for emotional spirituality, especially in the praise houses on the outlying Sea Islands. "In the churches they act like 'white folks,'" he concluded, "but in 'praise houses' they are 'cake walkers.'" Well into the twentieth century, the practices assailed by denominational leaders persisted throughout the region, most especially in the Deep South and mountain regions but sometimes in urban areas as well. Lydia Parrish, a folklorist of black song styles, recognized that such religious exercises remained an important part of black religious life even when hidden from the "more fashionable Negro preachers" and from white musicologists. Black and white worshippers spoke eloquently of the spiritual empowerment of emotional release. As one freedwoman said, "I stays independent of what white folks tells me when I shouts. De Spirit moves me every day, dat's how I stays in."[13]

The "shouts" (or "Egypt walking," "patting Juba," or "rings") frequently observed in black services in the low country and Deep South fascinated observers even as they embarrassed religious leaders. Northerners such as the Quaker pioneer missionary in the Sea Islands Laura Towne saw, if only through their own ethnocentric lens, that many of the religious customs prevalent in these regions represented "the remains of some old idol worship," as Towne put it, or "Africanisms" in the anthropological language. The dances varied according to the songs and rhythm. Sometimes a stick or other homemade instrument drummed out the beat. Some were traditional slave shouts. As described by Thomas Wentworth Higginson in *Army Life in a Black Regiment*, his classic narrative of commanding a black army troop during the Civil War, practitioners would "heel &

toe tumultuously, others merely tremble & stagger on, others stoop & rise, others whirl, others caper sidewise all keep steadily circling like dervishes," with congregants "falling out" or "walking the pews" during services. Secret black societies often oversaw shout ceremonies held outside the routine Sunday services. They enforced strict rules of sacred movement: no crossing the feet (meaning, no dancing), no sexually suggestive motion (or "cake-walking"), and a prescribed order of song style from slow tempo to double-time. William Francis Allen described a ring shout he observed in 1863. It originated, he believed, from a "strange connection between dancing and religious worship which was so frequent among the ancients and which we find in the dervishes, shakers, etc." After a prayer service, the room was cleared and a ring of six dancers formed. A chanting singer stood off to the side. The most skillful dancers "moved very easily and quietly. The shouters seldom sing or make any noise except with their feet, but work their bodies more or less, as the chanter called out lines and the dancers and other singers provided the base," calling back refrains such as "Oh Lord, yes my Lord" to the chanter's line "Pray a little longer, Jericho, do worry me." Later in the twentieth century, such calls rang out in Pentecostal services, often with the accompaniment of guitars, tubas, tamborines, and drums.

James Weldon Johnson witnessed similar scenes of preparing the space for the shout, a ring forming and beginning to move, then quickening, the shuffling feet producing accents and hand-clapping providing contrapuntal rhythm. In this instance, there was no separate band of singers and dancers; those in the ring supplied the melody and rhythm. Gradually, a "frenzy" developed, with the finale becoming a "wild monotonous chant. The same musical phrase is repeated over and over one, two, three, four, five hours. The words become a repetition of an in-coherent cry." The ring shout, noted Johnson, was "looked upon as a very questionable form of worship. It was distinctly frowned upon by a great many colored people. Indeed, I do not recall ever seeing a 'ring shout' except *after* the regular services," when whispered invitations would circulate: "There's going to be a 'ring shout.'"[14]

Religious leaders, missionaries, and outside observers often suspected (with considerable justification) that the ring shout was an African rite grafted onto a Christian form. Daniel Payne, presiding bishop of the AME for much of the nineteenth century, penned a memoir of his experiences demanding worship decorum of believers who clung to slave religious practice. "The strange delusion that many ignorant but well-meaning people labor under" led Payne on a tour to teach dignified worship to his benighted southern church members. At one brush meeting, he witnessed congregants forming a ring after the service, "and with coats off sung, clapped their hands and stamped their feet in a most ridiculous and heathenish way. I requested the pastor to go and stop their dancing. At his request they stopped their dancing and clapping of hands, but remained singing and rocking their bodies to and fro." After a few minutes, Payne ordered the congregants to "desist and to sit down and sing in a rational manner," informing the pastor that "it was a heathenish way to worship and disgraceful to themselves, the race, and the Christian name. In that instance they broke up their ring; but would not sit down, and walked sullenly away." A congregational leader pleaded with the bishop, "'Sinners won't get converted unless there is a ring.'" Payne responded, "You might sing till you fell down dead, and you would fail to convert a single sinner, because nothing but the Spirit of God and the word of God can convert sinners." Retorted the ring leader, "'The Spirit of God works upon people in different ways. At camp-meeting there must be a ring here, a ring there, a ring over yonder, or sinners will not get converted.'" A dismayed Payne discovered that some of the most "powerful and popular preachers labor systematically to perpetuate this fanaticism. Such preachers never rest till they create an excitement that consists in shouting, jumping, and dancing." Although feeling "strongly censured" because of his efforts to "change the mode of worship or modify the extravagances indulged in by the people," Payne persisted in preaching that "liberty must be regulated and controlled by the Church of the living God."[15]

Ring shouts and similar customs spread from the low country to other parts of the South, following black migration patterns. In one North Carolina town, an AMA missionary described a service in which worshippers left their seats and surged to the altar. They stood in a circle, with mourners dancing in the middle. The minister was "himself in the circle jumping and keeping time to the wild songs of the crowd." Stationed after the Civil War near the historic location of Harpers Ferry, Virginia, the white missionary Sarah Jane Foster watched a group of congregants circle around the mourner's bench, "where the seekers kneel meeting after meeting till they find peace." Foster saw those in the circle "then join hands, taking also the hands of their kneeling friends, and begin to sing, swaying . . . or lifting and dropping their hands in regular time." The celebrants would "'sing over'" mourners, as "nearly all thought that [was] the way to be 'brought through.'" She also pointed out that "even the white Methodists are very much the same about here; so it is not to be wondered at at all." At another service in a South Carolina church, where she labored during the last year of her life before succumbing to disease in 1868, Foster described how the "living mass began to sing and revolve, going around with various rhythmic twistings and shufflings in time to the melodies that were sung." The believers there insisted that a "seeker should never go to bed till he finds peace. He must watch by the fire, and go out to pray whenever he hears the cock crow. They wandered off in the wilderness under religious excitement, and most of them met with strange mental experiences there. At a recent night meeting or 'sitting up,' I heard a man say that in the wilderness the devil met him wrapped in moss, and another said that he had to go down to the lowest pit of hell to find his own lost soul." Black believers kept the customs alive and influenced white religious expression. Shouts and holy dancing, for example, were carried into Sanctified (Holiness/Pentecostal) congregations in the twentieth century.[16]

As Foster observed in Virginia, conversion and baptism were seminal communal rites of passage. This was vividly evident in low-country black religious culture, for example, where lay elders guided teenage candidates donned in special clothes through a ritualized set of events leading to a final "coming through" experience. Local religious societies admitted "raw souls" to membership after they "proved the reality of their 'striving.'" This striving was a "long process of self-examination and solitary prayer 'in the bush,' and so unremitting must be the devotion during this stage that even attendance at school is thought to interfere with the action of the Spirit. After a probation in the 'society' follow baptism and church-membership." Seekers often described being "held back" by an evil spirit, symbolic of the uncertain life struggles of a young person. Such a struggle defined "passing through," the route to conversion. "When I was converted I passed through many ordeals," reads one typical account. "It took me three weeks to come through with my religion. If I had not been a lover of those worldly things, it would not have taken me so long. I prayed every day all day long, in a big, open field . . . for three weeks I ate only four pones of bread about the size of your hand." Spiritual guides expressed no surprise over evil visions, for they expected seekers to pass through a difficult ordeal.

Dreams and visions quickened conversions. "When I was killed dead I saw the devil and the fires of hell," one seeker said. "I left hell and came out pursued by the devil. God came to me as a little man," offering to escort him to paradise. Others told of being chased by the devil up dirt roads, encouraged by angels along the way. Subsequent to their visionary experiences, the candidates were examined by the church community. They had to recount a definite sign that validated their passing through, whether it was the "feeling that a load of sins" had been released, or a dream of "travel" in which the sinner felt himself to have "seen hell and been rescued therefrom. Sometimes the prayer is that the pardon of sin may be assured by the sight of a shooting star." As one black believer from Georgia told an interviewer, "Things just come to me. I can see them and tell folks for it is just like a vision." And when God gave him those visions, he considered it his "bounden duty to tell 'em."[17]

These dreams, visions, and trances exasperated black and white religious reformers, the denominational leaders who sought to inculcate mental and behavioral modernity among their parishioners. A white South Carolinian bemoaned that the freedpeople, once "cut loose from us, and our Churches, and gone to themselves," delighted in recounting "Visions and Trances, they See and hear a great many Wonderful things." W. D. Siegfried, a missionary to the freedpeople, explained how candidates for conversion would "boisterously harangue congregations, by the hour, with the details of 'the wonderful things, which the Lord has revealed to them.'" These revelations and visions were "generally linked to some Scripture incident or sentiment which they remember to have heard, not *read*," indicating the continuing centrality of the oral tradition in black folk religious practice. In 1911, a black minister resigned himself to the fact that "one can preach 'till he busts' against this practice, but it will go on just the same." Dreams and visions also shaped white folk religious expression. Through the twentieth century, Appalachian mountain religion retained the older southern legacy of lengthy conversions involving days of wrenching soul torment and spectacular dreams. Mountain Christians saw little value in form devoid of spirit, for "the Spirit moves like the wind, touching and electing whom it ordains." They waited in the "sweet hope" that, in God's time, the Spirit would move in their soul.[18]

Conjuring/Spirits

Conjure, a form of healing and counterharming that borrowed from both Christian and African-based religious elements, was primarily the province of poor southern blacks who were its main practitioners (although whites formed a substantial clientele base). Religious and cultural reformers, both black and white, condemned conjure as another area where irrational fears hindered progress and uplift. In conjuring and other southern religious customs, spirits from another world (the "hants" and "hags" pervasive in the rural southern imagination) directed behavior, making it difficult to teach the kind of self-directed rationality, the mental modernity, that was the cultural project of white and black reformers. "It is this old time religion, that keeps the poor colored people back, and Conjuration, for the people are full of it," complained an exasperated contemporary. Fears of unseen powers—signified by specially concocted mixtures of roots and plants placed in bags—compelled frequent recourse to conjure men. Conjure doctors claimed to have "power superior to that of anybody else" due to their skillful manipulations and expertise in folk pharmacopoeia. They possessed spiritual sanction to engage in special tricks, poisoning, and snake charming, and believed they had been given a "calling from God to be doctors among the people; . . . the general idea of the people is, that these men have the power to do just what they have a mind to."[19]

Belief in conjure—or at least a willingness to suspend disbelief—pervaded much of the Deep South. "I believe it is safe to say that at least *three-fourths* of the mass of negroes have a tendency to believe in it," lamented one clergyman, "and one-fourth, you could not preach out of a belief in its truth. It is said to be so common and popular that it is practiced not only by the people of the church, but even that their leaders are often known as Conjure doctors." Afro-Christian believers talked "freely at their religious gatherings of 'tricking' and 'conjuring,'" related another observer, and told "marvelous tales of the power of those endowed with supernatural gifts." As one Mississippian put it, "Folks back then were religious and superstitious; they believed in divinities and ghosts as well as in signs and hoodooing. 'Our religion and superstition was all mixed up.'" Missionaries in white communities, especially in up-country and mountain regions, made similar observations. "I told you of the superstitions of the colored people but I found the white people were not entirely free from such ideas," wrote Esther Douglass, an AMA missionary, to a colleague in the field. "The woman who lived with me went one day to the house of a wealthy white family," she continued, "and was told that the end of world was near because it was warm—just like Bible supposedly says." She met another minister who "told wonderful stories which he thought proved that witch doctors and fortune tellers were all right." H. S. Beals in eastern North Carolina noted that "more than half the white people here believe in witches." Such beliefs were particularly common in Appalachia, a region that served as a repository of Anglo-Celtic cultural customs, much like the Sea Islands preserved African-derived belief structures.[20]

The conjurers preached to a receptive audience. Fear of hags, spirits riding in the nights, and ghostly presences haunted rural communities, especially, if not exclusively, among black southerners. Students and reformers associated with the *Southern Workman*, the journal of Hampton Institute in Virginia, collected data on religious folklore as part of a project to understand the obstacles to mental modernity in the southern countryside. Their reports constitute some of the best sources on the prevalence of dreams, visions, and conjuration in the black and white rural South in the late nineteenth century. "The hag in Negro folklore," a *Southern Workman* reporter discovered, was the "very essence of nightmare, about whose personality gather all the morbid fancies of distempered dreams. She oozes in at your key hold, pervades your room with her malicious but invisible presence, rides you in your sleep, and is so persistent in her persecutions of her victims that they sometimes pine away and die after a year or two of her nightly visitations."[21]

Conjuring supplemented and contended with the practice of black Christianity. Conjurers were "often devout individuals," wrote one correspondent. She reported on a woman who claimed a "special revelation from God," just as did "all the Conjure doctors I have ever heard of." The folklorist Newbell Niles Puckett discovered conjurers who were "called" to their profession just as preachers were called by God. "I tricks in the name o' the Lord," said a conjuring woman from Alabama. "It's a spirit in me that tells—a spirit from the Lord Jesus Christ." An ex-slave from Texas explained his conception of the relationship between conjure and Christianity this way: "There am some things the Lord wants all folks to know, some things just the chosen few to know, and some things no one should know. Now, just 'cause you don't know 'bout some of the Lord's laws, 'tain't superstition if some other person understands and believes in such. . . . When the Lord gives such power to a person, it just comes to 'em." He pointed to the mystical authority of "special persons" who enjoyed insider access to knowledge of supernatural esoterica.[22]

For religious reformers, Christianity and conjure were inherently contradictory. For many black southerners, they were complementary, able to address spiritual needs at different life moments. Some considered the Bible as the "greatest Conjure book in the world," as Zora Neale Hurston discovered on one of her anthropological expeditions. A sexton in an AME church who held voodoo circles in his house discerned no evident contradiction between his roles as church stalwart and practitioner of magic. In preparing her influential study *After Freedom*, anthropologist Hortense Powdermaker encountered conjure doctors who were also popular clergymen. Though claiming to be contemptuous of "luck" and signs ("I say luck is in god; conduct, in the people"), a black Baptist preacher in the 1930s pointedly added, "Now you understand I ain't saying they ain't no evil spirits in the land. The Bible says there is embodied spirits and the upper firmament is inhabited with them. I've made a study of ghostism, and I can tell you they is ghosts. . . . There's things goes on in the world that's evil. I ain't saying they ain't certain people that can conjure you. People that sell theirselves to the devil can put evil spells on other folks."[23]

In the practice of conjure, roots, herbs, and medicines possessed spiritual efficacy, as well as physical medicinal properties. One black Christian convert received divine assurance that " 'there ain't no such thing as conjurers,' " but he still believed in root doctors: "After all, we must depend upon some form of root or weed to cure the sick." Disease and pain came from spirits who left signs on earth signifying their presence. As one early folklorist explained, "If they dreamed of figures of the underworld, spirits were trying to convince them of their susceptibility to illness." The extent of the sickness depended on the size of the mental figure. Thus, a dream of a mule or a black horse could be understood as a sign of death. Conjure was tied up intimately with a sense of individual and communal health. When chronic misfortunes struck innocent individuals, social and supernatural explanations were invoked. The affliction of individuals stemmed from social causes; thus, communal ritual practices were involved in treatment.

Even if complementary to black Christianity, conjure also involved doing harm to one's personal enemies. Folk in her area, Esther Douglass reported, had maliciously conjured their enemies by grounding up "in a scarlet cloth pieces of toe or finger nails, bits of glass etc., and putting where the hated one would have to step over it. This they said would put a lizard in his leg and cause great pain in his limbs." The meaning of conjure, historian Yvonne Chireau has suggested, involved "an intense preoccupation with the nature of evil, misfortune, the acutely precarious, insecure aspects of life, and the impending hazards present in the natural and social worlds." Most conjure practices were "either aggressive quests for therapy or divination practices of prediction." People understood being "conjured," having a "spell" put on them, as evidence of ill relations with others in their social world. Conjure thus suggested, Chireau concludes, a "conflicted world of dissension and discord" for black southerners.[24]

Many southern believers, black and white, engaged in a Pascalian wager, trusting in their Christianity while also keeping one foot in the world of spirits invoked by conjurers and narrated in popular tales. It was self-evident wisdom to place some stock in both. Bernice White of Leflore County, Mississippi, recalled how the people she grew up with in the first part of the twentieth century were "still scared. Oh, they would talk about they see things at night, the people come back and talk to them. Every once in a while I hear that now. I don't believe it. I never believed it, but I didn't take a chance on it not being true." Deeply held notions that imparted spiritual meanings to objects in the natural world thus remained a resilient part of southern understandings of the supernatural.[25]

Dreams, Visions, and Salvation Narratives

The dreams and visions surrounding conversion stories represent another side of supernaturalism in southern belief. White and black southern evangelicals understood visions, signs, and wonders as harbingers of deep spiritual experience. The conversion moment—a sacred instant in which God's spirit infused the soul—remained a central rite of religious expression in the region, one transcending denomination, gender, and race. For many southern Christians, crying, screaming, and physical torment heralded the working of God's spirit. Public conversion tales formed a central part of the extemporized liturgy common in southern churches. They provided narrative structure and order to the worship experience while also allowing a space for the apparently spontaneous movement of the spirit.

Anthropological observers of African American life provide some of the best accounts of the conversion saga as community ritual. Zora Neale Hurston, daughter of a Baptist minister in an all-black town in Florida, was a lifelong religious skeptic who knew intimately of the entirely ordinary lives of churchgoers in her hometown: "They plowed, chopped wood, went possum-hunting, washed clothes, raked up back yards and cooked collard greens like anybody else." Even with her doubts and questions, she enjoyed the oral artistry of the salvation narratives. She felt moved in churches "not by the spirit, but by action, more or less dramatic." Candidates for membership were pursued by "hellhounds" as they "ran for salvation" (perhaps the same "hellhounds" that dogged legendary bluesman Robert Johnson as he ran from the "blues falling down like hail"). They would dangle precariously over the fires of hell, call on Jesus, see a "little white man" on the other side calling them, and finally traverse to heaven. In publicly describing their spiritual journeys, they sometimes strayed from the scripted narrative expected of them, relying instead on extemporaneously created variations: "These visions are traditional. I knew them by heart as did the rest of the congregation. Some of them made up new details. Some of them would forget a part and improvise clumsily or fill up the gap with shouting. The audience knew, but everybody acted as if every word of it was new." Converts added individual touches to tales of redemption already sanctioned by the community. "The individual may hang as many new ornaments upon the traditional form as he likes," Hurston explained, "but the audience would be disagreeably surprised if the form were abandoned."[26]

Church members ritually challenged the validity of conversion experiences, frustrating the advocates of systematic spirituality. Candidates often were " 'sent back to seek further,' until they can come with the usual stranger visions and physical demonstrations," one northern observer discovered. Congregants at Gillfield Baptist Church in Petersburg, Virginia, one of the oldest black churches in the South, pronounced one self-proclaimed convert "not to understand her self or the Principles of Christ's dealings with his people." They voted to send her back "to the Throne of God's Grace, which is able to make her wise unto devotion."[27]

In the belief systems brought to these shores by the forced African migration, spirits used the mouths of the possessed to articulate particular messages. The spirits were said to mount and "ride" their carriers. In variants of African American religious practice, individuals were not mounted and controlled by independently acting spirits. Believers inspired by visions of divine origin recited the imagery of their own salvation rather than serving as a channel for the direct unmediated voice of a spirit. After the messages of the Holy Spirit were heard and approved, they were communally celebrated. "It's not anything you can touch, of course, but you know it's there. It's about the only thing that is real to you while it's going on," said the veteran Holiness preacher Charley White. A vision was something like a dream, he continued, but "it's not exactly like that neither. When God gives you a vision your whole body kind of soaks up the message, like a biscuit soaks up red-eye gravy. And sometimes you can hear the message as well as feel it. And sometimes you can see it."[28]

These visions and conversion rituals were central moments in the spiritual lives of southern believers who rejected acculturated worship forms. Rossa Cooley, successor to the pioneer northern missionary Laura Towne in the Sea Islands, observed the continuity of religious customs among black Christians in an area where African traditions directly influenced belief and behavior. The young candidates in her area, still termed "seekers," had to "'see visions and dream dreams,' which are interpreted to [them] by a 'spiritual father' or a 'spiritual mother,' who is closer after having been seen in a dream." The seekers ceased all other activities and stayed all night in the woods, and then related their stories to church elders who judged their authenticity. In Liberty County, Georgia, Esther Douglass held a series of meetings designed to "counteract the influence of the false teaching." Parents in the homes she visited put their youngsters "under the instruction of an ignorant 'godfather' or 'godmother' to be 'brought through by a course of dreams.' How far this turned them away from simple trust in Jesus we could not tell. Their teachers were not satisfied till their 'seeker' promised to join the church." Douglass frequently encountered ministers who used loud praying and incantatory singing, "keeping time with bodies rocking," until they achieved the desired ecstatic inspiration. Douglass "told them that God was a God of order and we did not allow such things. They were angry and went out."[29]

In certain parishes, particularly in Louisiana and in the Sea Islands, candidates for conversion depended on church mothers, who "settled quarrels and difficulties among members, visited the sick, encouraged the dying, washed and coffined the dead, mourned over those believed to be lost, draped the church in black for the dead," and presided over the dress and conduct at funerals. Church mothers and local laypeople, with or without ministerial assistance, enforced the ritualized conversion journeys. As the unofficially sanctioned oracles of dreams and visions, they powerfully influenced the quality of individual religious experience. "By virtue of her supposed sanctity and religious activity," one missionary explained, the church mother was "gifted with power to make spiritual excursions into the other world." For the reformers, the power of these "gospel mothers" and "old shepherds" provided a persistent example of the lack of "system" and "intelligent worship" in their churches. In post–Civil War New Orleans, a city with a tradition of older black women renowned for their esoteric spiritual powers, the black missionary Charles Satchell encountered the powers of these spiritual guides. In his parish, younger women dubbed "gospel mothers" assisted older "church mothers," who exercised control over members, Satchell fumed, "on the ground of being sent to them by the Spirit." The consequences of crossing their will could be severe: "If a member can keep the right side of these officials he need have no fear of church displeasure; they can gain access to the church. But woe to that disciple who is so unfortunate as to be out of their favor." Pastors came and went, but the mothers, the deacons, and other active laypeople preserved distinctive Afro-Christian practices. Women active in the church assumed privileged positions, and congregants considered them to have special access to the Spirit. Clifton Taulbert, a churchgoer in Tulsa, remembered the formidable woman who headed the Mother's Board of his church in the 1940s and 1950s. Services could not begin without her: "Once Mother Byrd had taken her position, God could begin to move."[30]

In conversion narratives and practices, as in conjure stories, folk tales, and blues lyrics, participants adapted a set of prototypical experiences and story patterns, with local references and peculiar incidents constantly added to the storehouse of available lore. Likewise, salvation stories varied by individual but eventually settled into familiar formulas that assured hearers of their authenticity. The theology of the active supernatural eventually found its way into both white and black Pentecostal churches in the twentieth century. In such ways black and white worshippers influenced each other to an extent they rarely comprehended. This was most especially true of the sects that, as one writer marveled, "grew up like mushrooms" in the South. The early history of Holiness and Pentecostal sects provide especially compelling evidence of the extent and meaning of racial interchange in southern religious expressive culture.[31]

Racial Interchange in Early Southern Pentecostalism

Racial interchange at the margins of southern religious culture powerfully shaped the most important new religious movement of early-twentieth-century America: Holiness/Pentecostalism, often colloquially called the "sanctified church." Pentecostalism revived notions of spirit possession embraced in southern folk belief. If the theological fatalism of Pentecostalism fit the pessimistic theology common to white southern belief, the sanctified faith in the working of the Spirit closely paralleled historic African American practice. Limited and circumscribed by the dominant Jim Crow culture, sanctified churchgoers nonetheless created cultural forms and styles that exerted an enormous influence on twentieth-century popular cultural expression, spawning figures as diverse as Oral Roberts, Little Richard, Sam Cooke, Jimmy Swaggart, Al Green, and Elvis Presley.

Pentecostalism was not born in the South, but it attracted white and black evangelicals who were disaffected by the embourgeoisement of the region's dominant religious institutions. Early Pentecostalism functioned much like the camp meetings of the nineteenth century. In both cases, ordinary believers emotionally embraced a democratic religious community that impelled close bonds, a strict moral code forbidding worldly pleasure, and hypnotic worship practices and music that induced receptivity of bodies to the Spirit. African Americans delivered messages that, at times, white seekers embraced. Once these initial enthusiasms settled into institutional routines, believers usually settled into racially separate religious organizations.

Pentecostals claimed to be restoring the pure and primitive message of Christianity. But besides being theological primitivists, they were also, as historian Grant Wacker has argued, pragmatists. They sought to restore the purity of the original church, as did all primitivists, but they did so with a masterly use of the press and (later) radio and television. The early saints were both Holy Ghost idealists and this-worldly realists. They spoke in tongues, were "slain in the Spirit," preached and lived with moral conviction that sometimes slid into fanaticism, and fought each other fiercely. They also built churches and denominations and quickly mastered the world of print and electronic media.

Pentecostalism was a twentieth-century extension of the nineteenth-century Holiness movement, a set of doctrines that embraced eighteenth-century Methodist ideas of the soul's quest for perfection. Holiness believers looked for a work of God following conversion—what believers referred to as a "second blessing" or "sanctification"—when the Holy Spirit infused and completely purified the soul. In the antebellum era, the informal Bible studies of the New York Methodist Phoebe Palmer, who revived John Wesley's musings about achieving an ideal state of spiritual purity, popularized the Holiness movement for an urban, northern audience attracted by the widespread ideas of perfectionism. Palmer and her followers converted sanctification into a distinct and discrete event following conversion, one wholly cleansing the believer of sin. Holiness was mostly unknown in the South until after the Civil War, largely because of the movement's connection with social radicalism, especially abolitionism. By the late nineteenth century, however, Holiness had been denuded of some of its earlier theological and political implications. It then spread quickly, especially among Methodists in the Southeast.

Twentieth-century Pentecostal doctrine added speaking in tongues as evidence of the movement of God's spirit. The significance of tongues speech was heatedly disputed among the faithful. Some assumed it was a required "initial evidence" of sanctification. Others called it a "third blessing" following conversion and sanctification. Still others interpreted tongues speech as just one of many gifts that God bestowed differentially on individuals. Holiness teacher

Charles Fox Parham's revivals at his Bible school in Topeka, Kansas, in 1901 set a theological precedent for the emergence of the new Pentecostal doctrines. The second baptism of sanctification—the ultimate cleansing from sin explained by Holiness theologians—was necessary but not sufficient, he preached. Only the final Holy Spirit baptism could complete the initiate's spiritual quest. When God's power suffused the human vessel, the believer spoke in tongues, a practice that was evidence of the "latter rain" of the Holy Spirit. The early Pentecostals looked expectantly for the imminent and catastrophic coming of the "end times" (in contrast to the more optimistic postmillennialism common to many in the nineteenth-century northern Holiness movement), and espoused a literalist biblicism that very nearly merged into fundamentalism. Like the fundamentalists, too, the Pentecostals shunned the consumption of tobacco and alcohol and what they perceived as adornment in dress (jewelry for women and neckties for men being the most vilified worldly baubles). However, Pentecostals remained distinct from fundamentalists because of the doctrine of tongues speech as evidence of the baptism of the Spirit, an innovation too closely akin to antinomian anarchy for the guardians of a literalist evangelical orthodoxy.

Racial interchange permeated early southern Holiness and Pentecostalism. The Fire-Baptized Holiness Church, one of many small offshoots of the growing Holiness movement of late-nineteenth-century America, prepared the ground for biracial Pentecostalism. The Fire-Baptized faithful envisioned the second baptism of the believer and complete sanctification as a process of being cleansed of all sin by fire, with emotional rapture following. Exulted one early believer, "It seems clear to us that history is repeating itself and that in these last days we are being permitted to witness the same marvelous and miraculous displays of divine power which the early disciples witnessed in those first days." At one meeting in Beniah, Tennessee, in 1899, a Holiness pioneer reported, "The Lord put the holy dance upon a number of the saints. . . . Such jumping, and screaming, and shouting, and dancing before the Lord, we have seldom seen." This Holiness minister then traveled to Abbeville, South Carolina, at the invitation of William E. Fuller, ruling elder of the Colored Fire-Baptized Holiness Association. The two held meetings in private homes for blacks and white factory workers. "These poor and needy people are hungry for the pure gospel," one minister commented of the cotton mill workers who flocked to his services. The "big, proud, worldly church, and the unsaved preachers . . . have no real interest in them, and do not want them in their 'heathen temples.'" Interested black seekers met in a ramshackle building on the outskirts of town. The impoverished setting could not offset the rich spirit: "Such singing, such shouting, such dancing, such praying, it has never before been our privilege to hear." The black participants, he observed, "dance before the Lord differently than our white people," a feature of the meeting "peculiarly fascinating" to the only white man there.[32]

William Fuller had been present at the establishment of the Fire-Baptized Holiness Association of America (soon renamed the Fire-Baptized Holiness Church) in 1898, held at the home of the white southern Holiness leader R. B. Hayes. Originally a Baptist from South Carolina, Hayes became a traveling evangelist, working closely with white and black fellows in the new Fire-Baptized sect in the late nineteenth century. Hayes landed himself in trouble for inviting black worshippers and a choir to attend a service he led in Georgia. Challenged for espousing racial equality, he insisted that he was simply extending the message of entire sanctification to all. The efforts of Hayes and Fuller resulted in many black accessions to the young church, many of whom later converted to the ranks of Pentecostalism. Eventually, blacks formed their own organization, the Fire-Baptized Holiness Church of God of the Americas. Fuller served as its overseer until his death in 1958. The church was "connected with the white people for ten years," he later recounted, until in 1908, "owing to the growing prejudice that began to arise among the unsaved people, it was mutually agreed that we have separate incorporations." Fuller's early preaching to whites and blacks, as recorded in the Holiness paper *Live Coals of Fire*, was replaced with a career in the tiny black Holiness group. Even in their own church annals, white Pentecostals soon forgot their early contact with black figures such as Fuller.[33]

Established evangelicals scorned the Holiness sects in part for their theology, and even more so because of the class of people they attracted—lower-class whites, factory workers, ordinary black laborers. "There are some people who think that nobody but poor folks and 'niggers' ever shout. If that is true it is because nobody but the poor folks and the 'niggers' have anything to shout about," wrote North Carolina Holiness advocate A. B. Crumpler. "In this country the proud, supercilious, ungodly whites look upon us with scorn and contempt because we hold meetings for the colored people, and preach the gospel to their former slaves," said another Holiness leader. Black Holiness preachers also met considerable opposition from black Baptist and Methodist denominations, who recognized the clear and present danger posed by the young sects.[34]

Frequent reports from the turn of the century attest to the biracial services and racial interchange that coexisted with the racially separated world of mainstream southern Protestantism. Between 1880 and 1920, scores of independent evangelists, musical itinerants, and faith healers combed the South in the name of Holiness and Pentecostalism. Whites and blacks in the movement formed a tenuous but burgeoning network of sanctified churches and denominations. In Kingstree, South Carolina, around the turn of the century, a biracial team of

Holiness evangelists set up a tent and divided the salvation altar into white and black sections. By their account, the services came off harmoniously, with a "profound interest manifested among the people, both white and colored, and a real Holy Ghost awakening." The black Holiness exhorter later led some camp meetings in which blacks and "some of the leading white people of the community came out, and showed much interest." After being sanctified in 1914, one former AME teacher, claiming to be healed of cataracts, spent the next twenty years as a traveling evangelist for both white and black listeners. At one meeting in Georgia, he recounted how "white and colored were at the altar. Seeking for Salvation. The meeting was so powerful that men seemingly could not stay on their jobs." Whites in Jacksonville Heights, Florida, placed such "great faith in the gospel that was preached to them, until they would send handkerchiefs to the meeting, and God would manifest his power through the prayer of faith." He continued his work through the 1920s and 1930s, reporting on "large gatherings, white and colored." The biracial mingling in early Holiness and Pentecostalism sometimes agitated locals who perceived the services as potential harbingers of social equality. At an annual encampment for blacks in Hearne, Texas, worshippers built a brush arbor to accommodate white inquirers. People flocked there, having never heard the full gospel of sanctification. White converts said they could not "seek Baptism at a colored altar." A young minister preached to crowds of whites and blacks in separate services. At his next appointment, he met men with pistols who threatened him for putting whites "on a level with the d—niggers." While he was waiting to take the train out of town, another crowd beat him with clubs, fracturing his wrist. The persecution honored the young minister with admission into the fellowship of suffering saints.[35]

Emergence of Southern Pentecostalism

The relationship between white and black believers in southern Holiness movements and Pentecostalism emerged most interestingly and ambiguously in 1906, at the Azusa Street revival in Los Angeles. There, Pentecostalism first drew widespread public attention. Four key figures in the expansion of Pentecostalism into the South were present: William J. Seymour, a Louisiana native who led the Azusa Street revivals and the early Apostolic Faith Mission; Charles Harrison Mason, a black Mississippian by birth who was converted at the Los Angeles meetings and later founded the Memphis-based Church of God in Christ; Gaston B. Cashwell, a white North Carolinian captured by the exciting movement of the Spirit he read about in the Pentecostal press and by his own experience of tongues speech under Seymour's preaching; and Howard A. Goss, a working-class white Missourian electrified by the sheer physical presence of his white and black brethren. All four veterans of Azusa carried the message to white and black southern communities from Texas to Virginia.

As a young man, the native Louisianan William J. Seymour traveled frequently, worked odd jobs in Indianapolis and Cincinnati, and contracted smallpox, which permanently damaged his left eye. In 1903, the thirty-three-year-old prophet attended a series of meetings in Houston led by Charles Parham, the white Holiness minister who witnessed tongues speech among his Bible school students in Topeka in 1901. While in Houston, Seymour met a black woman named Lucy Farrow, a future Pentecostal missionary; she was then a governess to Parham's children. Segregation laws (and Parham's own segregationist views) compelled Seymour to sit in the hallway. Parham's exhortations taught Seymour of the baptism of the Holy Spirit, evidenced by speaking in tongues, the culmination of conversion and sanctification. Parham and Seymour later preached together in street evangelistic crusades in Houston.

In 1906, Seymour himself began teaching the tongues doctrine, the key innovation that distinguished Pentecostalism from its Holiness antecedent. Using some packing cases as his pulpit in a small tumbledown building on Azusa Street in south central Los Angeles, Seymour preached quietly but earnestly for a handful of listeners. Since the former warehouse had a seating capacity of about thirty, the "crowds" reported to be present were small. Over time, Seymour's revivals attracted a diverse crew of whites, blacks, Mexicans, Europeans, and Asians. The press played the event for prurient fun. "The devotees of the weird doctrine practice the most fanatical rites, preach the wildest theories and work themselves into a state of mad excitement in their peculiar zeal," reported the *Los Angeles Times*. "Colored people and a sprinkling of whites compose the congregation, and night is made hideous in the neighborhood by the howlings of the worshipers, who spend hours swaying forth and back in a nerve-racking attitude of prayer and supplication." Just after the opening of the revivals, a Holiness writer noted how "some months ago, among some of the colored people in this city, re-inforced after a little with some whites, there began something which was called the 'gift of tongues.'" He attributed the movement to immature believers who would "run after the hope of exceptional or marvelous things, to their own further undoing."[36]

For the early Pentecostals, however, there was no such thing as bad publicity; the *Los Angeles Times* gave the movement "free advertising," one early believer happily reported. The Pentacostals' makeshift press network furthered the excitement that "the fire spreads," to use their favorite descriptive metaphor. Seymour established the *Apostolic Faith* to publicize the awakening. Some 50,000 copies of the paper circulated nationally. Reports in the religious press drew the attention of Holiness seekers in the South such as Charles H. Mason, Gaston Cashwell, and Howard Goss, each of whom eventually headed for Los Angeles.

With Lucy Farrow's charismatic presence and piano playing, the Azusa mission proved instrumental in spreading the word. An early white participant and the revival's most meticulous recorder, William Bartleman, remembered that "Brother Seymour was recognized as the nominal leader in charge. But we had no Pope or Hierarchy. We were brethren." On Sunday morning, April 15, 1906, Bartleman witnessed the "colored sister [Farrow] speak in tongues." According to one account, Farrow

> walked across the room and went over to the piano and started to play. . . . And then all at once she broke out in singing in a language that I could not understand. . . . And then I recognized that it was like that other color[ed] lady speaking in tongues. And then I recognized that she must be singing in tongues. And when she started singing in tongues and accompanying herself on the piano, and it all seemed to be so harmonious and beautiful, we became tremendously interested in that phenomena. And we noticed that those who were down on their knees praying, begun speaking in other tongues. And that was my first introduction in Pentecost . . . nobody trying to urge them on to something, it was just simply God opening the windows of heaven and throwing down upon them, the blessings that they themselves could not contain.

As Bartleman later reminisced, "It was not all blessing. In fact the fight was terrific. But the fire could not be smothered. Strong saints gathered in prayer and gradually the tide rose in victory."

Seymour attempted to restrain emotions by preaching doctrinally careful sermons. He insisted on the priority of salvation first over spectacular demonstrations of spiritual ecstasy. He saw the movement of God's spirit as validated first by the evidence of love in the believer. Tongues speech was not the most important signifier of a true faith. Despite these attempts at deliberate self-control, early participants remembered Azusa as a time when the Spirit broke down intellectualism and other man-made barriers. An English visitor to the revivals exclaimed how "extraordinary" it was that "white pastors from the South were eagerly prepared to go to Los Angeles to the Negroes, to have fellowship with them, and to receive through their prayers and intercessions the blessings of the Spirit," and even more so that they would return to their congregations and report on that. As another participant said of the gathering, "I, being southern born, thought it a miracle that I could sit in a service by a colored saint of God and worship, or eat at a great camp table and forget I was eating beside a colored saint, but in spirit and truth God was worshipped in love and harmony."[37]

Racial and theological conflicts worsened after the initial enthusiasm of the revivals waned. Seymour had invited his erstwhile mentor Charles Parham to Los Angeles to help lead the fledgling movement. In Los Angeles, however, Parham was disgusted by the "hypnotic influences, familiar-spirit influences, spiritualistic influences, mesmeric influences, and all kinds of spells, spasms, falling in trances" that he saw at Seymour's services. The meetings were a dangerous "hot-bed of wildfire," he wrote caustically, with respectable whites lapsing into the "unintelligent, crude negroisms of the Southland, and laying it on the Holy Ghost." Until his death in 1929, Parham ranted that the Los Angeles meetings were just a "modification of the Negro chanting of the Southland" rather than the "result of Pentecostal baptism." By that time, the movement had evolved out of Parham's hands. In the last two decades of his life, he propagated scurrilously racist theological doctrines such as Anglo-Israelism, the origins of what later became the Christian Identity Movement. He imagined, for example, that God's punishment of mankind for the mixing of races in Noah's time would be paralleled by similar catastrophes for miscegenation in the modern era.[38]

Aside from such critics, Seymour faced all manner of dissent, personal jealousies, and legal tussles. Dismayed at the misunderstanding of the tongues doctrines, Seymour desired unity for Christians of all races. "One token of the Lord's coming is that He is melting all races and nations together, and they are filled with the power and glory of God. He is baptizing by one spirit into one body and making up a people that will be ready to meet Him when He comes," he wrote in the *Apostolic Faith*. In the *Doctrines and Discipline* of his Apostolic Faith Church, Seymour urged that "our colored brethren must love our white brethren and respect them in the truth so that the word of God can have its free course, and our white brethren must love their colored brethren and respect them in the truth so that the Holy Spirit won't be greaved. I hope we won't have any more trouble and division spirit." Seymour wanted worshippers of any color to feel free "in spite of all the trouble we have had with some of our white brethren in causing diversion, and spreading wild fire and fanaticism. Some of our colored brethren caught the disease of this spirit of division also." Despite Seymour's professed desire for unity, the Azusa mission dwindled to a small black congregation. After Seymour's death in 1922 and his wife's passing a few years later, it was sold. Seymour himself nearly vanished from historical memory until his rediscovery by Pentecostal historians working in the wake of the civil rights movement.[39]

Despite its problems, the Azusa Street revivals spun off a corps of black and white evangelists who spread the new gospel and encouraged cultural interchange in religious settings. Howard A. Goss's career shows the influence of racial interchange in early Pentecostalism. After a childhood in rural Missouri and a youth spent working in mines, Goss sold his worldly possessions and followed

Charles Fox Parham to Houston, gathering there with other early converts. "I started out with my pockets empty of money," he recounted in his autobiography, "but my heart brimful of zeal and courage for the Lord." Drawn to Los Angeles by press reports of the Azusa revival, Goss heard Sister Lucy Farrow and witnessed fellow mourners lining up, being touched, speaking in tongues. Feeling his heart become hungry again for "another manifestation of God," he "went forward that she might place her hands upon me. When she did, the Spirit of God again struck me like a bolt of lightning; the Power of God surged through my body, and I again began speaking in tongues. From that day to this I have always been able to speak in tongues at any time I yielded to the Spirit of God." Unlike more established white evangelicals, Goss endorsed fervent bodily exhibitions: "I have never seen dancing that was of God that did not touch someone in the audience." Public religious dance in white churches, he acknowledged unabashedly, was "drawn from the colored work, there their freedom from inhibition, one of their most attractive traits[,] made its appeal." He assured his (perhaps discomfited) readers that such joyous expressions were "entirely controlled by the pastor, and stopped or started at his signal. . . . He knew his congregation, no doubt, and allowed only what was beneficial." Like most other early Pentecostal advocates, Goss encountered much opposition, which he blamed on coldness and laxity in the established churches.[40]

The most significant white southern convert from the Seymour meetings was Gaston B. Cashwell. He came from a Holiness tradition in North Carolina that descended from the Fire-Baptized Holiness Church, which provided him an intermediary point from Methodism to Pentecostalism. Although Cashwell was deeply affected by the new Pentecostal doctrines and practices, his enthusiasm was chastened by the fire-baptized movement's early sexual and financial scandals. In the early twentieth century, he continued his Holiness ministry, preparing his entrance into Pentecostalism. At one 1903 revival in Dunn, North Carolina, he reported that the "colored saints" had invited him to preach on a Sunday evening. The house was "packed with both white and colored and the Spirit of the Lord was there, the people rejoiced and God blessed them. They seemed to be filled with the Spirit, and the white people of the community say they live it." Cashwell converted to Pentecostal doctrine and practice a number of early church leaders, including A. J. Tomlinson of the Church of God (Cleveland, Tennessee), as well as early organizers of the Assemblies of God (founded in 1914 in Arkansas and later headquartered at Springfield, Missouri). Cashwell's success in transmitting the message also influenced several figures in the early Pentecostal Holiness Church (PHC), centered in the Southeast and the second largest white grouping after the Assemblies of God.[41]

The Holiness press kept white and black southerners such as Cashwell and

Charles H. Mason intrigued by the new powers of the Spirit apparently descending on believers in Los Angeles. Struck by the reports, Cashwell set out for Southern California in search of further inner enlightenment. "I had been preaching holiness for nine years," he explained in the *Apostolic Faith*, the paper of the Azusa mission, "but my soul began to hunger and thirst for the fullness of God." At first he recoiled from the interracial nature of the early Pentecostal services. The prospect of receiving the baptism of the Spirit at the hands (literally) of the diminutive black minister Seymour caused "chills to go down my spine." Nevertheless, the power fell on Cashwell in December 1906: "The Lord opened up the windows of heaven and the light of God began to flow over me in such power as never before. I then went into the room where the service was held and while Sister Lum was reading of how the Holy Ghost was falling in other places, before I knew it, I began to speak in tongues and praise God."

Cashwell then returned to North Carolina, rented a tobacco warehouse in the small town of Dunn, and initiated a series of seminal meetings that served the same purpose for the South as the Azusa revivals had for Los Angeles. The preachers and people came to Dunn, he later recounted, and "went down for the baptism with all the earnestness they could command, and were soon happy in the experience, speaking in tongues, singing in tongues, writing in tongues, shouting, leaping, dancing and praising God. They returned to their respective homes to scatter the fire. Great Pentecostal revivals broke out in practically all the churches. Some of the preachers and some of the laymen held back, but the majority went right into the experience. A great revival had come, and no one was able to stop it." One of Cashwell's converts from Durham, North Carolina, reported in April 1907 of how "nearly the whole of North Carolina is being stirred among the holiness people, white and colored."[42]

In October 1907, Cashwell began publication of the Atlanta-based *Bridegroom's Messenger* to spread the Pentecostal word. The weekly paper tied together early Pentecostals in a regional ecumenical network of conversation and reassurance about the spreading glory. In the first issue, Cashwell castigated contemporary religious institutions. "With all their bishops, elders, preachers, and colleges," established churches reminded him of "the wooden Indian that stands at a door, a bunch of cigars in his hand, yet lifeless, blind, deaf, and dumb, so knowing nothing of the Spirit of God that gives life to the soul, body, and spirit." By contrast, Cashwell ecstatically surveyed the coming of Pentecost to the Southland: "The power is falling from the Atlantic to the Mississippi River. The cities and country are filled with the glory of God, healing, working of miracles, divers kinds of tongues."

In the early twentieth century, many of Cashwell's converts organized southern Pentecostalism into a variety of denominations and other church institutions. For them, freedom's coming through what they referred to as the "latter rain" of the Holy Spirit also necessitated doctrinal discipline to restrain spiritual chaos. In the process, white Pentecostals gradually dissociated themselves from the racial interchange of their earlier origins. The early biracial Pentecostal services produced some genuine sentiments of Christian interracialism, but by the 1920s black and white believers had settled into racially distinct and separate organizations.[43]

Early White Southern Pentecostalism:
The Pentecostal Holiness Church, the Church of God
(Cleveland, Tennessee), and the Assemblies of God

Gaston B. Cashwell's converts spread Pentecostalism in the Southeast, where some of them eventually coalesced into the Pentecostal Holiness Church in 1911. A union of several smaller groupings, the PHC adhered to basic evangelical doctrines, adding to them characteristic Pentecostal emphases on the baptism of the spirit, divine healing, and premillennialism. The PHC's support came largely from the southeastern states, especially the Carolinas and Georgia. The other major white Pentecostal denomination, the Assemblies of God (formed in 1914), drew most of its members from the Upper South and lower Midwest.

One of the PHC's early constituent groups was the Fire-Baptized Holiness Church, led in its early days by Joseph H. King. Born in 1869 to a sharecropping family in South Carolina, J. H. King's early religious experiences were sparse. "What passed as the Gospel in these churches was almost no Gospel at all," he wrote of his upbringing. "Regular prayer services at any church in all the community I never heard. . . . Darkness covered the masses mentally and morally." In 1897–98, when King was in charge of a Methodist circuit in northeastern Georgia, he converted to the doctrine of fire-baptism as the experience of sanctification. By the time of the first Fire-Baptized Holiness convention in Anderson, South Carolina, in 1898, he considered himself entirely sanctified. In 1900, King became editor of the church's paper, *Live Coals.* "In spite of his youth," a Pentecostal historian later wrote of King, "he was a man of somewhat sober judgment and was very conservative in his religious behavior."[44]

King took the fire-baptized messages of salvation and sanctification to the Oklahoma Territory. A few years later, a preacher and theologian named F. M. Britton organized the Fire-Baptized Holiness Church of Oklahoma City, which became one nucleus for Pentecostalism in the southwestern region. Later, many of King's church members in Georgia attended Gaston Cashwell's Pentecostal revival being held in Dunn, North Carolina. King himself became one of Cashwell's original converts. Originally devoted to spreading the "two-stage" doctrines of Holiness, after Cashwell's preaching, "it was not long until a major portion of the members of the Holiness Church had received the baptism of the Spirit and spoke in other tongues." King's own newly renamed Pentecostal Holiness Church resolved that officers of the denomination should "admit no preacher or teacher into any of the churches who preach or teach against the baptism of the Holy Ghost."[45]

Together with George Floyd Taylor, King sent out the *Pentecostal Holiness Advocate* for thirty years beginning in 1917. As editor, King allowed much prayer testimony as potential evidence of God's prophecy. But as veterans of the excitement and disorder of the Fire-Baptized Holiness Church, PHC leaders also balanced individual messages from God with sobriety and wisdom from Bible study and authoritative ministerial messages. Pentecostal believers were "baptized with fire from heaven's altars," as evidenced in tongues speech and rapturous behavior, but were then stabilized by preaching "that instructs, corrects, reproves, and perfects in Christ," explained one church leader. Most southern Pentecostals eventually settled on the notion that tongues speech was the onetime "initial evidence" of spirit baptism. PHC members understood dreams, visions, conversations, messages picked up from tracts, and prophetic deliverances in tongues speech all as potential direct contact with the Divine. Tongues simply added a new form of dialogue to a preexisting enthusiasm.[46]

The white southern evangelical trek from Holiness to Pentecostalism came in myriad ways. One such path may be charted in the life of George Floyd Taylor. The theologian and future historian of early Pentecostalism first encountered Holiness ideas of sanctification in the late 1890s. Taylor's search for spiritual fulfillment coincided with enthusiastic tent crusades in North Carolina. Taylor recalled "strange manifestations and demonstrations in those meetings. People would laugh, . . . scream, jump, dance, run, slap their hands, and praise the Lord." In the early twentieth century, Taylor spent a year futilely seeking the spiritual drama of sanctification. In 1906, he prayed for divine wisdom on the question of tongues speech. Taylor eventually spoke in tongues under the exhortation of Gaston B. Cashwell, the white southerner who himself had received his Pentecostal baptism at the hands of William J. Seymour. Taylor also interpreted Pentecostalism as essentially modern in its innovative theology and readiness to accept and utilize technological advances. For example, believers no longer had to rely on strained biblical prophecies or outmoded Calvinist dogmas, for God's spirit was empirically evident both in the New Testament and in the contemporary phenomenon of tongues speech. Despite their premillennial theology, which implied skepticism about improvement in this world, early Pentecostals such as Taylor also embraced optimistic views of technology and new thought about the health of the body. Their primitivism, in other words, did not preclude their pragmatism. For them, supernaturalism was "the spiritual equivalent of modern scientific discoveries, a tapping of the powers of spiritual nature."[47]

Taylor produced one of the earliest extended treatises on Pentecostal doctrines, *The Spirit and the Bride*, in 1908. Taylor separated conversion from sanctification, seeing the latter as a consecration and preparation for the final gifts of the Spirit. As an early church leader, Taylor soon recognized that the enthusiasm of Pentecostal practice required the restraining force of ecclesiastical organization. "The first evidence of the Baptism is the manifestation of tongues," he said. "This may or may not be accompanied by emotions. We must not mistake emotions for the manifestation." For Taylor, Pentecostalism was not about emotional release but represented a means to induce order from the proliferation of sects and doctrines that competed for the allegiance of believers. The gifts of the Spirit, as Taylor knew, were powerful but troublesome. "Freedom of the Spirit," he wrote, "is encouraged and enjoyed by all so far as 'consistent with sobriety.'" The word of God captured in the uncertain ways of dreams, visions, and heteroglossolia left considerable leeway for controversies. PHC authorities fought what they saw as "fanaticism" in their church, establishing the doctrinal and behavioral boundaries needed for institutional growth. As leader of the newly formed PHC (five years old in 1916), Taylor felt he should discipline spontaneous expressions with the written word. The constant bickering in Pentecostal groups, over everything from wearing neckties to understanding the place of tongues as either *one* or *the* evidence of God's spirit, seemed evidence of an unseemly "fanaticism." On the other hand, Pentecostals also feared "formalism," the quenching of God's spirit. Although salvation was never "altogether a shout," wrote one early believer, shouting was a "very definite part of our salvation." The effort by early Pentecostals to teach restraint and more carefully structure the church hierarchy came at some cost, as splinter groups challenged the centralization of the church, as well as the "amount of emotional manifestation which should be encouraged in religious expression."[48]

Leaders of groups such as the PHC, including George Floyd Taylor, often were educated in colleges or Bible schools. They set up their own colleges and printing presses and enforced doctrinal orthodoxy. Ministerial standards adopted in 1917, for example, required prospective PHC clergymen to have read the Bible through twice and to have studied a series of other books that inculcated fundamental tenets, including conservative doctrines of original sin and premillennial dispensationalism. This widespread view, common in the conservative evangelical world, held that God had divided the history of the world into seven predetermined periods, or "dispensations." In the end times, Christ would return to gather the saints prior to the final conflict between good and evil that would climax human history. Like other evangelicals, Pentecostals created a variety of intricate charts that laid out biblical prophecies and helped the faithful visualize and comprehend the byzantine prognostications of premillennialist scholars.[49]

In the up-country of Tennessee and North Carolina, in the rural Southeast, and in newly opening southwestern areas such as Oklahoma and western Texas, Holiness and Pentecostal converts constructed enduring religious institutions, including the Church of God (Cleveland, Tennessee). In 1886, a former Baptist preacher named Richard Spurling in East Tennessee asked his small congregation to "come out" with him to pursue true holiness. After his death in the 1890s, his son R. G. Spurling Jr. continued urging God's people to unite. "In this way," a Church of God historian later wrote, "the minds of the people were continually agitated, and gradually prepared for the work of the Spirit that was to follow." A decade later, three men came to Cherokee County, Tennessee, delivering the message of the second blessing subsequent to conversion. "The people knew but little about the bible," Spurling said, "but they prayed, and shouted and exhorted until hundreds of hard sinners were converted."[50]

These were the humble origins of what became the Church of God (Cleveland, Tennessee). The church owed its growth in the early twentieth century to its domineering and charismatic overseer, Ambrose Jessup Tomlinson. Looking back, Tomlinson insisted that the manifestation of tongues that famously hit Los Angeles in 1906 first struck in the backwoods of Tennessee in the late nineteenth century: "It was the same thing, the same Spirit, the same power and the same manifestations." The former Quaker from Indiana came to the Tennessee mountains in the late nineteenth century to farm and distribute free scriptures provided by the American Bible Society. Traveling through the region in 1901, he despaired at the "poverty and ignorance that I am yet unable to avert, but glory pours into my soul as I resolve to make a mightier effort than ever to lift these poor whites from their ignorance and poverty. I am waiting here today for further orders by the Spirit." Unhappy with the turmoil and divisions in the Christian world, A. J. Tomlinson joined the Christian Union being formed from the preaching of Richard Spurling and William F. Bryant. The duo formed the base of a Holiness network headquartered in Beniah, Tennessee. Southern Baptist churches excommunicated both for countenancing the "modern theory of sanctification," and vigilantes targeted Bryant and Spurling as religious deviants. In 1903, Tomlinson began to edit the *Way*, the journal of the young church. He turned himself into a fledgling religious entrepreneur, even insisting that his more backward fellows dress up appropriately and professionalize their demeanor. Following his sanctification, Tomlinson continued the quest for ever higher states of religious experience. "Some one may say we can never reach oneness of doctrine, only oneness in spirit," he explained, "but I affirm that we can or else the word of God is mistaken." Tomlinson insisted that all Christians should unite wholly on points of doctrine and practice—and come together under his divinely ordained leadership. Under its founder's teachings, the denomination took on a highly centralized theocratic structure.[51]

The exhortations of the pioneering southern Pentecostal G. B. Cashwell, himself fresh from the Azusa revivals, introduced Tomlinson to the third and final blessing of the Holy Spirit and the experience of tongues speech. In early 1908, as Tomlinson described it, "the Spirit came upon me and down I went on the floor, right by the side of the rostrum.... Before I arose again the Spirit obtained such control that He spoke and sang for Himself. Hours passed into eternity while under His control." Tomlinson declared faith in divine healing, feet-washing, the premillennial Second Coming, bodily resurrection, and sanctification subsequent to the new birth. While the movement of Pentecostalism was in its infancy, he believed that "as the apostolic order is more thoroughly reached the gifts will be bestowed more abundantly."[52]

Through the early 1910s, Tomlinson reported frequent spells of the anointing of the Spirit. At the Church of God's General Assembly in 1912, for example, Tomlinson recounted how "the Spirit came upon the audience so strong that I was obliged to discontinue for a spell while the people fell on their faces and wept. At another time while I was speaking on the government of the church the power fell so strong that the people were held until after dark, and I lay on the floor under the power of the Spirit for five hours." In 1912, Tomlinson ordained a "colored brother" in Florida, after discussion about whether to set "the colored people off to work among themselves on account of the race prejudice in the South." The next year, thousands of the faithful joined a camp meeting full of "weeping, shouting, dancing, visions, music under the power as well as music and singing in every service. The people were carried by the Spirit . . . like the waves of the sea." Tomlinson consistently encouraged his church folk to wait expectantly on such emotional manifestations. Doctrinal instruction was necessary but not sufficient, he knew, for believers also hungered for "testimonies, talking in tongues, interpretations, signs, wonders, dancing, and whatever else the blessed spirit of God dictates. Our people must be free in the Holy Ghost. This freedom must not be taken away from them." The gift of tongues, for example, was "to be controlled, and at certain times and places must not be exercised, but speaking in tongues as the Spirit gives the utterance is controlled by the Spirit and should not be interfered with by rules and regulations." The faithful hardly needed encouraging in this regard. The yearly minutes of the young Church of God record meetings halting altogether to hear attendees speaking in tongues, often interpreted to be God's message to resolve whatever controversy was then occupying the assembly. At the same time, the yearning for respectability remained strong. For example, one assembly decreed that all use of the despised term "holy rollers" by the press would be "considered and treated as a slanderous and malignant offense."[53]

The Church of God attracted common folk in Tennessee and the Southeast who felt increasingly estranged from the southern evangelical establishment. One convert, a native of the mountains, knew that it was unacceptable to wear overalls to urban Baptist or Methodist services but that he would be welcomed at the Church of God: "The services that they held were something like ours had been at home but somehow there seemed to be *more power* in their meetin's than we'd ever had. Of course we had seen shoutin' before, but not the kind that they were doin' there." He came to the altar at one service and his "built-up emotions and feelin's came surgin' out" as he "sobbed and cried for the blood of Jesus and its cleansing power." He prayed for sanctification and "was submissive to His every impulse and let Him have His way. What I did I don't remember, but they say I was joyous in the spirit."[54]

Tomlinson maintained a pristine doctrine of tongues as evidence of God's spirit and a militant premillennialism, preaching that Christians were living through "the last great conflict" prior to Armageddon and the return of Jesus. "Remember we are now in the last great conflict," he wrote confidently, meaning that it was "time to press the battle and wage a strong warfare against the devil and all his allurements and devices." He advised members that God was "raising up a people to engage in this last great struggle and conflict against formalism, perverted Scriptures and theories of men, who will sacrifice their lives . . . rather than surrender any part of the truth." He yearned for a phalanx of men "filled with such holy zeal and Godly courage, that we could all together burst forth under the power of this mighty baptismal fire and rush to every quarter of the globe like mad men . . . until every tribe, kindred, tongue and people could hear, and thus end this Last Great Conflict." Tomlinson named himself General Overseer for Life of his young denomination, and annual church assemblies confirmed his theocratic mission: "Each Assembly brings stronger ties and greater evidences that God has set me as Overseer of the church. Gleams of light, angels, Jesus were witnessed by many either in vision or reality, around and over me at certain periods to force people to know that I was in the place God designed."[55]

Tomlinson's visions for Christian unity did not survive his own theocratic egotism. The Church of God split in the early 1920s, when charges flew that Tomlinson had mismanaged the church treasury. Soon, the original "Christian Union" had two bitterly divided descendants: the Church of God (the original church body) and the Church of God of Prophecy (formed by Tomlinson following his ouster). Each was based in the small town of Cleveland, Tennessee; and each supported its own educational institutions, presses, official newspaper, and church hierarchy. Despite the split, Tomlinson continued his work through the 1920s and 1930s, increasingly indulging his taste for spectacles and parades. He adopted the gospel country tune "Great Speckled Bird" as the church's own, interpreting the lyrics to suggest that the body of Christ on earth should consist of a "compound of all races and colors" and that the Church of God would be known by all races under "one rule, one faith or doctrine—all one." By the 1940s, there were three divisions of the Church of God, all derived from the original Christian Union dreams of poor white Pentecostal pioneers in the Tennessee mountains.[56]

Black Holiness and Pentecostalism

Holiness revivals also took hold in black church communities in the late nineteenth century, provoking the same friction with black Baptists and Methodists as it had with white believers. Like their white counterparts, early black Holiness believers in the South normally were refugees from Baptist and Methodist churches searching for higher spiritual experience. One early black Holiness convert was William Christian. Like his colleague Charles Harrison Mason, the future organizer of the Church of God in Christ, Christian turned away from Baptist churches, fearing they had lost the simplicity of primitive Christianity. William Christian perceived declension where others saw progress as ministers joined Masonic societies, peddled everything from pencils to tombstones, and promoted a restrained piety over ecstatic worship. In a series of dreams, Christian received divine instructions to form the Church of the Living God, Christian Workers for Fellowship, the first African American Holiness organization in the Mississippi/Arkansas Delta region. Within twenty years Christian claimed about 10,000 members in the area. William's wife, Ethel, also left her Baptist affiliation because, as she put it, "strange revelations began to unfold" from the Bible telling her to seek out an "unadulterated doctrine." Following her husband's death in 1928, she took over leadership of the Church of the Living God. Many black Holiness groups subsequently splintered off from William Christian's work, including the Church of the Living God, the Pillar and Ground of Truth (one of many smaller black Pentecostal bodies founded by women, and the home church of soul singer and Motown star Marvin Gaye and his father).[57]

Black Holiness groups, including Christian's, sprouted up in the late nineteenth century. In 1894, the United Holy Church of America established itself in the working-class tobacco town of Durham, North Carolina. Early on, the United Holy Church led interracial revivals at the First Baptist Church of Wilmington, North Carolina, in a tabernacle that proved too small for the "ever increasing crowds of all races and denominations." Shortly thereafter, the group secured a larger structure that could hold 4,000 congregants.[58]

The most significant black Holiness movement resulted from the collaboration (and, later, the split) between two Baptist ministers in Mississippi: Charles Price Jones and Charles Harrison Mason. The first, Charles P. Jones, claimed entire sanctification in 1894. Then pastoring a Baptist church, he was "not satisfied with a faith that brought no fruit, or else fruit of a poor quality, scripturally, and a religion that none of the signs spoken of in the Scriptures followed." He fasted three days and nights and, as God had promised him, was sanctified "sweetly in His love. New visions of Christ, of God, of truth, were given me," he later wrote, and "the earnestness of the Spirit was mine. I was sealed unto the day of Redemption." He subsequently accepted a call to Mt. Helm Baptist Church in Jackson, began publishing the *Truth* as an organ for the black Holiness movement, and organized a series of Holiness convocations. His enemies removed him from that pulpit, ending Jones's days in the Baptist ministry. As he publicly explained to his former colleagues, he was "walking but from corrupt and unscriptural denominationalism; from unscriptural names and methods; from man-made constitutions and institutions, and returning to New Testament names and the leadership of the Spirit of God." Jones joined with Charles Harrison Mason and others to form a nondenominational fellowship called the Churches of God in Christ.[59]

The Church of God in Christ (COGIC) emerged as the largest and most influential expression of black Pentecostalism. It sprang from the work of Jones, who later made his name as a prolific gospel songwriter and hymnologist, and the evangelist and organizer Charles Harrison Mason. While his colleague Charles Jones was something of a scholar and held a more prestigious Baptist pulpit, Mason was a quintessential folk preacher, one whose exuberant doctrinal readings could not be contained by the reigning denominational orthodoxies. Born to parents who had been slaves, Mason grew up intending to be a minister. "It seemed that God endowed him with supernatural characteristics," his daughter later said, "which were manifested in dreams and visions, that followed him through life." Mason's parents moved to Plumersville, Arkansas, in 1878, where Mason forsook his mission to preach until he was stricken with tuberculosis. He understood the disease as God's punishment for ignoring the call and his healing as a miraculous reprieve and divine message to pursue his spiritual duty. Mason attended Arkansas Baptist College briefly in the early 1890s but left school after a few months, declaring that God showed him "there was no salvation in schools and colleges." He "arose and bade them a final farewell, to follow Jesus, with the Bible as my sacred guide." In 1897, Mississippi black Baptists ordered him to vacate his pulpit for the offense of preaching holiness doctrines. He then found an abandoned gin house to use for a revival. After their conversion to holiness beliefs, Jones and Mason formed the Churches of God in Christ in 1897.[60]

In the early 1900s, Mason walked from town to town in the Mississippi Delta teaching Holinesss. James Delk, a white man converted under Mason's preaching in Conway, Arkansas, was one of a large crowd standing around a cotton wagon listening spellbound to Mason's sermons and songs for over an hour one day in 1904. "That day Brother Mason made an impression on me that I have never forgotten and can never forget," he later reminisced. "Brother Mason attended college very little but has as wide experience with human nature and an understanding of his fellow man such as no other man seems to have." Shortly thereafter, Delk himself founded a COGIC congregation in Madisonville, Kentucky, an offense to local racial mores that earned him a beating by local vigilantes.[61]

Charles Harrison Mason was not satisfied with the second blessing of sanctification. Like other early Pentecostals, he yearned for a yet more profound spiritual transport. He found it at the Azusa Street revival upon receiving the final Holy Spirit baptism at the hands of William J. Seymour. During a night of prayer, Mason saw a vision. He felt compelled to chew a dry roll of paper; he tried to swallow it and looked up to see a man at his side. Awaking from the vision, he realized that "God had me swallowing the whole book" and that he had to turn to God alone for answers. He cried out for the culmination of the work of sanctification. Soon he felt himself levitated from his seat. "There came a wave of glory into me," as he described it, "and all of my being was filled with the glory of the Lord. So when He had gotten me straight on my feet there came a light which enveloped my entire being above the brightness of the Sun. When I opened my mouth to say glory, a flame touched my tongue which ran down in me. My language changed and no word could I speak in my own tongue." Upon returning home, he felt that the "Spirit had taken full control of me and everything was new to me. I soon found out the Lord was teaching me and giving me new songs. I asked Him to give me the interpretation of what was spoken in tongues for I did not understand the operation of the spirit. . . . The Lord stood me up on that day and I began to speak in tongues and interpret the same. He soon gave me all kinds of spiritual utterances," as well as "all kinds of drawings and spiritual writings . . . done without any thought of my mind."[62]

When Mason added tongues speech as part of his theological arsenal, Jones "disfellowshipped" his former Holiness comrade. Legal tussles ensued, resulting in Mason's establishing the COGIC, and Jones remaining in Mississippi with his Holiness faction, renamed as the Church of Christ (Holiness), U.S.A. Lacking an incorporated organization of their own, white Pentecostals used ordination in COGIC to access valuable privileges such as reduced-rate clergy passes on the railroads. For Mason, this development exemplified Christian unity. For the white Pentecostals, however, it was more a pragmatic concession to legal reality until they could form their own recognized entities. Even in the most open and flexible of southern religious groups, even among white believers who were relatively receptive to substantive interchange with black brethren, race hierarchies were preserved.

Early Pentecostals recognized Mason's special powers of discernment; and some in his congregations might have perceived Mason's direct appropriation of conjuring traditions in the service of his preaching. When theologians exhausted themselves confounding people with intellectual eloquence, wrote one admirer, Mason would pick up a stick "shaped in the exact likeness of a snake in its growth, or a potato shaped in the exact likeness of the head and ears of a pig in its growth, and demonstrate with such authority and power that thousands of hearers are put on a wonder. It appears that he is reading his message from a scroll which is concealed within some one of the recesses of the object from which he is preaching." Mason was not shy about his bringing his version of root-work to white Pentecostals, either. When Mason went to the formative convention of the Assemblies of God in 1914, he used the sweet potato as an homiletic device to illustrate the movement of God's spirit. He took the trunk of two saplings grown in the shape of a hand and foot (the former with five fingers and the latter with five toes) and gave the object this interpretation: "It's God's time to cut off His children from worldliness setting them apart in His will baptized in the Christ mind." Mason illustrated God's message in memorable ways: "As he turns it over and from side to side God's mystery comes out of it; God's warning to His people is given, God's understanding is made known to them that are sanctified . . . among all classes and types, the people are captivated for they hear the voice of God, pertaining to the signs." Mason's followers respected his supernatural gifts: "The manifestations of these powers is clear, plain and simple in unfolding the mystery of godliness." Criticized for importing conjure into the churches, the COGIC founder pointed to the scriptures indicating that Jesus employed the same kinds of healings and spirit possessions that he himself also preached.[63]

Mason's preaching skill garnered considerable attention in and around Memphis and in Pentecostal circles more generally. He proudly recounted that in his early career, the Holy Spirit through him "saved, sanctified and baptized thousands of souls of all colors and races." Mason enticed crowds of whites and blacks to see him in action. In Nashville, for example, he attracted a sizable audience to a city auditorium in 1916. "Many of the best white people of the city attended the meeting," Mason claimed. "The Holy Spirit through me did many wonderful things." A series of services in Little Rock in 1919 reportedly produced the same effect, as "God so wonderfully wrought His power among both white and black, sanctifying, baptizing, and healing." In 1933, the church's newspaper, the *Whole Truth*, noted that "both white and colored testified of the wonderful healing power of God" at the COGIC annual convention in Rocky Mount, North Carolina. During these years, Mason traveled with a white minister named W. B. Holt; the two sometimes were arrested for violating Jim Crow customs, for Christian interracialism was legally actionable in the apartheid South.[64]

Jones and Mason both served long careers as church leaders—Jones until 1949 and Mason to 1961. But it was Mason who best captured the spiritual zeitgeist, as the Church of God in Christ rapidly became the largest black Pentecostal denomination in the country. Mason's creation became a significant force in American cultural life, in large part through its recapturing of the black sacred musical traditions spurned by established denominationalists, music that inspired secular and religious American popular song form later in the twentieth century.

COGIC meetings resounded with spirited expression and powerfully hypnotic music employing repetitive chanted phrases. At one COGIC service in the 1930s, an observer recounted how individual prayers sometimes lasting more than an hour filled the interior of the building with a "confusion of sounds." Gradually, the "muscular twitchings become observable, and automatic motions of limbs become more frequent in some. . . . Still others get worked up to a state in which they seem to writhe in pain and go through several forms of bodily contortions, even doubling up with the head drawn between the knees so as to form a ball of the body"—the kind of behavior from which the derisive term "holy rollers" originated. Zora Neale Hurston described how the sermon in the sanctified church was "not the set thing that it is in other Protestant churches. It is loose and formless and is in reality merely a framework upon which to hang more songs. Every opportunity to introduce a new rhythm is eagerly seized upon. The whole movement of the sanctified church is a rebirth of song-making! It has brought in a new era of spiritual-making. . . . Shouting—which is just possession —is prevalent in Negro Protestant churches and is universal in the sanctified churches. They protest against the more highbrow churches' efforts to stop it." Sanctified services were really "drama with music," Hurston concluded.[65]

Sanctified churches grew as congregants moved out of their former Baptist and Methodist affiliations. While serving as a Baptist preacher in Nacogdoches, Texas, Charley White heard of sanctified people who were said to "put some kind of spell on folks." Initially he was unreceptive to the movement of the Spirit: "I'd been telling other folks about their sins, and how they ought to live. What would they think when they saw me on the altar." Finally humbled, he received the gift of the Holy Ghost:

Was not nothing to it after I got myself straightened out. It sure felt good. I'd never been anyways near this close to God before. The Church of God in Christ people made me a preacher in their church right then. . . . And then all my congregation at Richardson's Chapel followed me into the Church of God in Christ, the ones that wasn't already there. So Richardson's Chapel become a Church of God in Christ church instead of a Baptist church. It didn't belong to the Baptists. It belong to the people there and me—we built it.

Ministers such as Charley White helped proselytize for COGIC and other black Holiness and Pentecostal groups. Black and white southern migrants brought their new churches to storefronts and roadsides in the North and West.[66]

Women played a key role in the Pentecostal expansion as well. Women's voices in the pulpit, in prophesying, and in church leadership were far more common in what were perceived to be fringe sects. Common Pentecostal understandings of the latter days, in which "your daughters shall prophesy," and a generally egalitarian understanding of human relationships before God meant that men and women in Pentecostalism enjoyed some degree of equality even while Pentecostal organizations gradually restricted women's leadership roles.

As in every other Pentecostal denomination, women formed the majority of COGIC members; and like virtually every other sanctified group, Mason's church afforded some leeway for women's authority, short of leadership positions in the church hierarchy. COGIC women established some churches for the denomination but were not authorized to pastor them. Mason also rejected the ordaining of women as bishops. COGIC women who worked for the church usually took the status of missionaries, a category given over nearly exclusively to them. Mother Arenia C. Mallory, for example, became president of the Saints Academy (a COGIC school) in Lexington, Mississippi, in 1918. But if COGIC women were limited in positions of pastoral authority, they were given free reign in the women's auxiliary that stood behind Mason's work.[67]

In addition to COGIC, black Pentecostalism spawned any number of other sects and churches. Some grew to be established denominations; others dwindled or were irreparably divided after the passing of a charismatic founding mother or father. Women created many of the black Pentecostal sects, including the Mount Sinai Church of Bishop Ida Robinson (about 465 churches in the 1990s), Bishop Lillian Tate's the Church of the Living God (with about 500 churches by the 1990s), and Bishop Mary Daniels's the House of God (with 412 churches). One of the more significant of these denominations originated in 1908 from the work of Mother Mary Magdalena Tate, first chief overseer of what became the Church of the Living God, the Pillar and Ground of Truth, Inc. Tate called together "the humble people of the southern sections of the country into the true light of the gospel of Jesus Christ in true holiness." She preached Holiness to people who had not heard the new word, teaching the new faith in the "homes of both white and colored." Upon delivering her message to a black Presbyterian church in a small Tennessee town, she proudly recounted that "never will it be forgotten how the power of God lifted physically strong men as well as women from off their seats while she preached and taught the people that night. . . . Grown men shouted, leaped, and wept for joy." In 1908, she conducted the first general assembly of the church in Greenville, Alabama, where dozens were sanctified. The sect grew slowly through the years.[68]

In most early Pentecostal groups, female leadership gradually gave way to a more conventional male-dominated hierarchy. Nevertheless, through the twentieth century, independent Pentecostal churches provided opportunities for women that were unavailable elsewhere. For example, Mother Mable Smith unofficially pastored the Rescue Temple COGIC in Greensboro, North Carolina. Her husband, ostensibly the church's pastor, provided her political cover. She traveled through the state as an evangelist, song leader, and administrator. Although she headed women's work for the church, she also demonstrated that women did not have to be confined to the prescribed roles of missionaries and evangelists. Before a 1991 COGIC convention in North Carolina, she proclaimed:

> I was not called to be a missionary. God told me that I was a prophetess. Yes a prophetess! As a prophetess I was not called to fry fish and chicken, roles that have been designated for missionaries. God sent me forth to establish churches. In fact he has used me to establish seven of them. I don't have the title of a pastor but I'm doing the work. I don't have the title of a district superintendent but I assist my husband who is a district superintendent in supervising the Churches in the district that I personally hewed out. My ministry has not been certified by man but it has been sanctioned by God. God has used me to pray for the sick and see them recover, and I have conducted numerous revivals in convention halls with hundreds of people in attendance. After all God places no restrictions on women, only men do. After God has removed the yokes from our necks [men] have tried to put them back on us.[69]

"Crackers and Niggers Be Shouting Everywhere": Music, Race, and Religious Cultures

Holiness and Pentecostal denominations generally remained much smaller than their mainstream Protestant (meaning mostly Baptist and Methodist) counterparts, but they exercised an outsized influence on southern and American religious life because of their culturally innovative practices, most especially in music. The persistence of vernacular conversion visions and rituals, conjure, and the tongues speech and ecstatic worship of Pentecostalism suggests that the practice of religion often has eluded the control of religious specialists and official theologies. The transformation of singing practices and hymnology also illustrates the interaction of tradition and innovation in popular piety. The rise of southern sacred vernacular music in the nineteenth century and its development and popularization in the twentieth demonstrate the lasting impact of racial and cultural interchange in southern religion.

Just after the Civil War, Charles Satchell of the American Baptist Free Mission Society moved to New Orleans, organized several black churches and associations in the area, and set about acquiring the accoutrements essential to proper worship. With northern financial assistance, Satchell's flagship congregation in New Orleans bought an organ and recruited a "reasonably fair choir of singers." Satchell forecast a finer style of worship for his church: "I think when we get fairly on the way, with the improvements in singing, order in worship &c., the people who may attend will see the advantages of an enlightened state of things, and it will be the leaven that will work until old fogyism and the tyranny of the old churches, with the popish idea of old shepherds and gospel mothers, lords over God's heritage, will be unknown." A choir, AME bishop Daniel Payne believed, could be shaped into a "power and efficient auxiliary to the pulpit. Two things are essential to the saving power and efficiency of choral music—a scientific training and an earnest Christianity."[70]

Satchell and Payne's efforts presaged a generation who taught congregants to sing "scientifically and correctly," as AME bishop Levi Coffin put it. A younger colleague of Payne's, Coffin grew up as a slave in Maryland and later edited the *A.M.E. Church Review*, the church's high-toned intellectual periodical. As a young man, he possessed a gift for singing, and older congregants depended on him to furnish song leading. But he was self-conscious that "these home-made tunes were but makeshifts, and I only awaited an opportunity to take up the study of vocal music, and prepare myself to do scientifically and correctly the work that I was forced to do by guess."[71]

Denominational reformers such as Coffin experienced some success, especially in larger urban congregations that increasingly adopted acculturated worship forms. Antebellum southern sacred song, such as the spirituals and lined-out hymnody, intermixed with musical influences from missionaries, popular tunes, and the writings of black and white gospel hymnists. In the process, southern religious music diversified, and not always in the manner that missionaries and reformers desired. Worshippers altered tunes from varied sources into incantatory cadences that allowed for improvisation even within the formulaic structures of gospel songs. Urban black churches used hymn books with "little of the genuine negro element left in them," Mary Allan-Olney noted, but congregants nevertheless massaged new tunes with older styles of vocal expressiveness. A few lines sung out by the leader would simply be repeated, each time getting louder. Soon the "ordinary Sabbath school songs" would be transformed into music reflecting the distinctive style of African American culture. During the singing, congregants often rose up spontaneously and related conversion experiences, "always talking in a scream, as if crying." The congregations supplied rhythm with clapping and bodily movement, "gradually increasing to a stamp as the exercises proceeded, until the noise was deafening." The noted anthropologist Melville Herskovits also documented how an ordinary gospel hymn would be converted into a song "typically African in its accompaniment of clapping hands and foot-patting, and in its singing style. All that is left of the original hymn is the basic melody which, as a constant undercurrent to the variations that play about it, constitutes the unifying element in this amazingly illuminating music."[72]

In both white and black churches, congregational demands for newer gospel hymns of the Moody-Sankey variety (scorned by one denominationalist as "pious jigs") compelled publishers to respond. Over time, the hymnody of sentimental Victorianism overpowered the guardians of musical and theological orthodoxy, who preferred the "classical" Protestant music of eighteenth-century vintage. By 1913, a prominent Southern Baptist seminary professor advised ministers to adapt to the styles desired by congregants: "One of the severest tests of the devotion and adaptability of the cultured minister is his ability and willingness to lay aside the fringes and adornments of culture and so come at the heart of realities as to hold and help the plain man in his worship. Popular gospel hymns, sung with verve and vigour, may not satisfy the artistic taste of the cultured, but they serve the purpose of worship for the common man far better than more elevated efforts."[73]

Religious publishers eagerly pushed for printed hymnals and other ways to help acculturate southern sacred musical styles into the American Protestant mainstream. The black Baptist entrepreneur Richard Henry Boyd almost singlehandedly built the largest black-owned publishing house in the country, the National Baptist Publishing Board. His agency sold everything from hymnals to church pews to black dolls. Boyd compiled and printed formal anthems for church choirs and published hymnals for use in Sunday schools. He also put out cheap pocket editions for mass use, allowing each church member to "select and sing the old metered songs of his or her choice." Like the gospel hymnists, Boyd believed that doctrine could be "more easily taught in poetry set to music than it can be by dry prose." His publishing house also recognized the desire of congregants for compilations of black sacred music drawn from the folk tradition, especially the spirituals. In 1916, Boyd's agency produced the *National Jubilee Melodies*, one of the first collections that brought these African American classics into printed circulation. "These melodies express the emotion of the soul of the Negro race as no other collection of music — classically or grammatically constructed could possibly do," he wrote of this anthology of what W. E. B. Du Bois called the "sorrow songs."[74]

In the early twentieth century, black religious publishers mixed "classical" Protestant music (such as the Isaac Watts hymns) and the spirituals with newer gospel compositions from black and white authors, signaling the diversification of black sacred music. In 1909, a group of black Methodists printed *Soul Echoes: A Collection of Songs for Religious Meetings*, an anthology dominated by contributions from the pioneering black gospel composer Charles Albert Tindley (credited with classic tunes such as "He'll Understand It Better By and By" and "I Will Overcome"). Again, congregational demand for music in the black vernacular remained strong despite the penchant of reformers for classical Protestant music. The seminal songbook *Gospel Pearls*, edited by black Baptist musician and arranger W. M. Nix in 1921, was perhaps the single most significant collection of African American sacred music in the twentieth century. The compilation took in classical Protestant hymnody, the black spirituals, standard gospel songs from the Moody-Sankey era, and innovative choruses of Holiness-Pentecostal invention. The introduction of *Gospel Pearls* warned of the "tendency to get away from that fervency of spirit and song that characterized the church and altar worship of other days, and which contributes so much to the stability of our religion." The hymnbook thus sought to preserve the "good old soul-stirring hymns of days gone by" while providing space for newer compositions. Anglo-Protestant hymnody intermingled with gospel tunes of the late nineteenth century, spirituals ("jubilee songs"), and early black gospels from songwriters such as Charles Albert Tindley, Lucie Campbell, W. J. Harvey, Thomas Dorsey, and Carrie Booker Persons.[75]

Gospel Pearls was the first official hymnbook for the nation's largest black denomination, the National Baptist Convention. By bringing "trills and turns" into the music, Nix's own performances at convention meetings enthralled listeners, and his melismatic and blues-inspired improvisations defined black gospel styling. "Hymn singers, they couldn't put this stuff in it," black gospel musician and composer Thomas Dorsey said of his colleague Nix. "What he did, I wouldn't call blues, but it had a touch of the blue note there. Now that's the turn and the feeling that really made the gospel singers." Gradually, the sacred forms of "white" hymns and folk religious harmonies from shape-note books, black spirituals, Holiness-Pentecostal rhythms and raptures, and gospel from both traditions mixed with the secular forms of the blues, reaching a synthesis in the gospel blues of the mid-twentieth century.[76]

Shape-Note Singing and White Religious Expression

For much of the nineteenth century, white southerners only grudgingly accepted aesthetic cultivation in sacred spaces. Controversies over musical instruments (particularly organs) tore apart some congregations that could afford to purchase them. "I verily believe God will not suffer this *Beast* to rule in Baptist churches," a South Carolinian exclaimed of the organ. Yet he found it "little use to speak and argue against it," as it became a staple of church life. The organ, fretted one Presbyterian, was "a kind of *luxury*" that forced believers "either to abandon our church or witness the profanation of God's worship." Choirs outfitted in robes, moreover, took from congregations the "right to praise God in singing. For there the general aim and style of the singing is offensive. May say they might as well go to the opera house at once." Qualms about the theology of performance troubled believers who were talented in music but scorned "mere display" as sinful. "Harmony is voluptuous," a nineteenth-century Virginian pondered in his diary. "It requires no pious emotions for a man to love harmony. In fact, by singing base and suffering my mind to be distracted from the words, by the 'lascivious pleasing' of chords, I am often unfitted for the other exercises of the Sanctuary." He felt that "mere accompaniments" should have no place in sacred music. Nevertheless, he sang in church because people enjoyed his voice.[77]

Southern evangelicals who had been suspicious of vocal display thus gradually accepted stylistically refined music as spiritually acceptable, even uplifting. By the mid-nineteenth century, larger congregations were moving away from a capella hymns lined out by individuals to congregational singing accompanied by pianos and organs. Soloists and other special performances graced urban worship services. Church leaders ridiculed the slow and seemingly discordant style of singing characteristic of rural upcountry and mountain congregations. Denominationalists initiated training programs in schools, encouraged the use of professional music ministers in wealthier churches, and promoted revivals with professionally skilled song leaders.[78]

In the mid-nineteenth century, educational entrepreneurs established singing schools to provide rudimentary musical training for plain-folk southerners. Educators generally used a simplified form of notation known as shape notes, a system of representing sounds on the page based on four shapes. Each shape stood for a note on a scale that retained fixed intervals, obviating the need to learn different key signatures. Of the many shape-note books published in the antebellum era, the *Sacred Harp* and the *Southern Harmony* proved the most influential. The key figures in the evolution of the *Sacred Harp* were Benjamin Franklin White, born at the beginning of the nineteenth century in South Carolina, and his brother-in-law William "Singing Billy" Walker. White published the *Sacred Harp* in 1844 and promoted revised editions of it until his death in 1879. With tunes based primarily on Celtic melodic fragments, each part was written to be melodically interesting by itself. Shape-note musical conventions featured chairs set in a square pattern facing inward and performers belting out tunes loudly, lending Sacred Harp singing the peculiarly vigorous quality that survived to be recorded in the twentieth century (and seen in the film adaptation of Charles Frazier's novel *Cold Mountain*). The shape-note style also penetrated black religious communities in the rural South, deeply influencing gospel singers such as R. H. Harris and his pioneering quartet, the Soul Stirrers.

Musical education through instruction in the shape-note method spread rapidly after the Civil War through the efforts of Aldine Kieffer, grandson of a shape-note pioneer, and his brother-in-law Ephraim Ruebush. Combatants on opposite sides of the Civil War, Kieffer and Ruebush reunited in the 1870s to found the Shenandoah Training School, a singing normal institute in Dayton, Virginia. The two also collaborated in publishing the *Musical Million*, a journal sent to some 10,000 subscribers. Kieffer and Ruebush hired Jesse Aikin, editor of the *Christian Minstrel*, who replaced the original four shaped notes with the seven of a regular octave. Kieffer pushed his work in musical reformation and the new-fangled seven-note system as the same "practical common sense" that fit an age of progress and science. Washing away the "old customs, old ideas, [and] old methods," he believed, would help southerners overcome their deficiencies in making a joyful, instead of discordant, noise.[79]

Kieffer and Ruebush's Shenandoah Normal School in Virginia trained numerous students and imitators, who formed a variety of schools and music publishing companies throughout the region. The most widely influential graduate of the Kieffer-Ruebush school, and the most important white musical promoter of the early twentieth century, was James D. Vaughan. Like the early black gospel pioneers, he spread popular music through church communities. The native of Lawrenceburg, Tennessee, grew up as a Methodist. As an adult, he joined the Church of the Nazarene, a Holiness sect that still practiced camp meetings and older features of southern religious life. After years of teaching school and singing with his siblings, Vaughan established a normal school of music, launched his own publishing company, and hired promotional touring singers. The publisher's star foursome traveled stylishly in a Model A, providing them the mobility to introduce the music, as well as Vaughan's sheet music, far afield. When a Vaughan group came to Kentucky in 1912, a local churchgoer expressed his amazement about how the shape-note music craze had "swept across the hills, hollows, and flatlands like a wildfire fanned by a strong wind." Vaughan also produced early phonograph recordings and broadcast his music on one of the first radio stations in Tennessee, WOAN. Through the 1930s, Vaughan continued to sell 200,000 songbooks a year and sent his publication, *Vaughan's Family Visitor*, to subscribers throughout the country. Into the 1920s and 1930s, shape-note singing remained part of small-town and rural southern life, especially among groups outside the mainstream denominational orbits.[80]

One of Vaughan's star pupils, Virgil O. Stamps, worked lumber in rural Texas prior to founding the most important gospel music publishing company of the twentieth century. He worked for the Vaughan company until, in a dramatic break with his mentor in 1924, he set up a rival enterprise in Dallas. Two years later, Jesse R. Baxter, another singing school recruit, joined forces with Stamps. Together, the two possessed the drive, expertise, and venture capital that propelled the Stamps-Baxter Company to become the dominant market leader in southern gospel music through the middle decades of the twentieth century. The Stamps All-Star Quartet, led by Frank Stamps (brother of V. O.), toured the South beginning in the late 1920s and later recorded for RCA Records. By World War II, Stamps-Baxter had overtaken Vaughan as the leading gospel music publishing house in the region. The company sponsored all-night singing fests, promoted its products on radio shows, and influenced black quartet singers. The Stamps-Baxter firm also hired black songwriters such as Cleavant Derricks, a Baptist minister from Chattanooga, to produce tunes for black quartets and churches that would find their way onto race records. Addressing concerns that the aggressively commercial tactics employed by Stamps-Baxter might cheapen the music, Wallace Fowler, a quartet singer and country music songwriter, responded, "If we sing hymns to practically every beat except the tango and the mambo, it's because it doesn't matter how you honor the Lord, just so you honor him." Southern gospel increasingly found a mass-media audience through radio and phonographs, accounting for about 20 percent of the material recorded by white and black performers for Columbia Records in its early years.[81]

By the 1930s, successive generations spawned by the *Sacred Harp* and *Southern Harmony* tradition, shape-note writers, and the original Kieffer-Ruebush singing schools had formed a variety of competing gospel publishing firms. Each supported its own touring quartets that hawked songbooks in a variety of venues from church services to radio programs, uniting what had been a diverse set of intraregional musical styles. The original idea of singing schools and musical conventions, to train ordinary folk to read simple music and vocalize harmoniously, had metamorphosed into what became the entertainment conglomerate of "southern gospel." Although meant primarily for whites, southern gospel also influenced black performers, who sought the largest audience possible for their innovative styles.

Professional Gospel Music

The rise of "southern gospel" and "black gospel" in the twentieth century illuminates the separate and shared traditions of the white and black evangelical South. From the early intermingling of Protestant hymns and African styles into spirituals, to the mixing of white and black country and gospel sounds on the radio, two streams of musical religious culture traveled beside each other, never merging but often intersecting. The gospel business, according to music historian Bill Malone, evolved from shape-note singing schools and evangelical revivals "but drew much of its dynamism and much of its personnel from the Holiness-Pentecostal movement of the late nineteenth century and early twentieth century. By 1900 a great stream of religious songs, fed by the big-city revivals of the era, flowed into American popular culture." Publishing houses within and outside denominations cranked out paperback hymnals for church meetings and singing schools. Beyond the church walls, white and black secular and religious musicians traded licks, vocal styles, and lyrics. Evangelistic itinerants spread the message through the music of the people. Brother and Sister George Goings took the Holiness gospel through Tennessee and Kentucky in the last years of the nineteenth century, introducing tunes (such as "There's a Little Black Train A Coming") that later would be recorded by minister-performers such as J. M. Gates. As Malone explains, "whether black or white, Pentecostal evangelists such as George Goings, armed with guitar and Bible, accompanied perhaps by a mandolin-strumming or tambourine-shaking wife, and preaching on street corners, under brush arbors, in tents, or in storefront churches, took their places alongside the shape-note teachers and gospel quartets as major agents in the fashioning of the southern gospel music repertory."[82]

Opportunities beckoned everywhere for songwriters and performers. As a result, the Vaughan and Stamps-Baxter outfits, with their myriad competing quartets, songbooks, hymnals, and salesmen, could not retain their most talented employees. One of them, a native of Spiro, Oklahoma, named Alfred E. Brumley, emerged as the premier white gospel songwriter of his era. Brumley worked with a music company in Arkansas, taught in singing schools, played piano, and composed hymns. Brumley left the Stamps-Baxter empire to form his own business with Eugene Bartlett (composer of the gospel standard "Victory in Jesus") in Hartford, Arkansas. In 1931, Brumley penned his classic "I'll Fly Away." Eventually becoming Brumley's signature tune, "I'll Fly Away" perfectly captured the fond hopes for a future life that permeated white gospel music lyrics. During his long and productive career, Brumley composed some 700 songs, including "Turn Your Radio On," "He Set Me Free," and a bluegrass standard later made famous by Ralph and Carter Stanley (and much later by Bob Dylan), "Rank Strangers to Me":

> Everybody I met Seem to be a rank stranger;
> No mother or dad, Not a friend could I see.
> They knew not my name And I knew not their faces—
> I found they were all Rank strangers to me.

Brumley's songs usually painted a blissful picture of a benevolent God, who would gather his children in heaven on "some glad morning," where no one would be a rank stranger. In later years, any number of brothers duets carried country gospel forward. The powerful Louvin Brothers duo, for example, with Ira supplying a piercingly high tenor and Charlie providing a lead voice, warned of the dangers awaiting the uncoverted in "Are You Afraid to Die" and looked forward to the joys of heaven on "I'm Going Home." Their marriage of religion and commerce is evident on the phantasmagorically kitschy cover to their gospel album *Satan Is Real*, featuring the gawking white-suited brothers standing in front of a giant devil-with-pitchfork figure on the burning coals of hell.

The sounds of up-country singing—lined-out hymnody, *Sacred Harp* tunes, and the widespread gospel tunes—eventually found their way into the repertoire of bluegrass, traditional gospel, and newer country groups ranging from Roy Acuff and the Smokey Mountain Boys, Flatt and Scruggs, the Louvin Brothers, the Stanley Brothers, Bill Monroe's bands, the Osborne Brothers, and dozens of others. The familiar themes of focusing on the joys of salvation and eternal life and avoiding worldly entanglements dominated country gospel, heard in such classics of the genre as "Working on a Building":

> I'm working on a building, I'm working on a building
> I'm working on a building, for my Lord, for my Lord.
> It's a holy ghost building, it's a holy ghost building,
> It's a holy ghost building, for my Lord, for my Lord.

Whether performed by the slicker vocal quartets or by the more country sounding string bands and bluegrass groups, songs in the genre typically portrayed surviving the harsh journeys of life, with a "Bible for my roadmap," to get to "my last stop in heaven some sweet day." Lester Flatt and Earl Scruggs sang of "working on a road, that leads to glory / I want to shake my Saviour's hand." The "gospel highway" would lead to final escape and rest. Aside from "I'll Fly Away," perhaps the best-known song of the genre was "I Saw the Light," which Hank Williams adapted freely from the lyrics and music of Albert E. Brumley's "He Set Me Free":

> I wandered so aimless, life filled with sin,
> I wouldn't let my dear Saviour in:
> Then Jesus came like a stranger in the night,
> Praise the Lord I saw the light.
> (refrain) I saw the light, I saw the light, no more sorrow no more night,
> Now I'm so happy no sorrow in sight, praise the Lord, I saw the light.[83]

Holiness/Pentecostal churches raised up many of the most innovative gospel musicians. Pentecostals were known for up-tempo, rhythmically expressive music. More conservative members worried about the prevalence of sacred songs set to "ragtime" in their churches, fearing that believers would "work themselves into a frenzy playing and singing in the effort to please their listeners. . . . Jazzy music and singing is merely a substitute, and instead of appealing to deep spirituality it caters to the natural man." Still, the Pentecostals served as a ready market for new gospel tunes and enthusiastic singing that complemented the cadence of their services.[84]

The white singer James Blackwood remembered that Pentecostal churches were the "first denomination to use our type of Gospel music. They were more given to singing songs with a beat. They weren't afraid to clap their hands and pat their feet." Doyle and James Blackwood formed the nucleus of the most important white gospel quartet of the twentieth century, the Blackwood Brothers. The natives of Choctaw County, Mississippi, became the standard-bearers for the new age of white gospel performers. Growing up, Doyle Blackwood (born 1911) and brother James (born 1919) were consumed with ambition to become professional gospel singers. They practiced while working in the fields, imitating the performers of their day and developing a strong-throated style that could fill auditoriums with sound. "We promised each other to learn everything about Gospel Music and Gospel Singing," James later said, "until such time as we could set out on our own, and do our very best to establish our name of Blackwood as a household word in gospel singing circles." When the family purchased a Victrola record player in the early 1930s, the boys learned to mimic the vocal effects of early quartet groups, who were smoothing out and introducing more sophisticated harmonies to the coarser and more antiquated shape-note sounds.

Enrollment in a singing school provided the Blackwoods an opportunity to perfect their quartet style. They formed their first group in the mid-1930s and began recording on a radio show in Kosciusko, Mississippi. Immediately popular with listeners, they sought larger audiences from a more widely broadcast station in Jackson. The Blackwoods pursued singing opportunities avidly, performing several times a day on the radio. The Stamps-Baxter firm arranged the business side of their tours (as well as a company piano player to accompany the quartet), while the Blackwoods promoted the burgeoning publisher's products; the relationship was profitable for both parties. During World War II, while working in a shipyard in San Diego, the Blackwoods introduced southern gospel quartet music to the West Coast. Later, they recorded their own discs and sold them through mail order, thus circumventing the old publisher-performer relationship and establishing the beginnings of their business empire. Meanwhile, they continued singing on the radio, producing other sides for RCA Records, and pioneering bus concert tours of the country (later a staple of popular music entertainers). After the war, the Blackwoods settled in Memphis, where they reigned as the kings of white gospel. James Blackwood attended the same Pentecostal church (the First Ascendant Assembly of God Church) as Elvis Presley. The brothers eventually bought out the copyrights to the Vaughan publisher songbooks and merged them with their own record label. One of the major touring black gospel quartet groups, the Golden Gate Quartet, often was paired with white groups, including the Blackwoods, but the tensions of the 1950s made such racial intermingling on the musical stage suspect and increasingly rare.[85]

Gospel quartets increasingly followed popular styles, provoking a perplexed James Vaughan to ask, "Why should people who love the Lord and clean Christian society have to listen to music of the 'juke box' to find a medium of expression toward God?" Despite such concerns, the music of southern Protestantism and the tunes of the juke box intermingled frequently through the twentieth century—as did the musical worlds of white and black southerners.[86]

Blues and Black Gospel

Black gospel emerged from a tangled history of nineteenth-century spirituals, Moody-Sankey hymns, and a variety of twentieth-century sources, including Holiness-Pentecostal forms, as well as the blues and bawdy music. Early controversies over the relationship between the blues and sacred song gradually disappeared as the forms increasingly intersected in the commercial world of popular music. In the early twentieth century, however, the tension was very real, as the two forms vied for the soul of black American performers and their audiences. As a young man, W. C. Handy worked as a janitor for a white Baptist church. He listened each Sunday as his own father, a black Baptist minister, pounded the pulpit. With his earnings, the young Handy bought a guitar and proudly brought it home. "A guitar!" his father exclaimed. "One of the devil's playthings! Take it away. . . . Get it out of your hands. Whatever possessed you to bring a sinful thing like that into our Christian home? Take it back where it came from! You hear?

Get!" Handy dutifully exchanged the instrument for a dictionary—a temporary retreat for the man who popularized the blues form for a wider American audience, even if he was not the "father of the blues" as proclaimed by overeager publicists of the time.[87]

The blues and religion competed for souls, a theme often played out in blues music and in the frequent migrations of performers from one genre to another. The bluesman and preacher Son House was conscious of his own sin as he wavered between preaching the gospel and singing the devil's music. When he bowed to pray in his room, according to one of his autobiographical compositions, the blues came along and drove his spirit into exile. "I can't hold God in one hand and the Devil in the other," he said in 1965 just before performing "Preachin' the Blues," one of his classics from 1930. "Them two guys don't get along together too well. I got to turn one of 'em loose. So I got out of the pulpit." Son House's struggles duplicated those of a generation of talented men and women who saw the church as an avenue for respectability but could not reconcile themselves to the self-abnegation required of evangelicals. Son House took his 1930 recording of "Preachin' the Blues" from Bessie Smith's 1927 version of the song, adding in his own autobiographical struggles:

Oh I have religion this very day,
But the womens and whiskey, well they would not let me pray.
Oh, well, I wish I had me a heaven of my own
Well, I'd give all my women a long, long happy home.
Oh, I got to stay on the job, I ain't got no time to lose
I swear to God, I got to preach those gospel blues.
Oh I'm going to preach these gospel blues and choose my seat and sit down.
When the spirit comes sisters, I want you to jump straight up and down.

The choice was clear for those of Son House's generation, including a South Carolina native and guitarist named George Scarborough. A churchgoer all his life, Scarborough tried to parlay his talents into a career of sacred music. Eventually, he stopped playing gospel because he did not want it known that he played the clubs on Saturday night and the churches on Sunday. Restrictions against the "devil's instrument" eventually eased, "but they had outlawed it before," he reminisced. Musicians in a later era would mix genres freely, but Scarborough felt that he "had to make a choice. Right, I felt like I had to make a choice."[88]

Many bluesmen saw themselves as the conscience of the community, at the periphery of Christianity and alternative forms of supernaturalism. The blues conflated the Christian and African (the trickster and subsequent bad man) and mixed in a variety of Euro-American folk beliefs. Bluesmen often referred to themselves as "devils," linking themselves to the prodigal son archetype, those who returned to religion after a debauched sojourn. "I was a great musician," said one who struggled with his calling, "and at times, after I had spent seasons at fasting and praying, I would get tired of it and go back to the ways of the world. You see, the devils knows how to tempt a man. He always reminds him of the things he likes best, and in this way he can get his attention." B. B. King said of the bluesmen and religion that, while "a lot of them didn't go the way of church," they still possessed the "same feeling" as church people. The bluesmen invoked sacred power while singing about profane things. Rubin Lacy, a well-known blues guitarist and later a Methodist preacher, claimed to tell more truth in his blues than many people would in church. "Sometimes the best Christian in the world have the blues quicker than a sinner do, 'cause the average sinner ain't got nothing to worry about. . . . But a Christian is obliged to certain things and obligated not to do certain things. That sometimes cause a Christian to take the blues."[89]

Rural southern bluesmen served as folk theologians. They explored the nature of good and evil, commented profoundly on the nature of human relationships, and lampooned the hypocrisies of supposedly respectable community leaders. The preachers and the bluesmen saw themselves as ferocious competitors in a zero-sum game. But they offered two apparently contradictory but ultimately complementary versions of black folk spirituality—a close parallel to the relationship between conjure and African American religion discussed earlier. The country blues offered a theodicy, but one that reinforced enmity in human relations, hence the frequent emphasis on using conjure as a force of revenge on one's enemy. Many blues portrayed the inability of humans to sustain relationships, improve their condition, or encounter the Sacred as something other than a trickster.[90]

The blues also presented a medium for older African-derived spiritualities driven underground by the relentlessly assimilationist program of established religious leaders. The visionary experiences of both converts and bluesmen drew from a long tradition of African American folk visionary thought that entrusted spirits to guide individual lives. With a narrative structure remarkably similar to the conversion narratives, Robert Johnson, the great Mississippi Delta bluesman of the 1930s, sung of how "me and the devil was walking side by side," personified the blues as "walkin' like a man," and expected his spirit to be laid by the roadside. Johnson lyrically embellished his version of the mythic Faustian bargain at the crossroads, where he received special dispensation to play the guitar. Many other bluesmen followed in his steps, adding their own variations on the prototypical tales of selling out to the devil. They may have done so precisely because they were not that frightened of the evil presence. Closer to the trickster gods of Africa than to the darkly powerful Satan of Western Christianity, the devil in African American folklore was a force at once attractive, amusing, and frightening, just as were the bluesmen themselves to black southerners.

In the mid-twentieth century, those who came from rural traditions, both white and black, purchased instruments from mail-order catalogues, listened and imitated musicians played on the radio, and gradually created musical forms that merged what had been highly distinct secular and sacred styles. In the popular tune "Life's Railway to Heaven," written by the white Georgia Holiness pioneer Charles Tillman, the train was a vehicle carrying both physical and spiritual deliverance. In "When the Train Comes Along," Henry Thomas, an itinerant musician and preacher, waited at the depot for Jesus to take him in:

I'm praying in my heart, I'm cryin' out of my eyes
That Jesus has died for my sins.
I will meet you at the station, I'll meet you in the smoke
I will meet you at the station when the train come a[long].
When the train come along, the train come along.

In southern religious imagery, trains were the path to salvation. Blind Lemon Jefferson, a gifted guitarist and troubadour, added songs about traveling across the Jordan River, where "Jesus gonna be my engineer," expressing the popular notion of the train as a vehicle to Canaan land. Through the twentieth century, the train found its way into innumerable song lyrics, as well as personal testimonies. One conversion narrative relates how the seeking mourner stood on a platform at a train station, then "knelt to pray. As I knelt Jesus handed me a ticket. It was all signed with my name. I arose to my feet and handed it in at the window and was told to take my place with the three men standing on the platform and wait." The train also symbolized transport in the other direction for sinners who were not right with God. In more than 300 recordings made in the 1920s, the Reverend J. M. Gates, a well-known pastor in Atlanta, recorded classics of chanted sermonizing and singing such as "Death's Black Train Is Coming." His rendition of the well-traveled song sold over 35,000 copies and helped to establish Gates as one of the most popular artists for Columbia Records. Just as Bessie Smith and other pioneers brought vocalizations of earlier eras to recorded blues, Gates imported African American folk sermonic forms to his prolific output of three-minute record sides:

O, The Little Black Train is coming.
Get all you business right.
You'd better set you house in order
For that train may be here tonight.[91]

In addition to Gates, hundreds of preachers, songsters, and bluesmen took their turns at commercial recording. Some eagerly sought out these opportunities, while others were discovered accidentally by talent scouts for fledgling record companies and folklorists such as the father-and-son team of John and Alan Lomax. Altogether, these artists left a legacy that makes clear the ubiquity of particular sermonic forms, song styles, and lyrical lines, as well as the diverse array of styles that shaped southern sacred music. In addition to the ubiquitous blues-influenced forms that made their way onto race records meant for a religious audience, white and black performers borrowed freely from just about every musical tradition they could find. Thus, blues runs and African American syncopation found their way into the styles of white singers, while "white" lyrical themes, instrumental adaptations, and harmonic structures influenced scores of black religious performers. For example, a hillbilly mandolin graces the black Pentecostal Ford Washington McGee's 1927 rendition of the "white" gospel hymn "Rock of Ages, Cleft for Me" (in stark contrast to the polyphonic Sanctified revelry of his first recording, "Lion in the Tribe of Judah"). McGee's talented piano player, Arizona Dranes, belted out barrelhouse lines and nascent rhythm-and-blues lines in her records in 1926 and 1928. The black gospel singer Alex Bradford saw her perform some years later in Bessemer, Alabama, where he remembered that "crackers and niggers be shouting everywhere."

Ignoring race lines, an ever-growing storehouse of songs, lyrics, tunes, and sermonic lines passed back and forth among musicians and recording preachers and songsters. "O Death," "John the Revelator," "Please See My Grave Is Kept Clean," and numerous gospel tunes from the late nineteenth and early twentieth centuries coursed through white and black southern sacred song. For example, a variety of white and black country and gospel singers recorded "John the Revelator." The best-known version (partly because of the recording's inclusion on Harry Smith's "Anthology of American Folk Music," which introduced a subsequent generation to the music of this era), features the ferociously growling Texas street guitarist and singing evangelist Blind Willie Johnson asking, "Who's that writing," his wife Angeline answering "John the Revelator," and Blind Willie punching back with frightening intensity, "Hey, book of the Seventh Seal." Johnson's recorded output reveals a mastery of his highly individualized form of gospel blues, with skillful slide guitar runs backing religious lyrics sung with passionate intensity. Beyond that, pioneering bluesman Charley Patton, perhaps the largest single influence on the first generation of Mississippi Delta blues music, recorded several religious songs, sometimes using pseudonyms (such as "Elder J. J. Hadley") foisted on him by record companies seeking to differentiate their gospel and blues product lines. Even in his sacred recordings, notably the chilling two-part "Prayer of Death," Patton's wicked guitar runs (with a single blue note taking the place of the final word on the obligatory line "I'll meet you on that other shore") lend an air of devilish power.[92]

Through the interwar years, a number of musicians combined the blues and religious song, importing blue notes, instrumental virtuosity, and the skills of charismatic soloists into what had been highly communal forms of sacred expression. "The Baptist style of singing gospel," writes gospel music historian Clarence Boyer, "inspired the development of gospel groups and soloists who heretofore had been attracted to the music but found no way to participate, given their sense of moderate vocal and physical indulgence." The classic example is Thomas Dorsey. The native of Villa Rica, Georgia, and son of a Baptist minister deserved the title often bestowed upon him, the father of black gospel music. But a coterie of people working together, writing hymns and performing them in the unique pastiche that was black gospel, elevated the music to its place in the African American sacred canon. In his youth, Dorsey paid the bills by spinning out hokum and sexually punning tunes (such as "It's Tight Like That") even while yearning to put his soul in the hands of the Lord. An ambitious and aspiring musician, performer, and writer, Dorsey learned to emulate all sorts of styles around him, from the rollicking piano in clubs and brothels to the sophisticated jazz riffs of the 1920s. A series of personal tragedies, including the death of his beloved wife, convinced him that God would provide for a religious musician. He then served up the classic anthem of God's reassurance, "Precious Lord, Take My Hand." The spectacular success of this moving song and his subsequent career justified his faith.

Dorsey's younger years as a musician took him to juke joints, blues haunts, and Holiness storefront churches, as well as attendance at some of Chicago's largest and most respectable Baptist congregations. Gradually, he married blues feeling to gospel message. "Blues is as important to a person feeling bad as Nearer My God to Thee," he later said. "I'm not talking about popularity. I'm talking about inside the individual. This moan gets into a person where there is some secret down there that they didn't bring out.... When you cry out, that is something down there that should have come out a long time ago. Whether it's blues or gospel, there is a vehicle that comes along maybe to take it away or push it away." Aside from differences in the words, "you take that blue moan and what they call the lowdown feeling tunes and you shape them up and put them up here and make them serve the other purpose, the religious purpose."[93]

The prolific female black gospel songwriter Lucie Campbell collaborated closely with Dorsey in popularizing the gospel sound through organizations such as the National Convention of Gospel Choirs and Choruses. Campbell was born near Duck Hill, Mississippi, in 1885 but spent her adult life in Memphis. A successful composer, she copyrighted her first song, "Something Within," in 1919, and her final tune, "Come, Lord Jesus, Abide with Me," in 1963. In the intervening years, she presented one new song yearly to the huge annual meetings of the National Baptist Convention and helped to shape Dorsey's work into a thriving business enterprise. Her compositions, published in collections such as *Gospel Pearls* and *Inspirational Melodies No. 2*, sprang from a deep feeling for the black experience of turmoil and migration, making Campbell a close analogue to Dorsey.[94]

Sister Rosetta Tharpe, a guitarist who moved from street evangelism to performing gospel tunes at New York City's finest clubs, followed Dorsey in infusing popular tunes, blues feeling, and a nascent rhythm-and-blues sound into black Protestant music. Born in Arkansas to a family active in the Sanctified church, Tharpe took the rhythmically expressive music of her upbringing and brought it to the world of the street and commercial marketplace of commercial recording, nightclubs, and concert-hall music. Accompanying herself on guitar, at first as a solo act and later with larger groups and jazz bands, Tharpe could "pick that box, baby. Oh she could pick that box," as one listener remembered. Traveling through the country in the 1920s and 1930s, Tharpe served as a music evangelist first alongside her mother (a preacher for the Church of God in Christ) and then with her husband. Like blues instrumentalists, Tharpe picked her guitar with an insistently rhythmic one-note sound that accompanied a large variety of religious lyrics drawn from all eras of American sacred music. The style was a staple of numerous other street performers and evangelists, including Blind Lemon Jefferson and Blind Willie Johnson. In 1938, she appeared at the Cotton Club in New York City, a performance that transported her to celebrity status even as it alienated much of her Sanctified audience. From there, Tharpe produced numerous recordings for Decca Records. "She sings in a night club because she feels there are more souls in the nighteries that need saving than there are in church," a black newspaper reported of her choice to bring jazzy guitar sound and gospel lyrics to New York nightlife. Tharpe's ready transition from the world of Sanctified religion to the market of popular religious recordings traced a path that brought black religious music to a popular mainstream through the course of the twentieth century.[95]

Other musicians and arrangers took folk and popular cultural styles and integrated them with sacred lyrics. Memphis-based Baptist minister and songwriter W. Herbert Brewster brought the religious pageant, a miniature sacred opera set on the church stage, into national renown. During his illustrious preaching career at the East Trigg Baptist Church in Memphis, he published over 200 religious songs. Many of his best-loved tunes were included in religious dramas that depicted black history, including "From Auction Block to Glory." As he later reminisced, "the fight for rights here in Memphis was pretty rough on the Black

Church. The lily white, the black, and the tan were locking horns; and the idea struck me that I wrote that song 'Move on up a Little Higher.' We'll have to move in the field of education. Move into the professions and move into politics. Move in anything that any other race has to have to survive. That was a protest idea and inspiration. . . . In order to get my message over there were things that were almost dangerous to say, but you sing it." Brewster used "vamp" sections, in which soloists repeated lines against antiphonal responses from backup choruses, the lyrics and music building line by line to an explosive conclusion.[96]

This musical formula came out of Holiness and Pentecostal worship, which emphasized call-and-response dialogue and intense audience involvement. Gospel legend Mahalia Jackson made Brewster's tune "Move on up a Little Higher" famous. Surrounded in her hometown of New Orleans by the blues and Pentecostal music, she was happiest in congregations where she could hear foot-tapping and hand-clapping. The Sanctified church next door to her home Baptist church introduced her to drums, cymbals, tambourines, and triangles. "Everybody in there sang and they clapped and stomped their feet and sang with their whole bodies," she remembered. "They had a beat, a powerful beat, a rhythm we held on to from slavery days, and their music was so strong and expressive it used to bring the tears to my eyes. . . . First you've got to get the rhythm until, through the music, you have the freedom to interpret it." Jackson avoided the temptation of pop music stardom, which endeared her to her gospel music fan base.[97]

Black gospel quartets, a counterpart to the southern gospel groups popular among whites, elevated innovative styles to a new level of musical sophistication. The jubilee style of quartet singing emerged in the mid-1930. Singers cast sermonic themes in narrative form. Among black migrants, gospel quartets sang in nearly every community venue—churches, revival celebrations, community outings, and labor union meetings. The foursomes enhanced their appeal by adding special rhythmic touches to their performances. The Soul Stirrers, Blue Jay Singers, Dixie Hummingbirds, Swan Silvertones, and numerous other groups further refined the black gospel quartet sound. Formed in Norfolk, Virginia, in 1934, the Soul Stirrers mixed older spirituals (set to a twentieth-century beat) along with newer gospel songs to draw an audience of both white and black listeners on their radio show, broadcast from WBT in Charlotte, North Carolina. Their lead singer, who grew up learning the shape-note tradition that found its way from white singing schools into rural black congregations, created much of the vocal style that would become standard in black gospel quartets. Subsequent groups employed multiple leads who engaged in religious versions of competitive "cutting contests," introducing what later was termed "hard" gospel. Ira Tucker of the Dixie Hummingbirds and the Sensational Nightingales's Julius Cheeks epitomized this skill. These performers "talked to crowds, raising audiences to an emotional fervor with the use of bluesy vocal intonations, heavy musical instrumentation, and amplified sound systems." By the early 1950s, at the zenith of the quartet era, many groups alternated two lead vocals: one for hard gospel and the other for more traditional spirituals, known as jubilee singing. Packaged shows that traveled throughout the South featured intense competitions between star performers.[98]

In the 1960s, secular popular music drew from an abundance of talented performers who had been honed in the gospel music world among both whites and blacks. As an art form emerging on the street, moving into the concert hall and recording studio and later back to the community, black gospel quartet singing "moved full circle from the folk tradition to popular culture and then back to its folk roots again." Along the way, it left an indelible mark on American popular arts. Sam Cooke was the perfect exemplar of the gospel crooner as pop star. Born in 1931 in Mississippi, he grew up in Chicago as the son of a minister in the Church of Christ Holiness (the creation of the Mississippi black Holiness pioneer Charles Price Jones). As a teenager, he performed for the Highway QCs, a group that served as a farm team for the major-league black gospel groups of the era, including the Soul Stirrers. Later, Cooke became a lead singer for the Soul Stirrers, where he developed a style elegantly described as "sophisticated sanctification." In the 1950s, he struck out on his own and became the famous mellifluous voice of doo-wop and soul classics ranging from the chart-topper "You Send Me" to social commentary such as "Chain Gang" and "Change Gonna Come." Curtis Mayfield provides another example of the deep influence of the "beat" of the Sanctified church and the politicization of lyrics handed down in folk and commercial traditions, most notably in his classic anthem written to celebrate the 1963 March on Washington, "People Get Ready," with its moving gospel quartet harmonies accentuating the lyrical transformation of the train image as the vehicle to freedom's coming:

> People get ready, there's a train a'comin
> You don't need no baggage, just get on board
> All you need is faith, to hear the diesels hummin'
> Don't need no ticket, just thank the Lord.[99]

People raised as cultural products of this racial interchange in religious expression entered the public world of broadcasting and performing in the mid-twentieth century. Radio orators, barnstorming evangelists, gospel singers, bluegrass pioneers, and pop stars—nearly all with roots in the low-church southern religious traditions—profoundly influenced American popular culture. Any number of country and soul singers and black gospel stars, from Hank Williams and Bill Monroe to Ray Charles and Sam Cooke, come to mind. Hank Williams's "Honky-Tonk Angels" bore a marked resemblance to the white gospel classic "Great Speckled Bird" made famous by Roy Acuff; Bill Monroe's innovative jamming on mandolin often backed gospel harmonizing that was obviously influenced by black quartet singing; Ray Charles's "Baby What I Say" was a gospel vamp backed by an eroticized refrain; and Sam Cooke set a model for later singers such as Al Green in his move from gospel to soul and back again.

Perhaps more than anyone else, Elvis Presley illustrates this point. The young Elvis borrowed freely from sacred performers in creating his own musical persona. He memorized an entire catalogue of church music from both white and black traditions and could produce it on command. Along with his friends in Memphis, Presley enthusiastically sampled African American religious culture both in person and on the radio. Unlike the rowdies who satirized southern religious solemnities, Presley was affected by his encounter with African American Pentecostalism. He intuitively grasped its kinship to his own Assemblies of God background. He listened avidly to black religious orator W. Herbert Brewster on the radio and frequented local meetings of the Church of God in Christ.

Whites and blacks borrowed theologies, performance styles, and cultural practices freely (if often unwittingly) from one another. Elvis, for example, absorbed the sounds, the rhythms, and the stage manner that shaped his own electric performances. White secular and religious performers learned from—some might suggest they stole—doo-wop (with its own roots in black gospel quartets), religious holy-roller dancing, and the melismatic singing that coursed through African American church music. In the process, they created entertainments that shaped American popular culture. Sacred passion, expressed most obviously in white and black southern Pentecostalism, was at the heart of R & B and rock and roll. Later in the twentieth century, Pentecostalism became one of the fastest growing religious groupings in America, confounding a generation of interpreters who condemned it as the opiate of primitive people unable to adapt to modernity. These primitives instead provided much of the soundtrack for the twentieth century. Like the black Pentecostals in COGIC, white Pentecostal churches were training grounds for a remarkable number of figures (Presley, Johnny Cash, Oral Roberts) who left their mark on American popular culture.[100]

Later in the twentieth century, ordinary white and black southerners seized new opportunities elsewhere, leaving the South for northern and western cities. Southern religious cultures accompanied them and readapted to new settings. Radio, professional gospel publishing companies, and television supplied the means to transmit these traditions to a new generation, despite the homogenizing efforts of denominational reformers and the scorn of national elites. In the 1950s and 1960s, these traditions were transformed again by their incorporation into political struggles. Black southern religious culture energized the civil rights movement, especially in the freedom songs adapted from spirituals and popular tunes and given politicized lyrics, while white religious and cultural expressions pervaded segregationist culture and, later, the religious right. As Lillian Smith recognized, the ties of "common songs, common prayer, and common symbols" bound white and black southerners "on a religio-mystical level," even as the "brutally mythic" idea of white supremacy delayed freedom's coming.

Racial interchange in southern religious cultures thus led outward in different directions. One way was toward Christian interracialism, expressed most vividly in the freedom songs of the civil rights era, the music that provided hope and inspiration that the beloved community might be realized, if only for a transcendent moment. Chapter 4 takes up this complex story of religion, race, and culture in the civil rights era.

Ours was an evangelical freedom movement that identified salvation with not just one's personal relationship with God, but a new relationship between people black and white.

—Andrew Young, from *An Easy Burden: The Civil Rights Movement and the Transformation of America.*

We stood up. Me and God stood up.—Ethel Gray, Mississippi civil rights activist

Chapter Four

Religion, Race, and Rights

Writing to Ralph McGill in 1962, a black Georgian queried the white southern moderate editor of the *Atlanta Constitution* on the unconscious assumptions that distorted the views of even the best-intentioned white southerners. In a previous editorial, McGill had excoriated religious institutions for doing "nothing at all" to address the region's social ills. With clergymen delivering sermons that were "routinely irrelevant," the South's churches had "placed themselves on the sidelines." The correspondent quickly pointed out that McGill, of course, referred to white churches. Had so many black ecclesiastical buildings "been burned and bombed because they were on the sidelines?" he inquired. "Have they not provided the meeting-places, theme-song, and leaders for the center of the non-violent protest?" In McGill's language, "Christianity" and "the churches" unconsciously signified "white" in both cases. "When one views the churches and Christianity without regard for color," the letter concluded, "it becomes strikingly clear that Christianity and the churches have never been more relevant (taken as a whole)—or less on the sidelines."[1]

This correspondent speaks to the common understanding that black churches and activist ministers sparked a moral crusade to redeem America. Such a view captures part, but only part, of the complicated and ambiguous relationship between religion and the civil rights movement. Leaders of the freedom struggle knew firsthand of the numerous congregations that closed their doors to movement meetings. "The preachers, number one, they didn't have nothing to do with it," two local activists recalled of the movement in Mississippi. "Teachers number two, they didn't have nothing to do with it. Until things got when they could tell they wasn't gon' kill 'em, and then they went to comin' in." In Holmes County, a Mississippi civil rights worker reported, "We got turned down a lot of times from the black minister. . . . He mostly was afraid because they [whites] whooped a few of 'em and bombed a few churches. The preacher didn't want his church burned down, and them old members was right along in his corner." There was good reason, of course, for this fear. In the early summer of 1964, forty-one black churches in Mississippi, of various denominations and geographic locations, went up in flames.[2]

This contrast between the institutional church and individual church people, previously explored in Chapter 2, emerges strikingly clearly when one looks at the freedom struggle of the 1950s and 1960s. A white student stationed in southwest Georgia in 1965 tellingly concluded that the movement was "saturated with religion," but for him the "most shocking discovery . . . (because it is at such variance with the impression one gets from the national news media) was to find how conservative and separate from the movement are most Negro churches." He generally found religious leaders "far more conservative than the people in many cases." Black churches were a "very active" stumbling block, another activist observed, often still beholden to a theology "based on a heaven-centered world view coupled with a demeaning view of the power of man. These two tenets fulfill the function of keeping the Negro in his place." White churches, too, refused "to take any meaningful step in the direction of integration," with most clergy unwilling to "allow any type of integrated meeting within their sacred walls." The longtime South Carolina NAACP organizer Septima Clark understood that the tenure of local black ministers often depended on the approval of whites. Even with their congregations' support, they could be "run out of town if the white power structure decided they ought to go." Ministers who shied away from involvement were not necessarily opposed to the movement but might have been "just afraid to join it openly. It's simply a contradiction: so many preachers support the Movement that we can say it was based in churches, yet many preachers couldn't take sides with it because they thought they had too much to lose."[3]

When one looks beyond the church itself, however, the empowerment provided by the tradition of intense personal evangelicalism appears powerfully evident. As Charles Payne has written, "faith in the Lord made it easier to have faith in the possibility of social change," even if in the Delta towns he studied, such as Greenwood, the movement grew despite ministerial recalcitrance. Those on the movement's front line, in the words of one participant, had that "something on the inside." Susie Morgan joined the freedom movement in Mississippi one Sunday when "something hit me like a new religion." For many ordinary southerners, nothing else besides this "something on the inside," this religious vision of redeeming the South, could have sufficed for the sacrifices required in the struggle. Jim Crow, one black South Carolinian recalled, "just violated your person, your values, your truths, your beliefs, but you couldn't give up. You just had to keep that fire burning . . . and you had to pray."[4]

Religious thought and practice, so much a part of the reign of theological racism through American history, could turn against the dominant systems of white supremacist ideology. African American Protestantism empowered the most important social struggle in twentieth-century American history, one that fundamentally redefined citizenship for disfranchised peoples. Civil rights leaders employed multiple arguments, many of them involving constitutional protections. But beneath that ran the powerful stream of black Protestant ideas (translated sometimes through Gandhian notions of civil disobedience and active resistance) that pushed forward a leadership that otherwise remained cautious and circumspect.

Evangelical Protestantism among black southerners historically appeared to be apolitical. Critics called it "otherworldy" or "compensatory." But the implicit potential of southern folk faith—what contemporary scholars might call the "hidden transcript" of religious belief and behavior—bears close attention, for it defeated an enemy far superior in number and resources. Robin D. G. Kelley has argued that "we need to recognize that the sacred and the spirit world were also often understood and invoked by African Americans as weapons to protect themselves or to attack others. . . . Can a sign from above, a conversation with a ghost, a spell cast by an enemy, or talking in tongues unveil the hidden transcript?" One might add, can one's private and communal prayer when facing down racist sheriffs and voting registrars, shotguns blasted through a window, or snakes thrown on one's front porch serve as the antidote to the poison of apartheid? The freedom struggle brought the hidden transcript to the surface. The assassins who bombed the 16th Street Baptist Church in Birmingham and numerous other ecclesiastical buildings recognized this as clearly as anyone.[5]

Freedom Songs: The Sacred Music of the Movement

"You sing the songs which symbolize transformation, which make that revolution of courage inside you," a movement veteran said of the music that accompanied the black freedom struggle of the mid-twentieth century. The civil rights struggle had legislative aims. To that extent, it was a political movement. More than that, it was a religious crusade sustained by deeply Protestant imagery and fervor and a vision of Christian interracialism encapsulated in the idea of the beloved community. And it arose out of a religious culture steeped in the rituals of mass meetings, revivalistic preaching, and sacred singing. Black churchgoers unified themselves through freedom songs, connecting local people to the larger aims of the struggle. "Somehow through the music a great secret was discovered," as civil rights leader Andrew Young expressed it: "that black people, otherwise cowed, discouraged, and faced with innumerable and insuperable obstacles, could transcend all those difficulties and forge a new determination, a new faith and strength, when fortified with song. The music was not a political or economic gift to the people from the authorities, nor could it be taken away by them—music was the gift of the people to themselves, a bottomless reservoir of spiritual power."[6]

Freedom songs arose in a variety of ritual contexts. They came at the beginning and end of mass meetings, as crowds energized themselves with music. Traditional Protestant hymns familiar especially to older church people (such as "Leaning on the Everlasting Arms," a favorite of black Montgomerians, and other tunes from the nineteenth-century songbook), often began the proceedings. Newer lyrics, sometimes composed on the spot in specific response to frightening situations and then disseminated through word-of-mouth and traveling troubadours, increasingly took their place as the movement progressed. Sometimes they were accompanied by piano or organ, sounding much like lined-out hymnody dating from the nineteenth century. Participants propelled the music forward with singing, shouting, bodily movement, and rhythmic accompaniment of spirited hand-clapping and foot-stomping, legacies from the rituals of antebellum African American sacred music and motion. In this sense, freedom songs transmitted movement history across time. The transformation of received communal forms into freedom songs unlocked the potential power of southern religious expressive culture. Reflecting on the role of song, the journalist Pat Watters described the "mystical, ecstatic experience" that overcame him when he was surrounded by powerful sacred music in mass gatherings. It was the ultimate irony, as he saw it, that "southern cultural proscriptions" made it "impossible for whites to enter such churches, hear such eloquence, feel the southernness of those meetings."[7]

Freedom songs soothed congregants surrounded by hostile whites, National Guardsmen, and tear gas outside their sanctuaries; fortified marchers as they tramped down streets; accompanied the black working men and women who stayed off the buses for 381 days in Montgomery, Alabama; and sustained the thousands of black citizens who faced incarceration for the audacious act of trying to exercise their constitutionally protected rights. As protesters filled penitentiaries throughout the South, they sang to each other and to the sheriffs arresting them, following the example of the Apostle Paul and Silas in the New Testament. Dozens of new verses spontaneously arose in jail cells, pickets, and boycott lines.

The sacred music of the movement flowered in the 1960s, as movement faithful converted widely known spirituals, hymns, church anthems, and popular songs into versions of civil rights manifestos. In the spring of 1961, an interracial group of thirteen riders from the Congress of Racial Equality (CORE) set out on a fateful Greyhound bus trip from Washington, D.C. (in part replaying the Journey of Reconciliation in 1947, recounted in Chapter 2). Their route took them to North Carolina, then westward through the states of the Deep South and then southward again to New Orleans. Initially, the riders met only limited resistance. In Alabama, mobs firebombed one bus in Anniston and attacked another group of riders in Birmingham (while local police conspicuously absented themselves). Several riders, including two whites, were severely beaten. Despite the Kennedy administration's advice for a "cooling-off period," a new set of riders insisted on making their way from Birmingham to Jackson, Mississippi. As they traveled, they sent up a renewed version of "Hallelujah, I'm A-Traveling," a song used in black protest movements since the 1940s:

I'm paying my fare on the Greyhound bus lines
I'm riding the front seat to Jackson this time
Hallelujah, I'm a-traveling,
Hallelujah, ain't it fine,
Hallelujah, I'm a-traveling,
Down freedom's main line.

A later verse told a bit of civil rights history:

In Nineteen Fifty-Four, the Supreme Court has said,
Looka here, Mr. Jim Crow, it's time you were dead.
Hallelujah, I'm a-traveling . . .

State authorities (who had made a deal with the Kennedy administration) escorted the riders to jail when they arrived in Jackson. In Mississippi, jail sometimes meant the city penitentiary. Other times it meant places such as Parchman farm, a gigantic convict labor camp in the Mississippi Delta controlled by U.S. senator and state power broker James O. Eastland. The protesters sang through the evenings; true to form, the authorities tried to stop them. Jailed activists took up the old gospel song "I Woke up This Morning with My Mind Stayed on Jesus," and again converted the tune to their own uses: "Woke up this morning with my mind (My mind it was) Stayed on freedom." While in jail, Robert Zellner, son of a white Methodist minister from Alabama and a SNCC activist, invented new verses such as "Ain't no harm in keep'n' your mind, In keepin' it stayed on freedom," and "Singin' and prayin' with my mind, My mind it was stayed on freedom."[8]

Through the winter and spring of 1961 and 1962 in the small city of Albany in southwest Georgia, thousands of African American citizens sustained the struggle. Black churches supplied an organizing base and spiritual inspiration. Thus, Albany serves as an excellent case study in the work of freedom songs.

For years, black church people sang "Don't You Let Nobody Turn You 'Roun'":

Don't you let nobody tun you 'roun',
Turn you 'roun'
Don't you let nobody turn you 'roun',
Keep the straight an' the narrow way.

In Albany, the protesters faced a dilemma. Historically, civil rights leaders baited local authorities by violating segregation ordinances, anticipating that the federal government would trump segregationist law by applying federal civil rights statutes. This time, however, the judicial system proved to be a hindrance rather than an ally. Albany's sheriff, Laurie Pritchett, a close student of nonviolent tactics, realized that civil rights strategists planned to fill the jails, create a crisis, and exert public pressure on exposed and embarrassed authorities. He also understood that protesters desired dramatic confrontations with local officers. Pritchett refused to provide that forum. Instead, he allowed defined and limited street protests and then secured a federal court injunction against further picketing. This was a turning point, for now activists had to break the federal court order. As they filled the jails, freedom songs, especially "Ain't Gonna Let Nobody Turn Me 'Roun,'" became anthems of unity. "Ain't gonna let nobody tun me 'roun," they sang. "I'm gonna keep on a-walkin, keep on a-talkin, Marching up to freedom land." As police officers escorted them into paddy wagons, they spun out variations on the verses. "Ain't gonna let Chief Pritchett, turn me 'roun', turn me 'roun', turn me 'roun,'" a group of young women chanted as officers escorted them into police vehicles. "Ain't gonna let no injunction, turn me 'roun', turn me 'roun', turn me 'roun,'" they responded upon hearing of the federal court order against their demonstrations.

Following the Albany campaign, which ended inconclusively, organizers turned their attention to Birmingham, Alabama. The city's de facto boss was police chief Theophilus Eugene "Bull" Connor, a clumsy tactician of racial repression. Local black Baptist minister Fred Shuttlesworth, who had endured years of bombings and racial harassment from Klansmen and policemen, encouraged Martin Luther King Jr. and the Southern Christian Leadership Conference to attack segregated institutions in the "Magic City." In the spring of 1963, the movement reached an impasse when boycotts failed to open up city stores. Support from adults waned. Organizers recruited hundreds of black schoolchildren to fill up the city's jails, creating a renewed crisis situation that forced the city to the negotiating table. "I'm on my way, to freedom land, Oh, yes, I'm on my way," the children sang while lining up to be carted off in police wagons:

If my mother don't go, I'll go anyhow
If my mother don't go, I'll go anyhow
If my mother don't go, I'll go anyhow
Oh yes, Oh Lord, I'm on my way
I'm on my way, to freedom land . . .

"We Shall Overcome," the anthem of the freedom struggle, captured the movement's religious, interracial, and nonviolent emphasis. The song dated from the antebellum era. South Carolina slaves sang a tune titled "I'll be Alright," which soon entered the black sacred music repertoire. In the early twentieth century, the pioneering gospel songwriter Charles Albert Tindley composed the gospel song "I'll Overcome Someday." Another version, with the words "I Will Overcome," emerged from black workers on the picket lines in Charleston, South Carolina, in the 1940s. Tobacco workers and CIO organizers picked up on the tune and compelling lyrics. From there, folk singer Pete Seeger carried the song through the country and introduced it to the songster and activist Guy Carawan at the Highlander Folk School in Tennessee in the 1940s and 1950s. At Highlander, the tune became identified with the freedom struggle. Carawan, Seeger, and others introduced it to SNCC in 1960. Later in the 1960s, activists substituted the final words "some day" with the more insistent "to-day." And as with the other tunes, new verses arose spontaneously, addressing the needs of specific situations. Birmingham residents in 1963 sang, "We shall go to jail, we shall go to jail / We shall go to jail, today." The turmoil in Birmingham ended in triumph for the Southern Christian Leadership Conference and especially for Martin Luther King Jr. On August 28, 1963, over 250,000 Americans marched to the Lincoln Memorial and heard King deliver his most famous speech. The march was alive with freedom song, including a benediction of "We Shall Overcome." In this way, music symbolized the entire epochal struggle of the civil rights era. The freedom songs remain some of the most powerful and politically potent ritual music in American history.[9]

The Religious Culture of the Movement

It is sometimes said that the civil rights movement emerged from "the black church," a falsely singular term for what was in fact a multifarious set of institutions. Historians cite evidence such as churches that served as gathering points for mass meetings. For black southerners, the church was the center of cultural life, remembered Lucille Fisher Parker (the daughter of Miles Mark Fisher, longtime pastor in Durham and author of a pioneering study of slave songs), because "you were more *free* to do things in the church than any place else, so like the labor, blacks got involved in labor unions and they were able to meet in the church, [and] the NAACP in the church." Lorena Poole alternated between Baptist and AME services in her mill-town home of Graniteville, South Carolina. Whites and blacks lived in neighborhoods next to each other, and there was considerable hostility. Her mother, a teacher, was afraid to join the NAACP, and a cross burned next door suggested to Poole that "they were trying to scare the rest of the blacks I guess from joining." Her father carried a rifle and insisted he would "take somebody out" if they harassed him. "I saw so much, so many things that were wrong that inspired me," Poole recalled. In her spiritual haven of church, she found an "escape from those things that were happening" in her community, "and the church would always relieve me of the pain I was suffering inside, whatever. And I'd always end up finding a way to deal with it once I got that spiritual feeling or uplift in church. I made that my life."[10]

But activists also contended with the reality that "the black church" was not, as a rule, behind the movement. Because of indifference, fear, theological conservatism, or coercion and terrorism, many congregations simply avoided involvement. "We have learned, and our students 'learned' with us, that deacons and preachers, especially in the wealthier churches, are generally conservatives," a Mississippi civil rights volunteer wrote of his trying experiences seeking places to hold freedom schools. Thus, the relationship between religion, race, and rights during the 1960s is more complicated than often portrayed, particularly in the recent deification (and oversimplification) of Martin Luther King's life and work. Still, a movement based on secular ends, namely the extension of citizenship rights in the American nation-state, drew its sustenance from spiritual understandings, language, and motivations. It was a fundamentally Protestant imagery of Exodus, redemption, and salvation that inspired the revivalistic fervor of the movement. And it was church activists—most visibly Martin Luther King Jr. but also figures such as Jo Ann Gibson Robinson, Fred Shuttlesworth, John Lewis, and Fannie Lou Hamer—who infused the struggle with their religious passion and steely commitment.[11]

That faith in the Lord could spark action in the face of physical threat also was evident in the bravery of the Reverend J. A. DeLaine of Clarendon County, South Carolina. Working together with the South Carolina NAACP organizer Modjeska Simkins, DeLaine organized school desegregation suits that eventually led to landmark cases such as *Briggs v. Elliott* and others that were eventually subsumed into the omnibus *Brown v. Board of Education* decision in 1954. Simkins and DeLaine mapped out a strategy for the *Briggs* case in DeLaine's home. DeLaine certainly needed all the help he could get. The Reverend L. B. McCord, a white minister who served as school superintendent in DeLaine's home county, declared that "integration of the races would definitely be sinful." Local white Methodist churches took their stand for "continued racial segregation in the schools, state and federal installations of all kinds, churches and all ways of life where it has always been practiced."

Discouraged by the lack of progress, NAACP lawyer Thurgood Marshall threatened to withdraw from the Clarendon County case. The black plaintiffs found only one person willing to step forward to file a complaint, and this only on a bus transportation (not a school equalization) case. In response, DeLaine rounded up several dozen local African Americans to sign an equalization petition presented before the Clarendon County school board. DeLaine paid a heavy price. After arsonists torched his St. James AME church, he received this threatening letter addressed to the "Rev. J. A. Delane, Collard": "We have been notified by the best of authority that you are the one that started the school segregation mess at Manning, S.C. and that you was run out of Manning for your dirty filthy work. Maby you don't know Lake City but you are goin to fin out real soon. Several hundred of us had had a meeting and pleged ourselves to put you where you belong, if there is such a place." Charleston police turned the letter over to the FBI. A year later, gunmen fired on DeLaine. Hidden in the back of a car, he eventually escaped the state and moved to Buffalo, New York. During this turmoil, DeLaine received support from South Carolina's Methodist Woman's Society of Christian Service. He wrote to them appreciatively: "Regardless to the outcome of this struggle I shall every remain unmovable in my confidence in the GUIDING HAND OF GOD which has guided me during these perilous days when even Night-Riders thought to do something to make my life miserable and bring me into open shame. I feel like God has fought a wonderful battle for me."[12]

That "something on the inside" also empowered the working women and men of Montgomery, Alabama, during their bus boycott in the mid-1950s. In the next year after the *Brown* ruling, black residents of Montgomery protested the separate and unequal rules that governed bus transportation in their city and humiliated black riders. A seamstress named Rosa Parks refused to give up her seat to a white passenger and was arrested. Organizers deliberately portrayed Parks as a humble working woman who simply was tired. Of course, she was much more than that. She had been trained in activism through her work with the NAACP and workshops at Highlander Folk School. The black Alabamians initially sought not an end to segregation on public transportation but simply more equitable treatment for black citizens riding segregated bus lines. The city resisted. In short order, the black community mobilized.

Martin Luther King Jr. built his reputation in part out of the miracle of Montgomery. But recent memoirs, documentary histories, and scholarship have demonstrated that the remarkable solidarity shown during this turning point of twentieth-century American history depended not only on charismatic leaders such as King and folksy orators such as Ralph Abernathy but at least as much on women's savvy. The Montgomery Women's Political Council stood behind the boycott, kept it going on a day-to-day basis, filled the mass meetings that inspired those who trudged the streets, and through their sheer persistence often dragged along ministers and other male community leaders. This is not to underestimate the ministerial eloquence of King and his comrades; the women involved certainly did not. But it is to recognize that this leadership depended to a large degree on persistent organizers such as Montgomery labor leader E. D. Nixon and women such as Jo Ann Gibson Robinson, Mary Fair Burks, and Rosa Parks. In addition to them, thousands of ordinary maids and laborers kept each other informed and, consequently, the boycott effective through phone trees, women's missionary society meetings, labor organizations, and social gatherings.

Mary Fair Burks, longtime member of the Dexter Avenue Baptist Church in Montgomery, did not suffer pious fools gladly. She sympathized with Martin Luther King Jr.'s predecessor in the pulpit, the legendary iconoclast Vernon Johns. A great social gospel orator and an eccentric who wore clothes hardly befitting the stereotype of the carefully coiffed southern preacher, Johns was a devastating critic of the black bourgeoisie. One Sunday, Johns launched a particularly vigorous assault on the complacency of the comfortable church members. As Burks recalled, "I looked all around and all I could see were either masks of indifference or scorn. Johns's attacks, his patched pants, and his Thoreauvian philosophy of plain living and high thinking did not endear him to his congregation." Eminent pewholders ousted the pointedly undiplomatic Johns and replaced him with Martin Luther King Jr., a quiet and studious seminarian who seemed more in keeping with the status and demeanor expected of a Dexter Avenue divine. Burks herself was ready for action. Since girlhood she had entered white-only restrooms and sat at forbidden lunch counters, scampering away before being caught—she delighted in her own "private guerilla warfare." Shortly before hearing Johns's sermon, she had been arrested for a trivial violation of local segregation laws. She then helped to found the Women's Political Council and served as its president for years, before relinquishing those duties to Jo Ann Gibson Robinson. Burks was one of many in Montgomery who combined church activism, deep religious faith, and grassroots political organizing. The success in

Montgomery came about largely through their dogged efforts, even if the national spotlight shone on King and other public spokesmen.[13]

Burks's friend and fellow agitator Jo Ann Gibson Robinson arrived in Montgomery in 1949 to teach English at Alabama State. Soon the harassment and mistreatment of black Montgomerians on city buses reduced her to tears of rage. Following the arrest of Rosa Parks, Robinson prepared leaflets and pamphlets for the incipient uprising. By then, she was president of the Women's Political Council. She mailed copies of the Montgomery Improvement Association's newsletter to supporters around the country, helping to raise funds for the boycott's spontaneously jerry-rigged and frequently financially imperiled private transportation system.

On December 2, 1955, Montgomery ministers met with an AME Zion congregation to discuss a possible boycott of the city buses. "When the Women's Political Council officers learned that the ministers were assembled in that meeting," Robinson later recounted, "we felt that God was on our side. It was easy for my two students and me to leave a handful of our circulars at the church, and those disciples of God could not truthfully have told where the notices came from if their very lives had depended on it. Many of the ministers received their notices of the boycott at the same time, in the same place. They all felt equal, included, appreciated, needed. It seemed predestined that this should be so." Local clerics quickly discovered that the congregants were "quite intelligent on the matter and were planning to support the one-day boycott with or without their ministers' leadership. It was then that the ministers decided that it was time for them, the leaders to catch up with the masses." Churches that had been relatively quiescent served during the boycott as "channels of communication, as well as altars where people could come for prayer and spiritual guidance." After the initial one-day trial, attendees at a mass meeting demanded that the action be extended. As congregants offered up prayers for "misguided whites," the people "felt the spirit. Their enthusiasm inundated them, and they overflowed with emotion." Some months later, when Robinson, Burks, and other women took their turns being arrested, supporters came to the Dexter Avenue church for a mass meeting. Robinson felt that "certainly the Spirit from above must have been among the crowd, for people were mentally, spiritually, psychologically serene inside. Even I, always demanding proof for statements, felt a special peace within myself. A quiet calm seemed to invade and relax me. At the very beginning of the movement, I had put myself in the hands of the unseen power from above, and since then there had been no turning back." Robinson's fears for her career and her life were calmed; her thoughts were "in the *now!*" For Robinson, faith was indeed the substance of things hoped for, as well as an eminently useful tool for pursuing justice.[14]

Local white reaction to the boycott made the job of sustaining support easier. On one day of arrests, the Reverend M. C. Cleveland, an older pastor of the Day Street Baptist Church and a man "so upright and so cautious" that he never attended a single mass meeting, sat "forlornly in the jailhouse, signing a piece of paper." When authorities harassed a man well-known for being the "epitome of prudence and conformity," the old strategies of accommodation appeared more bankrupt than ever. At the same time, veteran southern liberals such as Clifford and Virginia Durr expressed their support, sometimes publicly but more often privately. A "white friend" wrote to Martin Luther King Jr. early in 1956, telling him that although the White Citizens' Council would meet that night, "they can't make you ride and you are not breaking any law, so continue in the spirit of Christ. He is your real leader. Don't forget him!" A "fellow Suffer" from the Sixteenth Street Baptist Church in Birmingham told King that Negro mothers had "prayed that God would send us a leader such as you are. Now that the Almighty has regarded our lowly estate and has raised *you* among us, I am indeed grateful. . . . The Arm of God is everlastingly strong and Sufficient to keep you and yours." Mass meetings kept the spirit up in Montgomery. Ninety days into the boycott, one minister exulted that "it was in Montgomery that God chose us to play this all-important role. We must accomplish the will of God." Because the white church would not practice what it preached, he urged one crowd, "we must grab whites with a spiritual hand, and tell them we love you as though you were our very own."[15]

The Montgomery movement received material assistance from two white ministers in town: Robert Hughes and Robert S. Graetz. Hughes was a Methodist minister with a degree from Emory whose activities earned him the enmity of the Klan. Local authorities tapped a phone Hughes used to talk with Harrison Salisbury of the *New York Times*; shortly thereafter, the Klan acquired information from the bugging. Segregationists tried to compel Hughes to turn over a list of members of the Alabama Council on Human Relations, a group he chaired. Hughes refused, was jailed for contempt of court, and had his clerical credentials revoked by the North Alabama Methodist Conference.[16]

Like the young Martin Luther King Jr., Robert S. Graetz was new to town and fresh out of seminary in 1954. By his own account, the young Lutheran minister had grown up with conventional racist ideas but rethought his positions after taking college courses in race relations. The church hierarchy sent Graetz to pastor Trinity Lutheran, a modest black congregation in Montgomery. Although this church previously employed white preachers, parishioners were wary of Graetz. Such suspicion diminished considerably when he participated in the bus boycott, but it did not disappear entirely until a bombing at his home. Driving in his new automobile along the street one day, he was sandwiched between two other cars when the driver of one leaned out the window to say, " 'That's the nigger-lovin' preacher in front of you!' " Graetz realized how easily he could be targeted. Simply to attend a human relations meeting took an act of courage. The moderate Methodist ministers he met usually had brief tenures marked by heavy congregational pressure to vacate their pulpits. Women offered behind-the-scenes support, sometimes against the wishes of their husbands. Graetz noted how "wives became actively involved in our councils, while their husbands took part in White Citizens' Councils and other organizations working to preserve segregation." In one instance, a husband took out a newspaper advertisement publicly disclaiming any support for his wife's work on the Alabama Human Relations Council. Graetz opened his church to the NAACP Youth Council advised by Rosa Parks, with whom he attended strategy sessions at Highlander Folk School.[17]

Black southern communities faced their own internal divisions on responding to the mounting civil rights crusade. Ralph Abernathy, King's close colleague and friend in Montgomery, recognized the generational and class conflicts in the black community. For him, this partly explained how church people joined the movement even while the ministerial and denominational establishment held back. Abernathy's father was a landowner who raised his own food for his family and was the principal deacon and financial contributor to a Baptist church in rural Alabama. A strict disciplinarian and a man concerned with rising in the world, Abernathy's father was part of an older generation accustomed to the delicacies of working within the Jim Crow system. They fought with younger pastors and church members who were frustrated by the word *wait*—which, as Martin Luther King later pointed out, almost always meant *never*. "Many of the older clergy were in favor of sweeping social change," Abernathy wrote, "but they were willing for it to come about slowly, when white society was ready to accept it. They preached a strict adherence to the law and peace at any price." As Abernathy concluded of the older clergy, "the last thing they wanted to see destroyed was their precarious credibility among white leaders, who occasionally gave them minor posts of honor in the community in order to use them to keep the rest of us in line." In private, they might "join the rest of us in denouncing the oppression of the white establishment," but publicly they would "say nothing to incur the wrath of those they privately denounced." The older generation inveighed against injustice in general. It was up to his generation, Abernathy realized, to preach about "this *particular* act or this *particular* white man [who] was vicious and unjust; or that this *particular* practice—in force for generations—should be abolished." Abernathy had no problem in doing so, in part because local policemen ignored attacks on his church property. After Abernathy's own house was bombed and he rushed home from out of town, he encountered a group of policeman visiting his neighborhood. When another explosion deto- nated in the distance, one of the policemen informed him, "'That would be your First Baptist Church.'" The police had known all along.[18]

Abernathy saw his role as moving congregants to act in accordance with the principles of the fledgling movement. He taught them the theology of nonvio- lence but also the "techniques of survival." Both Abernathy and his new friend Martin Luther King Jr. worried that they did not have the resources to "confront the formidable white leadership arrayed" against them in "every state capitol and county courthouse in the South. We were two young and inexperienced black preachers in an old and cynical society—and we knew it." But they also had that something within, and they knew that, too.[19]

Martin Luther King was Abernathy's friend and colleague in Montgomery. A man who has been thoroughly dissected and studied from every angle—in his personal life, his upbringing, his experiences at Morehouse College in At- lanta and at northern seminaries and universities, his pulpit leadership, his civil rights activism and increasing radicalism in the later 1960s—King was formed first by his father's preaching in the milieu of the black Baptist church. His fa- ther, "Daddy" King, was an early NAACP organizer and a charismatic preacher known to "walk the benches." Early in life, the young King avidly memorized gos- pel songs and Bible verses. As he matured, he questioned the literal truth of the Bible and disdained what he saw as his father's rigid fundamentalism. In college and graduate training, however, he determined that "behind the legends and myths of the Book were many profound truths which one could not escape."

King's "conversion," as he described it, diverged from the standard evangeli- cal model; it involved the "gradual making of the noble ideas set forth in my family and my environment, and I must admit that this intaking has been largely unconscious." While he may not have been saved in the traditional ecstatic ca- tharsis, he experienced his own crisis moment on January 27, 1956. Sitting in his kitchen after receiving a threatening phone call—one of many during those early days of the Montgomery bus boycott—he realized "religion had become real to me and I had to know God for myself. And I bowed down over that cup of coffee, I never will forget it." He heard the voice of Jesus urging him to "fight on"; "He promised never to leave me, never to leave me alone." At that moment King "experienced the presence of the Divine as I had never experienced Him before. . . . My uncertainty disappeared. I was ready to face anything." His vision that troubled evening steeled his resolve. Three nights later, following the bomb- ing of his home, an angry crowd gathered outside. King calmed them, possibly preventing an ugly confrontation. In doing so, he sealed his growing reputation as an orator with near magical powers of persuasion.[20]

Although new to town, King was "committed to the preaching of a social Gospel that would awaken the Christian churches and mobilize them in the fight against segregation." Knowing little substantively about the philosophy of non-violence, the young King applied for a firearms permit and purchased a gun to keep at home. As the bus boycott episode gained national attention, he consulted with veterans of nonviolent civil disobedience. The Fellowship of Reconciliation sent Glenn Smiley, its national field secretary, from Texas. The white pacifist clergyman, who had worked with FOR and had been imprisoned during World War II as a draft resister, advised King in all he knew about nonviolence. Smiley's impressions of King were mixed: "So young, so inexperienced, so good," perhaps a "Negro Gandhi," or possibly "an unfortunate demagogue destined to swing from a lynch mob's tree." Smiley set up meetings with white churches and encouraged interracial ministers' associations and prayer groups. He pushed King to develop a small grassroots interracial organization that could organize spontaneous protests and avoid dependence on charismatic leaders—something like the SNCC eventually became.

Bayard Rustin, the brilliant political strategist and committed advocate of nonviolent resistance, became another influential theorist and adviser to King (although his homosexuality and political radicalism forced him to keep his distance from the SCLC). Rustin came to Montgomery partially at the behest of Lillian Smith. They had worked together during the 1940s, he as race relations director and she as a board member of the Fellowship of Reconciliation. Bayard Rustin persuaded King to accept nonviolence as a fundamental philosophical principle. As a short-term stratagem, Rustin insisted, it would be dismissed as a political ploy, not as the satyagraha ("soul force") that empowered the Indian independence movement. King was deeply influenced by Rustin's philosophical nonviolence but less so by Smiley's organizational ideas. King developed SCLC more as a small and hierarchically controlled organization dependent on a cadre of leading ministers.[21]

King's own theology emerged from the Old Testament teachings of the moral absolute of justice, a historic black Christian emphasis. To that, King added in diverse and to some extent contradictory influences, including liberal Protestantism, his own reading of Niebuhrian neo-orthodoxy, and Gandhian maxims. Mixed together, the philosophical brew inspired active nonviolent resistance to injustice, and a faith and hope that conquered despair. Local whites admonished the young preacher to stick to the gospel and let other issues alone. King would have none of it, for he recognized that there remained a "material connection between man and his environment and this connection means a material well being of the body as well as the spiritual well being of the soul is to be sought." More than any theology or philosophy, King's oratorical artistry moved people in ways that were difficult to articulate but unmistakably present. Andrew

Young remembered King's "strong biblical metaphors, drawing upon his scholarship and sophisticated knowledge. Martin had the ability to make us feel as if we were more than our daily selves, more than we had been—a part of a beautiful and glorious vision that was enabling us to transcend ourselves. It was a marvelous quality he had, not ever fully captured on the printed page or in recordings, to lift the people to another place so that they could almost feel themselves moving." At that point, parsing King's intellectual and theological influences mattered less than understanding his ability to move the spirit of people.[22]

No one represented the movement's fire—a "fire you can't put out," as his biographer has expressed it—more than the Reverend Fred Shuttlesworth, who served in Birmingham during fateful crusades in the infamously tough industrial town. Shuttlesworth grew up surrounded by ministers who would not attack segregation directly; it seemed pointless. Though raised a Methodist, he began attending Baptist churches with his wife, Ruby, and was immersed in 1944. Later he attributed this switch to Providence, for in the AME a presiding bishop could have curtailed his controversial activities. A white Baptist missionary encouraged Shuttlesworth in his studies. He first attended an AMEZ Bible institute, where his frequent disagreement with teachers convinced him to trust his own reading of the Bible. Later he attended Selma University, a college led by the longtime black Baptist convention president D. V. Jemison, where he enrolled in general studies rather than in the theological curriculum.[23]

Shuttlesworth gradually made his name locally as a willful preacher with a "'combative spirituality.'" For example, he refused to accept a job offer from one church until they eliminated the annual call (the customary practice of granting Baptist pastors one-year tenures and voting each year on whether to retain them). He told this congregation, "Once you vote on me, you don't vote on me again. So if you and the Holy Spirit can get together, we can make some progress." A Selma University teacher convinced a substantial Baptist congregation in town to hire Shuttlesworth at a stable level of income needed to support his family. He was quickly embroiled in conflicts with his Selma congregation over control of a separate fund overseen by a group of powerful deacons, and over Shuttlesworth's practice of printing in the church bulletins the exact amount of members' contributions. While working on a bachelor's degree from Alabama State, the determined preacher took on additional jobs, angering the deacons and resulting in his resignation. His experience at Selma established the pattern for Shuttlesworth's career; he was headstrong, self-assured, and perceived by some as erratic or dictatorial but by others as a spiritual leader called by God.[24]

Electrified by the *Brown* decision and his sense of God's hand moving in history, Shuttlesworth's civil rights career blossomed in the 1950s. He felt divinely inspired to defy a response to the banning of the NAACP in Alabama imposed by state authorities. Resisting more senior ministers who urged caution, Shuttlesworth and his followers organized the Alabama Christian Movement for Human Rights (ACMHR). He saw the new group as part of a "worldwide revolution which is a divine struggle for the exaltation of the human race." Repeated attempts on his life only enhanced his personal authority and charisma. In 1957, white terrorists exploded dynamite at his home, nearly killing his wife and children. Shuttlesworth emerged from the severely damaged building uninjured.[25]

Through the 1950s, Shuttlesworth felt optimistic about the triumph of justice. Even in white churches, he noted, one could hear some figures "at last pleading for justice and reason. We have arisen to walk with destiny, and we shall march till victory is won." At the same time, he condemned whites who sang "Amazing Grace" in their church choirs even while marching "at night in robes to burn crosses." Shuttlesworth grew close to Carl and Anne Braden, the white couple from Louisville who suffered ostracism and arrest for their support of civil rights. Although initially fearing Braden's Southern Conference Educational Fund as a communist front, Shuttlesworth used the Bradens' connections to publish information about Birmingham in the northern press, significantly aiding the civil rights effort in the city.[26]

After the sit-ins at lunch counters in Greensboro and the birth of the SNCC, Shuttlesworth met with former SCLC executive director Ella Baker and told her to inform King that Birmingham was the thing that could "really shake up the world." Even while sitting in an Alabama jail, Shuttlesworth smuggled out pieces of writing, including a petition signed by inmates to desegregate courthouse facilities in the county. Following his release, Shuttlesworth led an interracial conference assembled at the Gaston Motel in Birmingham on integrating the South. The success of the gathering convinced Shuttlesworth to pressure King and the SCLC leadership to choose Birmingham for their next crusade. "There are certain places that have symbolic meanings," as one participant put it, including the town infamously known as "Bombingham." After the meeting, true to form, bombers struck Bethel Baptist Church (where Shuttlesworth had preached) for the third time since 1956. Shards of shrapnel sprayed everywhere. Shuttlesworth later said, "I have always been a symbol of the Negro freedom movement here, and that is why the church where I used to be pastor has been bombed again. This is Birmingham's shame and America's tragedy."[27]

Shuttlesworth threw his energies into the civil rights movement, and, as one of his congregants said, "everything he did and said spoke to that." Shuttlesworth told black Birminghamians that he possessed no "magic wand to wave nor any quick solution by which the God of segregation can be made to disappear" but had only "myself—my life—to lead as God directs." After suffering a severe beating while trying to enroll his daughter in a school, he lay near death on the ground but heard the voice of God telling him, "You can't die here. Get up. I got a job for you to do." While considered headstrong and even neurotic for his apparent desire for martyrdom, Shuttlesworth reminded supporters of how many of the "Biggest Preachers (I'll call no names) pleaded with me to call off the Mass Meeting; how many tried to take a stand against the Movement, and would have publicly except for public sentiment. . . . You cannot imagine how tedious and painstaking it has been to forge together this organization in Birmingham; nor how difficult to keep in line moving forward." Of his courageous actions, he later reflected, "I really tried to get killed in Birmingham. I exposed myself deliberately, and I felt [that] if I did give my life that the country would have to do something about it." Shuttlesworth placed himself squarely in the "contest for justice and righteousness" from the Old Testament to the present, seeing the biblical parable of good and evil being waged "between God and Eugene [Bull] Connor." During the Birmingham demonstrations in 1963, Shuttlesworth reminded his colleagues frequently that "this is my town, and I know this town; I know them rednecks." He was contemptuous of Billy Graham's advice for King to "put the brakes on a little bit." Shuttlesworth was not one to hit the brakes. When James Farmer of CORE came to Montgomery, Shuttlesworth escorted him through a mob surrounding a church. Miraculously, the crowd of hostile whites opened up and allowed them to pass. Farmer attributed this to Shuttlesworth's well-deserved reputation for near insanity in pursuit of justice —the "crazy nigger" syndrome, Farmer satirically called it. For Shuttlesworth, it was more akin to God opening up the Red Sea.[28]

Birmingham's young people kept the movement alive in the spring of 1963, reciting daily the ten commandments of nonviolence, including "remember always that the nonviolent movement seeks justice and reconciliation—not victory" and "pray daily to be used by God in order that all men might be free." Working alongside Shuttlesworth in Birmingham, SCLC organizer Andrew Young explained to cautious elders, "This was a movement led by the spirit. We had spent the better part of six months nurturing and drawing out that spirit which we now saw alive in the thousands of young people who were determined to go to jail to gain their freedom. Caution would now destroy the movement."[29]

Andrew Young was the more polished and smooth-talking counterpart to Shuttlesworth's rougher persona. Hailing from New Orleans, Young was the son of a well-established family of dentists affiliated with Straight College, a Congregationalist school for African Americans established by the American Missionary Association. He received a strict (and very good) education but eventually felt that much of this early training "had to do with accommodating myself to the injustices I saw all around me. I could not square that philosophy with what I read to Gran from her Bible." He could not see how enjoying the perks of the black talented tenth translated "into uplift for my classmates and the folks on Rampart Street." His parents' faith inspired social responsibility, "but theirs was an individual effort, helping one person at a time." Young understood that "it was going to take more than good works to change segregation; it would require a change in the social order." In working with the United Christian Youth Movement and the National Council of Churches (NCC), he sensed a spiritual awakening that freed him from the stifling career expectations of his upbringing.[30]

In the early 1950s, after working for the National Council of Churches in New York, he told a friend, "In our present situation you must be a little outside the structure of the church to do the church's work, otherwise you get caught up in the grinding wheels." Invited to join the SCLC, he teamed with Dorothy Cotton, Septima Clark, and others to set up adult citizenship schools at the Dorchester Center, a site near Savannah used since Reconstruction for summer gatherings of the Congregationalist Convention of the South. The citizenship schools were a natural extension of the historic educational role of the American Missionary Association in the South. Young and his comrades focused their work in the Deep South, where they registered voters and recruited a collection of home-grown activists whose names would become legendary in civil rights history, among them Aaron Henry, Amzie Moore, and Fannie Lou Hamer. At Dorchester, Young caught a "new attitude, a new determination in the air, in the voices of the people, in the music." He felt that the winding roads he had followed through his life had led him "to the right place at the right time," and he was "grateful to be part of this historical, spiritual transformation of the South." Two years later, after the movement encountered obstacles in Albany, Young and others retreated to Dorchester and sketched out plans for the upcoming Birmingham campaign.[31]

The Birmingham crusade and other successes in the 1960s drew considerable media attention. But there were numerous struggles further from the public eye, including uphill battles to organize protests in lesser-known locales such as Tuscaloosa, Alabama. Well into the 1960s, when Willie Herzefeld came to Tuscaloosa to pastor Christ Lutheran Church, there was no local movement. There was instead only "one man who was going around spouting off": Herzefeld himself. He was troubled by the "apathy of the Baptist ministers in the city," and about being seen as a man who had no "real lasting ties with the community, who was concerned primarily about creating trouble." But he knew that "if the Lord Christ were here on earth, right now, in the South, he would preach against segregation. He would probably be crucified by the whites and any number of Negroes here, but . . . he would preach against this, this lovelessness, which is really the problem." Herzefeld teamed with T. Y. Rogers, pastor of First African

Baptist Church in Tuscaloosa, who had apprenticed as an assistant to Martin Luther King at Dexter Avenue Baptist Church in Montgomery. Seeking to take down segregation signs at the county courthouse, Rogers and Herzefeld first had to confront over twenty clergy colleagues who threatened "to go over to the newspaper and make a statement that the Baptist ministers had nothing to do with the efforts that we were making." This put Herzefeld "in opposition, right quick, with the religious power structure." Despite such resistance, he managed to gather over 800 participants to march on the courthouse on June 9, 1964. When white authorities responded with tear gas and beatings, driving the protesters into a church building, the church members were stunned; they had presumed that local whites would be well-disposed.[32]

Younger men and women with evangelical roots in the rural South found a home in the movement, including John Lewis, the native Alabamian, SNCC organizer, and future congressman. Lewis's boyhood church in rural Alabama was a "colorful, vibrant place," where people whose "lives were circumscribed by the rhythms and routines of hard work" found time for fellowship and "pure singing, the sound of voices fueled by the spirit, people keeping rhythm with a beat they heard in their hearts, singing songs that came straight from their soul, with words they felt in every bone of their body." He also knew that these religious institutions were cowed by segregation. His boyhood preacher never addressed daily issues such as the cheating of sharecroppers, and the minister omitted any mention of the *Brown* decision or the acts of violence that followed. "It also did not escape my notice," Lewis recollected, "that that minister arrived and departed in a pretty nice automobile, and that he went back to a very comfortable home in Montgomery, more comfortable than the homes any of us lived in."[33]

Listening to Martin Luther King's voice on the radio transfixed the young Lewis. It was the first time he had heard the clarion call of the black freedom struggle. Unable to attend Morehouse College as he wished, Lewis enrolled at a small black Baptist seminary in Nashville, where a professor introduced him to Hegel and to religious ideas outside biblical literalism. His studies gave him the "philosophical and theological underpinnings" for what he had "sensed and deeply felt" and set in relief the contradictions he saw all around him. At the seminary, he also met James Bevel, a future colleague in the movement. He began attending meetings led by James Lawson at Clark Memorial Methodist Church in Nashville. This former Methodist missionary to India was a crucial mentor in the philosophy of nonviolence for a generation of young activists, black and white. Listening to Lawson, Lewis heard for the first time of the pantheon of nonviolent avatars, from Thoreau to Gandhi.

Lewis, Andrew Young, and others in SCLC and SNCC applied these lessons in nonviolent but very active resistance to injustice. SNCC sent its intrepid corps to some of the South's hottest spots in the early 1960s—New Orleans, Louisiana; Nashville, Tennessee; Albany, Georgia; Danville, Virginia; McComb, Mississippi; Selma, Alabama. Often the students joined and fortified ongoing local struggles, with the intent of becoming a part of "the people" rather than assuming the mantle of "leaders." For example, in southwestern Virginia in May and June 1963 (the same time as the internationally publicized crusade in Birmingham), black ministerial leaders of the Danville Christian Progressive Association picketed city hall, demanding an audience with the mayor. Their grievances were many, given Danville's reputation as a strictly segregated town that boasted of its "high moral and spiritual tone" and its "loyal and intelligent" white working-class population. They were arrested. On June 10, nearly eighty locals and SNCC volunteers walked from the Reverend Lawrence Campbell's church to the city jail, singing hymns in front of the waiting policemen. After a prayer directed at the police, asking forgiveness for those who knew not what they did, the officers turned fire hoses onto the crowd. Deputized garbage collectors wielded nightsticks, injuring several dozen protesters. Through the next week, several hundred black Danvillians faced physical abuse and jailing as they sought access to city hall. Finally, on June 22, policemen kicked down the door of the black High Street Baptist Church and took away three SNCC workers, who were charged with "inciting the colored population to acts of violence and war against the white population."[34]

John Lewis, chairman of SNCC at the time of the Danville episode, saw his fellow activists as akin to the early church apostles, "going out with virtually nothing but the clothes on our backs to bring the gospel of freedom to the people." Lewis "felt the spirit, the hand of the Lord, the power of the Bible . . . but only when they flowed through the church and out into the streets. As long as God and his teachings were kept inside the walls of a sanctuary, as they were when I was young, the church meant next to nothing to me. My work, my commitment to community, had become my church, both during the movement and now, as I was making my way on my own. My work was my religion, my entire life." As Andrew Young explained and John Lewis's experience confirmed, the nonviolent approach sought to "transform, rather than defeat, the oppressor and the oppressive situation," to bring the historically subjugated to an understanding and forgiveness toward those who oppressed them. "In the process of citizenship schooling, the boycott, mass meetings, and demonstrations," Young continued, "people grew in understanding and gained a sense of their own worth, power, and dignity." Such a philosophy received its severest test in Mississippi, where white supremacy reigned supreme and challenges to the repressive order were dealt with summarily.[35]

"The Bible, My Lord, and My 30-30":
Mississippi and the Radical Religious Vision

SNCC targeted places that other organizations feared or avoided. Foremost among these was Mississippi. The obstacles to opening what was memorably described as the "closed society" by University of Mississippi historian James Silver were formidable. Historically, legal injustices perpetrated in Jim Crow's courts worked in tandem with extralegal violence dealt out more unpredictably, and thus more hauntingly, on black bodies throughout the state. During times of crisis, the terror predictably intensified. In 1944, near the town of Liberty in Amite County, Mississippi, six white men abducted the Reverend Isaac Simmons. This sixty-six-year-old minister owned more than 200 acres of land and, more important, the oil rights to that acreage. Pressured to give up the property, Simmons hired an attorney in Jackson. White abductors shot him in the back three times, cut his tongue out, and dumped the body. Following the murder, Simmons's son, who had watched the execution, filed charges against the killers. No one was convicted. The Magnolia State reached new heights of infamy in the case of Emmitt Till, a teenaged black Chicagoan brutally murdered while visiting relatives in the state in 1955. As was customary, a local jury acquitted Till's killers; much more unusually, the case made national headlines. In a lesser-known hate crime coincident with the internationally publicized Till murder, the Reverend George Lee, a man active in the NAACP and other organizations, was gunned down in Belzoni following his public addresses urging blacks to exercise their right to vote. The FBI conducted only a perfunctory investigation of his killing.[36]

A long line of activists carried forth the freedom struggle in Mississippi. Many were World War II veterans returning to the state, including Medgar Evers and Amzie Moore. Black churches played a relatively small role in developing this leadership. "Church people are somewhat active in community organizations but there has been no cooperation from the ministers of Deacons boards or the churches," read one very typical report from a local activist in Bolivar County, which included some all-black towns such as Mound Bayou. "Negro churches very negative," a white activist in Natchez notated in his journal. "Presently no church is open for freedom or civil rights meeting. Boycott stopped by cooperation of Negro ministers with whites. Public statement in local newspaper thanked the Negro ministers for bringing the boycott to an end." There were some exceptions, notably including Aaron Johnson, pastor of the First Christian Church in Greenwood, Mississippi. Johnson joined the NAACP in the 1950s, bailed a number of civil rights workers out of jail, and opened his church building for freedom meetings. Most of Johnson's pay came from the denominational office of the Disciples of Christ in Indianapolis, allowing him to survive even when attendance declined and his local salary fell to a pittance. Such activist clerics were the exception rather than the rule. In one part of Mississippi, residents recalled that a local ministerial leader, the Reverend J. J. Russell, was "the onliest preacher [who] stayed with us," while other clergymen "knowed so many of their members was afraid, and they's afraid they wouldn't get no money." Before his assassination in June 1963, state NAACP president Medgar Evers complained bitterly of the black clergymen in the state who dared not even mention the NAACP in their pulpits. The preachers' reliance on income from the congregants and the sharecropper churches' dependence on landlords forced religious institutions into positions of subservience.[37]

In much of Mississippi, women were at the forefront of the struggle. Black evangelical Protestantism, some scholars have argued, afforded women the same sense of power and proprietorship that landownership provided for men. The moment of freedom for black Mississippian Bee Jenkins came when she faced down a group of state troopers. Confronting the risks of joining a civil rights march, she "walked outta the house, looked up, said a prayer, and went and got in the marching." Despite the presence of law enforcement, she knew that "I had somebody there who was on my side. And that was Jesus; he was able to take care of me. That who I can depend on and put my trust in." For some men, also, religious faith was a prime mover. Cleveland Jordan, a deacon at Zion Baptist in Greenwood, boasted a "formidable knowledge of the Bible." Referring to black preachers connected to the white establishment through patronage and bribery, he blasted mere "grip toters and chicken eaters." One of his primary targets was the Reverend H. H. Humes, president of the General Missionary Baptist Convention, the state organization of over 400,000 black Baptists. Humes published a newspaper advising submission among sharecroppers and spied on organizing activities among black farm workers. The Delta Council, an organization of powerful white planters in the Mississippi Delta, kept agents in the black community. In Hattiesburg, the Reverend R. W. Woullard colluded with State Sovereignty Commission chairman Van Landingham, a former FBI employee who compiled dossiers on blacks and white sympathizers in the movement. Woullard also attempted to dissuade local activist Clyde Kennard from desegregating Mississippi Southern College. Authorities sentenced Kennard to hard time at Parchman Farm for the alleged offense of stealing chicken feed. At the huge penal colony, he contracted cancer. The state refused to treat him; the medical care following his release came too late to prevent his death. In part because of such brutality, the movement grew slowly in Hattiesburg.[38]

The police-state tactics of the Mississippi establishment intimidated many civil rights organizations. It would be more productive to focus on locales where some victories could be secured, they reasoned. But Christian SNCC organizers respected the "spirit" of the deeply evangelical local people with whom they worked. Black SNCC activists fused their evangelical heritage with lessons in radical nonviolent politics learned from James Lawson at Vanderbilt during the late 1950s. For Lewis, the freedom struggle was a "holy crusade," with the blood of civil rights martyrs redeeming the South from its former self-professed Redeemers. The young students who integrated lunch counters in Greensboro and inspired the original SNCC organizing conference also grew up in black churches. Two of the four initial pioneering student demonstrators in Greensboro attended Shiloh Baptist Church. Pastored by Otis Harrison, the church led an NAACP membership drive in 1959 and provided mimeograph materials for student sit-ins.[39]

SNCC's language in its early days was steeped in theology. Its real impulse went beyond integration, one participant explained, for beyond that lay the "redeemed community and the Kingdom of God." Racial prejudice, wrote one SNCC idealist, was a "judgment on the lie we have been living. . . . For though the days of lynching may be over, the lynching of personhood continues. It is a spiritual issue." The nonviolent character of the movement exhibited a "noble, dignified understanding of oneself," one that could "deal with the rabid segregationist as a person." The final goal of the student movement, the editor of SNCC's paper, the *Student Voice*, said, was the "retaining and creating of personhood," a task made difficult given that mass movements were "necessary to save the South and America." The radical organization's "distinctively idealistic belief that fortitude, determined action, and fearlessness would result in momentous social change," white SNCC worker Mary King later reminisced, "stemmed to a great degree from the Protestant upbringings of most of its workers." She connected her vision specifically to Wesleyan theology, that "through grace and redemption each person can be saved." This view reinforced the belief that the "good in every human being could be appealed to, fundamental change could correct the immorality of racial segregation, and new political structures could be created." The freedom struggle "abounded in the biblical ethos of the southland, black and white," King concluded; it was "part of the climate in which the movement was working." Belle Bennett, Louise Young, and Thelma Stevens each had enacted that same faith in the teeth of Jim Crow earlier in the century. Building on their legacy, black and white students used and transcended their church training in the freedom struggle.[40]

Christian students dramatized the appalling persistence of theological racism through "pray-ins" at churches. In the words of one participant, they showed that "the house of all people, fosters segregation more than any other institution." As the "best place for reconciling moral problems," they believed, the church was a legitimate target for direct action. In 1963, Ed King, a young white

Methodist chaplain at Tougaloo College near Jackson, organized protests in collaboration with the campus NAACP Youth Council. The Mississippi Conference of Methodists would not admit King to membership, preventing him from obtaining a pastoral appointment in the state. A Methodist district assigned specifically to African Americans welcomed him. In January 1963, twenty-eight Methodist ministers published in the *Mississippi Methodist Advocate* a pamphlet titled "Born of Conviction," affirming freedom of the pulpit and nondiscriminatory church membership policies. The pastor of the largest Methodist congregation in the state, W. B. Selah, backed the statement. But the Mississippi Association of Methodist Ministers and Laymen damned integration as a "crime against God" and drummed out all but seven of those twenty-eight signatories; those who remained indicated that the state Methodist hierarchy hung them out to dry. Later, Ed King helped northern Methodist clergy who came into the state as part of Freedom Summer in 1964, and was a delegate in the Mississippi Freedom Democratic Party. King led groups of students from Tougaloo College and other institutions to flagship white denominational congregations in Jackson. Three women from Tougaloo College (two black, one white) attempted to enter Capitol Street Methodist in the heart of Jackson on World Wide Communion Sunday in 1964. After being arrested and bailed out, they tried again. Others sought seating at Trinity Lutheran and Galloway Methodist. State officials blocked all their efforts. By mid-1964, thirty-seven pray-in participants had been arrested, including twenty-three Methodist clergymen at five different churches. The pray-ins and the arrests spread quickly to other regions of the South.[41]

Freedom Summer in 1964 arose from SNCC's efforts to publicize the difficulties of voter registration for tens of thousands of black Mississippians. Violent racist groups immediately made their own plans to counter the outside agitators. Sam Bowers, the Laurel resident who revived the state's White Knights of the Ku Klux Klan, intoned that "a Solemn, determined Spirit of Christian Reverence must be stimulated in all members." His words signaled that the counter-revolution against the southern freedom movement would dredge up virulent varieties of theological racism. The white Mississippi establishment lived up to its reputation, forming its own Sovereignty Commission as a state-sanctioned way to harass the "outside agitators." When Freedom Summer workers arrived in the spring of 1964, the State Sovereignty Commission turned over their identifying information (including license plate numbers) to policemen and Klan members. In June, two white northern SNCC volunteers, Michael Schwerner and Andrew Goodman, teamed with black Mississippian James Chaney to investigate church burnings in Neshoba County. A local member of the Mount Zion Methodist Church, near Philadelphia, arranged for Chaney and Schwerner to speak to his congregation on Memorial Day about Freedom Summer. The congregation also agreed to host a freedom school. A group of Klansmen arrived at Mount Zion just as a congregational board meeting was beginning. The men assaulted members of the congregation and later burned down the church building. Five days later, Klansmen abducted and murdered the three sncc workers, burying them in an earthen dam in a remote area of the county. They were discovered only weeks later, when mounting national public pressure compelled an investigation.[42]

The fact that many churches and ministers shrank from the conflict did not spare them from being targeted. In midsummer 1964, three black churches burned in Pike and Amite counties, despite the fact that the parishioners in these congregations had not been politically active. McComb, Mississippi, gained a reputation as the "bombing capital of the world," with numerous violent attacks during and after Freedom Summer. In its initial efforts, the Council of Federated Organizations (cofo) in Mississippi made little headway against these sinister elements. Churches closed themselves off, and only a few residents risked putting themselves on the front lines. Freedom Summer revived the struggling movement in McComb, as local youth shamed religious leaders into involvement. Congregations such as St. Paul's Methodist Church in McComb finally agreed to permit political gatherings.[43]

Even if ministers were recalcitrant, deacons and other parishioners could be educated and motivated. Amzie Moore, a local store owner and activist, chided one minister, "You preaching holiness, you say God can do everything. Now don't come back off your profession. If God can do everything and we done dedicated and give this church to God and if God can't take care of his own house, it's got to go, cause we gonna have the meetings. . . . All these preachers, Baptists, Methodists, claim like they had so much God, but they didn't believe the God they served could keep this white man off him. I used to tell them that [the] white man was their God.'" As people caught this spirit of resistance, they publicly attacked the timidity of their leadership. In response, local ministers tried to "build their images and redeem themselves," as one contemporary observer put it.[44]

Violence aimed at civil rights centers continued well beyond Freedom Summer and the passage of the congressional civil rights acts of the mid-1960s. Attempting to separate cofo from its local support base, segregationists employed indiscriminate violence against African Americans in McComb. On September 7, 1964, Klansmen bombed the homes of a black minister and school principal, neither of whom had been noted for acts of rebellion. Two nights later, the Reverend James Baker, a minister and farmer near Summit, suffered the same retribution. C. C. Bryant's Society Hill Baptist Church in McComb was blasted to the ground that same month, after the congregation transgressed sacred southern mores by using its mimeograph machine to run off practice copies of the

Mississippi voter registration form. The tactics persisted even after J. Edgar Hoover turned over to the governor a list of highway patrol officers who were Klan members and after agents of the Justice Department moved into communities with civil rights projects. A SNCC worker surveyed the damage to both buildings and spirit: "Who now? My mother, father, sister, brother. God damn, how much blood do they want. They got the church—Society Hill—the movement church. Its doors were closed this summer, but it has always been the center of the movement in South McComb. All the Freedom School kids belong to Society Hill. It's Bryant's church. The NAACP holds its meetings there. I spoke there this summer. SNCC workers were there the past Sunday and the Sunday before. . . . The church is demolished. It was a terrible blast. The police are here, certain again to see that all clues are removed and destroyed." In 1964, over 1,000 movement activists were arrested; dozens suffered beatings. COFO and SNCC members pondered painful questions. Could the sacrifice be justified? "We had told a lot of people to put down their guns and not be violent in Mississippi," SNCC organizer Dave Dennis later recalled, "and I wasn't so sure that the nonviolent approach was the right approach anymore. And I had to do a lot of soul searching about that." For many in the movement, the beatings administered the next year to John Lewis and scores of others attempting to march across the Edmund Pettis Bridge in Selma, Alabama, marked the nadir for the philosophy of nonviolence and soul force.[45]

Advocates of nonviolence and self-defense contended for the soul of the movement in the mid-1960s. The violence perpetrated by white supremacists made some shrink from the conflict and others reject nonviolence as a response. Yet many held to the faith. For example, the Reverend J. J. Russell of Holmes County, Mississippi, opened his church to movement meetings, even though "most of the churches was afraid," as he remembered. He joined the SCLC and later received funding for construction of the Holmes County Community Center, which endured despite Klan harassment. For his own protection, when driving home, Russell turned off his car lights and used special signals to indicate his arrival. One of his churches, Bell Chapel, was burned; others had windows shot out. Despite the harassment, and unlike Hartman Turnbow and many Delta activists, Russell himself never carried a gun. Instead he trusted his personal talisman, the Bible, which he called "the best weapon of all times. When I get out, I pull it up. The policeman starts tremblin' he have his pistol—'n' he goes to shaking. When I go in the courthouse, we would go in and carry the Bible. And they'd be shaking. They never did stop me on the road; they'd stop everybody but me." For others, though, the gun was a talisman of equal strength with the Bible. One SNCC worker reported of talking with a civil rights leader in Lee County and trying to determine "how to convince him (or to decide whether we *should* convince him) to leave his pistol home when he comes to mass meetings. After an intensive discussion of non-violence at one of our meetings, [he] told me, 'I believe in the Bible, the Lord, and my 30-30.'"[46]

In Greenwood, the marketing hub for cotton from the Delta, activists sustained themselves despite a fear campaign directed against them. When Medgar Evers and Aaron Henry, who had been scheduled to speak at Locust Grove Baptist Church in March 1963, were locked out, they moved to Reverend Aaron Johnson's First Christian congregation, where dozens registered to vote. The opening of Johnson's church was the first breakthrough for SNCC's intrepid organizer Sam Block. A day after the meeting, he later recounted, "as I walked the streets I met a lot of people, and the thing that they remembered most about that meeting was the songs we were singing. And they asked me when we were going to have another meeting and sing those songs." In response to SNCC's activities, Greenwood city officials cut off commodities to poor sharecroppers in the region, punishing those who SNCC sought to help. Black ministers generally were wary of opening their churches as distribution centers for food; most refused to become involved. SNCC workers who assumed the duties of sorting and distributing the commodities were fired upon. When the police arrived, they asked if civil rights volunteers had been associating with "that nigger Sam Block. That nigger is the most dangerous nigger in Mississippi."

Greenwood police arrested Block following his remarks to the press about a failed arson attempt directed at SNCC headquarters in town. A packed meeting at Aaron Johnson's church protested the outrage. During the following two days, more than 150 residents tried to register to vote. SNCC organizers in Greenwood turned increasingly to direct action. The resulting marches and demonstrations incited full-blown confrontations with city officials and attracted national attention to the Delta cotton center. The Reverend David L. Tucker, a young AME minister, led a group of forty-two prospective voters to register. Upon returning to Wesley Methodist Chapel, police dogs attacked them, enraging the community and getting the attention of Martin Luther King and Robert Kennedy.[47]

Grassroots organization depended on black southerners whose deep religious faith emboldened them to action. Unita Blackwell, a poor woman from Mayersville, Mississippi, was a church worker and mother in 1964 when SNCC came calling. She was one of the first to volunteer for voter registration. "I was in Issaquena County and we were just there," she later recalled. "It wasn't that we just went looking for the movement; the movement came to us. I was teaching some children about God and they came and asked me about registering to vote. They said, 'Well, you know they doing it over in such-and-such county.'" As many civil rights workers discovered, intimidation worked. Some of the deacons in Blackwell's church were "upset at the time. They were scared of white folks." Blackwell persevered anyway: "I had found it in the Bible that all men were created equal and I didn't understand that how come that this was my constitutional right and I couldn't have that. I got mad and I was determined that I wasn't gonna take no more. I realized that I was angry and that I had really felt this all of my life. . . . I didn't know what I was doing at first and [SNCC] acted like I was really doing something by talking to the people about civil rights." Like so many other civil rights believers, Blackwell mixed together the language of evangelicalism ("I had found it in the Bible") with the tenets of the American civil religion, how "this was my constitutional right and I couldn't have that." The two were inseparable in her mind.[48]

They were also inseparable in the mind of Fannie Lou Hamer, who personified the fortitude and vibrant religious imagery of the movement. Daughter of a sharecropper in Ruleville, Mississippi, she experienced sexual abuse and later sadistic torture at the hands of local policemen. Hamer rose to prominence in the 1960s as a liaison between "local people" and national civil rights leaders. With her wicked sense of humor, spirited singing voice, and uncompromising stance on justice, Hamer articulated a liberation theology that sustained her through years of struggle and turmoil. "She compares herself frequently to Job . . . without a trace of self pity or some warped sense of pride," wrote one northern admirer serving in Mississippi. "Her faith in God is pervasive and in a sense dominates her life. . . . There is a prophetic, messianic sense about her—an awareness, an electricity, a sense of mission which is very rarely absent." As a girl, Hamer had joined the Strangers Home Baptist Church in her hometown. She quoted the Bible expertly and led congregational song, qualities that served her admirably in the 1960s. In 1962, at a SNCC meeting in a rural church, Hamer and a few others volunteered to register to vote. This serious act of political defiance against the state regime earned them a beating in the county jail. After their release, they experienced economic and verbal harassment. For example, the mayor of Ruleville canceled the tax-exempt status of Williams Chapel Missionary Baptist Church, Hamer's congregation, reasoning that by welcoming in SNCC field secretaries the congregation had been using the building for "purposes other than worship services."

Hamer eventually won a seat in the Mississippi Freedom Democratic Party's delegation (sent as a protest against the all-white official state delegation) to the Democratic National Convention of 1964. Hamer incited Lyndon Baines Johnson's special ire as she delivered an impromptu national address explaining why the Freedom Democratic Party would not settle for the compromise of taking two seats on the official state delegation. Queried by reporters, Hamer told of the black Mississippians who had risked their lives simply for trying to exercise citizenship rights. Hamer led the participants in her favorite freedom song,

"This Little Light of Mine," a tune known by Sunday schoolers everywhere. In Hamer's version, the sweet ditty became a manifesto of freedom:

> This-a little light of mine, I'm gonna let it shine, let it shine
> Let it shine, let it shine.
> We've got the light of freedom, We're gonna let it shine . . .
> Tell Chief Pritchett, I'm gonna let it shine . . .
> Voting for my Freedom, I'm gonna let it shine. . . .[49]

Hamer's political stance required spiritual sustenance. "Before 1962," she later wrote, "I would have been afraid to have spoken before more than six people. Since that time I have had to speak before thousands in the fight for freedom, and I believe that God gave me the strength to be able to speak in this cause." She deployed her knowledge of the Bible in public rebukes of the timid. As she told one group of black Mississippians, "We are tired of being mistreated. God wants us to take a stand. We can stand by registering to vote—go to the court to register to vote." Christ would side with the sharecroppers in Mississippi during their struggle. Answering the inevitable charges that civil rights workers were agitators and communists, she retorted, "If Christ were here today, he would be branded a radical, a militant, and would probably be branded as 'red.'" Christ was a "revolutionary person, out there where it was happening. That's what God is all about, and that's where I get my strength." Summing up her life's work, she explained, "We can't separate Christ from freedom, and freedom from Christ." She criticized southern churches for doing "too much pretending and not enough actual working, the white ministers and the black ministers standing behind a podium and preaching a lie on Sunday." It was "long *past* time for the churches to wake up" and address fundamental life issues. Ephesians 6:11–12 provided the spiritual basis of the freedom struggle: "Put on the whole armor of God, that ye may be able to stand against the wiles of the devil. For we wrestle not against flesh and blood, but against principalities, against powers, against the rulers of the darkness of this world, against spiritual wickedness in high places." Women such as Fannie Lou Hamer "placed Jesus where his experiences, as passed through the traditions of the Black church, could be used in the freedom struggle."[50]

Besides the charismatic former sharecropper Hamer, other Mississippi women also served as movement stalwarts. Victoria Gray Adams, a self-described "Christian activist," was born to a poor family in 1926. Early in life she became a "conscientious objector to the closed society" of Mississippi, in part due to her visits to Detroit and other northern cities. When SNCC volunteers arrived in south Mississippi, she was a successful entrepreneur in Hattiesburg. She was ready for civil rights action, although the local churches generally were not. Two young SNCC staffers, Hollis Watkins and Curtis Hayes, called a meeting at the St. John

Methodist Church. Perhaps they expected "a great welcome, with the churches open to them, where they could go out and share their mission with the people in the community and all would go well," but only one church provided space. At this meeting, Adams shot her hand up during the "altar call," which at that service consisted of the "invitation for people to come and participate in seeking first-class citizenship." In her own words, she knew intuitively that "I might even lose my life because of raising my hand, but I knew that I had to do what I had done, and that brought the most important turning point in my life." Later, civil rights groups brought in ministers and others from outside Mississippi to help with marches. The locals "didn't have anywhere to put them," Adams realized, "because at this point people were not yet liberated enough in our parts to be willing to open up their homes" or to find them hotel rooms. More local people would have to be involved. She told the Starlight Church members "how wonderful it was to have these people come and share our journey and fight with us and for us and all that, but trying to say we too have got to do something." She remembered a scripture from Isaiah 6: "And I heard him say, 'Whom shall I send, whom can we send and who will go for us?'" Then "all of a sudden I found myself standing there saying that and realizing that it wasn't what somebody else said: at that moment it was my word of truth." She was the one who said here am I, send me, I'll go.[51]

Students and other activists far removed from the black southern evangelical ethos admired the strength of the indigenous tradition of resistance represented by Adams and Hamer. Leaders invigorated the people with prayer, song, testimony, and preaching. In the process, they learned of the evangelical fire that inspired churchgoers steeped in religious belief. Meetings in Greenwood surged with feelings evoked by prayer and music. As one participant expressed it, "The religious, the spiritual was like an explosion to me, an emotional explosion. I didn't have that available to me [before]. It just lit up my mind. The music and the religion provided a contact between our logic and our feelings." Ethel Gray had rattlesnakes thrown on her porch but afterward said proudly, "We stood up. Me and God stood up." As the journalist Pat Watters later suggested, King did not teach the people the "spirit of forgiveness, the philosophy of redemptive love. He drew it from them, learned it from them, had it, like the SNCC kids, in his own heart." Evangelical women in the struggle had it in their hearts also.[52]

Evangelical Women in the Freedom Struggle

In many local communities, evangelical organizations such as United Church Women (renamed as Church Women United in 1971) provided one avenue for white and black women to work toward a desegregated society. United Church

Women began in 1941 as an interdenominational fellowship of those who sought "integration in the total life and work of the church and to the building of a world Christian community." Rather than forming new committees and programs, UCW organizers intended the group to act as a clearinghouse for programs within denominations. The original national board included Mary McLeod Bethune, as well as five white southern women. The *Church Woman*, the organ of UCW, featured articles on Christian citizenship, temperance, and moderately liberal social themes of poverty and racism. Louise Young remembered her work with United Church Women as "the most fruitful on breaking down racial practices," as her UCW chapter had been "truly integrated and truly effective." Edith Mitchell Dabbs, born in South Carolina to a Southern Baptist ministerial family, led white women's Christian progressive organizations while working with black Sea Islanders. Her husband, James McBride Dabbs, was a member of the Fellowship of Southern Churchmen and a critic of white southern hypocrisies. Edith Dabbs found that suspicions and tensions ran high even in UCW. It was nearly impossible to find white churches that would allow integrated meetings under the group's auspices. Still, Dabbs felt that in UCW she "got to know the most liberal women" that she had met anywhere.[53]

Race was "peculiarly our problem. It is in our thinking, consciously and unconsciously, all the time," wrote one southern UCW member in 1955. In the 1950s and 1960s, UCW took part in local civil rights action. When the State Board of Education in Georgia revoked the license of a teacher who had joined the NAACP, the local UCW resolved to "reaffirm our faith in the public schools, in academic freedom and in the loyalty and integrity and ability of our teachers, without regard to race or creed." UCW endorsed the sit-in movement of the early 1960s and participated in biracial committees that negotiated local racial conflicts.[54]

In "Assignment: RACE," a project carried out from 1961 to 1964, UCW worked to "mobilize and train women in local church councils and denominational groups to work toward improved race relations." Carrie Meares, a South Carolina native, former African missionary, member of the national Christian Social Relations Committee for UCW in the 1940s, and world YWCA adviser, founded the project. In Greensboro, North Carolina, for example, women supported ministers who fostered racial harmony. In Atlanta, UCW looked after the welfare of women jailed during protest demonstrations and sponsored programs to ease tensions arising from school desegregation.[55]

Meares collected statistical surveys summarizing the efforts of individual councils in supporting civil rights legislation, equal employment opportunities, and equal access to public accommodations. Reports varied widely and showed how much white paternalism and black suspicion lingered in particular chapters. A UCW group in Georgia highlighted its work in helping the "Negro race develop a more Christ like attitude in achieving their goals." One white UCW chapter praised the progress it perceived it had made in "developing a sense of responsibility among the Negroes," while another group condemned the "misguided aggressiveness of outside agitators, including the National Council of Churches." Distrust of the council had "all but destroyed UCW," they believed. In marked contrast, a black UCW chapter complained, "We can't in any way get the cooperation of the white people"; their pleas for white ministers to attend biracial prayer services had elicited no response.[56]

As such reports indicated, UCW's work produced mixed results, but at times it significantly addressed the tensions gripping the South. During 1964–65, about 50 northern women contacted more than 300 white and black southern women of "every faith and shade of opinion" in a program called "Wednesdays in Mississippi." UCW members sent supplies to students in the Freedom Summer project and "tried to dispel some of the misconceptions" about Freedom Summer's makeup and goals. One volunteer later commented, "Even some of the most hostile women in the South seemed to have been impressed by the sincerity and respectability of the team members." A follow-up team in 1965 included one Philadelphia (Pennsylvania)–to–Philadelphia (Mississippi) group that sought to allay racial strife in a town made infamous the previous year by the murders of three civil rights workers nearby. By the end of the visits, 400 white and black women from North and South had participated. "We were careful not to offend the mores of the community by flaunting our own integration," an organizer noted, "but it was known that women of both races moved and worked together as much of the time as was feasible." Many of the southern women later attempted to open up their own churches to black members. "They could not have done this without meeting—through our teams—women who were already hard at work on these efforts," she proudly concluded. A northern woman who visited Jackson found a meaningful fellowship among white and black women at the Pearl Street Baptist Church, a black congregation in the state capitol. There, she gathered with twenty-nine UCW members, notably including Myrlie Evers, wife of the slain state director of the Mississippi NAACP. For all the optimism such fellowship engendered, she also reminded UCW that "religious extremes and hatred of the National Council of Churches, suspicions—these certainly blanket the area. The communist conspiracy theory is rampant and evident even in the churches as in the civil life."[57]

In reporting to funders of these projects, Meares cited the success of desegregation in the Alabama chapter of United Church Women and the organization's progress toward fair housing. "Hundreds of women," Meares continued, "have a deep sense of frustration, futility and guilt as they see the tragic gap and distance between their convictions as Christians and the daily practice of their church and their community. . . . Assignment: Race provides a channel through which conviction can be deepened and 'know how' gained, and the power thus released mobilized for *action* to effect change in church, council and community." Participants in UCW sensed the irritation among African Americans who saw "the state and local courts upholding white people, so-called 'good Christians,' in their defiance of the Supreme Court ruling," and the "quiet conniving of the white man" in resisting desegregation. "The Negro often asks why the white Christian does not take the initiative in matters relating to this issue," wrote one member, and why the church "takes a stand only after the demonstration. United Church Women are in danger of losing Negro women at this crucial point." A black UCW participant added, "The mood of the Negro today is threefold: *Determination, Anger, Sorrow*."[58]

During the 1960s, black women assumed executive positions in UCW. Claire Collins Harvey, one of Jackson's black elite, was the daughter of Malachi Collins, the first black mortician in Hattiesburg, Mississippi, and founder of a funeral home chain, an important avenue of entry for black entrepreneurship. In 1939, Harvey attended the World Christian Conference and became involved in UCW. In 1940, she co-sponsored the Farish Street branch of the YWCA and became the first female trustee of Tuskegee Institute. In 1961, she founded Womanpower Unlimited, an interracial human relations group aiding civil rights workers. When the Freedom Riders came to Jackson in 1961, Harvey established an interracial network of some 300 women who provided resources for the jailed workers, initiated voter registration campaigns, and led boycotts of Jackson businesses. In 1971, Church Women United elected her as its first black president. Many black Christians, she explained in the *Church Woman*, still felt that "second-class churchmanship" was the "order of the day." For example, too many chapter meetings of Church Women United saw participants politely conversing but not getting to the palpable "levels of mutual hostility" that existed. As Harvey noted, many white women could "give lip service to integration" without making "any really basic changes in their attitudes and practices."[59]

Generations of training in segregation and acts of intimidation reinforced this kind of caution among sympathetic but cautious and fearful whites. The image of pure white southern womanhood provided no defense against threats directed at Claudia Thomas Sanders. In her short piece "This I Believe," the genteel Episcopalian churchwoman presented the gradualist case for acceptance of the Supreme Court's ruling on desegregating schools. She advocated moving "*slowly*" but also "*surely* because our social conscience and Christian ethics leave us no alternative." Sanders's article appeared in the 1957 pamphlet *South Carolinians Speak: A Moderate Approach to Race Relations*. The timing coincided with the tumultuous fall semester at Central High School in Little Rock, hardening segregationist attitudes into massive resistance. Mrs. Sanders authored her piece at the request of Episcopalian clergymen in South Carolina who sought to "steer a course between the excesses of the White Citizens Councils on the one hand and extreme excesses of the NAACP on the other." The pamphlet featured both opponents and proponents of desegregation, attempting to show that whites could discuss regional problems rationally, that freedom of speech still existed. Segregationists responded by engaging in a campaign of propaganda and intimidation directed at dissenters to regional orthodoxy.[60]

In Atlanta, Sarah Mitchell Parsons, another quintessential southern dissenter, grew up comfortably in white Georgia and began her adult life as a conventional Atlanta housewife. As a leader of the Woman's Society of Christian Service in the Peachtree Road Methodist Church, she gradually became aware of political matters. Her interest peaked initially in 1947 after hearing Henry Wallace speak at Wheat Street Baptist Church, a prominent black congregation that provided to the Progressive Party presidential candidate an integrated audience in a segregated town. Even while sitting "primly on the hard pew wearing my white gloves and hat," she surmised correctly that most men were registered to vote and most women not. Through the 1950s, she used her church affiliation and leadership post in the League of Women Voters to urge women to exercise their political voice. Well aware of the controversy that would ensue from her suggestion, she insisted that black women be allowed to join the league. "Once I started looking more closely at the world around me," she recounts in her autobiography, "I could never go back." During the 1960s, her "religious beliefs and . . . now active civil rights conscience collided. In the ensuing battle, traditional white southern Methodist ideology lost." Parsons articulated the shameful truth that "at the historical moment when the white churches of the Bible Belt most needed to prove their Christianity, they failed miserably. The shame of their stand against integration will endure as a blot on their history."[61]

Sue Thrasher presents an even more compelling example of progressive women of evangelical background engaged in the freedom struggle. Thrasher grew up on a farm near Savannah, Georgia, a devoted churchgoer influenced by her years in the Methodist Youth Fellowship. The church taught her values that she brought to the freedom movement. Ironically if inevitably, it was those values— "like the fatherhood of God and the brotherhood of man"—that led her to "turn away from the church later." As a student at Scarritt in Nashville, Thrasher authored a resolution restating words from the Methodist book of discipline about human equality before God. She had been moved to action when she witnessed a Fijian student denied service at a local greasy spoon. The student council at Scarritt rejected the resolution, fearing it might result in picketing. The situation was "very different than the endless talk about interracial gatherings and working behind the scenes," she realized.

While at Scarritt, Thrasher was perceived as a radical. Gradually, she actually became one after attending James Lawson's instruction in active nonviolent resistance. After finishing at Scarritt, she abandoned plans to enter the mission field and chose instead to work at a Methodist publishing house, a job that kept her in close contact with the freedom movement. She came to know Carl and Anne Braden, white radicals who suffered severely in the 1950s after they sold a house to a black couple in a white neighborhood in Louisville, Kentucky. Thrasher produced articles for their paper, the *Southern Patriot*. The job trained her for later forays into historical journalism for the liberal magazine *Southern Exposure*, where she published pieces on the history of southern radicalism in the 1930s and 1940s. Thrasher also worked with the Southern Student Organizing Committee, a group of white southern college students who supported SNCC activists. In her own words, she was a "good Christian girl trying to do something about racial inequality." She was also the product of three generations of southern evangelical women who helped to transform their society.[62]

The efforts of black and white women from multiple generations—including Ella Baker, Fannie Lou Hamer, Rosa Parks, Virginia Durr, Jo Ann Gibson Robinson, Dorothy Tilly, Sandra Cason, Fannie Lou Hamer, Victoria Gray Adams, Dorothy Burlage, Sue Thrasher, Constance Curry, and Joan Browning—blossomed in a period of intense student activism in the South through the early and mid-1960s. The Christian Faith and Life Community at the University of Texas nurtured many younger women, notably Sandra Cason (later Casey Hayden). The native Texan attended the state university in Austin in the mid-1950s. Through the local YWCA, she learned (in her own words) a "democratic manner of work." She also joined the Christian Faith and Life Community, a project in which participants tried to "create meaning through intentional living." She experienced what she described as the "creation of empowering community" and later "understood the movement on this model. Our image of ourselves in the southern Freedom Movement was that of the Beloved Community, created by the activity, the experience, of nonviolent direct action against injustice." Her southern white female comrades, including Constance Curry and Jane Stembridge, constituted her "base community inside the movement in these early days." Like Thrasher, she also studied James Lawson's lessons on nonviolence, interpreting them as "at heart a presentation or demonstration of oneself. It was the acting out of a self-understanding of oneself as essentially free—existentialism carried to the streets."[63]

As a leader of the Christian Faith and Life Community, Hayden inspired others who were quiet revolutionaries during the civil rights years. One was Dorothy Dawson Burlage, a native of South Texas near San Antonio. A tradition of paternalism mixed with rank racism dominated race relations in her home area. Her pastors frequently exegeted scriptural passages to explain why "blacks should be manual laborers working for white people." While attending the University of Texas, she became involved in the National Student Association and the YWCA. "Though my framework for challenging segregation was becoming secular as well as religious," she later wrote, "I still felt that my Christian background was the major source of my social ethics." As with many of her SNCC comrades, the movement became her spiritual home, even as the organized religion that had nurtured her seemed increasingly irrelevant: "I was at home with the ideals of the Southern Freedom Movement, with its religious tradition and its commitment to nonviolence and creating a Beloved Community. The movement became my new spiritual home." Later, she organized a voter education drive in Raleigh, North Carolina, which served as a direct model for the larger effort during Freedom Summer in 1964. She tried to run her program in the democratic and nonhierarchical way she had learned from Cason in the YWCA. She also cooperated with Septima Clark on a citizenship school project for the SCLC following training with Andrew Young and Dorothy Cotton at Dorchester, Georgia.[64]

Like Burlage, progressive southern women in the civil rights era discovered that their "sense of place" lay in the movement. As one participant later said, "If this sense has to do with feeling at home, or secure, or belonging, then mine lies in the Beloved Community and Freedom Movement of the early sixties, with our vision of a truly integrated society." The same feeling of place also inspired Joan Browning, a native of Telfair County, Georgia. She came from a family of self-sufficient country folk; her parents read the *Progressive Farmer* and were proud of being good stewards of the land. The Methodism that nurtured her was "an exuberant, joyful, life-affirming faith." Browning also witnessed the ugly legacy of white supremacy in Georgia, notably in the powerful political personages of the Talmadge family. She moved from home to attend Georgia State College for Women in Milledgeville (where, in an earlier generation, Katherine Du Pre Lumpkin attended school). While there she attended an AME congregation that reminded her of the rural roots she now missed. "I went there to worship," she later reflected, "not to break some racial barrier." Threats of violence compelled her to leave town. "The warmth and friendliness of a small community," she remembered sadly, "meant ostracism from the very thing I sought." Her actions had "unknowingly aroused white segregationists' worst nightmares." While only intending to explore "new dimensions of my own Christianity," Browning wrote, in fact she had challenged the white South's deepest mores about miscegenation, and consequently was forced into internal exile.[65]

Following her expulsion, Browning attended an annual student seminar at Paine College titled "The Christian Student and the University," where she observed Lawson's techniques of nonviolent civil disobedience. These "echoed and expanded lessons" from her childhood, showing "how to be a Shiloh witness that God is love." She practiced nonviolence by picketing stores in Augusta, Georgia, where the meeting was held. The next morning, protesters attended a mass meeting of the black Tabernacle Baptist Church, where Browning felt as "welcome and loved as if I were in my home church at the end of a revival meeting." In 1962, Browning moved on to Atlanta, where she worked for SNCC as a volunteer and found her "spiritual exploration turning from organized Christianity to activism and into existentialism and eastern mysticism." In the freedom movement, she finally found an "all-inclusive true church." Her labor of love, she wrote, "grew naturally out of my beliefs about my role as a Christian in response to social sins. My role was that of 'witness' to spiritual values." The work had a huge cost, for "participation made us outcasts—women without a home." And yet the journey from her father's white Methodist church to Albany's black churches as a freedom rider seemed natural: "I did not believe I was taking sides. I thought I was merely witnessing to a universal belief."[66]

Christian Interracial Ministries

In addition to SNCC, theological students found other avenues of entrée into the revolution sweeping the South. The Student Interracial Ministry Program (SIM), a program run out of Union Theological Seminary, placed student interns in the center of southern communities in the struggle. Starting in four locales in 1961, the SIM project later grew to encompass twenty counties. Between 1960 and 1966, SIM harnessed the energies of more than 200 students, 66 of them in 1966 alone. One section of SIM placed a group of students in Southwest Georgia under the direction of Charles Sherrod. In his proposal to the United Presbyterian Board of Missions, the SNCC activist and ministerial apprentice suggested that an interracial group of male and female seminary students seek "in active witness and worship, in and with the world, to understand our 'call' in Christ in such a time as this." Sherrod felt that the "Christian 'revolutionary' is a freed man for others; the 'Movement' is one manifestation of the 'Church'; the 'missionary enterprise' can be interpreted in terms of the 'Movement' and the 'Church'; and so the process of becoming the Church is always moving!" The civil rights movement was simply "one context in which the Church can be found."[67]

Sherrod wanted the seminarians not to descend as theological interlopers but to live with the people. The students worked with social service agencies, taught German at Spelman College in Atlanta, served with Head Start in Baker County, helped tenant farmers' organizations, and registered new African American voters. White students encountered timidity and divisions within black communities, and they recognized the exaggerated deference shown to them by a cowed local black population as a nearly insurmountable barrier to real communication. Most of the local leadership, as one participant noted, was "composed of deeply 'religious' people," including ministers who pastored several once-a-month churches while holding down other jobs on the side. The part-time clergymen felt "threatened by the presence of people who were turning their city and indeed their churches upside down."[68]

Students stationed themselves in black and white neighborhoods and everywhere felt the stifling influence of the white church—astutely judged in one SIM letter as the "ideological arm of the Southern Way of Life." M. Katherine Havice and Edith Snyder, two SIM participants, rented a house in the white section of Albany. They learned that some of their neighbors at least dimly perceived the sinister force of segregationism. Some white ministers understood the ethical implications of Jim Crow, the women reported, but these individuals seemed the "most alone, frightened and frustrated group. The race situation is not freely discussed within this group, and we have come to know more about their positions than they know perhaps of each other's." Because of their "politically exposed and vulnerable positions," clergymen generally were reluctant to be progressive. Churchwomen in Albany identified with the pair in part as "symbols of liberated womanhood." Local women wanted to form discussion groups on race, but "pressure was applied which effectively discouraged any such meeting for the time being." As Havice and Snyder concluded, "If a person were to work more deeply into the Church structure she could provide real leadership for these women in a way that would not be subject to their relatives' fear of political and business pressure."[69]

Student Interracial Ministry volunteers sent back dispatches from all over the South detailing their personal and philosophical transformations. A Southern Baptist minister and SIM participant from Harrisonburg, Virginia, wrote that he had learned to listen to those he had "ignored before—poor people, oppressed people, scared people, dejected people, hopeless people." He concluded that "we can not afford to be moderate while others suffer" and that "Christianity must become revolutionary." Other seminarians realized that it was impossible to do God's work inside the white southern religious establishment, a closed system of "oppression and narrowness." The "typical" white sermon, as this participant discovered, concerned only "piety and personal morals and the struggle of Christianity with the evil forces of the world which, translated into the layman's language, means the struggle of the American way of life against communism." Working within the "ideological arm of the southern way of life" could lead only to complete frustration or total compliance. Impetus for change would have to come from the outside. The Student Interracial Ministry offered to free churches from their straitjacket. In his three-year retrospective, Sherrod reported some halting progress:

> I have seen the church moving, surging and falling, struggling to breathe, eager to learn the truth; I have seen it in stinking jail cells packed with people, singing and sweating people, brought before the Pilates of this day; I have seen the church under the stars praying and singing in the ashes of a burned down church building, in the winter shivering under a tent in the open country, in a home where people cried together without speech but with a common understanding; I have seen the church in a pool room. I have seen with my eyes whites protecting blacks with their bodies and blacks bleeding to shield whites from whites. I have seen ministers lead their congregation from Sunday service to the City Hall to condemn the state. I have seen ministers with three grades of education put Ph.D.s to shame.[70]

SIM provided one model for church people involved in the struggle. In 1963 and especially during Freedom Summer in 1964, the National Council of Churches experimented with other innovative ways to harness these energies. The National Council sponsored training sessions for volunteers in Freedom Summer, sent scores of clergy who served as minister-counselors into Mississippi during 1964, and invited lawyers to provide legal defense after arrests. The volunteers almost uniformly reported back on the caution they saw among the black clergy. "These fellows are scared and their people know it," wrote one participant of the ministers he talked to in the Mississippi Delta town of Indianola. "Unless they get going they and the 'Church' are going to get left way behind in this movement!" Others criticized many northern volunteers for their insensitivity to the fact that "the Negro revolt seems to gain its fire and momentum as a basically religious and moral movement," that the "religion" in the movement was not something to be manipulated as a tool or stratagem. They found white clergy to be consistently timid, paternalistic, or effectively Klansmen of the cloth. "For him the Christian action is benevolent paternalism and everyone stay in his place," one volunteer wrote of a kindly Presbyterian pastor in Vicksburg. Most white southern clergymen were more contemptuous of the outside agitators.[71]

The Freedom Summer project of 1964, which counted among its participants over 235 ministers from all over the nation, also gave birth to the Delta Ministry, one exemplifying the "servant" vision for the involvement of religious people in the freedom movement. Ministers involved with it admired Martin Luther King's ability to transcend the premises of neo-orthodox theology, especially its emphasis on the reality of evil, and the consequent moral imperative of active engagement in the world. The Delta Ministry followed the same path, drawing from the legacy of Christian interracialism in the South while also attempting to negotiate the traps of paternalism and heavy-handed mission work that characterized earlier efforts dating from Reconstruction.

In the fall of 1964, the National Council of Church's Commission on Religion and Race opened an office in Greenville, Mississippi. This became the first home for the Delta Ministry, which later rented the abandoned Disciples of Christ College near Edwards as a more permanent base of operations. Following unsuccessful attempts to mediate conflicts in Mississippi, and experiments with minister-counselors who volunteered during Freedom Summer, the Delta Ministry aimed to create a long-term program of community development and reconciliation in a state still rent by conflict and impoverishment. "Demonstrations . . . will be played down and citizenship schools, seminars, community service, inter-race dialogue, and voter registration will be the order of the day," explained an early participant. It began with a full-time staff of four from various denominations. Arthur Thomas, a veteran of Freedom Summer, was its first director. Thomas was an ordained Methodist minister who earned a graduate degree in economics from Duke. He had been interested in the labor movement in North Carolina and helped to organize the first interracial church in Durham. In 1963, he became a southern field representative for the Commission on Religion and Race. Robert Beech, a Presbyterian from Iowa, and Harry Bowie, an Episcopal priest from New Jersey, took charge of offices in Hattiesburg and McComb. "Both our black and white brethren there must come to sense our oneness with them in their struggle," Beech wrote of his decision to go south.[72]

A project of the National Council of Churches, the Delta Ministry combined social service and civil rights action, attempting to minister to immediate needs of food and clothing and underlying problems of "equal justice, education, political power, [and] economic development." The ministry supported black textile workers in the Greenville Mills, set up a city for tenant farmers driven off farm land, conducted Freedom Schools, and distributed food to the poor of any race. One worker from the Hattiesburg project reported that poor whites from the region began showing up for food distributions. They lolled about nervously, gradually taking some handouts and bringing along friends. "We began to talk about the problems that make people poor and keep them that way," he reported, "about the similarity between their troubles and those of the Negroes, and about segregation and prejudice itself." He received an invitation to preach at a local Holiness congregation. To share in the service itself was an experience, the minister said, "but to do so with men who had been pointed out to me previously as members of the Klan added yet another mixed feeling!" To these participants, the Delta Ministry Project exemplified the newfound power of ecumenicism.[73]

Those moments of contact and small triumphs were relatively few, however, in comparison to the rejection, fear, hostility, and apathy the participants more often encountered. Begun as a ministry of reconciliation, the Delta Ministry soon discovered that a "true reconciliation between unequal and alienated groups is not possible without justice." They determined to work with the poor, not becoming another middle-class reformist group but taking a stance of "responsible militancy" and demanding an answer to the question: "Will the Church support a ministry which is under fire because it is carrying out the Gospel of serving the poor and freeing the captives."[74]

That "militancy," a self-conscious identification with Mississippi's black poor, inevitably heightened suspicion. Whites involved in the Delta Ministry hoped to develop relationships with white southern clergy, but they usually were disappointed. The "hard" opposition of violent threats and attacks was expected. More surprising to the Delta Ministry idealists was the "quiet, determined, and effective attempt" on the part of Mississippi's white church leaders to "discredit the Ministry and get it out of the state." Local pastors refused them entrance into churches, ignored invitations for meetings, or simply felt, as one local pastor expressed it, that "any cooperation with Civil Rights workers in Mississippi would be extremely detrimental to any ministry he might be accomplishing among the members of the congregation." Delta Ministry participants longed for a "mutual relationship with the white churches" but mostly "met with only rejection because of the explicit Delta Ministry involvement with an integrated society and with the poor." White religious leaders throughout Mississippi lambasted the clerical troublemakers, and they withheld contributions from the NCC to wring dry the Delta Ministry's budget. "It becomes increasingly clear how difficult it is for ministers here," one observer wrote of white pastors sympathetic with the movement. "One admires their courage. But the power structure is on the side of the segregationists, and . . . they have things pretty well sewed up."[75]

The local black clergy and many congregants, too, shied away from the controversial clerics. Stationed in Hattiesburg through most of 1965, a Delta Ministry participant found that while most of the people in the movement were church members, few of them made a connection between religious teaching and movement activism: "This is not to say that people think of the Movement as unchristian, but rather that no one is making the motivations inherent in a Christian's approach to social, day-to-day problems clear." Until pastors began to "delineate Christian living to the parishioners in terms of involvement in the Movement," he felt that "no large-scale move in this direction" could occur. Meanwhile, a "kind of Cold War" froze relations between the Delta Ministry and the NAACP in town. The middle-class orientation of the NAACP ensured conflict with the liberation theology expressed in the Delta Ministry Project. National Council of Churches leaders were frustrated at the lack of effective local leadership for the poor black communities in particular. The Delta Ministry's major attempt to create a "model city" for displaced sharecroppers near Greenville — derided as "Mud City" by its critics — ended in failure when troops evicted the squatters. The ministry developed close connections with federal agencies such as the Office of Economic Opportunity, despite talk of avoiding the federal government and "its pernicious poverty program." One radical Delta Ministry critic concluded of the group's failed efforts, "As I said in the beginning never trust a Christian."[76]

Despite such obstacles, leaders of the group kept the faith. "This is really where the church ought to be," Andrew Young said of his time with this work. "Something dealing with the political, economic, and social realities of the time. Something that is not afraid to face death for something they believe in." In this "lifetime struggle," Young believed, the church would have to work patiently, realizing that the Kingdom would arrive and that "it does come each day for some people in some place. The food for a hungry mother in the backwoods of Holmes County represents the coming of the Kingdom, that even the right to vote in Belzoni and the very fact that you dare to run a candidate in there, does represent some progress. Not the coming of the Kingdom, but certainly the promise of it in our midst."[77]

Mississippi's white churches, of course, saw freedom's coming differently. They threw up considerable resistance to what Young hoped was the "promise" of the Kingdom "in our midst." The colossal moral failure of white southern churches was very real but certainly not preordained, for there was considerable (if ultimately ineffectual) effort within white denominations to move beyond their history and legacy of theological racism, even at times to tentatively embrace Christian interracialism.

The Civil Rights Movement and the White Churches

Into the early years of the civil rights movement, some optimistic observers held out hope for white southern religious institutions. Movement figures accorded some beneficial role to white churches at least in preparing their people for the change. Christian nonviolence, Andrew Young felt, "resonated with the strong moral foundation that was characteristic of Southern culture. The movement helped people to understand that segregation was morally wrong, and I believe that most whites were actually relieved when the laws were changed. It lifted them from a tremendous moral burden." The fact that the "white clergy urged forebearance" helped to bring about reconciliation. This was an essential part of a movement that was "trying to transform America, not triumph over white folk."[78]

There were more incipient rebels and reconcilers in the Upper South than elsewhere, but they could be found throughout the region. The war hardly converted white southern denominations overnight. For example, Southern Presbyterians in 1947 insisted that integration was not "desired by the best informed and wisest members of either the white or colored races in the Southland." Racial intermingling "socially and in religious conferences cannot successfully be effected without far reaching dangers." By 1954, these same Presbyterians strongly supported the school desegregation decision. Southern progressive religious elites, even those in conservative churches such as those in the Southern Baptist Convention, increasingly questioned segregation. Meanwhile, in Mississippi, Methodist bishop Marvin Franklin preached against "Hitler's paganism," the heretical idea of a master race. Pointing out that eight million sharecroppers earned less than $250 a year, he envisioned a postwar world based on justice for all. "Special privileges for the few, enslavement for the multitude, is not fair or right," he proclaimed. "No race, or class, or people must be exploited." H. Brent Schaeffer, a white Lutheran minister in Jackson and chairman of the Mississippi branch of the Southern Regional Council, headed a biracial group of ministers who called for cooperation to allow black Americans to "participate normally in the practice of [their] citizenship." In his view, the prevalence of contemporary global unrest, including black American aspirations for equal rights, came from the widespread desire for democracy. The Second Presbyterian Church in Richmond hosted an interracial meeting of the Fellowship of Southern Churchmen, with luncheon sessions at the Central YWCA. Participants agreed that no gathering in the city had "ever gone as far toward the goal of belittling the policy of segregation as did this one."[79]

In retrospect, this yearning for signs of hope and collective faith in a coalescing of moderate forces from religious communities appear naive. More typically, most white Christians avoided the fray altogether. Benjamin Mays lamented that during his life, the local white church had been "society's most conservative and hypocritical institution in the area of White-Negro relations," adding pointedly that most black churches did not have a "record of which to be proud." For white clerics, the most charitable explanation was simply that they sought to lead their congregations without alienating them from the outset, as an overly public stance might do. Many expressed the hesitating belief of one pastor who explained privately to Ralph McGill of the *Atlanta Constitution* that he could "do more on a personal relationship in my pastoral visitation" than in issuing public pronouncements. Most white ministers, he concluded, were perplexed about the wisest course of action. This attitude was hardly sufficient for many critics at that time or later. As a Greensboro, North Carolina, clergyman later recalled, "A lot could have been done to get the business power structure behind what was taking place . . . but no one person really emerged as a leader. The potential for leadership was fantastic, but they all hung back. The greatest reason was just the desire to avoid conflict."[80]

In particular locales, some whites attempted to take constructive action. In Little Rock, Marion Boggs pastored Second Presbyterian for twenty years. During the Central High School controversy, he led protests against Arkansas governor Orval Faubus's defiance of the Supreme Court. Prior to the opening of the 1957–58 school year, Boggs preached a widely noticed sermon titled "The Crucial Test of Christian Citizenship." Boggs insisted that the struggle for civil rights was "part for God's plan for the emancipation of mankind" and that segregation by law was in "direct contradiction to the Christian doctrine of the Dignity of Man." Some Presbyterian parishioners were heartened to see a minister uphold the Southern Presbyterian General Assembly declaration of 1954, which said that "enforced segregation on the basis of race is out of harmony with Christian theology and ethics." Churchmen from other parts of the South, however, bitterly rebuked Boggs. A doctor in Mississippi advised the moderate Little Rock clergyman to read the Book of Ezekiel to see "what God said about the sins of the Egyptians, there you can see what will happen to America if mixing of the races continues." He exulted, "Everywhere there is trouble except in my State and I thank my God I live in *Mississippi*."[81]

In the Southern Baptist Convention, a minority of progressive elites "weaned Southern Baptists away from support for segregation as public policy." In a shift "subtle rather than seismic," historian Mark Newman has argued, they gradually undermined the "mystic, sacred, and seemingly immutable character of segregation." The Southern Baptist Convention leadership advocated a positive response to desegregation even while their constituent churches shored up the ancien régime (a conflict explored further in Chapter 5). The Texas educator J. B. Weatherspoon was a godfather to a generation of white Southern Baptist progressives, including Foy Valentine and other inside agitators in the nation's largest Protestant denomination. Weatherspoon essentially wrote the sbc's endorsement of the *Brown v. Board* decision and defended it passionately at its 1954 meeting. "We recognize the fact that this Supreme Court decision is in harmony with the constitutional guarantee of equal freedom of all citizens, and with the Christian principles of equal justice and love for all men," the sbc resolved, in a move that the *Christian Century* magazine optimistically if mistakenly projected would "go a long way to secure acceptance of the controversial ruling." The resolution expressed faith in the public school system as "one of the greatest factors in American history for the maintenance of democracy and our common culture."

Weatherspoon influenced T. B. Maston, a Southern Baptist ethicist whose works were widely distributed and taught in Southern Baptist schools. Segregation, Maston insisted, "inevitably means discrimination, [and] is contrary to the spirit and teachings of Christ." Weatherspoon also mentored Hugh Brimm, head of the Christian Life Commission from 1948 to 1953, and Foy Valentine, its director from 1960 to 1987. Both men consistently attacked segregation and economic injustice. In the 1940s, Brimm spearheaded a new publication, *Light*, which reported on progress made in reducing race prejudice among Southern Baptists (including state Baptist Student Unions voting to hold meetings on a nonsegregated basis). This outlet for southern religious progressives endorsed Truman's program of civil rights, called for the abolition of the white primary, denounced Dixiecrats as fascists, and suggested that whites consider joining the NAACP. This remarkable public appeal appeared at a time when black Baptist leader D. V. Jemison assured white Southern Baptists that southern Negroes were content, and at a time when Truman's policies had inflamed southern segregationists into bolting the Democratic Party in favor of the Dixiecrat ticket headed by Strom Thurmond. Brimm condemned the "use of the sacred symbol of the Christian faith by the hooded promoters of race hatred and bigotry" as a "presumptuous sacrilege."[82]

Chaired by Foy Valentine, the Christian Life Commission of the Southern Baptist Convention (CLC) — which, as one member later said, was referred to in South Carolina Baptist circles as the "white NAACP" — insistently prodded Southern Baptists toward a recognition of their complicity in the region's unjust order. Raised as a devout Baptist in East Texas, Valentine interned for Clarence Jordan at Koinonia Farm and worked in interracial revival teams in the late 1940s. From the 1950s forward until his retirement in 1987, he fought to compel Southern Baptists to address issues of social justice, most especially through his work on the CLC first in Texas and later at the denominational headquarters in Nashville. He fought the standpat status quo of Southern Baptists, which in effect said, "Just don't make trouble, don't rock the boat . . . let's build these red brick buildings to make us look good." His response was to "lead, to pressure, to cajole, to plead" toward the ideal of "apply[ing] Christian principles in all of life." Valentine insisted, "We have been part of a culture which has crippled the Negro and then blamed him for limping." Valentine's CLC vigorously attacked the segregationist position, partly in response to the proliferation of prosegregationist hate literature. "Our Southern Baptist witness for Jesus Christ continues to be challenged more seriously and more fundamentally by the racial crisis than by any other ideological movement or moral problem in our time," CLC members insisted.[83]

In addition to Valentine, other white southern theological leaders attacked the religious mythologies that justified segregation. Vanderbilt professor Edward Leverett's *Segregation and the Bible*, published in 1958, demolished received folklore about the ancient biblical origins of the three races. The Genesis myth for segregation could not withstand any serious analysis, he pointed out, and neither could a presumption of racial purity based on irrelevant passages in Ezekiel about not intermixing lower animal and plant forms. The New Testament cut hard against "every single assumption of the argument for the doctrine of a limited or divided brotherhood. It supplies neither argument nor precedent for the restriction of membership on racial grounds, nor for the division of members along racial lines." Segregationists and integrationists alike stood in need of God's grace, he concluded. The Bible left in shambles any narrow idea of a chosen people.[84]

Veterans of groups such as the Fellowship of Southern Churchmen worked to reform the South. In the 1950s, radical Southern Baptist minister Will Campbell operated with a fairly conventional theology of social action. He was still in his phase of "liberal sophistication," as he later sardonically called it. In his childhood, this war veteran, Baptist preacher, and onetime chaplain of the University of Mississippi had learned that being a good Christian meant avoiding personal sins of the flesh. In theological school, he discovered that being a good Christian meant caring about suffering, paying workers well, and supporting desegregation. "That worked all right for me," he commented wryly, "until I realized that I had substituted one moralistic code for another." After his removal from the post of chaplain at the University of Mississippi and his increasing disenchantment with liberal Protestantism, Campbell took over the renamed Committee on Southern Churchmen and began publishing the journal *Katallagete* ("to be reconciled"). Through the civil rights years, Campbell journeyed intellectually back to his Anabaptist roots and challenged all sides of the religious war over civil rights. His brother, a redneck and drug addict, once had prodded him, "Your niggers are like my pills. They prop you liberals up and make you feel good." Liberal orthodoxy, Campbell decided, was as confining as southern fundamentalism. Church-based civil rights activities came from a vague humanitarianism rather than from a firm theological basis. Increasingly anti-institutional in theology, he devoted himself to reconciling adversaries. The churches, he believed, had become mere "adjuncts to human relations councils and civil rights organizations," forgetting that "what we have to say is far more radical, far more demanding, far more inclusive of all of society than anything the humanistically

oriented groups have said." More specifically, Christians should minister to segregationists as well as their victims. The racist could not be swayed by "facts";
rather, believers had to start from the assumption of man's profound involvement with sin, such that "we can say of the society in which we live that it is not
sinful because it segregates; rather it segregates because it is sinful." More so
than social gospel idealism or even the neo-orthodox radicalism of Howard
Kester and his fellows, Campbell's anti-institutional theology—expressed in his
widely quoted aphorism "We're all sons of bitches but God loves us anyway"—
probably moved a significant number of white southern Christians to question
their racially privileged status.[85]

Despite the prominence of segregationists in pulpits and in the pew, some
white southern ministers took up the cause. Generally they were the "moderates," those who counseled patience over justice, memorably skewered in Martin Luther King Jr.'s "Letter from a Birmingham Jail." A masterstroke of penetrating rhetoric and skillful public relations, King's essay damned the southern
moderate minister. Many of them deserved the bad press—but not all. King
himself had good relationships with southern radicals as well as some liberals
and even moderates, ranging from the pacifist Texan Glenn Smiley, to the Durrs
in Montgomery, to other lesser-known sympathetic whites scattered through
the region. He recognized that "here and there," churches were "courageously
making attacks on segregation, and actually integrating their congregation";
some church-related schools were "throwing off the traditional yoke of segregation," a process that would ease the transition to an integrated society: "You know,
when you can finally convert a white Southerner, you have one of the most genuine, committed human beings that you'll ever find," he once said.[86]

In many ways, the civil rights movement took on an evangelical Protestant
cast, a sort of regionwide revival movement. In what Fred Hobson refers to as
racial conversion narratives, whites used blacks as symbolic agents to redeem
their own souls. The civil rights movement, Hobson explains, "had always been,
for participating whites, in part about saving their own souls—about willing
themselves back into a religion they could believe in—and their feelings of rejection within the movement in its latter days suggested they were not worthy
after all." Sounding much like the Methodist expatriate and social theorist Lillian Smith, the Presbyterian providentialist James McBride Dabbs said that he
"had finally to oppose all division and separation, both within myself and within
that outer picture of myself, the world. When finally I realized what a division
segregation was, I had to oppose it too." Like many other white southern Christians, he saw the Negro as a savior, and the black church as a redeemer of the national soul. Many activists experienced the equivalent of conversions, sacred
moments when the grim reality of southern racism and the sacred calling of re-

deeming the soul of America moved them to action. Reporting on the gatherings in Albany, the journalist Pat Watters found himself succumbing to the spirit, his thoughts returning to "the powerful pounding of the music of the mass meetings as a counterpoint to my words of discovery and analysis." The "mystical, inspired and excited, ecstatic—and reverent mood of those meetings" helped him overcome his own conventionally southern education. Although he spent a "lifetime within the South's church-oriented society," only in these settings did he experience "real religious feeling."[87]

As objects rather than agents in this version of the conversion narrative, black southern Christians were skeptical. The burden of serving as redeeming agents for the sins and sicknesses of white society could be trying. "You know, sometimes I get awfully tired of trying to save the white man's soul," Thurgood Marshall once joked. Through the 1960s, such conversions had to withstand a pervasive white disillusionment with the breakdown of the apparent Christian interracialism implied in the term "beloved community." Black power did not fit any conversion narrative, for in it, black people were no longer available for the redemption of the white soul.[88]

The African American freedom movement, moreover, appeared to many white southerners as a grave threat, hence the ferocity of the anti–civil rights movement. Discredited after their defeat in the civil rights years, southern Christian conservatives experienced a resurgence through the 1970s and 1980s. While the progressives effectively won the fight over civil rights, the results were very different when the battles were seemingly over everything except race. Freed from the historic burden of defending segregation, southern conservatives roused themselves to preserve God-ordained hierarchies of gender and class.

It is time that all conservatives get together and stand like a stonewall against these dangerous errors that are creeping in.—Henry M. Woods, North Carolina Presbyterian

Chapter Five

Religion, Race, and the Right

In 1995, the Southern Baptist Convention, dominated by self-styled leaders of a "conservative resurgence," adopted a resolution acknowledging and apologizing for the historic support of the denomination for slavery and racism. The convention lamented the opposition of many white Christians in the previous generation to civil rights for black Americans, denounced "racism, in all its forms, as deplorable sin," and repudiated "historic acts of evil such as slavery from which we continue to reap a bitter harvest." The resolution noted that the "racism which yet plagues our culture today is inextricably tied to the past" and apologized to "all African-Americans for condoning and/or perpetuating individual and systemic racism in our lifetime." Drafted by eight white and eight black men, the racial reconciliation statement in the SBC joined a number of other like confessions emanating from other predominantly white southern denominations. One black Baptist participant in drafting the resolutions remembered this as a "high point" for him. During the civil rights movement, he said, "when we needed a friend, the evangelicals weren't there. It was like either apathy at the best, or abuse at the worst." The "surviving racist elements" among Southern Baptists may have complained, another participant noted, but the center of gravity had shifted because the conservatives realized that there was no longer a "price to be paid negatively in any significant way for embracing racial reconciliation."[1]

This repudiation of the historic legacy of slavery and racism in southern religious life came near the same time as parallel statements reaffirming orthodox views of women in the ministry and gender relations in the home. Five years after the racial reconciliation resolution, SBC delegates voted overwhelmingly to proclaim a new faith and message statement. Originally adopted in 1925 and revised in 1963 as an informal but important statement of belief and faith for Southern Baptists, the later adaptation added significant new sections that addressed God's plan for family relations. Dorothy Patterson, wife of the president of Southeastern Baptist Theological Seminary and a noted conservative evangelical spokeswoman, was a lead author of the new section of the statement:

> The marriage relationship models the way God relates to His people. A husband is to love his wife as Christ loved the church. He has the God-given responsibility to provide for, to protect, and to lead his family. A wife is to submit herself graciously to the servant leadership of her husband even as the church willingly submits to the headship of Christ. She, being in the image of God as is her husband and thus equal to him, has the God-given responsibility to respect her husband and to serve as his helper in managing the household and nurturing the next generation.

The terrain of battle in the southern culture wars had shifted, in effect, from race to gender.

The evolution of the Southern Baptist Convention provides a good case study of the transformation of southern religious conservatism in the twentieth century. Conservatives had been caucusing over their grievances since the early twentieth century, but they managed to enlist only a minority of disaffected believers in ideological crusades against the heresies of modernism. In the 1950s and 1960s, their anger at denominational leaders who endorsed desegregation in the South compelled them to coalesce. As they perceived it, there *was* a denominational elite from which they were largely excluded. This elite, these conservatives believed, produced modernist books, endorsed integration, and perhaps even were soft on communism. In later years, the list of sins changed—endorsing abortion rights replaced sanctioning integration, for example—but the coalitions essentially remained the same.

The forebears of today's religious/political right came unhinged from their traditional denominational loyalties first in the fundamentalist-modernist controversies of the earlier twentieth century, when conservatives perceived the decline of the evangelical South from true orthodoxy. These divisions reappeared during the civil rights years, when the moderate elites in charge of denominational leadership angered conservative Christians in local communities by supporting measures of desegregation. In more recent years, conservatives jettisoned racial arguments for white supremacy but staunchly defended gendered stations in life. For the contemporary religious right, in short, gender has supplanted race as the bedrock defining principle of God-ordained hierarchy.

Southern Religious Conservatism in Historic Perspective

Drawing from the pioneering work of Samuel S. Hill Jr., a generation of scholars in the 1960s and 1970s described southern religion as being in cultural captivity, or as a "culture-religion." As they perceived it, white southern Christians, slumbering in a reactionary form of evangelicalism, faltered before the moral challenge posed by the pernicious system of southern apartheid. Writing in the midst of a most stunning social revolution, these scholars could not help but see cultural captivity when stiff-necked deacons and ushers stood cross-armed at church house doors, defending segregation now, segregation forever. Southern social critics and the cultural captivity school advanced the understanding that something outside Christianity had entrapped the white southern soul.[2]

Yet when placed in historical perspective, the conservative theology and social views of the white southern evangelical establishment hardly seem surprising. Dominant castes and classes rarely have espoused theologies of equality. Most commonly, they have sanctified inequality. "We do not believe that 'all men are created equal' . . . nor that they will ever become equal in this world," a prominent Southern Baptist cleric said in the 1880s. The white southern theology of class and blood was premised on God-ordained inequality. It was an unstable foundation in the context of American liberal democracy but one common in human history.[3]

In the post–civil rights years, it is often assumed that any "true" Christianity necessarily requires acceptance of human equality. Whether or not this assumption is valid theologically, it certainly is not true if looked at historically. The belief that Christianity supports human equality has an uneven trajectory through history; it by no means arises naturally from ambiguous biblical texts. Because it is open to multiple readings, the Bible has proven readily adaptable to a wide variety of social systems, from the most conservative and hierarchical (such as feudalism and slavery) to the most egalitarian and the capitalist. In his famous sermon, "The Christian Doctrine of Slavery," antebellum Presbyterian theologian James Henley Thornwell enunciated the themes familiar to generations of southern conservatives: *God created the world. If inequality exists, then God must have a reason for it. Without inequality—without rulers and ruled, without hewers of wood and drawers of water—there could be only anarchy. Men cannot govern them-*

selves on a plane of equality. Realizing this, God sanctions Himself to head the church, men to lead women and children, slave owners to direct the lives of slaves, and white people to guide the destiny of black people. Slavery drew a variety of defenses, both biblical and secular. Thornwell's was among the most rhetorically skillful, for he exempted himself from the charge of a heretical racism based on ideas of polygeny (the separate creation of the races, as opposed to monogeny, the idea that all people are descended from Adam and Eve). "We are not ashamed to call him [the Negro] our *brother,*" Thornwell intoned to his audience. Instead, he preached on how order, properly conceived, secured liberty and restrained the anarchy of sin being loosed upon the world.[4]

White southern religious ideas of social and racial hierarchy did not have to be merely hypocritical cant. Like James Henley Thornwell's arguments, they could be grounded intellectually in a respected conservative vision of preserving godly order. Particular biblical passages clearly explained why spiritual equality does not (and must not) imply temporal equality.

With plentiful references to biblical texts, antebellum white southern ministers defined southern theology by sanctifying slavery. They borrowed heavily from a national tradition of conservative thought outlined by Federalist religious thinkers. Godly societies required such hierarchies as God clearly had ordained —of class, blood, and gender. Episcopalian divines, Presbyterian elders, and even Baptist and Methodist preachers aspiring to the status of "gentleman theologians" understood that formulating a distinctive theological tradition for their section constituted part of their calling as apostles of respectability. For biblical literalists, the Bible clearly delineated the spiritual equality and temporal inequality of man on earth. After the demise of slavery, southern theologians emphasized human weakness, fallibility, and dependence on God. For them, defeat in the Civil War shored up orthodoxies of race and place, while political redemption would restore divine sanction for man's earthly rulers.

Later, however, defending the specific political institutions and social customs of racial segregation proved more difficult. In the civil rights years, southern denominational leaders slowly endorsed desegregation. Partly as a result, segregationists used religious arguments secondarily, if at all, and often seemed embarrassed by the strained biblical diatribes preached by some theological ideologues. The folk theology of Christian racism was weak and incoherent in comparison to the moral force of the civil rights movement. Still, it played a significant role in making white southern Christians obsessed with conceptions of purity. Their beliefs had been set in a mythological context that gave them a properly religious sanction. The migration into and spread of fundamentalist ideas through the South provided some of that context.

Southern Fundamentalism:
The Invention of a Tradition

Fundamentalism—defined by one historian as militant and angry antimodernism in theology—emerged originally as an intellectual movement in nineteenth-century northern seminaries, Bible institutes, summer camp meetings, and interdenominational schools. The early theological fundamentalists kept alive the Scottish commonsense realist tradition that once had been pervasive in American thought. God's will, went their reasoning, was manifest in the world; his workings were abundantly evident for anyone who would examine them using the principles of Baconian inductive science. The order of the natural world, for example, glorified the workings of the Creator, and the movement of God's spirit in the individual soul left a sensory impression that only the willfully stubborn (meaning most of mankind) could ignore.

Premillennialism, another key tenet of fundamentalist doctrine, originated in the nineteenth century among conservative English theologians who schematized the world's history into seven "dispensations," or discrete periods leading to the millennium. They prognosticated that the return of Jesus to gather up his disciples would precede a time of tribulation and Armageddon, speeding human history to a catastrophic end. Human history, they imagined, already had entered the concluding era of the seventh dispensation. Fundamentalists also objected to the higher textual criticism of the Bible imported from German universities, which increasingly shaped American seminary education, as well as modern modes of scientific thought such as Darwinism. Fundamentalism was not synonymous with anti-intellectualism, at least in its origins. More accurately, early fundamentalism articulated an intellectual tradition drawn from eighteenth- and nineteenth-century schools of theology and philosophy against the assaults of modern theology, science, and psychology.[5]

Already stalwart conservatives in theology and politics, white southern churches in the early twentieth century were not ripe for any self-conscious fundamentalist movement. Southern denominational leaders generally beat back the brush fires of fundamentalist agitation that periodically flared up in particular areas. Nevertheless, conservative discontent gathered momentum. By World War I, some southern believers perceived a drift toward biblical liberalism, higher criticism, and social gospelism in the colleges and seminaries. The Great War of 1914–18 only reinforced the growing disquiet. Many southern evangelicals immediately seized on German theological liberalism as the philosophical underpinning for the Germanic orgy of blood in Western Europe. "It was Germany's acceptance of [Darwin's] theory of materialistic evolution that made possible the dominance of militarism and the building up of a great machine that has taken the multiplied power of the Nations and of the world to smash it," explained a Texas Methodist. "The attitude of German Christians in condoning and applauding the inhumanities of the German army," he added, "lends color to the charge that the German destructive criticism of the Bible is but part of the German program for military conquest of the world." Southern Protestant intellectuals saw the war as an ideal moment to free American theology from "servile dependence . . . upon German initiative and leadership in philosophy and theology."[6]

Learning from the successful inroads of conservative theology in the late-nineteenth-century North, itinerant teachers in the early twentieth century spread fundamentalism through the South. Southern preachers attended northern conferences such as those at Moody Bible Institute in Chicago. There, they joined a growing number of nondenominational institutions in training the first generation of American fundamentalist leaders. Later, these itinerant ideologues replicated such interdenominational ventures in the South, where they warned evangelical audiences about the liberalism invading their own religious institutions. Leonard G. Broughton, pastor of Atlanta's Tabernacle Baptist Church and the director of the Tabernacle Bible Conference, taught characteristic fundamentalist emphases (biblical literalism, commonsense realism in philosophy, and Baconian inductive science) through a series of conferences and institutes.[7]

Fundamentalist educational efforts faced the problem that established evangelicals looked suspiciously on Bible schools because of their interdenominational character and because they drew students and money away from the denominations' own colleges and seminaries. The first generation of Bible college graduates stirred up much of this controversy. The fundamentalists often came across as theological innovators intent on wrecking the modus operandi of moderately conservative biblical interpretation that had kept the peace for decades. For southern evangelicals concerned with the growth and harmony of their institutions, fundamentalists also aroused ire by siphoning off money and young zealots for interdenominational causes. Eventually, southern fundamentalists had to determine whether to operate within or outside of the regular evangelical groupings. Some defenders of orthodoxy sought to resist liberalism within their beloved southern institutions. Other southern conservatives formed separate fellowships and informal groupings that were organized similarly to their own theological leanings. Still others worked in interdenominational organizations even while remaining affiliated with their own historic traditions. Fundamentalists agonized over whether the denominations themselves were worth saving, or whether they already had gone over to the enemy.[8]

Thus, fundamentalism was a difficult sell in southern churches. By the early twentieth century, the major southern denominations were broadly and irenically evangelical. In general, churchmen in the region saw the fundamentalist-modernist row essentially as a northern problem, unnecessary in the pervasively evangelical South. Southern Baptists, Methodists, and Presbyterians were at peace with their own culture and generally gave troublemakers scant leeway. When one who might have been suspect, such as biology professor and college president William Louis Poteat, stayed connected to the evangelical network, he could teach evolution and suggest notions about the Bible that were vaguely modernist even while remaining in good standing among North Carolina Baptists—much to the frustration of fundamentalists who lobbed periodic volleys toward Poteat's citadel at Wake Forest. The southern fundamentalists also made little headway in converting church people to their gloomy premillennialism.[9]

Fundamentalists who remained within their own churches were only occasionally successful in pursuing their agenda. For decades leading up to the reunion of southern and northern Methodists in 1939, conservative southerners blocked the merger. In the 1920s, their spokesman, R. A. Meek, formed the "League for the Preservation of Southern Methodism," which doubled as an effort to implant fundamentalist ideas in the MECS. On the other side, proreunion bishops joined with allies in the Missionary Council and with Methodist women's leaders in the Friends of Unification. They advocated progressivism in social reform and theology. Both contending groups took over individual conferences. In 1925, the plan of unification won but 52 percent of the vote, short of the 75 percent needed. A unification supporter called the vote the "greatest spiritual tragedy of my life," seeing it as a victory for reactionary theologians and their lay constituency.[10]

Apart from blocking reunion, however, conservatives in the Southern Methodist Church found little success. Bishops and progressive women in mission societies slowed the spread of literalist ideas. The relatively tolerant and expansive evangelicalism inherent to Methodist theology left little room for more doctrinaire fundamentalism. In *The Fundamentals of Methodism*, Bishop Edwin DuBose Mouzon stressed that the experience and practice of grace preceded any dogma. "Men are not first theologians and then Christians," he explained, but "are first Christians, and after that they begin to meditate on the significance of the things they have felt and seen." Most churchgoers, another bishop noted in 1934, valued "the pragmatic test of experience and life value." Since the experience of grace preceded doctrine, modern science and biblical criticism could not undermine the essence of Methodism.[11]

In one sense, early southern fundamentalism failed. No ongoing forums or institutions survived the 1930s. Both the World Christian Fundamentals Association and the Baptist Bible Union, two important early groups, collapsed. In another way, however, the early fundamentalists left their mark. As historian William Glass explains, "Through their Bible conferences and preaching tours, the itinerants created a southern constituency for the fundamentalist interpretation of Christianity." Northern conservatives who were upset with the loss of their own denominational institutions (such as the Methodist Episcopal Church, the Northern Baptist Convention, and the Presbyterian Church U.S.A.) looked south and saw a land that still valued the theology of their fathers. Meanwhile, southern conservatives built up a network of institutions that carried on the southern wing of the national fundamentalist movement. Such figures as Robert McQuilkin at Columbia Bible College, one of the earliest fundamentalist institutes, and Lewis Chafer of Dallas Theological Seminary sought to train graduates who would restore conservatism to northern institutions and defend southern schools against the inroads of liberalism. Extension programs with informal courses in English Bible for full-time local pastors implanted authoritarian scriptural views in ministers and laypeople, and countered what unsettled conservatives saw as the lackadaisical evangelicalism in the materials commonly used in Sunday schools.[12]

Gradually, conservatives gathered their forces and began to coalesce those who believed they were witnessing the demise of evangelical orthodoxy in the region. William McCorkle, a longtime conservative Presbyterian minister and polemicist in North Carolina, remained committed to his denomination even while tracking and lamenting the decline of American Christianity to theological torpor. McCorkle was an early standard-bearer for grassroots denominational fundamentalism. Later, he would be remembered best for his sniping at University of North Carolina sociologist Howard Odum and other intellectuals in the state. McCorkle grew up in Talladega, Alabama, attended Washington and Lee College in Virginia, and ministered in Southern Presbyterian congregations from the late 1880s to 1932. As a pamphleteer and correspondent, he inveighed against Christian science, evolution, atheism, sectional reunion of the Southern and Northern Presbyterians, theological modernism, and political progressivism.

McCorkle carried on an extensive correspondence with aggrieved church folk who joined him in the crusade against the politicization of the church and against modernism. Conservatives wrote frequently to him for advice and exhortations. One lamented that at a Presbyterian church in Miami he found "so much ceremony in the service I could hardly realize that I was in a Presbyterian church. The sermon was really a lecture on friendship rather than a gospel sermon." Others joined the cleric in warning of the "leaven of the Federal Council of Churches and of pagan psychology." It was "only a question of time," forecast one concerned Presbyterian, "before our Church will be altogether consistent with Unitarianism." The fight for orthodoxy was on, so the fundamentalists believed, and those who should be leading it were slumbering. McCorkle monitored the rise of theological liberalism at the flagship Southern Presbyterian theological school, Union Seminary in Richmond. The president of Hampden-Sydney College in Virginia feared that "the great body of our ministers and elders appear to be asleep, and the poison of Modernism is creeping in the church at a fearful rate." It was "time that *all conservatives get together* and stand like a stonewall against these dangerous errors that are creeping in," another pastor insisted. Because the "*radicals get together*, and stand for false doctrine," the conservatives now needed to do likewise. The "surest way for a very ordinary individual to attract attention these days," he had concluded, was to "do something bizarre; and the surest way for a very ordinary minister of the gospel or teacher to become 'brilliant,' 'progressive,' 'a deep thinker,' etc. is to become unorthodox."[13]

While mounting assaults against evolutionists and theological liberals, McCorkle remained confident that there could be no "conflict between the intelligent, reasonable interpretation of the Book and the testimony of himself which God has given in nature." McCorkle defined his doctrinal views as the set of "basic truths of religion that are like water, sunlight, pure air, bread—things indispensable, necessary to life, not to be improved upon or superseded by any human inventions or scientific discoveries." Here, he expressed the common-sense realism that historically shaped evangelical thinking. McCorkle condemned the vague ideals that passed for liberal religious principles. They were, he said, "in fact a sort of sentimentalism, . . . moved . . . to tears under pathetic exhortations." Even Presbyterian churches, the historic home for Calvinism, were now asked "to pave the way for the scrapping of the whole Calvinistic system in due time, whenever it pleases any presbytery to scrap it in its examinations of candidates." McCorkle sought a "revival of loyalty to the spiritual mission of the church," turning back the efforts to "bring every social and reform question into our church courts." Even Prohibition, in McCorkle's view, represented an unbiblical effort to redeem the world through the coercive power of the state rather than by transforming individual lives. McCorkle felt that "no better plan can be devised to arouse the fierce and intolerant spirit of fanaticism in our churches than this injection of politics," one almost exactly duplicating antebellum southern critiques of the abolitionists. The more the church became entangled in legislating how the state would deal with alcohol, the greater would be the "injury done in the long run both to the peace of the church and to the cause of rational temperance."[14]

McCorkle also spearheaded a rearguard attack against the University of North Carolina in Chapel Hill, specifically targeting Howard Odum and his seminal academic journal *Social Forces*. McCorkle's pamphlet attacking Odum's "anti-Christian sociology" drew the attention of some wary university trustees. "There is constantly being held up before the youth of the land," one of them wrote to the Presbyterian leader, "something bordering on contempt for what we would denominate the old time religion and faith, and it seems to me that those that we would term the most highly educated are the very ones who are living furthest away from the faith of the fathers." Another educational overseer believed that it would be "far better to close all our schools than for pagan, godless evolution to be taught to our children." Those who would teach "science falsely socalled" (by which they meant Darwinian evolution) were "*pernicious infidels*" who would "plunge the human race into perdition."[15]

University leaders fired back. The editor of the up-and-coming University of North Carolina Press, W. T. Couch (who sponsored the publication of a number of controversial works), carried on a classic modernist-fundamentalist dialogue with the irascible McCorkle. After having grown up a minister's son and "about as thorough a Baptist as ever lived," Couch explained in one letter, he had discovered the forces of heredity and environment. Since then, he had determined that the general public was unqualified to assess work in fields requiring scientific expertise. There was no "greater danger in modern life than the disrepute into which religion can be brought by those who are ministering it," he chided. "I hate to see the profession which my father respected and which I think he honored so intellectually degraded." Because so many ministers were "abysmally ignorant," they were poor guides for the people in the age of secular experts. Couch articulated the modernist faith in science that would be espoused by Clarence Darrow in the media spectacle known as the Scopes trial in 1925. In response, William Jennings Bryan defended majoritarian democracy in education, the idea that local communities should control the contents of school curricula. This split reverberated through American religious and cultural life through the twentieth century and would be revisited during the civil rights era, when denominational leaders and local churches often fought over desegregation.[16]

Among the religious leaders condemned by Couch were the large number of clergymen associated with the Ku Klux Klan, which flourished during the same years in which southern fundamentalists also gathered strength. In the 1920s, at the height of what historians call the Second Ku Klux Klan, members of the order numbered, by some estimates, as many as five million nationwide. In the South, Christian Klansmen publicly demonstrated the order's pan-Protestant morality while avoiding association with one church or denomination in particular. One Baptist pastor joined because, as he justified it, "everyone of importance is a Klan member." In fact, the Alabama Klan ran an employment service that matched sympathetic preachers with churches that would employ them. When Commission on Interracial Cooperation secretary Will Alexander delivered a speech against the Klan at a Methodist gathering, as he later recollected, "it turned out that a large number of the ministerial delegates and lay delegates to that general conference *were* members of the Klan."[17]

The "life test" of Methodism championed by Bishop Francis Mouzon hardly prevented the major inroads made by the Klan in southern denominations. A number of Methodist ministers—Hubert Knickerbocker in Texas, Alonzo Monk and C. D. McGehee in Missouri, Earl Hotalen in Alabama—served as traveling lecturers and organizers during the order's height in the 1920s. A Methodist minister wrote in despair that "some of our Bishops are members, all but two of the residing Elders in this state were, at least 75% of our preachers, and dozens of our Churches have their entire official boards, or the large majority, within the organization." Bishop Mouzon responded in disgust that nothing had "so distressed" him as the fact that "so many of our preachers have been misguided and have gone into this organization." Earl Hotalen, an Alabama Methodist, crisscrossed the state on behalf of the Klan, collecting money for Billy Sunday and other crusaders while stumping for causes such as Prohibition enforcement and immigration restrictions. The robes worn by members, he assured listeners, were not emblems of secrecy or skullduggery but rather symbolized the purity of Jesus. The Klan would only unrobe when "rapists, thugs, gamblers, crooked politicians, and murderers no long encumber the earth." The struggle of the day, as he saw it, was "Klancraft versus Roman priestcraft and niggercraft." While unofficially related to the church, the Klan was "unofficially pervaded by the Church's terminology and ideas," as a Methodist historian later put it.[18]

In the South as elsewhere, scores of local Klaverns sponsored civic festivals ranging from parades and beauty pageants to clean-up campaigns. They also spearheaded more coercive crusades against racial tolerance and sexual misbehavior. Sidney Catts, a Baptist preacher and the governor of Florida, delivered pro-Klan messages in his region, and state Klan members burned some Catholic buildings and flogged vice merchants. When Alabama received national attention for its seeming encouragement of vigilantism, Alabama Baptists charged that such critics were merely minions of the state oligarchy. Indeed, it was many of the "Big Mules," the state's conservative industrial elite (especially around Birmingham), that led the fight against Klan members, whom they saw as rabble-rousers unconducive to the state's economic growth. Yet progressive religious leaders sometimes defended the order. The longtime southern progressive editor of the *Alabama Baptist*, Leslie Gwaltney, praised the original idea of the Klan, even if he regretted some excesses. He sought to harness the energies of all groups in support of the enforcement of prohibition and racial hierarchies. To place the "passion inflamer" of alcohol "in the hands of a child race not far removed from their savage haunts in the jungles of Africa," he warned, "would be to court tragedy unspeakable."[19]

Although the second Klan collapsed in the mid-1920s, pockets of activity remained prevalent in regions where the order's stress on Protestant morality meshed easily with the dominant culture. Church people who were members of the Klan defined Protestant Americanism and attacked racial progressives, as well as business elites—a confluence of sociopolitical views that historian Nancy MacLean termed "reactionary populism." Donald Comer, an evangelical leader in Alabama, convened a committee including ecclesiastical elites to fight such groups. Aware of this ministerial opposition, the Klan took action. For example, the hooded order savaged John Buchanan of Southside Baptist Church in Birmingham for activating anti-Klan forces in Alabama in the 1940s. "I am a KKK and proud of it," a Jefferson County Alabaman wrote in the 1940s, "and I say if some of these fat, greasy, panty-waist preachers would get intestinal fortitude enough to preach the Gospel, and keep their mouths out of things they know absolutely nothing about . . . the churches would have more people in them." Increasingly pushed to the margins and belittled by denominational leaders and seminary-trained biblical authorities, Christian theological racism nonetheless remained pervasive. It significantly shaped the white southern response to the black civil rights revolution.[20]

The Folk Theology of Segregation

Prior to the civil rights movement, the theology of segregationism was handed down as confirmed dogma. When he was a boy, one North Carolinian remembered, it was nearly universal to learn that God made different races and that "He expected them to stay that way, and that each should have his own churches and schools." Segregation was a "fundamental law of nature," another Tar Heel wrote, while the state superintendent of education declared that the loss of white supremacy would be a "violation of God's eternal laws as fixed in the stars." Only a proper ordering of the races would maintain white southern purity. The frequent references to "filth" and "social disease" pervading white supremacist literature suggests that segregationism was something deeper than custom. The social ordering of the races had been sanctified, and a properly religious cloak thrown over Jim Crow's skeleton.[21]

Most white pastors and local congregations accepted segregation either as divinely ordained or simply as the best and most workable social system for the South. While denominational leaders increasingly endorsed desegregation, their constituent churches shored up the received social hierarchies. Denominational leaders were embarrassed by diehard segregationism. They identified it as being the right-hand pole of the "extremists on both sides" that they so often condemned—the NAACP being the left-hand pole. Clergymen were not in the forefront and, indeed, were strikingly under-represented in the ranks of the Citizens' Councils and religious organizations that defended the southern social order. No matter what their political bent, clerics usually knew when to keep quiet. "Most hid their heads in the sand and spoke the language of the people in the church, even if they didn't believe it," one woman recalled of the pastors she knew. Later, white southern believers felt embattled within a culture they saw slipping from them. Fundamentalists then seized the opportunity to politicize churches and parishioners. But that was later, in a post–civil rights generation.[22]

More so than clergymen, who mouthed the language of moderation to evade uncomfortable disagreements, laypeople in the South articulated, defended, and enforced the theology of segregation. The work of deacons, lay associations, and church auxiliaries paralleled the efforts of businessmen's groups and Citizens' Councils in the workaday secular world. Indeed, their memberships overlapped. There was, moreover, a theology of segregation, even if it was lodged more among laymen's organizations and ministers outside church hierarchies than in the circles of organizational leadership. Most of these southern religious conservatives melded integrationism, modernism, and communism into a single three-headed devil. Their theology was intentionally and self-consciously reactionary. The latter-day theologians of segregation seemed to realize their effort was futile, as they easily interpreted their own failure as part of the preordained story of the decline of man leading to the millennium. With conservative politicians such as Eisenhower supporting (however reluctantly) the court's mandate in *Brown*, and denominational authorities acceding to the dismantling of Jim Crow, segregation seemed a lost cause.

Some of the exponents of this segregationist thought engaged in politics, while others were resigned to the inevitability of southern decline into "mongrelization." All of them held the conviction that the Bible either actively or passively supported white southern ideas about ordering the higher and lower classes in the social world. Methodist cleric W. B. Selah presented the standard southern segregationist view in his address "The Doctrine of Separate but Equal Opportunities for All Races." Lamenting the judicial tyranny of the *Brown* decision, he recommended instead the doctrine of separate but equal as commending itself to good men of both races, one that would assuage the fears of sexual amalgamation that induced good folks to "shudder." In another widely reprinted and redistributed address, Leon C. Burns, a Church of Christ minister in Tennessee, suggested that there was "no racial problem until this decree was handed down." The Supreme Court had capitulated to "left wing groups that for years have sought to foment hatred, strife, and even bloodshed between the white and colored races of the South." In the short term, Burns advocated the peaceful continuance of segregation customs not as a matter of law or principle but for the sake of expediency. For example, he pointed out, teachers trained in Negro colleges would lose their place under an integrated educational system. More pressing than such practical arguments, however, was the specter of mongrelization, the trump card in the segregationist hand. "The law of expediency so clearly set forth by the apostle Paul would demand that Christians of one nation be very careful to marry within their own nation," Burns reminded readers. By contrast, he warned, proponents of equality would not rest until there was full intermarriage—what southerners a century before feared as "domestic amalgamation."[23]

Clerics and Sunday school teachers from all denominations articulated the theology of segregation, even as they insisted that questions of sociopolitical customs were political and thus best left out of the church. In Jackson, Mississippi, Governor Ross Barnett attended the church pastored by Douglas Hudgins, the fastidious pastor of the state capitol's First Baptist Church. Aptly called by one historian the "theologian of a closed society," Hudgins articulated a pristine view of the soul's competency before God, the purity of a salvation enacted outside the social world. His views provided sanction for the segregationism of his congregants. Some fellow Baptists provided more pointed language to accompany Hudgins's politely silent endorsement of segregationism. One of his deacons outlined the commonly held view that "the facts of history make it plain that the development of civilization and of Christianity itself has rested in the hands of the white race." One of the institutions firmest in the grip of the segregationists was Mississippi College, a Baptist institution located in Clinton, just a few miles from Jackson. Its president, D. M. Nelson, fumed that integration was "based upon Karl Marx's doctrine of internationalism . . . the obliteration of all national and racial distinctions and the final amalgamation of all races"; it would "mongrelize the two dominant races of the South." A Baptist faculty member and frequent speaker at Citizens' Council meetings believed, with Governor Barnett, that "our Southern segregation way" was the "Christian way." His talks were popularly received by deacons and Sunday school teachers.[24]

Some conservatives argued that the Bible did not specifically advocate or condemn segregation. Instead, they insisted, as did C. T. Gillespie of Presbyterian Bellhaven College in Jackson, that it was a purely civil issue. Gillespie's primary argument lay with denominational resolutions that promoted the *Brown* decision as consonant with New Testament understandings of the brotherhood of man. On the contrary, argued the Presbyterian educator, segregation was a social arrangement that was godly or not depending on the behavior of men within it. Despite these protestations, Gillespie could not help but express political views on southern customs. In his well-known pamphlet *A Christian View on Segregation*, he blasted the ecclesiastical endorsement of desegregation as a capitulation to racial "amalgamation," the ultimate prize desired by communist infiltrators.[25]

In this sense, the Christian segregationists faced some of the same dilemmas as had their southern forebears in the defense of slavery: should the primary civil institution for regulating the rights and privileges of races be defined as a positive good ordained by God? Should it be understood as a sociopolitical question best left outside the domain of ecclesiastical discussion? Or might it be a necessary evil simply required by the history of the region, a way of enforcing order and ensuring the rule of the more advanced race? Like the southern divines writing about slavery, religious thinkers often began by assuming that segregation was a civil institution. Yet the logic of their arguments inevitably led them to uphold race separation as inherently godly and biblical. As one layman put it, segregation was the South's "shield and buckler—our refuge, our fortress. It is the first commandment and not the last."[26]

While segregationists peopled white churches, it was difficult to organize them into concerted action. But when compelled into the fray by civil rights agitation, white southern church people were politicized in spite of themselves. "Congregations have been divided and confused at the political action of the churches," a cleric named Joseph Simeon Jones in Burlington, North Carolina, wrote to a town newspaper in 1959. Many churches, he continued, refused to assign literature from the denominational publishing houses because it was "often used as a means of propaganda for liberation. The Negro has been hurt—deeply hurt by his would be friends. He has been led to believe that the only way he can respect himself is by forcing himself on people who do not want him." Jones was furious about Presbyterians advancing legal expenses for the NAACP in Alabama, a group he saw as "equal to the Communists by reason of accomplishing the Communist objective of division, strife, hatred, enmity, chaos, confusion." For Jones, atheistic communism, racial integration, and "Romanism" posed the greatest threats to the southern Protestant heritage. Jones recounted for a Presbyterian publication his long struggle in "trying to arouse" laymen who seemed blithely unaware of the encroachments of the "liberal, modernistic element of the church." Newly activated laymen and elders, he hoped, would serve as the true guardians of church traditions.[27]

Laypeople grew increasingly agitated about this "liberal, modernistic" element that they perceived in church literature disseminated by denominational headquarters. By 1946, many congregants already were censoring church publications that advocated social equality or were "Communistic in trend and in direct contradiction to the traditions and principles held by the vast majority" of white southern believers. The men's Bible class at the historic Galloway Methodist congregation in Jackson, led by prominent lawyer and future White Citizens' Council spokesman John Satterfield, forwarded a resolution to the Methodist Church hierarchy suggesting that articles about racial brotherhood were "foreign to what church literature should contain."[28]

Located mostly among laymen's organizations and clerics outside the denominational hierarchy, segregationist theology spread widely, even if it could not coalesce into a regionwide movement. It was well expressed by Carey Daniel, a White Citizens' Council leader and pastor of the First Baptist Church of West Dallas, Texas. Daniel authored a widely reprinted pamphlet, "God the Original Segregationist." In it, he rehearsed the familiar racial genealogy drawn from the vestigial remains of the Son of Ham tradition. In Daniel's view, the Canaanites ("the only children of Ham who were specifically cursed to be a servile race") temporarily were allowed to occupy a narrow strip of the Promised Land along the Mediterranean, including the fateful lands of Sodom and Gomorrah. The children of the servant people were to live in a different part of the country from the ancestors of white people. But "when they later dared to violate God's sacred law of segregation by moving into and claiming the land farther east," God commanded the chosen people to destroy them. "We have no reason to suppose," he surmised, that "God did not make known to Noah and his children His divine plan for racial segregation immediately after the flood." Anyway, the burden of proof rested with those who believed Jesus was not a segregationist, for God's son never specifically repudiated the system. A note attached to one copy of the pamphlet, mailed to the Atlanta-area Methodist bishop John Owen Smith, asked this supporter of desegregation in churches to "please read the enclosed and then ask God to forgive you for trying to mix the races."[29]

Believers throughout the region, most especially in the Deep South, connected the preservation of race purity with the fear of miscegenation and the defense of southern social customs. The pastor of a major congregation in Birmingham, Henry L. Lyon, repeatedly delivered an address titled "Why Racial Integration is UnChristian," which insisted that "separation of the races" was the "commandment and law of God." For clerics such as Lyon, racial segregation arose from the white South's most profound conceptions of the proper social ordering. By "integrating the races in schools, we foster miscegenation, thereby changing God's plan and destroying His handiwork," a South Carolina congregation added. "God created and established the color line in the races," a Texas Baptist editor pointed out, and man had "no right to try and eradicate it." The obvious fact that "God created the races and set barriers of color," wrote another Texan, meant that "an intermingling and intermarriage (which is the definition for the word integration) of the races God separated himself, is unthinkable, disgusting, and contrary to His divine plan!"[30]

The triad of sex, segregation, and the sacred (in the formulation of historian Jane Dailey) was rarely enunciated at the level of denominational leadership and in seminaries, but it was a commonplace among churchgoers in the region and ordinary ministers. It may be found sprinkled through letters to editors, newspaper columns, and frequently in private correspondence. Most arguments employed some form of received wisdom and familiar folklore—the immutable "nature" of the Negro, the "impurity" that would inevitably accompany integration, or time-honored scriptural staples such as the Old Testament story of Noah and his progeny. Denominational ethicists and theologians consistently showed how the ancient and cryptic Old Testament tales in no way buttressed the specific twentieth-century social system of segregation. But this biblical jousting was beside the point, for the theoreticians of Jim Crow were by definition suspicious of officially sanctioned modes of scriptural interpretation. In endorsing *Brown*, after all, had not the leadership of the white southern churches betrayed them? Christian desegregationists quoted Acts 17:26: "Of one blood has God made all nations." Segregationists, in response, explicated the second half of the verse, which referred to God assigning to his creatures the "bounds of their habitation." This scriptural reference, insisted one Georgian, seemed "definitely to teach the racial boundary line for all races and their integrity kept inviolate." Scripture thus proved that the races should have "segregated life and Social inter-mingling to themselves to preserve the true and pure strain of their respective races."[31]

White southern believers commonly relied on a simplified and distorted version of commonsense realism, a kind of segregationist natural law. They insisted that the obvious natural truths of the world could not be abrogated without "destroying the handiwork of God in the creating of the races." Asked a Memphis Methodist in a private letter to a religious leader, "Why do you think God made the color of people's skin different? Why did he endow them with different characteristics? Why were they made different and set apart if God didn't want them apart?" A segregationist crusader asserted, "Rather than intermarriage, each race needs to evangelize its own people." Segregationists in the region also paired integrationism with the social gospel. Until denominational agencies realized "that we are in the business of saving souls rather than trying to solve social ills," a couple in Alabama feared, it would be "necessary for those Southern Baptists with firm convictions toward segregation to take drastic action to preserve what we feel is God's will." The Almighty had revealed Truth in scripture and in the natural workings of the world, and it was folly to reshape society by warping biblical truths.[32]

To these dubious biblical interpretations were added more secular arguments that ultimately assumed center stage in the debate. In the context of the Cold War, white southerners seized upon the fight against Bolshevism just as avidly as did those in favor of civil rights organizing. "Integration is nothing but [c]ommunism, and it is strictly against God's Holy Word," an Alabama minister intoned. "Since God made the races, and appointed the bounds of their habitations," a Florida Baptist church suggested (in what amounted to an amalgamation of all the southern religious segregationist arguments), any attempt to "force racial union in social life would lead to the communist hope of producing a 'one world hybridized human,' against the Word and will of God." The NAACP has been sponsored and fostered by "Marxian Christians in our churches, and these Neo-Socialists, teachers and preachers in our schools," Mississippi judge Tom Brady argued, noting that "if God in His infinite wisdom had wanted a Mongrelized, mixed man, that man would have been on this earth." A layman from Macon, Georgia, asked, "What are we doing as Christians while this awful thing called integration, that should be called communism, is destroying our Christian way of life and our entire race? . . . It was God that made the difference, not man." Inveighing against school desegregation, one rural pastor argued that "in the first place the Bible teaches segregation and in the second place what the Supreme Court did is political and our Conventions had no right to try to deal with it. . . . If the Lord had wanted us to all live together in a social way, why did he separate us in the beginning? . . . What the Supreme Court did would finally bring us under a dictatorship."[33]

That integration would produce intermarriage and mongrelization, that blacks themselves preferred segregation, that Negroes were unclean and simply socially inferior, that civil rights organizations were communist-inspired—religious segregationists mustered all the arguments they could in defending the crumbling social system they mistakenly had regarded as timeless and sacrosanct.

Laypeople were not about to follow the progressive denominational elite in sacrificing the embattled customs of the white South. The Alabama Baptist Convention was one of a number of state religious organizations to condemn *Brown* and the government's attempt to enforce it in Little Rock. "Never in the history of the nation," the Alabama Baptists insisted, had a "federal government by judicial decree attempted to enforce a law against the overwhelming and persistent opposition of the majority of the citizens of an area," made worse by the fact that *Brown* was a court decision rather than a legislative act. Louisiana's and Mississippi's state Baptist conventions also remained hostile to desegregation through the 1950s, despite periodic pleas from missionaries about the effect of this policy on their work internationally. Georgia's state Baptist convention heard, and rejected, its own Social Service Commission's recommendation to endorse *Brown* and defend public education. Clerics on the fence could be bullied by activist laymen, as segregationist organizations quickly realized. The White Citizens' Council in Mississippi targeted moderate ministers, whom it called "*our most deadly enemy.*" These fears were certainly exaggerated, for most of the clergy was silent, or silenced, and moderate laypeople generally shielded their views from public knowledge. In Danville, Virginia, the Baptist pastor Harry Wilson discovered his colleagues generally to be apprehensive about encouraging racial brotherhood.

"So many of our ministers have just as much racial prejudice as anyone else," the Reverend Carl Pritchett, a progressive pastor in South Carolina, wrote to a colleague. "The social penalty for nonconformity is still so high it discourages forthright thinking and outspoken Christian interpretation."[34]

Looking at the determination of segregationist churchmen to silence suspect ministers, it is hardly surprising that the white church appeared to lack a moral conscience. Joseph Rabun, a Georgia minister and veteran of combat in the Pacific theater of World War II, found himself after the war in skirmishes with his own congregation. He regarded World War II as a conflict "fought against forces that would shackle and ground man down instead of set him free; that the war was fought against an ideology which held that because of race one man was better than another." Rabun saw the clear parallel between southern racism and the Nazi and Japanese ideology of the master race. In 1946, Rabun found Georgia's white supremacists united under Eugene Talmadge, head of a "Cracker" party that successfully employed racist demagoguery to capture the allegiance of ordinary voters. Talmadge's church membership happened to be in Rabun's congregation in McRae. Persuaded by Rabun to take action, the Georgia Baptist Convention condemned Eugene Talmadge's campaign to save the white primary (then under attack in the state). Testifying against the discriminatory practice, Rabun proclaimed that "the real issue is not a white primary, it is democracy." In response, numerous congregants in McRae told Talmadge that Rabun's days were numbered. Rabun resigned from his pulpit in 1947, a victim of the postwar racist reaction throughout much of the South; the following year, he continued his crusade by running for governor against Talmadge. Rabun's martyrdom would be repeated frequently in the coming years, as ministers who sympathized with ending segregation were hounded from pulpits.[35]

Most white Baptist congregations throughout the region silently complied with or actively supported the segregationist order, ignoring statements emanating from the denominational leadership in Nashville and Atlanta. A writer in the *Alabama Baptist* commented, "We heartily wish all men well, but we cannot believe that any of our parents, of any race, want their children to live in a hostile environment caused by unwise idealism." In Little Rock, James Wesley Pruden, a local fundamentalist Baptist minister and radio personality on his show "The Little Country Church," stirred up resistance to the desegregation of the city's Central High School. Pruden met with Governor Orval Faubus to plot strategy for massive resistance. The Council of Church Women in Little Rock condemned Faubus, but fundamentalist ministers successfully tied the defense of segregation to the critical fight against all forms of modernism. Meanwhile, segregationist women in Pruden's congregation founded the Mothers' League of Central High. They were mostly working-class mothers offended that middle-class whites could send their students to safe suburban schools while they would be saddled with a "mongrelized" Central High as the only choice for their children. Such efforts found support in other congregations. One Baptist church in North Little Rock dispatched a telegram protesting the "unholy invasion" of the National Guard in Little Rock and subsequent violation of the "customs, rights, and privileges" of white southerners. "If you had been spending as much time on your knees in prayer as . . . on the golf course," they telegrammed President Eisenhower, "you never would have sent troops into Arkansas."[36]

The White Citizens' Councils cajoled, exploited, and sometimes coerced ministers in ways akin to the Klan's methods during its heyday earlier in the century. Donald Collins was a Methodist minister in Alabama through the 1950s and 1960s. His memoir recalls the formation of the White Citizens' Council in Selma, Alabama. At a giant rally in 1954, the Christian men and women in attendance joined an "honor bound and Christian cause." The councils organized for action by individuals in the various denominations. In Alabama, the Association of Methodist Ministers and Laymen formed at Highlands Methodist Church in Birmingham on December 14, 1954, intending to "maintain our current racial customs in churches, schools, conferences, and jurisdictions." Supporters from six different Methodist jurisdictions, including most of the local Alabama Methodist conference leaders, comprised an interstate network of communication. They soon found a legislative sponsor for a measure allowing any local congregation to claim the title of a church property if at least 65 percent of the adult membership agreed to separate from the national ecclesiastical organization. The Dumas Bill (later declared unconstitutional) opened the way for local Methodist churches to secede from the larger denomination over the issue of racial segregation, while still retaining control over properties.[37]

Ministers in substantial local churches, but usually outside the highest channels of denominational leadership, often affiliated with local Citizens' Councils. Prominent Baptist clergymen, including Charles C. Jones in Jackson, Marion Woodson of Olanta, South Carolina, and Henry L. Lyon of Montgomery's Highland Avenue Baptist Church, supported the Citizens' Councils in various states. In Mississippi, the White Citizens' Council garnered ideas from prominent segregationist ministers such as G. T. Gillespie. In turn, the council distributed widely his pamphlet *A Christian View of Segregation*. In it, Gillespie dredged up the hoary tale of how Noah's three sons (Shem, Ham, and Japheth) "became the progenitors of three distinct racial groups, which were to repeople and overspread the earth." As the sons occupied the bounds of their habitations, God thus provided for "the distinct racial characteristics which seem to have become fixed in prehistoric times, and which are chiefly responsible for the segregation of racial groups across the centuries and in our time." The separation of languages, furthermore, frustrated those who would seek the "permanent integration of the peoples of the earth" (such as the United Nations). At Jackson's First Christian Church, Archibald Stimson Coody IV, a self-educated man known for his talent with books, held forth for years as a charismatic Sunday school instructor and folk segregationist theologian. As a speech writer for Senator Theodore Bilbo, an elder in his church, and a men's Bible class instructor for over thirty years, he fought against the "cult of equality" emanating from the federal government. In his apocalyptic view, white southern Christians faced a formidable phalanx consisting of the international conspiracy of communists, presidents, the Supreme Court, the NAACP, and the UN. An open member of the Klan, Coody advocated violence in defense of "Land and Race." During his years as a fixture at this church, just a short distance from the state capitol, Coody's pamphlets and other publications received considerable attention.[38]

In Montgomery, G. Stanley Frazer of St. James Methodist Church led opponents of the bus boycott. Frazer urged black ministers to preach the gospel and avoid "getting tangled up in transitory social problems." Meanwhile, Frazer himself was heavily entangled in "transitory" issues, serving, for example, on the mayor's citizens committee that outlined the city's response to black protests. Frazer composed a request to the 1956 Methodist general conference asking that Methodist publishing mediums "not be used as a channel . . . for furthering the program of those who demand drastic changes in the racial structure" of the church. In Birmingham, a white minister boasted that other denominations were envious because Southern Baptists had "stoutly held the line against undemocratic and subversive influences." In North Carolina, hardline Baptists insisted that unless segregation could be shown to be "in conflict with the Sermon on the Mount, or other teachings of Jesus, we should be able to uphold and to practice it; and to do so with a *good conscience.*" In Charlotte, Henry E. Egger of an Episcopal parish expressed his fears that "unadulterated socialism" lay behind the move to integration, while in Virginia an up-and-coming pastor named Jerry Falwell preached that if "Chief Justice Warren and his associates had known God's word," then the *Brown* decision "would never have been made."[39]

The few whites who openly defied Jim Crow drew the ire of the segregationist right. The Mississippi White Citizens' Council and associated groups targeted Will Campbell, a young World War II veteran and Southern Baptist minister. As chaplain of the University of Mississippi in the mid-1950s, Campbell extended a speaking invitation to Alvin Kershaw, an Episcopal minister from Ohio who publicly supported integration and contributed winnings from a game show to the NAACP. "Your actions . . . disgrace God's position," a white Mississippian blasted Kershaw after the Ohioan's sentiments became public knowledge. "God created and SEGREGATED the races," the letter continued, "and no individual, executive, court, or Congress has either the moral or spiritual right to defy his will by ordering or allowing racial integration." The exclusion of this speaker angered other scheduled participants. Most of them withdrew from the program, compelling the university chancellor to cancel Religious Emphasis Week (called by fraternities "Be Good to God" week) altogether. Campbell aroused more controversy when he invited the African American journalist Carl Rowan to stay at his home and otherwise violated regional orthodoxy. Campbell resigned his post and moved to Tennessee to direct a civil rights project undertaken by the National Council of Churches. "In the end," historian Charles Eagles concludes of the debacle, "even a white, Mississippi-born clergyman in a mainstream Christian denomination could not be allowed to speak at the University of Mississippi if he held racial views incompatible with the state's segregated way of life and if he were likely to discuss his unorthodox views publicly." At Millsaps College, a Methodist institution in Jackson, similar outside pressures compelled the administration to withdraw an invitation for an appearance by Glenn Smiley, the field secretary for the Fellowship of Reconciliation. In Smiley's stead the school substituted John Satterfield, a prominent Methodist layman and lawyer, who told the Millsaps students that it was "possible to have a Christian attitude and believe in segregation." Even a private Methodist institution such as Millsaps could not withstand the assault of mobilized segregationists, who were turning Mississippi into a closed society.[40]

Ministerial allies of the movement felt the intensification of massive resistance in the late 1950s. When an interdenominational group of ministers in Mobile, Alabama, signed petitions supporting desegregation, they experienced considerable intimidation and harassment. The president of a local bank advised Methodist minister Douglas Collins not to attend any conferences dealing with racial reconciliation. When Bishop Goodson of the Alabama Conference of the Methodist Church issued a pastoral letter proclaiming "I am determined for God to use me in the struggle for reconciliation for all people," Alabama Methodists responded with a petition asking that ministers "refrain from giving aid or encouragement to agitations, demonstrations, or to attend any meetings, or engage in any propaganda that may encourage disobedience to local, state, or federal officials." They also demanded that church boards cease using denominational publications "as propaganda media to promote racial views repugnant" to the southern church membership. Youth leaders, moreover, were to be discouraged from using Methodist programs "as a means of promoting integration" among students.[41]

The records of Methodist Church bodies overflow with protests and cries of anger emanating from the grass roots. Lay members of First Methodist in Clarksdale condemned bishops for political meddling and announced that their church was "irrevocably opposed to integration of the Negro and white races in the public schools and in the Methodist Churches of Mississippi." Integration, they said, would "promote social equality, which in the annals of History has led almost without exception to miscegenation of the white and negro races." In response to a resolution by the national Methodist Board of Social and Economic Relations, which praised students for their dignified manner during the sit-ins of the early 1960s, Methodists from around the South insisted that, as a district superintendent wrote to the national office, "agitation and wild demonstrations" only worsened racial conflict in the South. Another angered churchman wrote, "I think it's about time that the Yankee Methodists get back to religion and not advocate integration." The sit-down demonstrations, moreover, were "caused by agitators and Communists influence, and lunch counter integration is not a function of the Methodist church."[42]

When 300 ministers in Atlanta signed a manifesto in 1958 to preserve public schools and obey *Brown*, the General Assembly of Georgia promptly denounced the statement. For John Owen Smith, the pastor of the Glenn Memorial Methodist Church in Atlanta and a proponent of desegregation, this underscored the impotence of moral persuasion divorced from political action. Methodist laymen and church board members bombarded Smith with concerns about church policy. A. H. McAfee, lay leader of the major congregation in Decatur, Georgia, complained about an integrated camp program planned for a Methodist young people's gathering in Dahlonega, which would, he thought, "use our children as 'pioneers' for some wild, extreme idea of a few individuals in the North Georgia Conference, to create a disturbance in race relations." At the same time, opinion within white churches was hardly unified. The president of the Woman's Society of Christian Service in that same Decatur congregation wrote Smith that "it both grieves and embarrasses me personally to think that such a letter should be sent to our Bishop." When Smith warmly greeted black visitors to his church in 1960, one correspondent commented on the irony that "a handshake between a Christian minister and a Christian worshiper would call forth a letter of commendation. . . . Yet, as a native white Southerner I am well aware of the Christian courage required of any minister (or layman) who so publicly greets one of another race." A pastor in Alabama, one of the besieged minority seeking to stem the tide of white reaction, complimented Smith for giving moral sustenance to "many of us who feel that the church and its leaders have defaulted at the point of giving real direction at a crucial time in history. We do not mind the role of prophet, if we can just know that we have some support from the higher levels in our church."[43]

Laymen's groups split from progressive elites in the major denominational groupings, as the latter moved gradually to an acceptance of measures for desegregation. The process presaged the division and disintegration that eventually fractured the national Democratic Party. Church people defended their citadels of segregation in church and society in spite of strong pronouncements from governing authorities urging support of *Brown*. As a Methodist Layman's Union pamphlet argued, church members were fearful "lest such propaganda, progressively increasing in intensity all the while, will eventually disrupt or destroy the basic harmony in race relations that has existed thru the years, and coerce magnificently-functioning Methodist congregations to litigate for their freedom, self-respect, and property." Just because the Supreme Court had been carried away by "socialist" writings such as Gunnar Myrdal's *American Dilemma* did not "suddenly make evil that which from time immemorial has been right and proper." All efforts at integration, they assured readers, would be "met by a stone wall of resistance."[44]

Church people felt betrayed by their own ministers who expressed sympathy for desegregation. "We have been shocked time and time again by Preachers and so-called Ministers advocating mixing of the races," complained one layman in 1955. When Methodist bishop and desegregationist James May was featured in *Look* magazine, it appeared to this reader that "in all good conscience we cannot understand nor even remotely conceive how anyone with a heart, especially a father, would attempt to destroy the God given and natural instincts of all species to prefer their own kind," even if this had come to be called "prejudice." The worst were the theologians who did not have "enough on the ball to attract any attention from their failure to otherwise arouse interest, so they grasp the most horrible and sensational method possible in these times, clasp the Negro to their bosoms and use him to make up for what they lack."[45]

Independent publishers of the ephemeral polemical literature of segregation—tracts, pamphlets, short-lived newspapers, and newsletters—reached a fevered pitch in the days of massive resistance following *Brown*. In Birmingham, to cite one example, Merritt Newby published the *Dixie Religious Review*, a paper avowedly in defense of the "Rights of the States, Fundamental Christianity, Constitutional American Government, and Southern Tradition and Custom." Newby dedicated himself to the fight against "race-mixing in the churches, schools, parks, buses, communities and naacp-ism, socialism, communism, false equality and brotherhood doctrines, supreme court government, 'integrate-ism' and all other ism's." Typically for publications of this sort, pro-integration editorials from leading progressive churchmen were reprinted, with the editor heavily annotating the margins with his own conspiracy-laden readings of contemporary history. "The clergy has assumed authority which they do not have and there is no rule or law in either church that prohibits the right of vote by the member in the local church on any racial, political, economic, or social matter," the editor as-

sured readers of a progressive churchman's piece titled "The Christian's Obliga-
tions to All Races," which had emphasized that "at the heart of Christianity was
human equality."[46]

Newspaper editors such as Ralph McGill of the *Atlanta Constitution* received
much of the literature of the segregationist religious right. The Birmingham
Committee for Religious Truth, for one, corresponded with McGill frequently,
explaining for the alternately bemused and disgusted southern moderate the
biblical basis for segregation as law. In this group's view, God "forced segregation . . . and forbid integration, [and] even changed the Tongues of four Brothers, the Sons of Ham, and scattered them abroad." To Billy Graham's assurance
that enforced segregation was not Christian, the southern conservatives responded
that Graham's views followed those of the Methodist Church, "where headquarters instruct Methodists to socialize, Intermingle, and take the Negro into their
homes." A self-described "Bible Student" in Birmingham blamed communism
for turning Congress and the clergy against the white race. Methodist women's
publications dangerously taught the "white race to forget the Scripture," ignoring the biblical narration of how God had set apart the races and "confounded
them and changed their tongues." As the descendant of Ham, the contemporary
Negro would surely intermarry with whites if "turned loose as the Methodist
Synod, and other so called religious denominations advocate."[47]

For frustrated southern segregationists, the centralization of power in denominational headquarters, the racial revolution, and the communist threat all
betokened the decline of freedom in America. "We are losing ground because
the seat of control is already too far removed from the local church," worried
one Methodist. "Some race mixers would insinuate that we who oppose race
mixing are unchristian," wrote a North Carolina segregationist. But he liked to
turn the tables and "ask if it is Christian to pursue a course that would ruin America? True Christianity is truly patriotic. The finest type of Christians both among
the whites and Negroes are those with their racial integrity, and respect for each
other's race here in the South." A Savannah lawyer asked of his bishop, "Where
does the Bible teach Christianity by agitation?" When a meddling clergyman
"invades my neighborhood, my way of living, my home, and attempts to force
his personal philosophy on me, then he has taken the first step in destroying
Methodism in America," the attorney angrily said. "Communism is back of it [de-
segregation] all," pronounced another laywoman, for radicals had "infiltrated
the government, schools, colleges, and *even the church*." If a suspect pastor was
forced upon her home church, she vowed, "there will be many empty pews at
First Methodist."[48]

While Methodist women's leaders generally held progressive views on the desegregation of church and society, some Southern Methodist laywomen joined

in massive resistance. Any removal of the racial divide would have a "most destructive influence," one local chapter of the Woman's Society of Christian Service in South Carolina warned. These women specifically denied the prerogative of the national leaders of the Methodist Woman's Society of Christian Service to set policy on race relations. The national governing body, the South Carolinians insisted, was "not representative of the two million Methodist women they are supposedly representing." When the magazine *Methodist Woman* trumpeted the involvement of denominational women in the Selma desegregation movement, a church member from Georgia explained to her bishop that "we are probably more aware of the Communist Conspiracy than you are since we have seen it happening right here in Americus. We had good reasons to keep those agitators out of our Church. Didn't Jesus run the money changers out of the Temple. Those people were at our Church for a far worse purpose than money changing." The bishop had offended local Methodists by insisting that preachers should be active in the civil rights struggle. One well-publicized incident at Americus, in which blacks were denied admission to various churches in town, embarrassed the Southern Methodist hierarchy. Church people in town, however, complained bitterly of outside agitators. "The Government, backed by the armed might of the Nation, can inforce edicts detrimental to the best interests of the people," a local Methodist wrote to Bishop Smith, "but it is a hazardous, yea dangerous procedure for the governing body of a church to attempt to ram through laws not suited for a considerable part of the membership." The troublemakers seeking admission to the congregations, one churchgoer huffed, were "beatniks, prostitutes, derelicts. These boys and girls, white cohabitated with Negro men and women and the obscenity which was present on the streets of Americus was nauseating."[49]

Segregationist Christians fought on in the 1960s but suffered serious ideological defections. If supporters of the Jim Crow regime were to continue as the self-proclaimed defenders of law and order, they now faced the troubling reality that the law was on the side of desegregation, while blame for disorder lay squarely in the hands of fellow segregationists, who had been complicit with (or who themselves had been) instigators of violence. Conservative Christians still believed that racial separation was right in God's eyes, but they also knew that as a Christian citizen one must render unto Caesar what was Caesar's. Leon Macon, editor of the *Alabama Baptist* for fifteen years and an outspoken opponent of civil rights measures, faced this dilemma by the end of his term in 1965. During congressional debate over the Voting Rights Act, he attacked President Lyndon Johnson's efforts to enlist clergymen in his behalf. For the longtime Alabama Baptist, civil rights measures represented yet another step toward "an all-powerful centralized Federal government" that would "out-socialize the Socialists." Likewise, he opposed statements emanating from the Christian Life Commission of the Southern Baptist Convention that endorsed desegregation in church and society. To Macon, the stance violated the foundational principle of local church autonomy. Most important, as he expressed it, "the basic fear and cause of the opposition to the integration which the Civil Rights Bill intends to bring about has been the mongrelization of our society through intermarriage." Following the passage of the civil rights acts, Macon's only recourse was to suggest voluntary segregation, just as he believed the Jews had practiced for centuries. As a principled Baptist, moreover, Macon was unalterably opposed to state funding or tax advantages for private religious academies that could educate no more than a small elite of white students.[50]

Into the mid-1960s, battles raged in local congregations as determined laypeople (and sometimes ministers) clung to the segregationist line—now reduced simply to protecting their local churches. Determined segregationist factions steamrollered cowed congregations and blocked efforts to enact racially inclusive admissions policies. One of the better-known local controversies took place across the street from Mercer University in Macon, Georgia, the historic Baptist college in the state. Tattnall Square Baptist Church was pastored in 1964 and 1965 by Thomas J. Holmes. He arrived as Sam Omi, an African missionary student who in 1962 had desegregated Mercer, neared graduation. Once the dominant congregation in town, with more than 1,000 churchgoers, Tattnall Square had been reduced to 450 total members, fewer than half of whom regularly attended services. Holmes intended to improve its tattered facilities and salvage its battered reputation.

Upon taking the pulpit, Holmes sensed that trouble would arise with the deacons, two of whom were Klansmen. Holmes spent the first year preaching on the biblical message of the unity of mankind, while the deacons plotted to rid themselves of their suspect cleric. Holmes's supporters publicized these machinations and gave him a vote of confidence; but when the church voted on whether to admit Negroes, opponents packed the pews and turned down the measure. Although personally devastated, Holmes complied with the congregational vote. Sam Omi, already a veteran of the desegregation wars, decided to challenge racial exclusivity in the church. One Sunday, while Holmes was preaching (and unbeknownst to the embattled pastor), deacons on guard dragged Omi down the outside stairs of the church building, where he was whisked away by waiting police officers. By September 1966, the deacons forced the issue on pastor Holmes; he lost a vote of confidence by a count of 250 to 189, and thereafter resigned.

Meanwhile, the story had been picked up by the press, and the church's disgrace drew international attention. A few years later, Holmes penned *Ashes for Breakfast*, his memoir about the controversy, in order to expose the "ignominy of ministerial captivity by entrenched power structures within the church which have long fallen behind the thinking of the majority within the congregations." Holmes suggested how the "tragedy of this church is the nearly universal disgrace of the churches—they might have led the way to community, but, alas, they would not!" After this experience, Holmes joined a ministerial alliance that allowed him to fellowship with black clerics such as William Holmes Borders in Atlanta. By his own account, Holmes and his wife were able to

> sublimate our grief by merging it with that of other broken and bruised members of the human race. The fact that we were willing to suffer for a principle involving love and respect for Negro brothers and sisters has given us an introduction to the black community that we had never had before. The average Negro does not believe in the affirmations of the white community because he has seen too many pronouncements and not enough demonstration. But where there is evidence of genuine Christian love, black people respond magnanimously. We violated the mores of the segregated church and paid the penalty, but in the process we were liberated into the larger fellowship of God's people that transcends racial lines.[51]

Gender and Race in the Religious Right

After World War II, the American creed of democracy and equality effectively put white southern religious conservatives on the defensive. To justify inequality, they resorted to constitutional arguments ("interposition"), appeals to tradition, outright demagoguery, and obscurantist renderings of Old Testament passages. W. A. Criswell, who pastored the largest white Protestant congregation of his era, the First Baptist Church of Dallas, Texas, condemned *Brown* before the South Carolina legislature in 1955: "Let them integrate. Let them sit up there in their dirty shirts and make all their fine speeches. But they are all a bunch of infidels, dying from the neck up." Addressing the Supreme Court's decisions, he implored, "Don't force me to cross over in those *intimate things* where I don't want to go." At that point, however, the raw exercise of power that white supremacy entailed appeared naked, without any compelling theological justification. God-ordained racial inequality crumbled in the hypocrisy of endorsing equality while practicing racism. Most segregationist theologians eventually capitulated; Criswell himself later regretted his own "colossal blunder." Even when heartfelt as opposed to merely opportunistic, theological racism could not withstand the moral maelstrom unleashed by the civil rights movement.[52]

Though not renouncing their views, segregationists by the late 1960s and early 1970s knew better than to air them publicly. "I firmly believe in each race having its own schools, social organizations, and churches. . . . Of course, what I am suggesting will be considered ridiculous and absurd by today's liberal and brainwashed public and I will be labeled a dirty old racist and bigot," a white Alabama Baptist complained in 1974. What had been mainstream was now on the margins of acceptability, and he knew it. But a new battle for the soul of the white Christian South would result in a very different conclusion than the drama of the civil rights years.[53]

By the 1970s, many white southern believers accommodated themselves to the demise of legal segregation. Thus, in the recent controversies within southern church organizations, race has been one of the very few items usually *not* in dispute. Since the 1960s, southern religious conservatives, for the most part, have repudiated the white supremacist views of their predecessors, as seen in the 1995 Southern Baptist Convention resolution officially apologizing for the evangelical and denominational role in slavery and segregation.

Yet the standard biblical arguments against racial equality, now looked upon as an embarrassment from a bygone age, have found their way rather easily into the contemporary religious right's stance on the family. A theology that sanctifies gendered hierarchy has become for the post–civil rights generation what whiteness was for earlier generations of believers. For religious conservatives generally, patriarchy has supplanted race as the defining first principle of God-ordained order. Nowhere is this more evident than in the self-described "conservative resurgence" inside the nation's largest Protestant denomination.

Behind the recent battle for control of the Southern Baptist Convention has been a deep divide between those for whom human equality and autonomy reign as fundamental principles, and those for whom communal norms and strictures and a divinely ordained hierarchy remain determinative of social life. In some ways, the struggle replays a classic debate between philosophical liberalism and communalist conservatism. For the latter group, gender as a system of human social relations is fundamental to godly structures of religious, social, and political life. Of course, southern conservatism always has intertwined race and gender hierarchies, particularly in its emphasis on social purity. Shielding the body politic from corruption also took the form of protecting the white female body from defilement. The parallel with the proslavery argument is unmistakable. Foundational conservative principles of order and hierarchy and literalist biblical exegesis underlay each. Just as was the case with the antislavery biblical argument, liberals have been compelled to rely on broader readings of the biblical texts, which by definition leave them intellectually vulnerable within an evangelical culture that prizes strict constructionist readings of sacred passages —whether of the Bible or of the U.S. Constitution.[54]

In 1979, a group of conservative Southern Baptist men led by Paige Patterson and Paul Pressler, one a theologian and the other a lawyer and conservative district judge, set out to win control of the SBC. Earlier attempts by less well connected fundamentalists had failed. But this effort did succeed in formulating a strategy for ultimate victory: place the right men in the presidency of the convention, and then deploy the appointive power of the executive office to slot political and ideological allies in key positions. Patterson and Pressler, the two Texans who served respectively as the theologian and legal strategist of the movement, organized to purge the SBC of liberalism. They estimated, with remarkable prescience, that in ten years conservatives would own a controlling majority on seminary trustee boards and denominational agencies. An ugly battle through the 1980s for control of the SBC as an organization ensued. The annual meetings, attended by as many as 30,000 or 40,000 messengers from thousands of local churches, devolved into political brawls. By 1991, however, the conservatives emerged victorious, in what they referred to as a "conservative resurgence" (deliberately eschewing the word "fundamentalist," which they knew to be tainted by the stain of anti-intellectualism) and in what the defeated moderates condemned as a "fundamentalist takeover."[55]

The conservatives argued that theological modernism and political liberalism were weaning Southern Baptists away from their historical orthodoxy. The conservatives pursued their goal of putting the SBC back in the hands of believers in biblical inerrancy (showing their clear affinity for fundamentalist thought, despite their rejection of the term as a descriptor). By the late 1980s, the convention stood firmly in the control of men who swore by the inerrant nature of the Bible "in all areas of reality." The word "inerrancy," referring to a complete trust in the literal verity of the Bible, served primarily to smoke out skeptics who expressed the wrong kinds of deviance from the new theological orthodoxy (including support for women as ordained ministers or in other positions of clerical authority). The moderates responded that the fundamentalists were conducting a political purge. But the moderates lacked the capacity to fight with a single-minded will. By contrast, conservative leaders pronounced they were "going for the jugular," and it was the moderates' blood supply that would be stanched. As the SBC conservative intellectual Timothy George put it, the moderates "really never defined their movement in terms of a passionate goal that they could march behind." He saw a narrow isolationism in the moderates, despite their "presumed or pretended sophistication and intellectual patina." In the end, Southern Baptist moderates and progressives, who were often accused of being too preoccupied with matters of the world, turned out to be too spiritually and irenically inclined to organize themselves as a "movement culture" or engage in effective politicking. The conservatives, who proclaimed themselves defenders of the spirituality of the church, were also savvy operators imbued with a passionate belief in restoring orthodoxy. They understood at a visceral level how the personal, the political, and the theological were bound together.[56]

It was no accident that religious conservatives came to national prominence following the demise of race as the central issue of southern life. Underlying their political movements were philosophical positions that updated venerable defenses of social order as necessary for a properly ordered liberty. No longer saddled with the burden of defending discredited racist mythologies, the conservatives advanced unapologetically patriarchal arguments. In the late 1990s, when delegates to the Southern Baptist Convention approved the change to the Baptist Faith and Message that endorsed "wifely submission" to husbands, national commentators took note of what appeared to be a reactionary public message, but in fact this statement simply reiterated a time-honored position in southern religious life.

The authors of the statement rejected the concept of "mutual submission," for in that formulation the analogy of Christ and the church collapsed. Dorothy Patterson, the conservative woman in charge of the wifely submission manifesto, dissociated herself from the leadership of the Woman's Missionary Union of the SBC. In WMU literature, she complained, she did not see a "real lifting up of the responsibility of homemaking." Moreover, women's missionary leaders had separated themselves from pastors and churches and had stood "at every point publicly against the conservative resurgence"; they had "caricatured" the conservatives as being part of a "political" rather than theological movement. For example, the WMU leadership had refused to be brought under denominational control as were other agencies. According to Patterson, "they didn't want to be controlled by conservatives . . . and they didn't like the direction of the convention." The WMU leaders did not want to be called "feminist," but in fact there was a "great deal of sympathy toward feminism, whether that is something that's premeditated or whether it's just something [they] just kind of slide into." They had forgotten that, following the New Testament pattern, the pastoral role was to lead the congregation. Mark Coppenger, another SBC spokesman, saw in the WMU's magazine *Folio* and in certain seminary professors (in particular Molly Marshall, head of the social work school at Southern Baptist Theological Seminary until her abrupt firing in the mid-1990s) a suspiciously unorthodox view of man's and woman's possibly divine nature. Coppenger also criticized the WMU's implicit sponsorship of women in the ministry. For Coppenger, if "one were faithful to biblical inerrancy, then one would have to discount much of what the feminists were saying." Just as Christ headed the church, so the husband led at home. The issue of women in the ministry, as he saw it, was a "big part of the culture war. It's the perversion of the understanding of women in society."[57]

The restructuring of American religion outlined by the sociologist Robert

Wuthnow followed a pattern similar to the changes in American politics through the New Deal and civil rights years. Late in the Depression, senators led by figures such as the Southern Baptist Josiah Bailey effectively formed a coalition that stymied FDR's social reform plans. They argued that the Democratic Party had become a vehicle for the schemes of the New Deal, not the stalwart defender of decentralized and limited government as was the southern Democratic philosophy. Moreover, white southerners looked on with dismay as the party of their fathers became a multi-ethnic patchwork. They were especially uneasy as blacks deserted the party of Lincoln for the party of Roosevelt. A decade later, they stormed out of the Democratic National Convention in the Dixiecrat revolt of 1948. In subsequent years, many of the same figures (and their direct descendants) spearheaded the attack on the civil rights revolution.[58]

The relationship between race and contemporary white southern evangelical identity was forged in the wake of civil rights era controversies. That is not to say that race was the real issue behind the southern culture wars (such as the controversy over control of the SBC) of the 1980s and 1990s. It was not. It is to say, however, that moderates and conservatives, as well as a few liberals, coalesced during the civil rights years. The conservatives came together in part against the moderate and gradualist leadership of many Southern Baptist agencies in regard to race. Denominational critics argued strenuously that when the Christian Life Commission spoke in favor of desegregation, it did not speak for the majority of Southern Baptists; and, accordingly, the democratic principle supposedly determinative in Southern Baptist life had been breached. The descendants of this restructuring of southern politics and religion led the conservative movements of the 1970s, this time with more success. Divisions within the SBC had been evident during the Progressive Era, and of course during the modernist controversies of the 1920s. But the civil rights struggle sped up the process of re-forming southern denominations, fracturing them along the lines of conservatives, moderates, and liberals that typically form cross-denominational alliances. In fact, some tentative cross-racial conservative coalitions—organized particularly around the issues of abortion, public education, and women's rights —have distinguished contemporary southern evangelicals from their avowedly white supremacist predecessors.

The arguments made about civil rights brought to light differences within denominations known to exist but generally finessed or simply fought out and then forgotten. The new groupings on the right quickly left behind the dishonorable racist past of their predecessors but inherited their well-honed theological understandings of hierarchy, submission, and theological order. Abortion was the "stick of dynamite that exploded the issue," Southern Baptist Theological Seminary president R. Albert Mohler said of what he and others have praised as the "conservative resurgence" in American religious life. In Mohler's view, the southern progressive elite properly and usefully had critiqued cultural Christianity, the too-cozy relationship long existing between Southern Baptists and southern culture, but they had not understood the implications of a "naked public square" bereft of moral Christian foundations. Once the SBC had been separated from being merely a form of cultural Christianity, then southern Christians would find what it meant to be a "cognitive minority in a hostile culture." The era of cultural captivity had come to an end, and the era of culture wars inaugurated. Conservatives such as Mohler relished that battle.[59]

Later generations seem as likely to look upon gender strictures with the same regret as evangelicals ponder the history of proslavery and pro-apartheid theology — so much intellectual firepower and heartfelt biblical argumentation wasted on such futile causes. Over the long term, ideologies of inequality run headlong into the American creed of opportunity and equality. Eventually, theologies must adjust themselves to that social reality—as has been the case with the nearly complete demise of publicly articulated racial theologies among white southern conservative Christians.

Epilogue

The Evangelical Belt in
the Contemporary South

In Thomasville, Georgia, in the mid-1990s, a young white woman named Jaime
L. Wireman gave birth to a child she named Whitney, after the contemporary
black singer Whitney Houston. Wireman's husband, an African American man
named Jeffrey Johnson, worked odd jobs locally, and the two lived together in
a trailer just outside the southwest Georgia town. The child, born with a skull
not fully formed, died after just nineteen hours. Jaime Wireman wanted the
baby to be buried with her maternal grandfather in the cemetery of the Barnetts
Creek Baptist Church. After her burial, however, deacons of the church, who had
not known previously that the father was black, asked the family to remove the
child from the historically all-white cemetery. When the embarrassing incident
came to light, church members criticized the deacons' action and permitted the
child to remain in the cemetery. With some prodding from Whitney's maternal
grandmother, the deacons and the pastor of the church met the family, apologized for their actions, and asked for forgiveness. "Our church family humbly
asks you to accept our apology," the chairman of the deacon board told the family. "I believe people are sorry," the child's grandmother concluded. "She was just
a baby."[1]

This story of race and religion in the contemporary South allegorically retells the familiar themes traced through this book: theological racism, racial interchange, and Christian interracialism. Racial division runs headlong into an innocent childhood disrupted by the intrusion of an unjust social world. The culmination, on the face of it, brings healing. Just as important, the story puts into relief a paradox of southern, and American, religious history: namely, the deep tension between human spiritual equality in the eyes of God and divinely ordained social inequality in the everyday world.

The contemporary South still commonly appears as the land of the Bible Belt. Despite the rapidly increasing immigration from all parts of the world to the region, there is still justification for such a view. Scholarship in southern religious history, including titles such as *At Ease in Zion* and *Churches in Cultural Captivity*, furthers this seemingly timeless image of the "God-haunted" South, here referred to as the Evangelical Belt. Nevertheless, believers in the Evangelical Belt are often the most skeptical and uneasy about the culture that they ostensibly dominate. The title of another recent work, *Uneasy in Babylon: Southern Baptist Conservatives and American Culture* contrasts vividly with the earlier image of being "at ease in Zion." The South may be distinctive in the continued prevalence of born-again evangelicalism, but the region has never been Zion, and evangelicals not fully at ease in it.

There is another tension as well: that between involvement and noninvolvement with the state. In other words, the relationship between religion and public life in the Evangelical Belt is much more complex than may often appear in this much caricatured subject. Just what is God's and what is Caesar's is not always so clear. White southern evangelicals historically have preached a clear distinction between matters of morality, on which Christians were obligated to take a stand, and matters of politics, which evangelicals were supposed to avoid as divisive and detrimental to the advancement of God's kingdom. Thus, alcohol became a matter of public concern for evangelicals (and still is), while one's views on the tariff (in the nineteenth century) or the capital gains tax (in the twentieth) were largely outside the realm of evangelical discussion of politics and public life. This view, of course, hardly prevented antebellum white southern evangelicals from vigorously supporting and defending slavery. Nor did it block a heavy involvement in public life during the Civil War through army service, chaplaincies, and fast-day sermons. Moreover, evangelicals were vigorous proponents of new systems of racial control, namely segregation, in the late nineteenth century, and many defended that system during its declining years into the 1950s and 1960s.

The South's own self-image of being at ease in Zion has been shaken in recent years. Indeed, the very term "southern identity" itself has been called into question. What does it mean to call a region the "Evangelical Belt" when, according to the 2000 census data, 40 percent of those surveyed were either uncounted or unaffiliated with any church. The closest competitor to the category of "unaffiliated or uncounted" for the South was "Baptist," with 19 percent of the total regional population identified as adherents (a category more expansive than that of "members"). The category "historically black Protestant" registered at 12 percent. The only other group coming in at a figure of over 10 percent were the Catholics. In looking at current growth trends, moreover, evangelical hegemony appears on the wane. For example, while 27 percent of Tennesseans claim affiliation with the Baptists, the growth rate of the denomination has not kept pace with the rapid percentage growth of population in the Volunteer State.[2]

Statistics can tell many stories, of course. If the numbers crunched above show an Evangelical Belt that is, at best, holding its own, other tales from the tables suggest a different conclusion. In a poll conducted in 1998, 20 percent of southerners indicated they attended church services more than once a week, a rate more than double that for nonsoutherners. More southerners (almost 42 percent, in comparison to 33 percent for those outside the region) agreed with the statement that religion was "extremely important" in their lives. Six of ten southerners said they accepted the account of creation in Genesis over Darwin. A large proportion of the "unchurched" in the region still believes in God and afterlife. The predominance of southern preachers on the airwaves provides the oral soundtrack that many Americans associate with conservative Protestant Christianity more generally. "Several of my Christian friends had asked me why I seemed to slip into a Southern accent when praying or praising the Lord," one woman recently ruminated. "It dawned on me one night that I had been learning about prayer and ministry from several television ministers."[3] In other words, even if 40 percent of southerners are uncounted or unaffiliated, many register as believers if counted by other measures.

Tilt the prism another way and yet another perspective emerges. While the "distinctive South" still survives, the demographic distinctiveness of the South is in decline, in large part because of the influx of Latinos and Asians. Since the 1970s, religious diversity in the South has intensified. In 1999, more than one in five southerners affiliated with some faith outside of Protestantism. Latinos and Asians now make up almost 14 percent of southerners. Fourteen percent of Texas residents and 17 percent of Floridians were born outside the United States. In North Carolina, Latinos and Asians constituted less than 2 percent of the population in 1990, but that number rose dramatically in the subsequent decade. In North Carolina alone, the 77,000 Latinos counted in 1990 grew to 377,000 ten years later. Durham County's Hispanic population rose by over 700 percent in the 1990s, and Durham is now a "majority-minority" city: 48 percent white, 39 percent African American, 8 percent Hispanic, and 3 percent Asian.[4]

Still, a recognizable Evangelical Belt persists. According to the American Religious Identification Survey (ARIS), the South stands as having the highest percentage of churchgoers within the region who affiliate themselves with Baptists (23.5 percent), Presbyterians (3 percent), and black Protestants (14 percent, well over half of whom are Baptists). Combining the data for white Baptists and black Protestants and disaggregating blacks who are Baptist from the more general figure of black Protestant, one may see the considerable credence of the older notion of a "Baptist South." No other region comes close in terms of Baptist affiliation statistics. The Evangelical Belt as defined here is, in very many counties, effectively a Baptist Belt as well. One may compare the presence of Baptists in the region to the figure of 5.7 percent of Baptists within the region of New England and a national low of 3.8 percent in the coastal Northwest. The South also counts the highest percentage in any region of white non-Hispanic Methodists (6.9 percent) and a relatively high percentage of white non-Hispanic Pentecostal/Charismatic adherents (3 percent). Moreover, in the ARIS data, the South has the lowest count of those who responded "no religion" when asked generally about their religious beliefs and affiliations (10 percent within the region), and nearly the lowest count for white Catholics.[5]

The state-level data provide equally informative numbers. According to statistics provided in the North American Religion Atlas (NARA), evangelical Protestant members as a percentage of the total population peak in Alabama (32 percent, the highest in the region) and Mississippi (31 percent), followed closely by Tennessee (29.4 percent) and Kentucky (26.7 percent). A tabulation of mainline Protestant members—a figure that would include the substantial membership of United Methodists, for example—results in another 7 percent of the population of Alabama, 7.5 percent in Mississippi, 7.3 percent in Tennessee, and 6.7 percent in Kentucky. In terms of the entire South region, when measuring adherents as a percentage of total population, 19 percent are counted as Baptist adherents and 12.4 percent as historically African American Protestant. One may compare all these figures to the national average of 6.6 percent of Baptist members as a percentage of population, or 8.5 percent if measured in terms of adherents, and 7.4 percent of the national population listed in the historically African American Protestant category.

This is not to suggest that evangelical Protestantism has a uniform dominance across the region. On the contrary, evangelical Protestant adherents as a percentage of population are heavily concentrated in particular areas and counties of the region, numbering especially heavily in a broad swath that cuts directly through the historic cotton country and some upcountry regions of the Old South. A contrast of two states in the region makes this point clearly. In Mississippi, Baptist adherents (excluding historically African American Protestants) number 34 percent of the total population, and historically African American Protestant adherents account for another 29 percent. Just over 16 percent of Mississippians are "unaffiliated or uncounted." Jews exist in too small a number to form even a 1 percent slice on the pie chart. Some counties of Mississippi register 0 percent reporting "unaffiliated or uncounted." In Amite County, Mississippi, for example, 44 percent of the population counts itself as Baptist and 42 percent are adherents to historically black churches. With Methodists at 5 percent and Mormons racking up a surprisingly high 4 percent of the county's population, Amite County stands as one of the most religious microcosms in the entire country.

In Virginia, by distinct contrast, almost half the population goes into the "unaffiliated or uncounted" category—a larger percentage than that of the country as a whole. Baptist adherents, excluding those in historically African American churches, count for 12 percent of the state, a figure approximating the national average (in contrast to much of the rest of the South). The religiosity of Amite County, Mississippi, stands out against the relative indifference of Albermarle County, Virginia. The county that includes Charlottesville and the University of Virginia as its centerpiece ranks unusually high, by either regional or national standards, in the category of "unaffiliated or uncounted," almost 64 percent of its population. Baptist adherents account for only 8 percent of the population, and black Protestants just 3 percent. On the whole, Albermarle County looks more like the Pacific Northwest or other regions of high levels of indifference than it does most places in the South. In short, the South's religiosity is relatively high but varies considerably by place within the region. There is a clear "historically black Protestant belt" and an equally identifiable Evangelical Belt.

The particular demographic of the Evangelical Belt significantly influences the character of public life. Religion strongly influences politics, a fact becoming more evident as the conservative, "family values" wing of the Republican Party strengthens its hold on white believers in the region. In exit polling data from the 2000 election, 27 percent of voters surveyed in the South professed affiliation with evangelical Protestantism, the highest of any region (the next closest was the Midwest, at 25 percent; both contrasted starkly with New England, where just 1.8 percent claimed evangelical affiliation and 5.8 percent mainline Protestantism). Nationally, evangelicals voted in landslide proportions for George W. Bush over Albert Gore in the 2000 presidential race, by a combined margin of 78.7 to 19.4 percent. In this voting behavior in the South, the gap was almost the same, 80.2 percent to 19.0 percent in favor of Bush. One immediately notes the contrast with historically black Protestant adherents, 91 percent of whom cast a ballot for Gore, according to the exit polling data. As the most statistically evangelical Protestant of all the regions, the distinctive South clearly plays a key role in national elections. White southern evangelicals still live in the "solid South," but one that is solidly conservative Republican; the other solid South is that of historically black Protestants, who are even more highly partisan in the other direction.

Regional religious traditions appear even more significantly in data compiled by John Green of the University of Akron. He finds that the South has the highest percentage of those who self-identified (in his survey) as "evangelical" or "historically black Protestant" (41 percent and 16 percent, respectively), alongside the lowest percentage of Catholic adherents (12 percent), and the lowest number claiming to be non-Christian or secular (12 percent). The South as a whole tops the poll in terms of "high views" of the Bible (that is, those who endorsed some variant of the statement that the Bible is the inspired word of God). In this survey, 68 percent of southerners profess belief in the Bible as the inspired word of God. All religious groups in the South—evangelical, mainline, black, Catholic, "Other Christian," Jewish, and (most interestingly of all) those self-identified as "secular"—are more likely (usually considerably so) to profess a "high view" of biblical authority. Eighty-five percent of southern evangelicals claim a high view, as do 62 percent of mainline Protestants and 30 percent of secularists. The South, then, is the most solidly evangelical region of the country, and the South's white evangelicals are among the most conservative in terms of voting patterns, views of biblical authority, and attitudes toward significant social issues.[6]

The solidity of the Evangelical Belt in demography and public life is not necessarily all that it seems, however. Evangelicals influence but do not necessarily dominate or control public and political life. Politicians are obligated to speak to issues important to the evangelical right, but if they become associated too closely with that faction, then they risk losing the support of moderate and secular voters. Evangelicals have placed many of their own in seats of political power at local and state levels, but there they must forge coalitions and often move more to the center or else remain outvoted and exiled. Evangelical Belt Christians constitute a substantial voting bloc that politicians ignore at their peril. Thus, their social agenda is respected and feared, yet sometimes ignored when salient issues of economics are at stake. Their religious language has been adopted by political candidates, showing its wide influence but also paradoxically diluting its influence and meaning. In the contemporary South, then, evangelical believers are at ease in Zion and uneasy in Babylon at the same time.

Notes

Abbreviations Used in the Notes

AG   Assemblies of God Archives, Flower Pentecostal Heritage Center, Assemblies of God, Springfield, Mo.

ARC   Amistad Research Center, Tulane University, New Orleans, La.

BTV   Transcripts from "Behind the Veil: Oral Histories of African Americans in the Jim Crow South, 1940–97," Special Collections, Perkins Library, Duke University, Durham, N.C.

COHRO   Columbia University Oral History Research Office, Columbia University, New York City

CWUP   Church Women United Papers, General Commissions on Archives and History, United Methodist Church Archives, Drew University, Madison, N.J.

DC   Sherry Sherrod Dupree Collection (on African American Holiness/ Pentecostalism), Schomburg Center for Research in Black Culture, New York Public Library, Harlem Branch, New York

DOH   Duke University Oral History Program Papers, 1973–78, Special Collections, Perkins Library, Duke University, Durham, N.C.

ESCL   Special Collections Library, Emory University, Atlanta, Georgia

FAS *Reports* *Reports of the Freedmen's Aid Society of the Methodist Episcopal Church, 1866–1875* (Cincinnati: Western Methodist Book Concern, 1893)

FWP   Federal Works Project Interviews, Southern Historical Collection, Manuscripts Department, Wilson Library, University of North Carolina, Chapel Hill, North Carolina

GAPCC Minutes	Minutes of the General Assembly of the Presbyterian Church in the Confederate States of America
GAPCUS Minutes	Minutes of the General Assembly of the Presbyterian Church of the United States
GBCS Records	Records of the General Board of Church and Society, United Methodist Church, General Commissions on Archives and History, United Methodist Church Archives, Drew University, Madison, N.J.
GCAH	General Commissions on Archives and History, United Methodist Church Archives, Drew University, Madison, N.J.
MECSJ	Journal of the General Conference of the Methodist Episcopal Church, South
Narratives	George Rawick, ed., *The American Slave: A Composite Autobiography*, 41 vols. (Westport, Conn.: Greenwood Press, 1972–79). The narratives will be referenced by state and, where appropriate, by supp. ser. for supplemental series 1 and 2.
PHS	Presbyterian Historical Society, Montreat College, Montreat, N.C.
SBHLA	Southern Baptist Historical Library and Archives, Nashville, Tenn.
SCPL	Special Collections, Perkins Library, Duke University, Durham, N.C.
SHC	Southern Historical Collection, Manuscripts Department, Wilson Library, University of North Carolina, Chapel Hill
SOHP	Southern Oral History Program, Transcripts and Tapes of Interviews, Southern Historical Collection, Manuscripts Department, Wilson Library, University of North Carolina, Chapel Hill
THC	Institute for Oral History, Transcripts in Texas Historical Collection, Carroll Library, Baylor University, Waco, Tex.
WCJ	Journal of the Woman's Convention, Auxiliary to the National Baptist Convention
WHS	State Historical Society of Wisconsin (repository of the Student Non-Violent Coordinating Committee Papers)

Introduction

1. Joyner, *Shared Traditions*, 25.

Chapter One

1. Interview with Margaret Christine Nelson (Summerton, South Carolina) in BTV, TR-1.

2. For Murrell's view, see *American Baptist*, Feb. 25, 1868, Oct. 19, 1869. For Manly's view, see Charles Manly to Basil Manly Jr., May 28, 1866, in Manly Family Papers, reel 2, folder 179; and Basil Manly Sr. diary, entry for June 24, 1866, in Basil Manly Sr. Papers, SBHLA; Arthur Waddell quoted in *American Baptist*, Sept. 3, 1867. For more on Basil Manly Sr., see Fuller, *Chaplain to the Confederacy*.

3. Harvey, *Redeeming the South*, 31–33; Kellison, "Coming to Christ," 265.

4. Simon Richardson, *Lights and Shadows*, 181, 184, 197.

5. John Emory Bryant to "My Darling Wife," Dec. 22, 1878, in Bryant Papers, SCPL.

6. See Stowell, *Rebuilding Zion*, for a richly detailed recounting of the three "visions" for southern religious life after the Civil War.

7. The numbers from the 1906 religious census are summarized in Montgomery, *Under Their Own Vine and Fig Tree*, 343. These numbers include northern black church membership, but the great majority of the adherents would still have been in the South. The religious census numbers are at best rough guesses, given the vagaries by which some churches responded to the census requests and the varying definitions employed by denomination for the term "member." Thus, I have chosen to give round approximate figures so as not to imply that the exact figures given in the census are in fact precise.

8. Matthew Gilbert, "Colored Churches: An Experiment," *National Baptist Magazine* 1 (1894): 165. See also "The Colored Baptist Convention," *Southwestern Advocate*, July 29, 1875, and Dec. 27, 1869. For a fuller account of the drama of black religious institutions after the Civil War, see Montgomery, *Under Their Own Vine and Fig Tree*; Stowell, *Rebuilding Zion*; Harvey, *Redeeming the South*; and Dvorak, *African-American Exodus*.

9. Angell, *Bishop Henry McNeal Turner*, 24.

10. *Star of Zion*, Sept. 10, 1886. For a useful compilation of Turner's speeches and writings, see Redkey, ed., *Respect Black*.

11. Quotation from Angell, *Bishop Henry McNeal Turner*, 85.

12. Quoted in ibid., 249. For more on Turner and the rise of the African Methodist Episcopal Church in South Africa, see James T. Campbell, *Songs of Zion*.

13. Corey, *History of Richmond Theological Seminary*, 72; Donaldson, "Standing on a Volcano," 139–40; Harvey, *Redeeming the South*, 49.

14. Donaldson, "Standing on a Volcano," 157.

15. Ibid., 135–77.

16. Lynch to Bishop Matthew Simpson, Dec. 3, 1868, and Oct. 6, 1869, in Gravely, "Black Methodist," 7, 16.

17. MECSJ, 1874, 176–77.

18. Ibid., 458–60.

19. A. C. Ramsey, "Alabama Conference," *New Orleans Christian Advocate*, Dec. 9, 1875; Lane, *Autobiography*, 65–66, 84; "Some Plain Words," *Southwestern Advocate*, Feb. 26, 1874.

20. Holsey, *Autobiography*, 19, 23–25, 243.

21. L. H. Holsey, "Race Segregation," *A.M.E. Church Review* 26 (Oct. 1909): 109–23; Eskew, "Black Elitism," 666–77.

22. Bennett, "Religion and the Rise of Jim Crow," 27, 41–42.

23. Ibid., 143; Loveland, "'Southern Work,'" 395.

24. Bennett, "Religion and the Rise of Jim Crow," 129–30, 135, 152, 172, 180.

25. E. C. Haven, "No Separate Conferences for Whites," *Southwestern Advocate*, July 3, 1873; "The Question of Color in the Church," ibid., Apr. 9, 1874; "Bishop Foster to the Louisiana Conference," ibid., Jan. 14, 1875; Bennett, "Religion and the Rise of Jim Crow," 71. Much the same story held true for the Catholic Church in New Orleans as for the Methodists. Eventually, New Orleans Catholicism also became racially segregated, despite protests by older black Creole Catholics, who insisted that it was Catholicism's universality that would attract black converts. A substantial group of black Catholics, often

French-speaking Creoles descended from the free people of color, joined with black Americans to fight segregation in the church. They balked when the archdiocese put in place segregated parishes. Black Catholics used their paper, the *Crusader*, to articulate black grievances against segregation of the churches (similar to the role played by the *Southwestern Christian Advocate* for black Methodists). The racial divide continued to grow, however, speeded by the importation of priests with the Josephite order, whose mission it was to serve black Catholics, and by the Americanization of the church, which reduced the influence of French-speaking Creole leaders. As one member of the Josephite order wrote in 1909, "the white churches seem to be taking our coming as a good excuse to freeze the Colored out." The northern Catholic humanitarian Katherine Drexel's philanthropic support of black Catholic schools also inadvertently aided the segregation of Catholic parishes.

26. Sarah Jane Foster, letter from Charleston, Dec. 14, 1867, in Reilly, ed., *Sarah Jane Foster*, 171; Holt, "Making Freedom Pay."

27. Love, *History of the First African Baptist Church*, 58; Montgomery, *Under Their Own Vine and Fig Tree*, 276–77.

28. Montgomery, *Under Their Own Vine and Fig Tree*, 54, 88.

29. Tucker, *Black Pastors and Leaders*.

30. Ibid., 5–15; Armstead L. Robinson, "Plans Dat Comed from God," 73–74; Berkeley, " 'Colored Ladies Also Contributed,' " 182.

31. Tera W. Hunter, *To 'Joy My Freedom*, 48–49, 68–70; Rabinowitz, *Race Relations in the Urban South*, 199–204.

32. Woodworth, *While God Is Marching On*, 277, 286; "Prayer for the Country," *North Carolina Christian Advocate*, June 3, 1863.

33. Stowell, *Rebuilding Zion*, 65–69; Norvell Winsboro Wilson diary, entries for Dec. 31, 1864; Apr. 30, 1865; May 1, 1865; June 8, 1865; in Wilson Papers, SHC; *North Carolina Christian Advocate*, Aug. 12, 1864; Sparks, *Religion in Mississippi*, 134, 137.

34. Mary Jeffreys Bethell diary, entries for Aug. 7, 1865, and Jan. 1, 1866, SHC.

35. Cornelius, *Slave Missions*, 207.

36. Laura Comer diary, entries for Jan. 5, Sept. 4, 1862; Dec. 9, 1866; Feb. 6, 1867; July 5, 1868, SHC.

37. Dolly Lunt Burge diary, entry for Nov. 8, 1864, in James I. Robertson, ed., *Diary of Dolly Lunt Burge*, 98; Magnolia Wynn LeGuin diary, entry for Nov. 29, 1905, in LeGuin, ed., *Home-Concealed Woman*, 183.

38. Burr, ed., *Secret Eye*, 276.

39. Sara Chilton to "My Dear Lady" (Mrs. L. N. Brown of New Orleans), Oct. 24, 1875; Oct. 31, 1875; Nov. 13, 1875; undated, Nov. 1875; in Norton, Chilton, and Dameron Papers, box 1, folder 10, SHC.

40. Owen, *Sacred Flame of Love*, 100–105; MECSJ, 1866, 17–19, 34, 49; Farish, *Circuit Rider Dismounts*, 53–55.

41. "Endure Hardness," *New Orleans Christian Advocate*, Jan. 22, 1874; Farish, *Circuit Rider Dismounts*, 41, 53–55, 65–67.

42. See Harvey, *Redeeming the South*, ch. 1.

43. GAPCC Minutes, 1861, 51–52; GAPCUS Minutes, 1870, 539; Thomas Cary Johnson, ed., *Life and Letters of Robert Lewis Dabney*, 378.

44. GAPCC Minutes, 1861, 51–52, 58; 1864, 293.

45. Browder, *Heavens Are Weeping*, 255, 110, 156, 114, 122, 126, 159, 165, 173, 189.

46. Owen, *Sacred Flame of Love*, 119; Caldwell, *Reminiscences*, 3–4, 7–12; Stowell, "'Negroes Cannot Navigate Alone,'" 65–90.

47. Currie-McDaniel, *Carpetbagger of Conscience*, 160, 168.

48. William George Matton, "Autobiographical Sketch," SCPL; Board of Education, Freedmen's Aid Society of the Methodist Episcopal Church, ? Childress to J. F. Chalfant, July 14, 1867, copy in ARC.

49. *Religious Herald*, Jan. 24, 1867 (Andrew Broaddus).

50. *Biblical Recorder*, June 5, 1867; H. H. Tucker, "Letter from H. H. Tucker, D.D.," in Love, *History of the First African Baptist Church*, 322; Harvey, *Redeeming the South*, 34–38.

51. GAPCUS Minutes, 1869, 389; *Southern Presbyterian Review* 18 (1868): 6; McMillen, *To Raise up the South*, 175; Girardeau quotations from Adger, *My Life and Times*, 176–77; Dabney, "Speech of Rev. Robert L. Dabney," 5, PHS; and Thomas Cary Johnson, ed., *Life and Letters of Robert Lewis Dabney*, 320–21.

52. References for the last three paragraphs on Presbyterian evangelization among blacks come from James G. Snecedor to "Dear Brother" (sent to Presbyterian ministers), Nov. 16, 1909, in Snecedor Papers, box 2, PHS; Oscar Bickley Wilson diary, entries for June 15, 1899; July 22 and 23, 1896; Sept. 22 and 28, 1896; Dec. 14, 1896; Aug. 24, 1898; May 4, 1898, in PHS; GAPCUS Minutes, 1902, 292–93; 1910, 102, 104; and Ernest Trice Thompson, "Black Presbyterians."

53. Lydia Schofield diary, entries for Apr. 22 and 27, 1866, SHC.

54. George N. Greene to George Whipple, May 15, 1865, in AMA Archives, ARC; Luker, *Social Gospel in Black and White*, 15; De Boer, "Role of Afro-Americans," 316.

55. Joe Martin Richardson, *Christian Reconstruction*, 43.

56. De Boer, "Role of Afro-Americans," 412–32; Joe Martin Richardson, *Christian Reconstruction*, 98, 130.

57. Joe Martin Richardson, *Christian Reconstruction*, 147–51; FAS *Reports*, 1866, 12.

58. FAS *Reports*, 1866, 6–8, 12; 1871, 15, 21; 1878, 4.

59. A. S. Lakin to Rev. J. P. Chalfant, Dec. 14, 1865, in Records of the Freedmen's Aid Society of the Methodist Episcopal Church, Board of Education, ARC; FAS *Reports*, 1873, 11; McMillen, *To Raise up the South*, 75, 86; L. Mason Rice to J. E. Bryant, July 2, 1877, in Bryant Papers, SCPL.

60. FAS *Reports*, 1877, 61; 1878, 68, 74, 79; Litwack, *Trouble in Mind*, 91, 211; Butchart, *Northern Schools*, 69, 74–75.

61. Hahn, *Nation under Our Feet*, 179, 234; Allan-Olney, *New Virginians*, 148–50; Resolution of the First Baptist Antioch Association, 1868, quoted in Patrick H. Thompson, *History of Negro Baptists*, 44; Giggie, "God's Long Journey," 20, 36, 43.

62. Helen Dodd to Friends, Dec. 13, 1866, Dodd Family Papers, ARC; Sparks, *Religion in Mississippi*, 141; Meeting of the Colored Mens of the Mechanic and Laboring Men Association of Georgia, in Bryant Papers, box 2, folder for 1868–69, SCPL. An enumeration of the occupations of black men who held office during Reconstruction may be found in Foner, *Freedom's Lawmakers*.

63. Billingsley, *Mighty Like a River*, 30–34; Hahn, *Nation under Our Feet*, 145.

64. Montgomery, *Under Their Own Vine and Fig Tree*, 157, 179; see also Rabinowitz, "Holland Thompson."

65. Heard, *From Slavery to the Bishopric*, 42–44, 89–90.

66. Robert L. Hall, "Gospel According to Radicalism," 69–81, and "Tallahassee's Black Churches," 185–96; Zipf, "'Among These American Heathens,'" 130–34; Hahn, *Nation under Our Feet*, 134; John Paris, "Moral and Religious Status," SHC.

67. Clipping from July 29, 1867, in Bryant Papers, box 2, SCPL; *Southwestern Christian Advocate*, Jan. 4, 1877; *Texas Narratives*, supp. ser. 2, vol. 8, pt. 7, pp. 3062–63 (Lu Perkins); Edgefield Baptist Association (South Carolina) Minutes, 1871, SBHLA; *Arkansas Narratives*, orig. ser. 2, vol. 9, pt. 4, p. 68; *South Carolina Narratives*, orig. ser., vol. 2, pt. 2, p. 121 (Brawley Gilmore); *Arkansas Narratives*, orig. ser. 2, vol. 9, pt. 3, pp. 258–61 (Harriet Hill).

68. James Mallory, diary entries for Dec. 15, 1866; June 28, 1868; Oct. 13, 1867; Aug. 15, 1868; and Nov. 26, 1874; in McWhiney et al., eds., *Fear God and Walk Humbly*, 389, 379, 390–91, 459.

69. W. Wilkes, "Religious Schism and Defection," *Alabama Baptist*, Jan. 5, 1875.

70. Schweiger, "Transformation of Southern Religion," 256; *Religious Herald*, Sept. 9, 1866.

71. Wilson, *Baptized in Blood*; E. T. Winkler in *Christian Watchman and Reflector*, Jan. 4, 1872.

72. Charleston Baptist Association Minutes, 1865, 8, SBHLA; "The Signs of the Times," *South Carolina Baptist*, Apr. 20, 1866; D. P. Berton to Basil Manly Sr., Nov. 7, 1866, in Basil Manly Sr. Papers, folder 7, SBHLA.

73. "Some Causes of Our Troubles," *New Orleans Christian Advocate*, Oct. 15, 1874, p. 4.; Zipf, "'Whites Shall Rule the Land or Die'"; *South Carolina Baptist*, Sept. 27, 1867; David Butler, "The Victory—Rejoice," *Christian Index*, Nov. 19, 1874; *Biblical Recorder*, Dec. 7, 1887.

74. Poole, "Religion, Gender, and the Lost Cause," 585–86, 596; Alfred B. Williams, *Hampton and His Red Shirts*, 309–10; "There Is Hope for the Country," *Methodist Advance*, June 24, 1880, 180; Daniel Stowell, "Why Redemption: Religion and the End of Reconstruction, 1870–1877," paper delivered to the Southern Historical Association, Nov. 14, 1998; W. J. Sullivan, "The Color Line," *New Orleans Christian Advocate*, June 17, 1880; Farish, *Circuit Rider Dismounts*, 196–97, 221–22.

75. Charles N. Hunter, "Some of the Evils of Reconstruction," *A.M.E. Church Review* 4 (Jan. 1888): 277–84, reprinted in Angell and Pinn, eds., *Social Protest Thought*, 15–18.

76. Daniel Alexander Payne, *Recollections of Seventy Years*, 287–90.

77. Thornwell, "The Christian Doctrine of Slavery," in Adger and Girardeau, eds. *Collected Writings of James Henley Thornwell*, 398–436; Paul Harvey, "The Christian Doctrine of Slavery," in McDannell, ed., *Religions of North America*, 1:466–82. See also James O. Farmer, *Metaphysical Confederacy*.

78. GAPCUS Minutes, 1874, 592–95; Stephen F. Haynes, *Noah's Curse*, 139–42.

79. "Caucasian," *Anthropology for the People*, 29–30, 193, 213, 215, 228.

80. Hale, *Making Whiteness*, discusses "spectacle lynchings" with penetrating insight.

81. Litwack, *Trouble in Mind*, 208, 293, 297, 309.

82. Norman W. Brown, "What the Negro Thinks of God," *A.M.E. Church Review* 51 (Apr.–June 1935): 12–19; William E. Guy, "What the Black Man Thinks of the White Man's Religion," ibid., 43 (Jan. 1927): 141–44; C. S. (Charles Spencer) Smith, "Are Our Leaders Dead or Dumb?" *Christian Recorder*, Dec. 15, 1887; C. O. H. Thomas, "Politics, Ministers, and Religion," *A.M.E. Church Review* 11 (Oct. 1894): 275–86; all reprinted in Angell and Pinn, eds., *Social Protest Thought*, 135–39, 179, 313, 188–91, 203–5.

83. A. J. Powell, "The Mission of the African Methodist Episcopal Church to the Darker Races of the World," *A.M.E. Church Review* 19 (Jan. 1903): 585–95; George Wilson Brent, "The Ancient Glory of the Hamitic Race," ibid., 12 (Oct. 1895): 272–75; George Wilson Brent, "Origin of the White Race," ibid., 10 (Jan. 1893): 287–88. See also Maffly-Kipp, "Mapping the World," 610–26.

84. Litwack, *Trouble in Mind*, 491, 311.

Chapter Two

1. David Burgess, "Preachers, Beware!" *Prophetic Religion* 6 (Summer 1945): 37–38.

2. Interview with Anne Queen, DOH, box 5, folder 4, 17–18; interview with Randolph Taylor, May 23, 1985, transcript C-21, SOHP.

3. *Alabama Baptist*, Mar. 1, 1888 (P. S. Montgomery); Creech, "Righteous Indignation," 9–10.

4. S. M. Adams, "Politics and Religion," *Alabama Baptist*, May 9, 1889; Creech, "Righteous Indignation," 2; Goode, "Godly Insurrection," 155–69; Scott Hershey, "Our Washington Letter," *Alabama Baptist*, July 17, 1890; Hahn, *Nation under Our Feet*, 424, 439. The term "movement culture" comes from Goodwyn, *Populist Moment*.

5. Creech, "Righteous Indignation," 9.

6. Ibid., 7, 9–10, 216–18.

7. Last two paragraphs from Creech, "Righteous Indignation," 555–65, 287–88, 526, 231–33.

8. Watson quotation from Raybon, "Stick by the Old Paths," 231–45; "Preachers in Politics," *Biblical Recorder*, Apr. 27, 1892; *Alabama Baptist*, Oct. 6, 1892; E. B. Teague, "Despondency," *Christian Index*, Nov. 3, 1892.

9. *Christian Index*, Aug. 18, 1892.

10. J. W. Morgan, "Criticisms of the Convention," *Biblical Recorder*, Jan. 3, 1912.

11. Randal L. Hall, *William Louis Poteat*.

12. Gardner, *Ethics of Jesus and Social Progress*, 84, 112; Gardner, "Thy Kingdom Come," ms. of sermon delivered before SBC, May 17, 1911, in Sermons Delivered at Annual Meetings of the Southern Baptist Convention, SBHLA; Gardner, "Shall America Be a Christian Nation?" *Home Field*, Feb. 1915, 8–10; petition from students to Mullins, Feb. 21, 1910, in Edgar Young Mullins Letter Files, Boyce Library, Southern Baptist Theological Seminary, Louisville, Ky.

13. For this section on progressivism, I am indebted to Link, *Paradox of Southern Progressivism*.

14. Ibid., 34; GAPCUS Minutes, 1914, 80B; Josiah William Bailey, "Political Treatment of the Drink Evil," 109–24.

15. *Methodist Advance*, Jan. 11, 1888; Harvey, *Redeeming the South*, 215–17; Farish, *Circuit Rider Dismounts*, 309, 316, 321.

16. Thomas, *New Woman in Alabama*, 20–24, 30, 35; Cloyd, "Prelude to Reform," 48–64.

17. Sims, *Power of Femininity*, 55; Bennett, "Religion and the Rise of Jim Crow," 91, 94; John E. White, "Prohibition," 130–42.

18. Greenwood, *Bittersweet Legacy*, 40, 231.

19. Link, *Paradox of Southern Progressivism*, 53, 57.

20. Greenwood, *Bittersweet Legacy*, 223; Alexander McKelway, "Child Labor — A Challenge to the Church," Address at Annual Meeting of the Executive Committee of the Federal Council of Churches, Louisville, Kentucky, Dec. 9, 1909; "Justice, Kindness, Religion," Address at National Conference of Charities and Correction, 1913, in McKelway Papers, PHS; McKelway, "The Awakening of the South against Child Labor," in *Child Labor and the Republic* (New York: National Child Labor Committee, 1907).

21. Thomas, *New Woman in Alabama*.

22. Proctor, *Between Black and White*, 10.

23. Ibid., 102, 94, 106; Luker, *Social Gospel in Black and White*, 184; Proctor Papers, box 4, ARC; "Stop Burning Human Beings in America," Proctor Papers, box 3, folder 1, ARC; "The Atlanta Riots," typescript in McKelway Papers, PHS, article later published in *Outlook*, Nov. 3, 1906; "A Colored Church and Its Colors," Proctor Papers, box 3, folder 1, ARC.

24. MECSJ, 1910, 387; Kelly, *Race, Class, and Power*, 99, 106, 142, 170.

25. See Gavins, *Perils and Prospects*.

26. *Savannah Tribune*, Apr. 28, 1917.

27. J. William Harris, *Deep Souths*, 165; Luker, *Social Gospel in Black and White*, 95; Vinikas, "Specters in the Past," 535–64; Raper, *Tragedy of Lynching*, 22; Joseph Martin Dawson Oral History, 53, 65, THC; Powdermaker, *After Freedom*.

28. J. M. Hawley, "Facts Underlying the Race Problem," *Nashville Christian Advocate*, Jan. 14, 1904; Luker, *Social Gospel in Black and White*, 95; *Biblical Recorder*, Feb. 4, 1903.

29. Haygood, *Our Brother in Black*; Farish, *Circuit Rider Dismounts*, 196–97; Williamson, *Rage for Order*, 73–77.

30. Luker, *Social Gospel in Black and White*, 61, 100–101, 203–5; Andrew Sledd, "The Negro: Another View," *Atlantic Monthly* (June 1902): 69–71.

31. Sparks, *Religion in Mississippi*, 162–63; Bratton, *Wanted — Leaders!* 227–28.

32. J. William Harris, *Deep Souths*; Godshalk, "William J. Northen's Public and Personal Struggles," 140–61; Luker, *Social Gospel in Black and White*, 186.

33. Luker, *Southern Tradition*, 286–88.

34. Last two paragraphs from Luker, *Southern Tradition*, 309, 311, 342; Murphy, *Basis of Ascendancy*; and Murphy, *Problems of the Present South*.

35. Luker, *Social Gospel in Black and White*, 188; Egerton, *Speak Now against the Day*, 43–44.

36. MECSJ, 1914, 26–27.

37. Burr, ed., *Secret Eye*, 335; J. William Harris, *Deep Souths*, 173.

38. Correspondent from Atlanta to W. G. Sibley, Atlanta, May 22, 1912; and Sibley to Miss [Missouria] Stokes, Feb. 28, 1882; Stokes Papers, SCPL.

39. Hardesty, "'Best Temperance Organization,'" 187–94; Harvey Newman, "Role of Women in Atlanta's Churches," 17; Wills, *Democratic Religion*, 57.

40. "Woman Suffrage," *Raleigh Christian Advocate*, Apr. 2, 1873; Elna Green, *Southern Strategies*, 80.

41. Elizabeth Hayes Turner, *Women, Culture, and Community*, 277; Elna Green, *Southern Strategies*, 19.

42. Scott, *Natural Allies*, 93.

43. Statistics from W. B. Johnson, "The Story of Negro Baptists," *National Baptist Union*, Jan. 30, 1909; Burroughs quotes from NBC Journal, 1900, 196–97; and WCJ, 1903,

27–28; 1911, 42–44. For more on Burroughs's feminist theology, see Higginbotham, *Righteous Discontent.*

44. WCJ, 1903, 316–17; 1908, 273; 1911, 42–44; *Fifteenth Annual Report of the Executive Board and Corresponding Secretary of the Woman's Convention, Auxiliary to the National Baptist Convention* (Nashville, 1915), 50–52; WCJ, 1914.

45. Rouse, *Lugenia Burns Hope*; Salem, *To Better Our World*, 30–31, 64, 81, 88, 97; Tera W. Hunter, *To 'Joy My Freedom*, 136, 143.

46. See Dunlap, "In the Name of the Home"; *Christian Index*, June 7, 1888; Fair River Baptist Association (Mississippi) Minutes, 1884, 17, copy in SBHLA. For women and the war, see Faust, *Mothers of Invention*; Friedman, *Enclosed Garden*, ch. 1; and Harvey, *Redeeming the South*, 25–27.

47. *Baptist Record*, May 19, 1881 (Mrs. Jenny Beauchamp); SBC Annual, 1882, 38; SBC Annual, 1885, 34; *Biblical Recorder*, Apr. 21, 1886 ("Virginia").

48. Fourth Annual Meeting of the Woman's Missionary Societies, from Sketch and Constitution of the Women's Missionary Societies, May 1887 to May 1888, 3–4, SBHLA; WMU Organizational meeting, May 11, 1888, Richmond, Va., SBHLA; Constitution of WMU, 1888, SBHLA; Allen, *Century to Celebrate*, 117, 337, 354; SBC Annual, 1915, 30–31.

49. Annie Armstrong to T. P. Bell, July 8, 1893, in Frost Papers, box 1, folder 1A, SBHLA; WMU *Report*, 1894, 10; 1896, 9; 1897, 8; Armstrong to T. P. Bell, Dec. 13, 1893, Frost Papers, box 1, SBHLA. For a full recounting of Armstrong's life, see Sorrill, *Annie Armstrong*. For facts and figures on the financial successes of the WMU and the importance of WMU-inspired offerings in keeping alive Southern Baptist missions in the 1920s and 1930s, see Allen, *Century to Celebrate*, 150–55.

50. Woman's Missionary Union, Auxiliary to the Baptist State Convention of South Carolina, Minutes, 1912, 39–40; Woman's Missionary Union, Auxiliary to the Baptist State Convention of North Carolina, Report, 1919, 22, 93; Woman's Missionary Societies, Auxiliary to the Baptist State Convention of North Carolina, Minutes, 1895, 15; all in SBHLA; SBC Annual, 1917, 90; Allen, *Century to Celebrate*, 211. See also Patricia Summerlin Martin, "Hidden Work."

51. Allen, *Century to Celebrate*, 220–21.

52. Annie Armstrong to James M. Frost, Jan. 26, 1897, in Frost Papers, box 3, SBHLA; Annie Armstrong to J. M. Frost, July 19, 1892, in Frost Papers, box 1, folder 1, SBHLA; NBC Journal, 1902, 58–60; Allen, *Century to Celebrate*, 244–48.

53. Nannie H. Burroughs to Una Roberts Lawrence, June 29, 1935; Aug. 18, 1934; Aug. 23, 1938; in Lawrence Papers, box 1, folders 27 and 30, SBHLA.

54. Scott, *Natural Allies*; McDowell, *Social Gospel*, 144; Will Alexander Oral History, 224, COHRO; Dykeman and Stokely, *Seeds of Southern Change*, 95.

55. MacDonnell, *Belle Harris Bennett*, 126–27.

56. McDowell, *Social Gospel*, 7, 56–57.

57. Ibid., 26; MacDonnell, *Belle Harris Bennett*, 70, 85, 88, 236. For more detail on the connection between white Southern Methodists and black CME women, see Mary Frederickson, "'Each One Is Dependent on the Other,'" 296–324. Bennett became a spokeswoman for an expanded woman's voice in her church, the MECS. But even she found limited success in winning laity rights and in protecting the newfound power of women in their missionary societies. In 1906, the General Board of Missions recommended unifying mission boards with one-third women's representation, thus ensuring that "we are

in a helpless minority in a body where the membership is largely made up of men opposed to independence of thought in women," as one Methodist woman believed. These plans angered Bennett, who had worked to democratize Methodist church structure. Because they could not attend the church's general conference, women would thereby be ignored, she understood. The merger plan that was eventually adopted placed women's work under the General Board of Missions, with a subsidiary Woman's Missionary Council overseeing the various portions of women's work. Belle Harris Bennett accepted the deal, she later said, because she feared "something worse—complete subordination." The price was the loss of the *Our Homes*. Bennett's former colleague Lucinda Helm resigned as part of a personal protest against the way the plan for unification was formulated and its unequal male-female representation on the board.

58. McDowell, *Social Gospel*, 84–85, 107; Hammond, *In Black and White*; Hammond, *Southern Women and Racial Adjustment*.

59. Lumpkin, *Making of a Southerner*, 193.

60. Will Alexander Oral History, 98–99, 190–91, COHRO.

61. Luker, *Social Gospel in Black and White*, 196; J. William Harris, *Deep Souths*, 288; Dykeman and Stokely, *Seeds of Southern Change*; Jacqueline Dowd Hall, *Revolt against Chivalry*; Pilkington, "Trials of Brotherhood," 74–77.

62. Egerton, *Speak Now against the Day*, 48; Jacqueline Dowd Hall, *Revolt against Chivalry*, 97; Rouse, *Lugenia Burns Hope*, 107.

63. Lillian Smith to Mozell Hill, Mar. 11, 1957, in Gladney, ed., *How Am I to Be Heard*, 209.

64. Egerton, *Speak Now against the Day*, 425.

65. K'Meyer, *Interracialism and Christian Community*; Jasper Martin England Oral History, 38, THC.

66. Helen Lewis Oral History, May 17, 1996, Tape G-183, SOHP.

67. Flynt, "Alabama White Protestantism"; Cavalcanti, "God and Labor in the South"; SBC resolution, 1938, quoted in pamphlet "Church Answers Labor's Critics: Religious Leaders Endorse Organized Labor Movement," n.d., published by Organizing Committee, Atlanta, Georgia, in CIO, Virginia Industrial Union Council Papers, box 42, SCPL.

68. Shepherd, *Avenues of Faith*, 291, 270, 53.

69. Quotation from Randall Lee Patton, "Southern Liberals." The following paragraphs on Mason are taken primarily from Salmond, *Miss Lucy of the CIO*. Interestingly, Mason was also a devotee of spiritualism, a practice that salved the devastating loss of a best friend in 1929.

70. Salmond, *Miss Lucy of the CIO*, 133.

71. Brattain, *Politics of Whiteness*, 127.

72. Quotation from Randall Lee Patton, "Southern Liberals," 46.

73. Quotation from Dykeman and Stokely, *Seeds of Southern Change*, 95.

74. Jacqueline Dowd Hall, *Revolt against Chivalry*.

75. Louise Young Oral History, Feb. 14, 1972, transcript G-66, SOHP.

76. Ibid.

77. Thelma Stevens Oral History, Feb. 13, 1972, transcript G-58, pp. 19, 34–35, SOHP.

78. Knotts, "Bound by the Spirit," 145.

79. Ibid., 228, 235–36.

80. Goldfield, *Black, White, and Southern*, 51, 72; Shankman, "Dorothy Tilly," 95–108.

81. Goldfield, *Black, White, and Southern*, 72; Randall Lee Patton, "Southern Liberals," 178–79; Shankman, "Dorothy Tilly," 105.

82. Durr, *Outside the Magic Circle*, 19, 27, 32; Virginia Durr Oral History, vol. 3, 300–302, COHRO.

83. Lillian Smith to Martin Luther King, Mar. 10, 1956, letter reprinted in Burns, ed., *Daybreak of Freedom*, 201–2; Lillian Smith, "The Right Way Is Not a Moderate Way," speech delivered in absentia to the Institute of Nonviolence and Social Change, Dec. 3, 1956, reprinted in Burns, ed., *Daybreak of Freedom*, 312.

84. *Bible Way News Voice*, Nov.–Dec. 1947, in DC, box 1, folder 7.

85. Sullivan, *Days of Hope*, 137.

86. Ibid., 145; Pete Daniel, *Lost Revolutions*, 22; interview with Rev. I. DeQuincey Newman, Aug. 9, 1973, SOHP.

87. Dittmer, *Local People*, 2–3.

88. Charles Payne, *I've Got the Light of Freedom*, 80; Ransby, *Ella Baker*, ch. 1.

89. Charles Payne, *I've Got the Light of Freedom*, 80. The best full biography of Baker's life is Ransby, *Ella Baker*.

90. Dittmer, *Local People*, 30.

91. Quoted in Donahue, "Yearning," 106.

92. Sullivan, *Days of Hope*, 153–55; Egerton, *Speak Now against the Day*, 47; Goldfield, *Black, White, and Southern*, 72.

93. Thomas C. Allen, Annual Report of the Department of Interracial Cooperation, Virginia Council of Churches, 1946, in CIO, Virginia Industrial Union Council Papers, box 51, SCPL.

94. Interview with Jim Shumaker, DOH, box 6, folder 33–34; interview with Virginia French, DOH, box 2, folder 1, p. 13; interview with Henry Mitchell, Series F, SOHP; interview with Bob Brown, DOH, box 5.

95. Charles Jones Oral History, July 21, 1990, transcript A-335, SOHP.

96. Salmond, "Fellowship of Southern Churchmen," 179–99; interview with Jones, June 18, 1971, in Charles Miles Jones Papers, PHS; Morton, *Journey Is Home*, 180–90.

97. Pryor, *Faith, Grace, and Heresy*, 95; Report of the Judicial Commission of Orange Presbytery, Nov. 30, 1952; Judicial Commission: Orange Presbytery, Questionnaire and Interviews of Chapel Hill Officers, July 21, 1952; and interview with Jones, June 18, 1971; all in Charles Miles Jones Papers, PHS.

98. For details on the Jones controversy, see Charles Miles Jones Papers, PHS. Church authorities denied that Jones's well-known sympathy for desegregation had anything to do with his excommunication, but the record seems clear that his heterodoxy on race brought him to attention and disfavor among conservatives in the church.

99. See Danielson, "'In My Extremity,'" for a fuller analysis of Kester's relationship to radical and pacifist groups.

100. Quoted in Kester, *Revolt among the Sharecroppers*, 21.

101. The quotation, and these paragraphs on Kester, come primarily from Robert Frances Martin, *Howard Kester*, 63, and from my own perusal of the Howard Kester Papers and Southern Tenant Farmers' Union Papers, both at SHC.

102. Last three paragraphs from Kester, *Revolt among the Sharecroppers*, 21, 35, 37, and Robert Frances Martin, *Howard Kester*.

103. Sparks, *Religion in Mississippi*, 186.

104. Robert Frances Martin, *Howard Kester*, 114; Scotty Cowan to Nelle Morton, Aug. 1, 1949, FSC Papers, box 17, SHC; "We Affirm," pamphlet produced by the FSC, found in CIO, Virginia Industrial Union Council Papers, box 75, SCPL; David Burgess, "Preachers, Beware!" *Prophetic Religion* 6 (Summer 1945): 37–38.

105. David Burgess Oral History, p. 5, Series F, 4007-F, SOHP; David Burgess, "Preachers, Beware!" *Prophetic Religion* 6 (Summer 1945): 37–38.

106. *Prophetic Religion* 6 (Fall 1945). See also Minutes of Meeting of the Fellowship of Southern Churchmen, Warren Wilson College, Feb. 23–24, 1951, in FSC Papers, box 18, SHC; Robert Frances Martin, *Howard Kester*, 114, 129–30.

107. Salmond, "Fellowship of Southern Churchmen," 198–99.

108. Ibid., 179–99.

109. Zan and Westy Harper to Fellowship of Southern Churchmen, Mar. 29, 1952, FSC Papers, box 19, SHC; FSC Newsletter, Nov. 1955, copy in FSC Papers, box 21, SHC; Howard Kester to Field Foundation, Dec. 1952, FSC Papers, box 19, SHC.

110. Interview with Nelle Morton, p. 38, Series F, SOHP; Salmond, "Fellowship of Southern Churchmen," 197; Everett Tilson Oral History, Series F, SOHP.

111. J. C. Herrin Oral History; Nelle Morton Oral History, pp. 38, 58; Beverly Asbury Oral History; David Burgess Oral History, p. 6; all in Series F, SOHP; Morton, *Journey Is Home*, 189–90.

112. Horton, *Long Haul*, 26, 29.

113. Ibid., 115.

114. Ibid., 95.

115. Myles Horton Oral History, Series F, SOHP.

116. Ibid., pp. 5–6, 11.

117. Nelle Morton Oral History, pp. 13–14, 38, 58, Series F, SOHP; interview with Anne Queen, DOH, box 5, folder 4, 17–18; Randolph Taylor Oral History, May 23, 1985, transcript C-21, SOHP.

118. Parsons, *From Southern Wrongs*, 45–50; Pete Daniel, *Lost Revolutions*, 30, 206.

Chapter Three

1. E. B. Ingram diary, entries for July 10, 17, 1895, in Ingram Papers, SCPL; Gilmore, *Gender and Jim Crow*, 73; Winfield Henry Mixon diary, entries for Aug. 1 and May 1, 1903, in Mixon Papers, SCPL.

2. Woodworth-Etter, *Signs and Wonders*, 98–101; Jacobs and Kaslow, *Spiritual Churches of New Orleans*, 36.

3. Interviews with Ruth Johnson (Enfield, North Carolina) and Amy Jones (Memphis, Tennessee), in BTV, TR-2; Lillian Smith to Charles Johnson, June 10, 1955, in Gladney, ed., *How Am I to Be Heard*, 170.

4. Interview with Herman James, in BTV, TR-2.

5. Interview with W. C. Tims (Arkansas), in BTV, TR-1, 7; interviews with Money Alan Kirby and Anne Oda Kirby, in BTV, TR-1, folder for Arkansas.

6. Hatcher, *John Jasper*, 98, 36.

7. Orra Langhorne, "Southern Sketches," *Southern Workman*, Oct. 1891, 34; Conser, *Virginia after the War*, 39–40; extracts of letters of Frances Goodrich, Mar. 11 and Mar. 17,

1895, in Goodrich Papers, folder for 1894–95, SCPL; Toliver Vinson (Church of God), in Gillespie et al., eds., *Foxfire 7*, 206; *Florida Narratives*, vol. 17, p. 353 (Willis Williams).

8. Elizabeth Johnson Harris, "Life Story, 1867–1923," in Harris Papers, SCPL, also available online at ‹http://scriptorium.lib.duke.edu/harris›.

9. Evans, *Provincials*, 260–62.

10. *Baptist Home Mission Monthly*, July 1884, 174.

11. Missionary Baptist Convention of Texas *Proceedings*, 1882, n.p., in SBHLA; John E. White, "The Backward People of the South," *Our Home Field*, May 1909, 15–17; S. L. Morgan to Hight Moore, June 27, 1917, in Hight C. Moore Papers, box 3, folder 20, SBHLA.

12. *Savannah Tribune*, May 14, 1898; Sparks, *Religion in Mississippi*, 145; J. William Harris, *Deep Souths*, 194; Orra Langhorne, "Southern Sketches," *Southern Workman*, Oct. 1891, 34. See also *Baptist Home Mission Monthly*, Feb. 1881, 27–29 (R. Agnes).

13. Walter Hines Page, "Religious Progress of the Negroes," *Independent*, Sept. 1, 1881, 6–7; Richard Carroll, "Negroes on the Coast of South Carolina," *Savannah Tribune*, Apr. 22, 1911; Lydia A. Parrish, *Slave Songs*, 55; *South Carolina Narratives*, orig. ser., vol. 3, pt. 3, p. 5.

14. The preceding two paragraphs on the shouts come from Holland, ed., *Letters and Diary of Laura M. Towne*, 20, and Rosenbaum, *Shout Because You're Free*, 28–30, 41.

15. Daniel Alexander Payne, *Recollections of Seventy Years*, 255–56, 285–86.

16. Zipf, "'Among These American Heathens,'" 124; Sarah Jane Foster, letters from Harpers Ferry and Summerton, South Carolina, May 2, 1866; Feb. 12, 1868; and May 20, 1866; in Reilly, ed., *Sarah Jane Foster*, 105–6, 117, 176–77.

17. Preceding two paragraphs from Gannett, "Freedmen at Port Royal"; Wolfe, *Abundant Life Prevails*, 78, 80–81; *Southern Workman*, Apr. 1895, 59–61; and interview with Nick Waller in FWP, box 12, folder 204, SHC.

18. Williamson, *After Slavery*, 201; Siegfried, *Winter in the South*, 15; Richard Carroll, "Negroes on the Coast of South Carolina," *Savannah Tribune*, Apr. 22, 1911; Peacock and Tyson, *Pilgrims of Paradox*, 216, 148, 194. See also McCauley, *Appalachian Mountain Religion*.

19. *Southern Workman*, May 1878, 38–39.

20. Ibid., 38; Waters, ed., *Strange Ways and Sweet Dreams*, 142–44; Chireau, *Black Magic*, 11–20, 28; Zipf, "'Among These American Heathens,'" 123; Esther W. Douglass Memoir, 45–46, 81, in Douglass Papers, box 1, ARC.

21. *Southern Workman*, Apr. 1878, 31; ibid., Sept. 1878, 67; ibid., Feb. 1894, 26–27; Spencer, *Blues and Evil*, 13, 31.

22. Leonore Heron, "Conjuring and Conjure Doctors," *Southern Workman*, July 1895, 117; Chireau, *Black Magic*, 68–69; Comer, *Stars Fell on Alabama*, 218; *Texas Narratives*, supp. ser. 2, no. 2, pp. 16–17 (William Adams).

23. Zora Neale Hurston, "Hoodoo in America," *Journal of American Folklore* 45 (Oct.–Dec. 1931): 414; Powdermaker, *After Freedom*, 286; interview with "Preacher Goode," in FWP, box 17, folder 467, SHC; Dundes, ed., *Mother Wit from the Laughing Barrel*, 378.

24. Last two paragraphs from Clifton H. Johnson, ed., *God Struck Me Dead*, 141; Waters, ed., *Strange Ways and Sweet Dreams*, 76, 228–29; Esther Douglass Memoir, 55, in Douglass Papers, box 1, ARC; and Chireau, *Black Magic*, 70, 86, 101.

25. Chireau, *Black Magic*, 160–61, 210–11; interview with Bernice White, in BTV, TR-1.

26. Hurston, *Dust Tracks on a Road*, 275, 280; Hurston, *Sanctified Church*, 83.

27. *Baptist Home Mission Monthly*, Feb. 1881, 27–29; Minutes of the Gillfield Baptist Church, Petersburg, Virginia, Sept. 20, 1869, copy at SBHLA.

28. Charley White, *No Quittin' Sense*, 134.

29. Cooley, *School Acres*, 151; Esther Douglass Memoir, 56–57, in Douglass Papers, box 1, ARC.

30. Gannett, "Freedmen at Port Royal"; Lillie Barr, "Three Months on a Cotton Plantation," *Independent*, June 30, 1881, 1–2; *American Baptist*, Feb. 15, 1868; Aug. 18, 1868; Aug. 4, 1868; Taulbert, *Once upon a Time When We Were Colored*, 94.

31. See Clifton H. Johnson, ed., *God Struck Me Dead*, and Snyder, "Ordination of Charlie."

32. *Live Coals of Fire*, Feb. 9, 1900; Oct. 27, 1899; Nov. 3, 1899.

33. "Discipline of the Fire Baptized Holiness Church of God of the Americas" (Atlanta: Church Publishing House by the Fuller Press, 1962), in DC, box 7, folder 1; "Tenets of the Fire Baptized Holiness Church of God of the Americas," n.d., pamphlet in International Pentecostal Holiness Church Archives, Oklahoma City, Oklahoma; Synan, *OldTime Power*, 142–43.

34. "Sermon on Shouting," *Holiness Advocate*, Aug. 1, 1903; *Live Coals of Fire*, Oct. 27, 1899.

35. *Live Coals of Fire*, Nov. 3, 1899; Jan. 26, 1900; "Partly—Biography of N. Scippio and Wife" (1987), from *A Christian Worker's Handbook*, 9, 15, copy in DC, box 1, folder 16; F. F. Bosworth to Mother, Aug. 22, 1911, reprinted as "Beating in Tex. Follows Ministry to Blacks," *Assemblies of God Heritage* 6 (Summer 1986): 5, 14.

36. "Weird Babel of Tongues," *Los Angeles Times*, Apr. 18, 1906; "The Gift of Tongues," *Nazarene Messenger*, Dec. 13, 1906. For Holiness criticisms of Pentecostalism, see, for example, B. F. Haynes, "Fanaticism and Its Progeny," *Pentecostal Advocate*, Feb. 10, 1910; C. B. Jernigan, "Steadfast," *The Holiness Evangel*, Sept. 2, 1908; and *Pentecostal Advocate*, Nov. 25, 1909.

37. Material from preceding two paragraphs from Lovett, "Perspective on the Black Origins," 44; Wayne Warner, ed., *Touched by Fire*, 65–66; Doug Nelson, "For Such a Time as This," 198; interviews with A. G. Osterberg, in Record Group 2/4/9, AG.

38. Blumhofer, "'The Overcoming Life,'" 178–79; James R. Goff Jr., *Fields White unto Harvest*; "The Baptism with the Holy Ghost and the Speaking in Tongues," pamphlet by Charles Parham, 1906–7, 6, 9, 14, copy in DC, box 14, folder 1; *Apostolic Faith* (Baxter Springs, Kansas), Dec. 1911, June 1912, 7–8, copy in DC.

39. Seymour, *Doctrines and Discipline*, 10, 12.

40. Goss, *Winds of God*, 34, 42, 56, 90–91, 113, 129.

41. *Holiness Advocate*, Oct. 1, 1903, and Sept. 16, 1901, copies at AG.

42. *Apostolic Faith*, Dec. 1906, Apr. 1907; Synan, *OldTime Power*, 98, 100.

43. *Bridegroom's Messenger*, Oct. 1, 1907; Dec. 15, 1907; *Apostolic Faith*, Apr. 1907. For more on the crucial role of the Holiness/Pentecostal press in spreading the young faith throughout the South, see Stephens, "'There Is Magic in Print.'"

44. Joseph E. Campbell, *Pentecostal Holiness Church*, 201–2, 217.

45. Alexander, "Bishop King"; Joseph E. Campbell, *Pentecostal Holiness Church*, 240, 247, 412–13.

46. Joseph E. Campbell, *Pentecostal Holiness Church*, 204; Woods, "Living in the Presence of God," 276.

47. Trexler, "From Chaos to Order"; Robins, "Plainfolk Modernist," 85–88.

48. Woods, "Living in the Presence of God," 32, 245; Taylor, *Spirit and the Bride*, 128–29, 132, 135; J. M. Stalling, "Be Glad . . . and Rejoice," *Church of God Evangel*, Aug. 16, 1952, 6; Joseph E. Campbell, *Pentecostal Holiness Church*, 277, 280.

49. Joseph E. Campbell, *Pentecostal Holiness Church*, 275; Synan, *OldTime Power*, 127–28.

50. Church of God Publishing House, *Book of Minutes*, 10, 98–101.

51. "History of Pentecost," *Faithful Standard*, Sept. and Oct. 1922; A. J. Tomlinson diary, entry for Aug. 18, 1901, AG; "The Lord's Church," *Bridegroom's Messenger*, Mar. 1, 1909; Robins, "Plainfolk Modernist," 254–85, 379.

52. *Bridegroom's Messenger*, Feb. 1, 1908.

53. A. J. Tomlinson diary, entries for Jan. 18, 1912; May 17, 1913, AG; Church of God Publishing House, *Book of Minutes*, 13th Assembly, 201–2, 269; Conn, *Like a Mighty Army*, 313–14; "Manifestations of the Spirit," *Faithful Standard*, Sept. 1922, 1–2.

54. FWP interviews, box 23, folder 778, SHC.

55. Tomlinson, *Last Great Conflict*, 17, 97, 219; A. J. Tomlinson diary, entry for Nov. 17, 1919, AG.

56. Robins, "Plainfolk Modernist," 503.

57. Giggie, "God's Long Journey," 214; Charles Edwin Jones, *Black Holiness*.

58. William Clair Turner Jr., "United Holy Church of America," 52; *Standard Manual and Constitution and By-Laws of the United Holy Church of America, Inc.*, booklet in DC, box 7, folder 12.

59. Giggie, "God's Long Journey," 201; Sparks, *Religion in Mississippi*, 173; Jones autobiography, DC, box 1, folder 12; Charles P. Jones to Isaac Bailey, Mar. 26, 1898, in Bailey-Thurman Papers, ESCL; Charles Edwin Jones, *Black Holiness*.

60. *History and Formative Years of the Church of God in Christ*, 5, copy found in DC, box 3, folder 21; Giggie, "God's Long Journey," 213.

61. *History and Formative Years of the Church of God in Christ*, 19; Clemmons, *Bishop C. H. Mason*.

62. *History and Formative years of the Church of God in Christ*, 19. See also his description of his experience in *Apostolic Faith*, Feb.–Mar. 1907, 6–7.

63. Clemmons, *Bishop C. H. Mason*, 62; Mary Mason, *History and Life Work of Bishop C. H. Mason*, 88, 92, 94; Tucker, *Black Pastors and Leaders*, 87–100.

64. *History and Formative Years of the Church of God in Christ*, 5; Conkin, "Evangelicals, Fugitives, and Hillbillies," 287–322; Elsie Mason, ed., *From the Beginning of Bishop C. H. Mason*, 6; *Whole Truth*, Jan. 1933, issue found in AG.

65. Clark, "Sanctification in Negro Religion"; Hurston, *Go Gator and Muddy the Water*, 94–97.

66. Charley White, *No Quittin' Sense*, 120, 130.

67. See Butler, "A Peculiar Synergy," an extensive work on COGIC women.

68. *The Constitution Government and General Decree Book*, copy in DC, box 6, folder 8; materials for the Church of the Living God the Pillar and Ground of Truth, Inc., 70th Annual General Assembly, Nashville, 1978, convention program, in DC, box 6, folder 8.

69. Quoted in Best, "Loosing the Women."

70. *American Baptist*, June 25, 1867; Daniel Alexander Payne, *Recollections of Seventy Years*, 237.

71. Coffin, *Unwritten History*, 163–64.

72. Allan-Olney, *New Virginians*, 238–45; Kilham, "Sketches in Color"; Herskovits, *Myth of the Negro Past*, 223.

73. McGlothlin, *Vital Ministry*, 136.

74. *National Baptist Union*, Nov. 21, 1908, 7; Spencer, *Black Hymnody*, 80, 84. These paragraphs on black hymnody come from Spencer's very informative study.

75. National Baptist Convention Sunday School Board, *Gospel Pearls*.

76. Michael W. Harris, *Rise of Gospel Blues*, 68–70.

77. *South Carolina Baptist*, May 8, 1868 (G.); John Bailey Adger to F. W. McMaster, July 14, 1871, in Adger Papers, PHS; Aquila Peyton diary, entry for Mar. 12, 1860, Virginia Historical Society, Richmond.

78. For an example of this ridicule, see *South Carolina Baptist*, Aug. 22, 1867, which referred to the typical singing of rural congregations as an "inharmonious jingling of nasal sounds."

79. Ellington, "Sacred Harp Tradition," 30–31; Gavin James Campbell, "'Old Can Be Used Instead of New.'"

80. James R. Goff Jr., *Close Harmony*, 215.

81. Cusic, *Sound of Light*, 94–96; James R. Goff Jr., *Close Harmony*, 81–90, 165, 209.

82. Malone, *Southern Music*, 67–68, 76–78; Cusic, *Sound of Light*; Malone, *Singing Cowboys*, 32.

83. James R. Goff Jr., *Close Harmony*, 94–96.

84. Ibid., 41.

85. Ibid., 162; Cusic, *Sound of Light*, 103; Malone, *Southern Music*, 67–68; Pete Daniel, *Lost Revolutions*, 130–31.

86. Quotation from James R. Goff Jr., *Close Harmony*, 215.

87. Handy, *Father of the Blues*, 8, 10.

88. Interview with George Scarborough (Durham, North Carolina), in BTV, TR-1.

89. Spencer, *Blues and Evil*, 13, 31, 93, 113, 119, 121; Sparks, *Religion in Mississippi*, 179; J. William Harris, *Deep Souths*, 194; Spencer, *Protest and Praise*, 124.

90. Spencer, *Blues and Evil*, 95.

91. Clifton H. Johnson, ed., *God Struck Me Dead*, 147; Giggie, "God's Long Journey," 120–40; Gates, *Complete Recorded Works*. Gates's version of "Death's Black Train Is Coming" may also be heard on *Roots 'n Blues*, disc 1.

92. Preceding two paragraphs from McGee, *Complete Recorded Works*; Ken Romanowski, liner notes to Dranes, *Complete Recorded Works in Chronological Order*; Giggie, "'When Jesus Handed Me a Ticket'"; and Patton recording from *American Primitive*.

93. Last two paragraphs from Boyer, *How Sweet the Sound*, 21; J. William Harris, *Rise of Gospel Blues*, 99–100; and Kempton, *Boogaloo*. See also Palmer, *Deep Blues*, and Spencer, *Blues and Evil*, which provide some of the most recent compelling discussion of the relationship between the blues and African American spirituality.

94. Horace Clarence Boyer, "Lucie E. Campbell: Composer for the National Baptist Convention," and the Reverend Charles Walker, "Lucie E. Campbell Williams: A Cultural Biography," in Reagon, ed., *We'll Understand It Better By and By*, 81–108, 121–40.

95. Jackson, *Singing in My Soul*; Tharpe, *Complete Recorded Works*.

96. W. Herbert Brewster, "Rememberings," in Reagon, ed., *We'll Understand It Better By and By*, 81–108, 201.

97. Mahalia Jackson, *Movin' on Up*, 56–59.

98. Taulbert, *Once upon a Time When We Were Colored*, 95–100.

99. Lornell, *Happy in the Service*, 15–16, 22–24, 28–29, 37–38, 46, 66; Cusic, *Sound of Light*, 124.

100. For a fuller analysis of Elvis's religious upbringing, see Guralnick, *Last Train to Memphis*. For more on sacred passion in religion and music, see Chappell, *Stone of Hope*.

Chapter Four

1. C. Edwards (Macon, Georgia) to Ralph McGill, Sept. 22, 1962, in McGill Papers, box 24, folder 4, ESCL.

2. Youth of the Rural Organizing and Cultural Center, *Minds Stayed on Freedom*, 54.

3. Sparks, *Religion in Mississippi*, 227; "1965 Report Student Interracial Ministry" and "Statement by Edward A. Feaver on Student Interracial Ministry," in Sherrod Papers, box 3, ARC; Frederick C. Harris, *Something Within*, 88.

4. Watters, *Down to Now*, 46; Charles Payne, *I've Got the Light of Freedom*, 231; Charles Payne, "Men Led, but Women Organized," in Crawford, Rouse, and Woods, eds., *Women in the Civil Rights Movement*, 1–11; Frederick C. Harris, *Something Within*, 78; interview with Lillian Smith (Wilmington, North Carolina), BTV, TR-2, pp. 35, 56.

5. Kelley, " 'We Are Not What We Seem,' " 88.

6. Sanger, *"When the Spirit Says Sing!"* 16; Andrew Young, *Easy Burden*, 183.

7. Du Bois, *Black Reconstruction*, 124; Watters, *Down to Now*, 191.

8. Song lyrics for this section from Sanger, *"When the Spirit Says Sing!"*; Carawan and Carawan, ed., *Sing for Freedom*; "Eyes on the Prize," film series from Blackside Production; Watters, *Down to Now*; and *Voices of Freedom: Songs of the Civil Rights Movement*, Smithsonian Folkways Recordings, 1997.

9. Andrew Young, *Easy Burden*, 232.

10. Interviews with Ira Lee Jones (Tuskegee, Alabama); Josephine Dickey (Summerton, South Carolina); Lucille Fisher Parker (Tallahassee, Florida); and Lorena Poole, all in BTV, TR-2.

11. Vicki and Martin Nicklaus, open letter dated Dec. 25, 1964, in Nicklaus Papers, WHS.

12. Lochbaum, "Word Made Flesh," 139, 134.

13. Crawford, Rouse, and Woods, eds., *Women in the Civil Rights Movement*, 28. A collection of Vernon Johns's writings and sermons is forthcoming in Luker, *"The Man Who Started Freedom"* (see ⟨http://www.ralphluker.com/vjohns/index.html⟩).

14. Jo Ann Gibson Robinson, *Montgomery Bus Boycott*, 54, 64, 156.

15. Abernathy, *And the Walls Came Tumbling Down*, 168; Burns, ed., *Daybreak of Freedom*, 117, 136, 175.

16. Friedland, *Lift up Your Voice*, 27–29.

17. Graetz, *White Preacher's Memoir*.

18. Abernathy, *And the Walls Came Tumbling Down*, 114–15, 181.

19. Ibid., 169.

20. Baldwin, *There Is a Balm in Gilead*, 187–89; Burns, ed., *Daybreak of Freedom*, 17.

21. Abernathy, *And the Walls Came Tumbling Down*, 126–27; Burns, ed., *Daybreak of Freedom*, 22, 164.

22. Burns, ed., *Daybreak of Freedom*, 159, 132; Andrew Young, *Easy Burden*, 233.

23. Manis, *Fire You Can't Put Out*, 24, 26–27, 42.

24. Ibid., 51, 61.

25. Ibid., 79, 97, 112.

26. Ibid., 132–33, 138–39.

27. Ibid., 230–31, 296, 314.

28. Ibid., 141, 152, 196–99, 221, 231, 265, 347, 328.

29. Ibid., 328; Andrew Young, *Easy Burden*, 238, 241.

30. Andrew Young, *Easy Burden*, 42, 56, 65.

31. Ibid., 129, 139–40, 150, 154, 156, 190.

32. Interview with Willie Herzefeld, Pastor, Christ Lutheran Church, Tuscaloosa, and interview with T. Y. Rogers, "Civil Rights in Alabama" transcripts, vol. 2, COHRO.

33. John Lewis, *Walking with the Wind*, 20–21, 34.

34. SNCC [Dorothy Miller], "Danville, Virginia," pamphlet found in SNCC Papers, WHS.

35. John Lewis, *Walking with the Wind*, 187–91, 293–94; Andrew Young, *Easy Burden*, 251–52.

36. Dittmer, *Local People*, 30.

37. Rev. Owen Brooks, "Bolivar County Report," Beech Papers, box 5, folder 4, WHS; journal entry for July 19, 1965, in Wacker Papers, folder 5, WHS; Dittmer, *Local People*, 75–76; Charles Payne, *I've Got the Light of Freedom*, 42.

38. Frederick C. Harris, *Something Within*, 78; Dittmer, *Local People*, 80–81, 182.

39. Chafe, *Civilities and Civil Right*, 112–13.

40. "Report on the Raleigh Conference," in Zellner Papers, box 1, folder 58, WHS; "Across the Editor's Desk," *Student Voice*, Oct. 1960; King, *Freedom Song*, 273.

41. *Student Voice*, May 1960; Friedland, *Lift up Your Voice*, 102; Bette Poole et al., Appellants, against Ross Barnett, in Records of the General Commission on Religion and Race, folder 1, GCAH; Jackson Arrest Cases, folder 1, GBCS Records; Grover C. Bagby, "Memorandum on Arrests at Methodist Church Doors," Division of Human Relations and Economic Affairs, General Board of Christian Social Concerns of the Methodist Church, Nov. 8, 1965, GCAH; Silver, "Mississippi," 17–18.

42. Dittmer, *Local People*, 217, 237.

43. Ibid., 53–54, 217.

44. Ibid., 146–47, 150; Charles Payne, *I've Got the Light of Freedom*, 196, 199.

45. Mendy Samstein, "The Murder of a Community," *Student Voice*, Sept. 23, 1964; Dittmer, *Local People*, 104, 268, 305–7.

46. Youth of the Rural Organizing and Cultural Center, *Minds Stayed on Freedom*, 25–29, 54; "Lee County Report, Dec. 1962," in Rubin Papers, box 1, folder 8, WHS.

47. Dittmer, *Local People*, 131, 164.

48. Charles Payne, *I've Got the Light of Freedom*, 80; Vicki Crawford, "Beyond the Human Self: Grassroots Activists in the Mississippi Civil Rights Movement," in Crawford, Rouse, and Woods, eds., *Women in the Civil Rights Movement*, 21–22.

49. Robert Jackall diary, entry for May 25 and 26, 1967, in Jackall Papers, WHS; Dittmer, *Local People*, 137; Lee, *For Freedom's Sake*.

50. Fannie Lou Hamer, "Sick and Tired of Being Sick and Tired," *Katallagete*, Fall 1968, 26; Hobson, *But Now I See*, 17.

51. Greenberg, ed., *Circle of Trust*, 77.

52. Charles Payne, *I've Got the Light of Freedom*, 258, and "Men Led, but Women Organized," 5; Watters, *Down to Now*, 166; Bernice Johnson Reagon, "Women as Culture Carriers in the Civil Rights Movement: Fannie Lou Hamer," in Crawford, Rouse, and Woods, eds., *Women in the Civil Rights Movement*, 211.

53. CWUP, box 1, folder 30; interview with Louise Young, CWUP, box 78; Edith Mitchell Dabbs Oral History, Oct. 14, 1975, transcript G-22, SOHP.

54. Ida Milner, "Coming to Grips with Segregation," *Church Woman*, Oct. 1955, 19, 37.

55. Ford Foundation Grant application, CWUP, box 2, folder 21; Carrie Meares, "First Year of the Three-Year Project," report in CWUP, box 62.

56. "Report of Inventory," United Church Women Assignment: RACE, Southern Region, in CWUP, box 63.

57. Margery Gross and Frances Tenenbaum, "Wednesdays in Mississippi—1964–1965, Final Report," CWUP, box 62; Polly Cowan, "Wednesdays in Mississippi," *Church Woman*, May 1965, 14–15, 18; Mrs. Kyle Haselden to Polly Cowan, Aug. 30, 1965, in CWUP, box 62.

58. "The Churches and Race," Report of the General Department of United Church Women on Present Activities and Issues, Feb. 26–Mar. 1, 1963, CWUP, box 62; Jean Fairfax, "The Negro Mood: Notes on a Talk," typescript of talk delivered at Tennessee United Church Women State Work Session, May 1963, CWUP, box 62.

59. Clarie Collins Harvey, "The Black Woman: Keeper of the Faith," *Church Woman*, Nov. 1969, 15–18.

60. Pete Daniel, *Lost Revolutions*, 229, 249; Tyson, "Dynamite and 'The Silent South,'" 275–93.

61. Parsons, *From Southern Wrongs to Civil Rights*, 71.

62. Sue Thrasher, "Circle of Trust," in Curry et al., eds., *Deep in Our Hearts*, 209–51.

63. Casey Hayden, "Fields of Blue," in ibid., 339.

64. Dorothy Dawson Burlage, "Truths of the Heart," in ibid., 93, 110–11.

65. Constance Curry, "Wild Geese," and Joan Browning, "Shiloh Witness," in ibid., 34, 55, 63.

66. Joan Browning, "Shiloh Witness," in ibid., 40, 61, 81.

67. Willie J. Smith and Charles M. Sherrod, typescript copy of proposal for Student Interracial Ministry to United Presbyterian Board of Missions, Sherrod Papers, folder "Correspondence, General," box 1; and "For the Student Interracial Ministry—A Proposal," in Sherrod Papers, box 2; both ARC.

68. "1965 Report Student Interracial Ministry," Sherrod Papers, box 3, ARC.

69. M. Katherine Havice, "Review and Prospectus of Albany Project," in folder "Georgia—Albany," in Sherrod Papers, box 1, ARC.

70. "1966 Report: Student Interracial Ministry," booklet found in Student Interracial Ministry folder, p. 82, GBCS Records; "For the Student Interracial Ministry—A Proposal," in Sherrod Papers, box 2, ARC.

71. Donald Gall to Warren McKenna, Aug. 22, 1964, in Beech Papers, box 3, folder 5; M.

Laurel Gray, "The Shaw COFO Project: An Evaluation," and "Significant Activities of the Ministers with the COFO Group in Vicksburg, Mississippi, June 30, 1964," in Beech Papers, box 4, folder 5; all WHS.

72. Robert Beech, open letter dated May 17, 1964, in Beech Papers, box 1, folder 1, WHS. The best and fullest account of the Delta Ministry may be found in Findlay, *Church People*, esp. 111–39.

73. Robert Beech, "Report and Evaluations, Hattiesburg, September 1964–September 1965," in Beech Papers, box 5, folder 4, WHS; Dittmer, *Local People*, 336; Friedland, *Lift up Your Voice*, 109–10.

74. Paul Moore, "Report of the Delta Ministry," submitted to Executive Committee of the General Board, June 1, 1966, Beech Papers, box 5, folder 4; untitled manuscript (written by Beech) and "Goals for the Delta Ministry," typescript in Beech Papers, box 5, folder 1; all in WHS.

75. Beech, "Report and Evaluations"; James Corum to Robert Beech, Aug. 1, 1965, in Beech Papers, box 3, folder 1; Robert Beech to Bardwell Smith, Mar. 22, 1966, in Beech Papers, box 1, folder 4; Albert Gaeddert, "Excerpts from Reports by Albert Gaeddert on Summer Assignment in Mississippi, 1964," in Friesen Papers, folder 7; Jake Friesen diary, entry for Dec. 7, 1964, in Friesen Papers, folder 4; all in WHS.

76. Beech, "Report and Evaluations"; Friedland, *Lift up Your Voice*, 109–10; Findlay, *Church People*, 142; Rick Lapsansky to Frederick Heinze, n.d., 1965, in Heinze Papers, WHS.

77. Beech, "Report and Evaluations"; Findlay, *Church People*, 160.

78. Andrew Young, *Easy Burden*, 301, 251.

79. Donahue, "Yearning," 163; Sparks, *Religion in Mississippi*, 196; *Richmond Afro-American*, Dec. 21, 1946; May 4, 1945; Mar. 16, 1946.

80. Manis, *Southern Civil Religions*, 20, 25; R. L. Herrington to Ralph McGill, Oct. 5, 1962, in McGill Papers, box 24, folder 5, ESCL; Chafe, *Civilities and Civil Rights*.

81. Marion Boggs, "The Crucial Test of Christian Citizenship," sermon preached at Second Presbyterian, July 7, 1957, in Boggs Papers, PHS; Harmon E. Day to Marion Boggs, Dec. 19, 1960, in Boggs Papers, box 14, PHS.

82. Mark Newman, *Getting Right with God*, x, 67, 71–76; *Light*, Sept. and Oct. 1949, copy in Valentine Papers, Box 2A38, THC.

83. Julius Corpening Oral History, 8, THC; Mark Newman, *Getting Right with God*, 88; SBC Annual, 1954, 31; 1961, 84; 1964, 74, 229; 1965, 246; Foy Valentine Oral History, vol. 1, 59–62, 78, 124; vol. 2, 72–73, 79, 83, THC.

84. Tilson, *Segregation and the Bible*, 68.

85. Will D. Campbell, *Race and the Renewal of the Church*, 32, 36, 52, 56; and *Brother to a Dragonfly*, 201; Hawkins, *Will Campbell*, 45, 99; Will D. Campbell, *Forty Acres and a Goat*.

86. Baldwin, *There Is a Balm in Gilead*, 69, 78–79.

87. Hobson, *But Now I See*, 17; Ehle, *Free Men*, 20, 31; Watters, *Down to Now*, 116.

88. Hobson, *But Now I See*, 56.

Chapter Five

1. Gary L. Frost Oral History, THC; David Gushee Oral History, 5–6, THC.
2. Hill, *Southern Churches in Crisis*; Eighmy, *Churches in Cultural Captivity*.

3. *Christian Index*, Mar. 22, 1883.

4. Holifield, *Gentlemen Theologians*; Tise, *Proslavery*; Snay, *Gospel of Disunion*. For Thornwell's sermon and a fuller analysis, see Paul Harvey, "The Christian Doctrine of Slavery," in McDannell, ed., *Religions of North America*, 1:466–82.

5. Marsden, *Fundamentalism and American Culture*.

6. Sledge, "History of the Methodist Episcopal Church, South," 52.

7. Glass, "Development of Northern Patterns," published as Glass, *Strangers in Zion*, 63–70.

8. Ibid., 223, 430.

9. Ibid., 116.

10. Sledge, "History of the Methodist Episcopal Church, South," 129.

11. Ibid., 155.

12. Glass, "Development of Northern Patterns," 128–29, 216–17.

13. Frank Andrews to "My Dear Will," in McCorkle Papers, box 1, folder 16; Henry M. Woods to William Parsons McCorkle, Apr. 3, 1931, in McCorkle Papers, box 2, folder 22, both SHC.

14. McCorkle sermon, Jan. 26, 1902, in McCorkle Papers, box 3, folder 35a, SHC; letter from [illegible] to McCorkle, Dec. 2, 1931, and response by McCorkle, in McCorkle Papers, box 2, folder 23, SHC.

15. Edward Parker to William P. McCorkle, Aug. 19, 1925, and Sylvester Hassell to McCorkle, Sept. 19, 1925, in McCorkle Papers, box 1, folder 16, SHC.

16. W. T. Couch to McCorkle, Feb. 27 and Apr. 27, 1926, in McCorkle Papers, box 1, folder 17, SHC; Larson, *Summer for the Gods*.

17. Feldman, *Politics, Society, and the Klan in Alabama*, 37–40; Will Alexander Oral History, 190–91, COHRO. Italics mine.

18. Sledge, "A History of the Methodist Episcopal Church, South," 186–88; Feldman, *Politics, Society, and the Klan in Alabama*, 37–40, 59.

19. Feldman, *Politics, Society, and the Klan*, 184, 322.

20. Ibid., 312; MacLean, "Leo Frank Case Reconsidered."

21. Tyson, *Radio Free Dixie*, 21.

22. See Chappell, "Divided Mind," 45–72; Chappell, "Religious Ideas," 237–62; Oran P. Smith, *Rise of Baptist Republicanism*, 45–47. See also Chappell, *Stone of Hope*, ch. 8.

23. W. B. Selah, "The Doctrine of Separate but Equal Opportunities for All Races," 33–52, in Evaluation Report, Dallas Methodist Conference on Human Relations, GBCS Records; Leon C. Burns, "Christian Attitude toward Segregation," SHC.

24. Sparks, *Religion in Mississippi*, 228–31; Dittmer, *Local People*, 63.

25. G. T. Gillespie, *Christian View on Segregation*.

26. Tom Brady, "Segregation and the South," speech delivered to the Commonwealth Club of California, Oct. 4, 1957, in Bingham Papers, WHS.

27. Joseph S. Jones to *Greenville News*, letter dated May 6, 1959; Rev. Joseph H. Jones, "The Ku Klux Klan, the NAACP, and the Presbyterian Church," pamphlet; Joseph S. Jones, letter dated Oct. 29, 1959, to *Presbyterian Laymen*; all in Joseph Simeon Jones Papers, PHS.

28. Sparks, *Religion in Mississippi*, 197–98.

29. Carey Daniel, "God the Original Segregationist," pamphlet in Smith Papers, box 1, ESCL.

30. Lyon reference from Crespino, "Christian Conscience of Jim Crow," 36; Mark Newman, *Getting Right with God*, 50–51.

31. Rev. J. Davis Dimpson, "Non-Segregation Means Eventual Inter-Marriage," in Tilly Papers, box 2, ESCL.

32. Mark Newman, *Getting Right with God*, 51; David C. Stewart to James May, Oct. 4, 1955, in May Papers, ESCL; Billy James Hargis, "Integration by Force Not a Christian Crusade," in Henry Frank Beaty Papers, box 1, PHS.

33. Walter Dean to John Owen Smith, Mar. 17, 1961, in Smith Papers, box 1, ESCL; Tom Brady, "A Review of Black Monday," Address to the Indianaola Citizens' Council, Oct. 28, 1954, pamphlet in Bingham Papers, WHS; Mark Newman, *Getting Right with God*, 93, 99, 522, 549.

34. Mark Newman, *Getting Right with God*, 499, 502; Pete Daniel, *Lost Revolutions*, 182–85, 233, 236.

35. Brooks, " 'Winning the Peace,' " 574, 576 n. 33; Egerton, *Speak Now against the Day*, 424.

36. Pete Daniel, *Lost Revolutions*, 238, 255; Friedland, *Lift up Your Voice*, 34.

37. Collins, *When the Church Bell Rang Racist*, 16–19.

38. G. T. Gillespie, *Christian View of Segregation*, 9; Stephen F. Haynes, *Noah's Curse*, 117–18; Sparks, *Religion in Mississippi*, 230–33.

39. Collins, *When the Church Bell Rang Racist*, 16, 33, 39–41; Manis, *Southern Civil Religions in Conflict*, 83; Mark Newman, "Baptist State Convention of North Carolina," 1–28; Goldfield, *Black, White, and Southern*, 76.

40. Eagles, "Closing of Mississippi Society," 351–52, 370–72; Friedland, *Lift up Your Voice*, 23.

41. Collins, *When the Church Bell Rang Racist*, 49–51, 113.

42. Sparks, *Religion in Mississippi*, 236–37; P. M. Boyd to Dudley Ward, Apr. 2, 1960; Ray M. Earnest to A. Dudley Ward, Apr. 4, 1960; John W. Ward to Dudley Ward, Mar. 20, 1960; all in "Sit-In Demonstration, Race" folder, GBCS Records.

43. "A Relevant Gospel in Atlanta," in GBCS Records; A. H. McAfee to Cecil Myers, Apr. 6, 1962; R. W. Espy to John Owen Smith, undated; Ensley Tiffin to Smith, Aug. 26, 1960; Ralph W. Nichols to Smith, Sept. 21, 1961; all in Smith Papers, boxes 1 and 2, ESCL.

44. Pamphlet "The Methodist Layman's Union, a Pronouncement," folder for "Petitions by Local Churches against Integration," GBCS Records; Collins, *When the Church Bell Rang Racist*, 159.

45. Rucker Brothers to James W. May, Oct. 21, 1955, in folder "Feedback on *Look* article," May Papers, ESCL.

46. *Dixie Religious Review*, undated copy, Joseph B. Matthews Papers, box 142, "Communist Party: Negro, 1928–1961" folder, SCPL.

47. "The Gospel Truth about Segregation" and "Race Rows Blamed on Minorities," pamphlets in McGill Papers, box 24, folder 1, ESCL.

48. Ebenezer Myers to John Owen Smith, Aug. 15, 1961; Frank S. Cheatham to Smith, Nov. 7, 1961; Mrs. T. W. Brightwell to Smith, Feb. 13, 1961; all in Smith Papers, box 1, ESCL.

49. *Charleston News and Courier*, Dec. 8, 1955, clipping in folder "Petitions by Local Churches against Integration," GBCS Records; Grace Greene Pace to John Owen Smith, Sept. 7, 1965; Frank L. Butler to Smith, Aug. 18, 1965; Rev. Harry Moore to Smith, Aug. 16, 1965; all in Smith Papers, box 5, ESCL.

50. Mark Newman, *Getting Right with God*, 522.

51. Thomas J. Holmes, *Ashes for Breakfast*, 10, 122–23.

52. Manis, *Southern Civil Religions in Conflict*, 65; Wallie Amos Criswell Oral History, THC.

53. Mark Newman, *Getting Right with God*, 64.

54. See Hankins, *Uneasy in Babylon*.

55. See Morgan, *New Crusades*, and Hankins, *Uneasy in Babylon*.

56. Shurden and Shepley, *Going for the Jugular*; Timothy George Oral History, 11–12, THC.

57. See Paul Harvey and R. Marie Griffith, "Wifely Submission and the SBC," *Christian Century*, June 17 and 24, 1998, 31–33; Timothy George Oral History, 43–44, THC; Dorothy Patterson Oral History, 48–52, THC; and Mark Coppenger Oral History, 28–29, THC.

58. Sullivan, *Days of Hope*; Wuthnow, *Restructuring of American Religion*.

59. R. Albert Mohler Oral History, 46, THC.

Epilogue

1. *New York Times*, Mar. 31, 1996.

2. Statistics from Charles Lippy, "From Angels to Zen: Religion and Culture in the Contemporary South" (unpublished manuscript), and "North American Religion Atlas," developed by the Glenmary Research Center and the Polis Center, online at ‹http://www.nara.org›.

3. Brereton, *From Sin to Salvation*, 47.

4. Tweed, "Our Lady of Guadeloupe."

5. Data from the ARIS, 2001, provided by Mark Silk for the Religion by Region series of books, a project of the Leonard E. Greenberg Center for the Study of Religion in Public Life at Trinity College in Hartford, Connecticut. The ARIS researchers collected survey data compiled in over 13,000 telephone interviews nationwide that were focused on mapping patterns based on the self-identification of survey respondents to questions about religious beliefs and affiliations. Information about the ARIS project is available online at ‹http://www.gc.cuny.edu/studies/aris_index.htm›.

6. This data comes from my involvement with a major nationwide study that will culminate in a series of eight books studying religion by individual region. The Religion by Region project, overseen by Mark Silk of Trinity College's Greenberg Center for the Study of Religion in Public Life, was generously provided data by Professor John Green's study at the University of Akron. For more information, see ‹http://www.trincoll.edu/depts/csrpl/lilly_grant_press_release.htm›.

Bibliography

Researching this work has taken me to numerous archives and libraries seeking sources on a wide range of subjects. I have made no attempt here to list exhaustively all the sources consulted but to reference those that proved to be the most important in shaping the arguments, interpretations, and source material used in the preparation of this work.

Because of the long time period and variety of topics covered in this work, I have chosen to organize the bibliography topically rather than simply compile all titles into one list mixing together books on all the topics covered. For that reason, consulting the full form of a published work listed in the short form in the endnotes will involve finding the proper topic first to look under, and then finding the title there. Despite the extra step of such an approach, the topical approach to this bibliography offers the best chance for a reader to survey quickly the range of materials consulted on a given topic in this book, and to get a quick and admittedly incomplete overview of sources available on particular subjects. Also, it means that primary and secondary published sources are listed together under particular topics, rather than being separated out as is often in the case in conventional bibliographies. This is in accordance with the thrust of this book, which is to intermix original research on key understudied topics together with drawing on the wealth of research on other topics compiled over the last two generations of scholarship in the field.

Here, readers are encouraged to look over the topical organization of the bibliography before searching for specific works consulted and noted in short form in the endnotes. My hope is that organizing the reference material this way will assist readers who wish to delve further and deeper into particular topics covered in this book.

Archival Materials

Amistad Research Center, Tulane University, New Orleans, Louisiana
  American Missionary Association (AMA) Papers
  Samuel Stanford Ashley Papers
  Community Church of Chapel Hill, Records, 1953–59
  Dodd Family Papers
  Esther Douglass Papers
  Dunn-Landry Family Papers
  Ruth Grout Collection
  Fannie Lou Hamer Papers
  Henry Hugh and Adeline L. Proctor Papers
  Lincoln Academy Collection
  Charles Sherrod Papers
  Union Bethel African Methodist Episcopal Church, New Orleans
Assemblies of God Archives, Flower Heritage Center, Assemblies of God, Springfield,
    Missouri
  Archives Records Groups
  Bridegroom's Messenger
  Society for Pentecostal Studies Papers
Boyce Library, Southern Baptist Theological Seminary, Louisville, Kentucky
  James P. Boyce Correspondence
  John T. Broadus Correspondence
  Thomas T. Eaton Papers
  Edgar Young Mullins Letter Files and Letterpress Books
Collected Papers of the Student Non-Violent Coordinating Committee and the Delta
    Ministry, State Historical Society of Wisconsin, Madison, Wisconsin
  Meldon Acheson Papers
  Robert Beech Papers
  Steven Bingham Papers
  Harry Bowie Papers
  Jake Friesen Papers
  Frederick Heinze Papers
  Robert Jackall Papers
  Vicki and Martin Nicklaus Papers
  Larry Rubin Papers
  Daniel J. Wacker Papers
  George Weissman Papers
  Robert and Dorothy Zellner Papers
Columbia Oral History Research Office, Columbia University, New York
  Interview with Will Alexander
  Interview with Virginia Durr
  Interview with Willie Herzefeld
  Interview with T. Y. Rogers
Institute for Oral History, Transcripts in Texas Historical Collection, Carroll Library,
    Baylor University, Waco, Texas

Jimmy Allen Oral History

Warren Tyree Carr Oral History

Mark Coppenger Oral History

Julius Corpening Oral History

Wallie Amos Criswell Oral History

Joseph Martin Dawson Oral History

Jasper Martin England Oral History

Gary L. Frost Oral History

Timothy George Oral History

David Gushee Oral History

R. Albert Mohler Oral History

Dorothy Patterson Oral History

Paige Patterson Oral History

Foy Valentine Oral History

Foy Valentine Papers

International Pentecostal Holiness Church Archives, Oklahoma City, Oklahoma

Live Coals of Fire and *Live Coals*

Pentecostal Holiness Advocate

Library of the Sunday School Board, Southern Baptist Convention, Nashville, Tennessee

Edwin C. Dargan Papers

James Marion Frost Papers, 1891–1916

Frost-Bell Papers, 1891–1916

Presbyterian Historical Society, Montreat College, Montreat, North Carolina

John Bailey Adger Papers, 1871

Samuel Baird, Papers, 1838–82, Speech against Ecclesiastical Equality of Negro

Henry Frank Beaty Papers

Marion Boggs Papers

Robert L. Dabney, "Speech of Rev. Robert L. Dabney, in the Synod of Virginia, Nov. 9, 1867, against the Ecclesiastical Equality of Negro Preachers in Our Church, and Their Right to Rule over White Christians" (Richmond, 1868)

Edward Owings Guerrant, Correspondence, 1873–1916

Benjamin Helm Papers

Charles Miles Jones Papers

Joseph Simeon Jones Papers, 1954–67

Robert Matthew Lynn Papers, 1920–85

Alexander McKelway Papers

Minutes of the General Assemblies of the Presbyterian Church in the United States, 1865–1973

Samuel Cunningham Smith Sermons, 1965–71

James George Snecedor Papers

Robert Strong Papers, "Why Some of Us Are Not Leaving the PCUS," 1973 article

J. Leighton Wilson Papers

Oscar Bickley Wilson Diary, 1896–1900

Schomburg Center for Research in Black Culture, New York Public Library, Harlem Branch

Sherry Sherrod Dupree Collection (on African American Holiness/Pentecostalism)

Southern Baptist Historical Library and Archives, Nashville, Tennessee
Black Baptist Associational Minutes
William Owen Carver Papers
Una Roberts Lawrence Papers
Basil Manly Jr. Papers
Basil Manly Sr. Papers
Manly Family Papers
Hight C. Moore Papers
Sermons Delivered at Annual Meetings of the Southern Baptist Convention,
1866–1980
Isaac Taylor Tichenor, Diary
Whitsitt Controversy, Papers and News Clippings
Woman's Missionary Union, Auxiliary to the Southern Baptist Convention, National
and State Records (including annual meeting records)
Woman's Missionary Union, Executive Committee Minutes
Woman's Missionary Union of North Carolina, State Records
Woman's Missionary Union of South Carolina, State Records
Woman's Mission to Women, Minute Book, 1872–80, and Secretary's Report, 1
888–98
Southern Historical Collection, Manuscripts Department, Wilson Library, University
of North Carolina, Chapel Hill
Mary Jeffreys Bethell Diary
Leon C. Burns, "The Christian Attitude toward Segregation," sermon given at West
Seventh Street Church of Christ, Columbia, Tennessee, Sept. 12 1954, in John
Peacock Papers
Laura Comer Diaries
James McBride Dabbs Papers
William Porcher DuBose Reminiscences
Federal Works Project Manuscripts
Fellowship of Southern Churchmen Papers
Henry T. Harris Papers
Sylvester Hassell Papers
Cushing Biggs Hassell Papers
Howard Anderson Kester Papers
William Parsons McCorkle Papers
Samuel Lewis Morgan Papers
Edgar Gardner Murphy Papers
Norton, Chilton, and Dameron Papers
Rev. John Paris, "The Moral and Religious Status of the African Race in the Southern
States," handwritten manuscript in Paris Papers, folder for 1828–71
William Rutherford Savage Papers
Lydia Schofield Diary
Martha Schofield Papers
Robert E. Seymour Papers
Southern Oral History Program, Transcripts and Tapes of Interviews
Southern Tenant Farmers' Union Papers

Nannie (Haskins) Williams Diary
Norvell Winsboro Wilson Papers
Special Collections, Perkins Library, Duke University, Durham, North Carolina
"Behind the Veil: Documenting African-American Life in the Jim Crow South, 1940–97"
Iveson L. Brookes Papers
John Emory Bryant Papers
William Henry Chafe Interviews
CIO, Virginia Industrial Union Council Papers—Labor and Religion Fellowship Group Collection
Rebecca F. Clayton Diary
Duke University Oral History Program Papers, 1973–78
Lillie Moore Everett Papers
Frances Goodrich Papers
Gordon Blaine Hancock Papers
Elizabeth Johnson Harris, "Life Story, 1867–1923"
E. B. Ingram Papers
Joseph B. Matthews Papers
William George Matton, Autobiographical Sketch
Bessie Meachum Diary, in Townsend Family Papers
Winfield Henry Mixon Papers
Records of the Resource Center for Women and Ministry in the South, Inc.
Scarborough Family Papers
Missouria H. Stokes Papers
Special Collections Library, Emory University, Atlanta, Georgia
Bailey-Thurman Papers
Atticus Haygood Papers
James May Papers
Ralph McGill Papers
John Owen Smith Papers
Dorothy Tilly Papers
United Methodist Church Archives, General Commission on Archives and History, Drew University, Madison, New Jersey
Church Women United Papers
Records of the General Board of Church and Society, United Methodist Church
Records of the General Commission on Religion and Race, United Methodist Church
Virginia Historical Society, Richmond, Virginia
Sarah Payne Letterbook
Aquila J. Peyton Diary, 1859–61
John Pollard Diary

Religious Periodicals and Newspapers

Alabama Baptist
American Baptist

A.M.E. Church Review

Apostolic Faith (Pentecostal) (1906–15)

Baptist Home Mission Monthly (1860s–1900)

Baptist Standard (Texas)

Baptist World (Southern Baptist)

Biblical Recorder (North Carolina, Baptist)

Bridegroom's Messenger (1906–12, Holiness/Pentecostal)

Christian Index (Georgia, Baptist)

Christian Index and Southwestern Baptist (Georgia)

Christian Watchman and Reflector

Christian Recorder (1860s–1920s, African Methodist Episcopal)

Church of God Evangel (1910–60)

Church Woman

The Faithful Standard (Church of God, Cleveland, 1922–23)

Frontiers (1940s, Southern Baptist)

Georgia Baptist (late nineteenth century, black Baptist)

Home and Foreign Fields (1880–1900, Southern Baptist); continued as *Our Home Field*
   (1900–1920)

Independent (1870s–90s)

Katallagete (1960s)

Light (Christian Life Commission of the Southern Baptist Convention, 1947–50s)

Lighted Pathway (1929–50s, Church of God, Cleveland)

Live Coals of Fire (1898–1905, Holiness/Pentecostal)

Methodist Advance (1880s, North Carolina)

Methodist Layman (1920s–30s)

National Baptist Magazine (1890–1905, black Baptist)

National Baptist Union-Review (1900–1920, black Baptist; also named *National Baptist
   Union*)

New Orleans Christian Advocate (1870s–80s, Methodist)

North Carolina Christian Advocate (1860s–80s, Methodist)

Our Home Field (1900–1920, Southern Baptist)

Pentecostal Evangel (1914–50, Assemblies of God)

Pentecostal Holiness Advocate (1918–50, Pentecostal Holiness Church)

Prophetic Religion (journal of the Fellowship of Southern Churchmen, 1940s–50s)

Raleigh Christian Advocate (Methodist)

Religious Herald (1860s–1925, Virginia, Southern Baptist)

Royal Service (1915–60s, Woman's Missionary Union, Southern Baptist Convention)

Savannah Tribune (black newspaper in city)

South Carolina Baptist (1860s–70s)

Southern Presbyterian Review (1867–77)

Southern Workman (1870s–90s)

Southwestern Christian Advocate (Methodist, renamed *Southwestern Advocate*)

Star of Zion (1880s–1910s, African Methodist Episcopal Zion)

Student Voice (publication of the Student Non-Violent Coordinating Committee)

Word and Witness (1910–15, Pentecostal—replaced by *Pentecostal Evangel*)

Zion's Herald (1870s–80s)

Organizational Records

Black Baptist Associational Minutes, 5 microfilm reels, Southern Baptist Historical Library and Archives, Nashville, Tennessee

Consolidated American Baptist Missionary Convention, 1866–72, Southern Baptist Historical Library and Archives, Nashville, Tennessee

Freedmen's Aid Society of the Methodist Episcopal Church, Amistad Research Center, Tulane University, New Orleans, Louisiana

Freedmen's Aid Society of the Methodist Episcopal Church—Board of Education, Amistad Research Center, Tulane University, New Orleans, Louisiana

Journal of the General Conference of the Methodist Episcopal Church, South, 1862–1939, General Commissions on Archives and History, United Methodist Church Archives, Drew University, Madison, New Jersey

Minutes of the General Assembly of the Presbyterian Church, U.S., 1860s–1960s, Presbyterian Historical Society, Montreat College, Montreat, North Carolina

Minutes of the General Assembly of the Presbyterian Church in the Confederate States of America, Presbyterian Historical Society, Montreat College, Montreat, North Carolina

Minutes of the North Carolina Yearly Meeting of Friends, Southern Historical Collection, Manuscripts Department, Wilson Library, University of North Carolina, Chapel Hill

National Baptist Convention Journals, Southern Baptist Historical Library and Archives, Nashville, Tennessee

Southern Baptist Convention Annuals, 1865–2000, Southern Baptist Historical Library and Archives, Nashville, Tennessee

Books, Articles, Dissertations, Reference Works, and Other Publications

SOUTHERN AND AMERICAN RELIGIOUS HISTORY

Bailey, Kenneth K. *Southern White Protestantism in the Twentieth Century.* New York: Harper & Row, 1964.

Baker, Robert A, ed. *The Southern Baptist Convention and Its People, 1607–1972.* Nashville: Broadman Press, 1974.

Boles, John B. *The Great Revival, 1787–1805: The Origins of the Southern Evangelical Mind.* Lexington: University Press of Kentucky, 1972.

———. "The Rediscovery of Southern Religious History." In *Interpreting Southern History: Essays in Honor of Sanford W. Higginbotham,* edited by John B. Boles and Evelyn Nolen, 510–48. Baton Rouge: Louisiana State University Press, 1987.

———, ed. *Autobiographical Reflections on Southern Religious History.* Athens: University of Georgia Press, 2001.

Butler, Jon. *Awash in a Sea of Faith: Christianizing the American People.* Cambridge, Massachusetts: Harvard University Press, 1990.

Carwardine, Richard J. *Evangelicals and Politics in Antebellum America.* New Haven: Yale University Press, 1993.

Cash, Wilbur J. *Mind of the South.* New York: Knopf, 1941.

Conkin, Paul. *American Originals: Varieties of Homemade Christianity.* Chapel Hill: University of North Carolina Press, 1997.

———. *The Uneasy Center: Reformed Christianity in Antebellum America.* Chapel Hill: University of North Carolina Press, 1994.

Crowther, Edward R. "Holy Honor: Sacred and Secular in the Old South." *Journal of Southern History* 58 (November 1992): 619–36.

Dabbs, James M. *Haunted by God: The Cultural and Religious Experience of the South.* Richmond, Virginia: John Knox Press, 1972.

Dollard, John. *Caste and Class in a Southern Town.* New Haven: Yale University Press, 1937.

Finke, Roger, and Rodney Stark. *The Churching of America, 1776–1990: Winners and Losers in Our Religious Economy.* New Brunswick: Rutgers University Press, 1992.

Evans, Eli. *The Provincials: A Personal History of Jews in the South.* New York: Atheneum, 1973.

Flynt, J. Wayne. *Alabama Baptists: Southern Baptists in the Heart of Dixie.* Tuscaloosa: University of Alabama Press, 1998.

Harvey, Paul. "Religion in the American South Since the Civil War." In *A Companion to the American South,* edited by John B. Boles, 387–408. Malden, Massachusetts: Blackwell Publishers, 2002.

Haynes, Stephen F. *Noah's Curse: The Biblical Justification of American Slavery.* New York: Oxford University Press, 2002.

Heyrman, Christine Leigh. *Southern Cross: The Beginnings of the Bible Belt.* New York: Knopf, 1997.

Hill, Samuel S. *On Jordan's Stormy Banks.* Macon, Georgia: Mercer University Press, 1983.

———, ed. *Religion in the Southern States: A Historical Study.* Macon, Georgia: Mercer University Press, 1983.

———. *Southern Churches in Crisis.* New York: Holt, Rinehart, and Winston, 1967.

Holifield, E. Brooks. *The Gentlemen Theologians: American Theology in Southern Culture, 1795–1860.* Durham, North Carolina: Duke University Press, 1978.

Hughes, Richard T., and C. Leonard Allen, eds. *Illusions of Innocence: Protestant Primitivism in America, 1630–1875.* Chicago: University of Chicago Press, 1988.

Isaac, Rhys. *The Transformation of Virginia, 1740–1790.* Chapel Hill: University of North Carolina Press, 1982.

Leonard, Bill. *God's Last and Only Hope: The Fragmentation of the Southern Baptist Convention.* Grand Rapids, Michigan: Eerdmans, 1990.

Loveland, Anne C. *Southern Evangelicals and the Social Order, 1800–1860.* Baton Rouge: Louisiana State University Press, 1980.

Mathews, Donald. *Religion in the Old South.* Chicago: University of Chicago Press, 1977.

———. "The Southern Rite of Human Sacrifice." *Journal of Southern Religion* 3 (2000), ⟨http://jsr.as.wvu.edu/mathews.htm⟩.

———. " 'We Have Left Undone Those Things Which We Ought to Have Done': Southern Religious History in Retrospect and Prospect." *Church History* 67 (June 1998): 305–25.

McDannell, Colleen, ed. *Religions of North America in Practice.* 2 vols. Princeton: Princeton University Press, 2001.

Moore, R. Laurence. *Selling God: American Religion in the Marketplace of Culture.* New York: Oxford University Press, 1994.

Snay, Mitchell. *The Gospel of Disunion: Religion and Separatism in the Antebellum South.* New York: Cambridge University Press, 1993.

Sobel, Mechal. *The World They Made Together: Black and White Values in Eighteenth-Century Virginia.* Princeton: Princeton University Press, 1987.

Sparks, Randy J. *Religion in Mississippi.* Jackson: University Press of Mississippi, 2001.

Szasz, Ferenc Morton. *The Divided Mind of Protestant America, 1880–1930.* Tuscaloosa: University of Alabama Press, 1982.

Tise, Larry E. *Proslavery: A History of the Defense of Slavery in America, 1701–1840.* Athens: University of Georgia Press, 1987.

Tweed, Thomas. "Our Lady of Guadeloupe Visits the Confederate Memorial: Latino and Asian Religions in the South." *Southern Cultures* 8 (2002): 72–93.

Warner, R. Stephen. "Work in Progress toward a New Paradigm for the Sociological Study of Religion in the United States." *American Journal of Sociology* 98 (March 1993): 1044–93.

Williamson, Joel. *A Rage for Order: Black-White Relations in the American South Since Emancipation.* New York: Oxford University Press, 1986.

Wills, Gregory A. *Democratic Religion: Freedom, Authority, and Church Discipline in the Baptist South, 1785–1900.* New York: Oxford University Press, 1977.

Woodward, C. Vann. *The Burden of Southern History.* 3rd ed. Baton Rouge: Louisiana State University Press, 1991.

———. *Origins of the New South, 1877–1913.* Baton Rouge: Louisiana State University Press, 1951.

———. *The Strange Career of Jim Crow.* New York: Oxford University Press, 1955.

Woodworth, Stephen E. *While God Is Marching On: The Religious World of Civil War Soldiers.* Lawrence: University of Kansas Press, 2001.

Wuthnow, Robert. *The Restructuring of American Religion: Society and Faith Since World War Two.* Princeton: Princeton University Press, 1998.

Wyatt-Brown, Bertram. *Southern Honor: Ethics and Behavior in the Old South.* New York: Oxford University Press, 1982.

RELIGION, RACE, AND RECONSTRUCTION

Adger, John B. *My Life and Times, 1810–1899.* Richmond, Virginia: Presbyterian Committee of Publication, 1899.

Adger, John B., and John L. Girardeau, eds. *The Collected Writings of James Henley Thornwell, D.D., LL.D.* 4 vols. Richmond, Virginia: Presbyterian Committee of Publication, 1871–73.

Allan-Olney, Mary. *The New Virginians.* Edinburgh and London: Blackwood, 1880.

Amos-Doss, Harriet. "Race Relations in Religion between Planters and Freedmen during Reconstruction in the Black Belt of Alabama." In *Developing Dixie: Modernization in a Traditional Society,* edited by Winfred Moore and Joseph Tripp, 45–57. Westport, Connecticut: Greenwood Press, 1982.

———. "Religious Reconstruction in Microcosm at Faunsdale Plantation." *Alabama Review* 42 (October 1989): 243–69.

Angell, Stephen Ward. *Bishop Henry McNeal Turner and African American Religion in the South.* Knoxville: University of Tennessee Press, 1992.

Angell, Stephen W., and Anthony B. Pinn, eds. *Social Protest Thought in the African Methodist Episcopal Church, 1862–1939.* Knoxville: University of Tennessee Press, 2000.

Avary, Myrta. *Dixie after the War: An Exposition of Social Conditions Existing in the South, during the Twelve Years Succeeding the Fall of Richmond.* 1906. Reprint, New York, 1969.

Ayers, Edward. *The Promise of the New South: Life after Reconstruction.* New York: Oxford University Press, 1992.

Baker, Robert Andrew. "The American Baptist Home Mission Society and the South, 1832–1894." Ph.D. diss., Yale University, 1947.

Bennett, James Brinks. "Religion and the Rise of Jim Crow in New Orleans." Ph.D. diss., Yale University, 1999.

Blackburn, George A., ed. *Sermons by John L. Girardeau.* Columbia, South Carolina: State, 1907.

Boles, John B., ed. *Masters and Slaves in the House of the Lord: Race and Religion in the American South, 1740–1870.* Lexington: University Press of Kentucky, 1988.

Browder, George Richard. *The Heavens Are Weeping: The Diaries of George Richard Browder, 1852–1866.* Edited by Richard L. Troutman. Grand Rapids, Michigan: Zondervan, 1987.

Brown, Elsa Barkley. "Negotiating and Transforming the Public Sphere: African American Political Life in the Transition from Slavery to Freedom." *Public Culture* 7 (Fall 1994): 107–46.

Brown, William Wells. *My Southern Home; or, The South and Its People.* Boston: A. G. Brown, 1880.

Burr, Virginia Ingraham, ed. *The Secret Eye: The Journal of Ella Gertrude Clanton Thomas, 1848–1889.* Chapel Hill: University of North Carolina Press, 1990.

Burton, Orville Vernon. *In My Father's House Are Many Mansions: Family and Community in Edgefield, South Carolina.* Chapel Hill: University of North Carolina Press, 1985.

Burton, Orville Vernon, and Robert C. McMath, eds. *Toward a New South? Studies in Post–Civil War Southern Communities.* Westport, Connecticut: Greenwood Press, 1982.

Butchart, Ronald E. *Northern Schools, Southern Blacks, and Reconstruction: Freedmen's Education, 1862–1875.* Westport, Connecticut: Greenwood Press, 1980.

Caldwell, John H. *Reminiscences of the Reconstruction of Church and State in Georgia.* Wilmington, Delaware: J. Miller Thomas, 1895.

Campbell, James T. *Songs of Zion: The African Methodist Episcopal Church in the United States and South Africa.* New York: Oxford University Press, 1995.

Conser, Rev. Solomon L. M. *Virginia after the War: An Account of Three Years' Experience in Reorganizing the Methodist Episcopal Church in Virginia at the Close of the Civil War.* Indianapolis: Baker-Randolph, 1891.

Corey, Charles H. *A History of the Richmond Theological Seminary with Reminiscences of Thirty Years' Work among the Colored People of the South.* Richmond, Virginia: J. W. Randolph, 1895.

Currie-McDaniel, Ruth. *Carpetbagger of Conscience: A Biography of John Emory Bryant.* Athens: University of Georgia Press, 1987.

Daniel, W. Harrison. *Virginia Baptists, 1860–1902.* Richmond, Virginia: Virginia Baptist Historical Society, 1987.

De Boer, Clara Merritt. "The Role of African-Americans in the Origin and Work of the American Missionary Association, 1839–1877." Ph.D. diss., Rutgers University, 1973.

Donaldson, Bobby J. "Standing on a Volcano: The Leadership of William Jefferson White." In *Paternalism in a Southern City: Race, Religion, and Gender in Augusta, Georgia,* edited by Edward J. Cashin and Glenn T. Eskew, 135–77. Athens: University of Georgia Press.

Du Bois, W. E. B. *Black Reconstruction: An Essay Toward a History of the Part which Black Folk Played in the Attempt to Reconstruct Democracy in America, 1860–1880.* New York: Harcourt, Brace, and Company, 1935.

Dvorak, Katherine. *An African-American Exodus: The Segregation of the Southern Churches.* Brooklyn, New York: Carlson, 1991.

Eskew, Glenn. "Black Elitism and the Failure of Paternalism in Postbellum Georgia: The Case of Bishop Lucius Henry Holsey." *Journal of Southern History* 58 (November 1992): 637–66.

———. "Paternalism among Augusta's Methodists: Black, White, and Colored." In *Paternalism in a Southern City: Race, Religion, and Gender in Augusta, Georgia,* edited by Edward J. Cashin and Glenn T. Eskew, 85–109. Athens: University of Georgia Press, 2001.

Farish, Hunter Dickinson. *The Circuit Rider Dismounts: A Social History of Southern Methodism, 1865–1900.* Richmond, Virginia: Dietz Press, 1938.

Farmer, James O., Jr. *The Metaphysical Confederacy: James Henry Thornwell and the Synthesis of Southern Values.* Macon, Georgia: Mercer University Press, 1986.

Faust, Drew Gilpin. "Christian Soldiers: The Meaning of Revivalism in the Confederate Army." *Journal of Southern History* 53 (February 1987): 63–90.

Foner, Eric. *Freedom's Lawmakers: A Directory of Black Officeholders during Reconstruction.* New York: Oxford University Press, 1993.

———. *Reconstruction: America's Unfinished Revolution, 1863–1877.* New York: Harper & Row, 1988.

Foster, Gaines M. *Ghosts of the Confederacy: Defeat, the Lost Cause, and the Emergence of the New South, 1865 to 1913.* New York: Oxford University Press, 1987.

Fuller, A. James. *Chaplain to the Confederacy: Basil Manly and Baptist Life in the Old South.* Baton Rouge: Louisiana State University Press, 2000.

Gaines, Wesley J. *African Methodism in the South, or 25 Years of Freedom.* 1890. Reprint, Chicago: Afro-American Press, 1969.

Gannett, W. C. "The Freedmen at Port Royal." *North American Review* 101 (July 1865): 1–28.

Genovese, Eugene D. *A Consuming Fire: The Fall of the Confederacy in the Mind of the White Christian South.* Athens: University of Georgia Press, 1998.

Goen, C. C. *Broken Churches, Broken Nation: Denominational Schisms and the Coming of the American Civil War.* Macon, Georgia: Mercer University Press, 1985.

Gravely, William B. "A Black Methodist on Reconstruction in Mississippi: Three Letters by James Lynch in 1868–1869." *Methodist History* 11 (July 1973): 3–18.

———. "The Social, Political, and Religious Significance of the Formation of the Colored Methodist Episcopal Church (1870)." *Methodist History* 18 (1979): 3–25.

Hahn, Steven. *A Nation under Our Feet: Black Political Struggles in the Rural South from Slavery to the Great Migration.* Cambridge, Massachusetts: Harvard University Press, 2003.

Hall, Robert L. "The Gospel According to Radicalism: African Methodism Comes to Tallahassee after the Civil War." *Apalachee: The Publication of the Tallahassee Historical Society* 8 (1978): 69–81. Reprinted in Donald G. Nieman, *Church and Community among Black Southerners, 1865–1900.* New York: Garland, 1994.

———. "Tallahassee's Black Churches, 1865–1905." *Florida Historical Quarterly* 58 (October 1979): 185–96.

———. "'Yonder Come Day': Religious Dimensions of the Transition from Slavery to Freedom in Florida." *Florida Historical Quarterly* (April 1987): 411–32.

Hartzell, J. C. *Methodism and the Negro in the United States.* Cincinnati: Cranston and Curtis, 1894.

Harvey, Paul. *Redeeming the South: Religious Cultures and Racial Identities among Southern Baptists, 1865–1925.* Chapel Hill: University of North Carolina Press, 1997.

Heard, William H. *From Slavery to the Bishopric in the A.M.E. Church.* New York: Arno Press, 1969.

Higginson, Thomas Wentworth. *Army Life in a Black Regiment.* New York: Collier Books, 1962.

Hildebrand, Reginald Francis. *The Times Were Strange and Stirring: Methodist Preachers and the Crisis of Emancipation.* Durham, North Carolina: Duke University Press, 1995.

Holland, Rupert Sargent, ed. *Letters and Diary of Laura Towne.* 1912. Reprint, New York: Arno Press, 1969.

Holsey, Lucius H. *Autobiography, Sermons, Addresses, and Essays of Bishop L. H. Holsey, D.D..* Atlanta: Franklin Printing and Publishing Company, 1898.

Holt, Sharon Ann. "Making Freedom Pay: Freedpeople Working for Themselves, North Carolina, 1865–1900." *Journal of Southern History* 60 (May 1994): 229–62.

Hoole, W. Stanley, ed. "The Diary of Dr. Basil Manly, 1858–1867." Pts. 1–5. *Alabama Review* 4 (July 1951): 221–36; 4 (October 1951): 270–89; 5 (January 1952): 61–74; 5 (April 1952): 142–55.

Johnson, Thomas Cary, ed. *Life and Letters of Robert Lewis Dabney.* Richmond, Virginia: Presbyterian Committee of Publication, 1903.

Jones, Jacqueline. *Soldiers of Light and Love: Northern Teachers and Georgia Blacks, 1865–1873.* Chapel Hill: University of North Carolina Press, 1980.

Jones, John William. *Christ in the Camp; or, Religion in Lee's Army.* Richmond, Virginia: B. F. Johnson & Co., 1887.

Kellison, Kimberley Rae. "Coming to Christ: The Impact of Evangelical Christianity on Upcountry South Carolina, 1830–1890." Ph.D. diss., University of South Carolina, 1997.

Lane, Isaac. *Autobiography of Bishop Isaac Lane, LLD, with a Short History of the C.M.E. Church in America and of Methodism.* Nashville: Publishing House of the Methodist Episcopal Church, South, 1916.

Leigh, Frances. *Ten Years on a Georgia Plantation Since the War.* London: R. Bentley & Son, 1883.

Logsdon, Joseph, and Caryn Cosse Bell. "The Americanization of Black New Orleans." In *Creole New Orleans: Race and Americanization*, edited by Arnold R. Hirsch and Joseph H. Logsdon, 201–61. Baton Rouge: Louisiana State University Press, 1992.

Loveland, Anne C. "The 'Southern Work' of the Reverend Joseph C. Hartzell, Pastor of Ames Church in New Orleans, 1870–73." *Louisiana History* 16 (1975): 391–407.

McMillen, Sally G. *To Raise up the South: Sunday Schools in Black and White Churches, 1865–1915*. Baton Rouge: Louisiana State University Press, 2001.

McWhiney, Grady, et al., eds. *"Fear God and Walk Humbly": The Agricultural Journal of James Mallory, 1843–1877*. Tuscaloosa: University of Alabama Press, 1997.

Montgomery, William E. *Under Their Own Vine and Fig Tree: The African-American Church in the South, 1865–1900*. Baton Rouge: Louisiana State University Press, 1993.

Ochs, Stephen J. *A Black Patriot and a White Priest: Andre Cailloux and Claude Paschal Maistre in Civil War New Orleans*. Baton Rouge: Louisiana State University Press, 2000.

Owen, Christopher. *The Sacred Flame of Love: Methodism and Society in Nineteenth-Century Georgia*. Athens: University of Georgia Press, 1998.

Pearce, Larry Wesley. "The American Missionary Association and the Freedmen in Arkansas, 1863–1878." *Arkansas Historical Quarterly* 30 (Summer 1971): 123–44.

Pearson, Elizabeth Ware, ed. *Letters from Port Royal [1862–88] Written at the Time of the Civil War*. 1906. Reprint, New York: Arno Press, 1969.

Perdue, Robert. *The Negro in Savannah, 1865–1900*. New York: Exposition Press, 1973.

Phillips, Charles Henry. *From the Farm to the Bishopric: An Autobiography*. Nashville: Parthenon Press, 1932.

———. *The History of the Colored Methodist Episcopal Church in America, Comprising Its Organization, Subsequent Development, and Present Status*. Jackson, Tennessee: CME Publishing House, 1925.

Pierson, Rev. Hamilton Wilcox. *In the Brush; or, Old-Time Social, Political, and Religious Life in the Southwest*. New York: D. Appleton & Co., 1881.

Poole, W. Scott. "Religion, Gender, and the Lost Cause in South Carolina's 1876 Governor's Race: 'Hampton or Hell.'" *Journal of Southern History* 68 (August 2002): 573–98.

Rabinowitz, Howard N. "Holland Thompson and Black Political Participation in Montgomery, Alabama." In *Southern Black Leaders of the Reconstruction Era*, edited by Howard N. Rabinowitz, 249–79. Urbana: University of Illinois Press, 1982.

———. *Race Relations in the Urban South, 1865–1900*. New York: Oxford University Press, 1978.

Redkey, Edwin S., ed. *Respect Black: The Writings and Speeches of Henry McNeal Turner*. New York: Arno Press, 1971.

Reid, Whitelaw. *After the War: A Tour of the Southern States, 1865–1866*. New York: Harper & Row, 1965.

Reilly, Wayne E., ed. *Sarah Jane Foster, Teacher of the Freedmen: A Diary and Letters*. Charlottesville: University Press of Virginia, 1990.

Reports of the Freedmen's Aid Society of the Methodist Episcopal Church, 1866–1875. Cincinnati: Western Methodist Book Concern, 1893.

Richardson, Frank. *From Sunrise to Sunset: Reminiscence*. Bristol, Tennessee: King Printing Company, 1910.

Richardson, Joe Martin. *Christian Reconstruction: The American Missionary Association and Southern Blacks, 1861–1890*. Athens: University of Georgia Press, 1986.

Richardson, Simon Peter. *The Lights and Shadows of Itinerant Life: The Autobiography of Rev. Simon Peter Richardson, D.D., of the North Georgia Conference*. Nashville: Publishing House of the Methodist Episcopal Church, 1900.

Robertson, Archibald Thomas. *Life and Letters of John Albert Broadus*. Philadelphia: American Baptist Publication Society, 1901.

Robertson, James I., ed. *The Diary of Dolly Lunt Burge, 1848–1879*. Athens: University of Georgia Press, 1962.

Robinson, Armstead L. "Plans Dat Comed from God: Institution Building and the Emergence of Black Leadership in Reconstruction Memphis." In *Toward a New South? Studies in Post–Civil War Southern Communities*, edited by Orville Vernon Burton and Robert C. McMath Jr., 71–104. Westport, Connecticut: Greenwood Press, 1982.

Romero, Sidney J. *Religion in the Rebel Ranks*. Lanham, Maryland: University Press of America, 1983.

Rose, Willie Lee. *Rehearsal for Reconstruction: The Port Royal Experiment*. New York: Vintage Books, 1964.

Schweiger, Beth Barton. *The Gospel Working Up: Progress and the Pulpit in Nineteenth-Century Virginia*. New York: Oxford University Press, 2000.

———. "The Transformation of Southern Religion: Clergy and Congregations in Virginia, 1830–1895." Ph.D. diss., University of Virginia, 1994.

Schweninger, Loren. "The American Missionary Association and Northern Philanthropy in Reconstruction Alabama." *Alabama Historical Quarterly* 32 (Fall and Winter 1970): 129–56.

Shattuck, Gardiner H., Jr. *A Shield and a Hiding Place: The Religious Life of the Civil War Armies*. Macon, Georgia: Mercer University Press, 1987.

Silber, Nina. *The Romance of Reunion: Northerners and the South, 1865–1900*. Chapel Hill: University of North Carolina Press, 1993.

Smith, H. Shelton. *In His Image, But . . . : Racism in Southern Religion, 1780–1910*. Durham, North Carolina: Duke University Press, 1972.

Sobel, Mechal. "'They Can Never Both Prosper Together': Black and White Baptists in Nashville, Tennessee." *Tennessee Historical Quarterly* 38 (1979): 296–307.

Spain, Rufus B. *At Ease in Zion: Social History of the Southern Baptists, 1865–1900*. Nashville: Vanderbilt University Press, 1967.

Sparks, Randy J. *On Jordan's Stormy Banks: Evangelicalism in Mississippi, 1773–1876*. Athens: University of Georgia Press, 1994.

———. "'The White People's Arms Are Longer Than Ours': Blacks, Education, and the American Missionary Association in Reconstruction Mississippi." *Journal of Mississippi History* 54 (February 1992): 1–27.

Stetson, George R. *The Southern Negro As He Is*. Boston: G. H. Ellis, 1877.

Stowell, Daniel W. "'The Negroes Cannot Navigate Alone': Religious Scalawags and the Biracial Methodist Episcopal Church in Georgia, 1866–1876." In *Georgia in Black and White: Explorations in the Race Relations of a Southern State, 1865–1950*, edited by John C. Inscoe, 65–90. Athens: University of Georgia Press, 1994.

———. *Rebuilding Zion: The Religious Reconstruction of the South, 1863–1877*. New York: Oxford University Press, 1998.

———. "'We have Sinned, and God Has Smitten Us': John H. Caldwell and the Religious Meaning of Confederate Defeat." *Georgia Historical Quarterly* 78 (Spring 1994): 1–36.

Stout, Harry S., Charles Reagan Wilson, and Randall M. Miller, eds. *Religion and the American Civil War*. New York: Oxford University Press, 1998.

Thompson, Ernest Trice. "Black Presbyterians, Education, and Evangelism after the Civil War." *Journal of Presbyterian History* 51 (1973): 174–98.

Walker, Clarence Earl. *Rock in a Weary Land: The African Methodist Episcopal Church during the Civil War and Reconstruction*. Baton Rouge: Louisiana State University Press, 1982.

Washington, James Melvin. *Frustrated Fellowship: The Black Baptist Quest for Social Power*. Macon, Georgia: Mercer University Press, 1986.

Wheeler, Edmund L. *Uplifting the Race: The Black Minister in the New South, 1865–1902*. Lanham, Maryland: University Press of America, 1986.

Williams, Alfred B. *Hampton and His Red Shirts: South Carolina's Deliverance in 1876*. 1935. Reprint, Freeport, New York: Books for Libraries Press, 1970.

Wilson, Charles Reagan. *Baptized in Blood: The Religion of the Lost Cause, 1865–1900*. Athens: University of Georgia Press, 1980.

Wolfe, Michael C. *The Abundant Life Prevails: Religious Traditions of St. Helena Island*. Waco, Texas: Baylor University Press, 2000.

Zipf, Karen L. "'Among These American Heathens': Congregational Missionaries and African American Evangelicals during Reconstruction, 1865–1878." *North Carolina Historical Review* (April 1997): 111–34.

———. "'The Whites Shall Rule the Land or Die': Gender, Race, and Class in North Carolina Reconstruction Politics." *Journal of Southern History* 65 (August 1999): 499–534.

POPULISM, PROGRESSIVISM, AND SOUTHERN RELIGIOUS RADICALISM

Adams, Frank T. *James Dombrowski: An American Heretic, 1877–1983*. Knoxville: University of Tennessee Press, 1992.

Anderson, James D. *The Education of Blacks in the South, 1865–1935*. Chapel Hill: University of North Carolina Press, 1988.

Bailey, Josiah William. "Case for the South." *Forum* 31 (April 1901): 225–30.

———. "The Political Treatment of the Drink Evil." *South Atlantic Quarterly* 6 (1907): 109–24.

Bederman, Gail. *Manliness and Civilization: A Cultural History of Gender and Race in the United States, 1880–1917*. Chicago: University of Chicago Press, 1995.

Bode, Frederick A. *Protestantism and the New South: North Carolina Baptists and Methodists in Political Crisis, 1894–1903*. Charlottesville: University Press of Virginia, 1975.

Boyd, Richard. *The Separate or "Jim Crow" Car Laws, or Legislative Enactments of Fourteen Southern States*. Nashville: National Baptist Publishing Board, 1909.

Bratton, Theodore DuBose. *Wanted—Leaders! A Study of Negro Development*. New York: Presiding Bishop and Council, Department of Missions and Church Extension, 1922.

Brunner, Edmund. *Church Life in the Rural South*. New York: G. H. Doran Co., 1923.

Bryan, G. McLeod. *Dissenter in the Baptist Southland: Fifty Years in the Career of William Wallace Finlator*. Macon, Georgia: Mercer University Press, 1985.

Burbank, Garin. *When Farmers Voted Red: The Gospel of Socialism in the Oklahoma Countryside, 1910–1924*. Westport, Connecticut: Greenwood Press, 1976.

Campbell, Will D. *Brother to a Dragonfly*. New York: Seabury Press, 1977.

———. *Forty Acres and a Goat: A Memoir*. Atlanta: Peachtree Publishers, 1986.

Carey, John J. *Carlyle Marney: A Pilgrim's Progress*. Macon, Georgia: Mercer University Press, 1980.

Cashin, Edward J., and Glenn T. Eskew, eds. *Paternalism in a Southern City: Race, Religion, and Gender in Augusta, Georgia*. Athens: University of Georgia Press, 2001.

Cavalcanti, H. B. "God and Labor in the South: Southern Baptists and the Right to Unionize, 1930–1950." *Journal of Church and State* 40 (Summer 1997): 639–60.

Cloyd, Daniel L. "Prelude to Reform: Political, Economic, and Social Thought of Alabama Baptists, 1877–1900." *Alabama Review* 31 (1978): 48–64.

Compton, Stephen C. "Edgar Gardner Murphy and the Child Labor Movement." *Historical Magazine of the Protestant Episcopal Church* (June 1983): 181–94.

Creech, Joseph. "Righteous Indignation: Religion and Populism in North Carolina, 1886–1906." Ph.D. diss., Notre Dame University, 1999.

Curtis, Susan A. *A Consuming Faith: The Social Gospel and Modern American Culture*. Baltimore: Johns Hopkins University Press, 1991.

Danielson, Leilah. "'In My Extremity I Turned to Gandhi': American Pacifists, Christianity, and Gandhian Nonviolence, 1915–1941." *Church History* 72 (June 2003): 361–88.

DesBrunner, Edmund. *Church Life in the Rural South*. New York: George H. Doran, 1923.

Dittmer, John. *Black Georgia in the Progressive Era, 1900–1920*. Urbana: University of Illinois Press, 1977.

Donahue, Charles Donald. "The Yearning for a Prophetic Southern Culture: A History of the Fellowship of Southern Churchmen, 1934–1963." Ph.D. diss., Union Theological Seminary, 1995.

Doyle, Don H. *Nashville in the New South, 1880–1930*. Knoxville: University of Tennessee Press, 1985.

Dunbar, Anthony P. *Against the Grain: Southern Radicals and Prophets, 1929–1959*. Charlottesville: University Press of Virginia, 1981.

Durr, Virginia. *Outside the Magic Circle: The Autobiography of Virginia Foster Durr*. Edited by Hollinger F. Barnard. Tuscaloosa: University of Alabama Press, 1985.

Dykeman, Wilma, and James Stokely. *Seeds of Southern Change: The Life of Will Alexander*. Chicago: University of Chicago Press, 1962.

Egerton, John. *Speak Now against the Day: The Generation before the Civil Rights Movement in the South*. Chapel Hill: University of North Carolina Press, 1995.

Eighmy, John Lee. *Churches in Cultural Captivity: A History of the Social Attitudes of Southern Baptists*. Edited by Samuel Hill. Knoxville: University of Tennessee Press, 1972.

Ellis, William. *"A Man of Books and a Man of the People": E. Y. Mullins and the Crisis of Moderate Southern Baptist Leadership*. Macon, Georgia: Mercer University Press, 1985.

Fair, Harold Lloyd. "Southern Methodists on Education and Race." Ph.D. diss., Vanderbilt University, 1971.

Flynt, J. Wayne. "Alabama White Protestantism and Labor, 1900–1914." *Alabama Review* 25 (1972): 192–217.

———. "Dissent in Zion: Alabama Baptists and Social Issues, 1900–1914." *Journal of Southern History* 35 (November 1969): 523–42.

Gardner, Charles Spurgeon. *The Ethics of Jesus and Social Progress.* New York: George H. Doran Co., 1914.

Gaston, Paul M. *The New South Creed: A Study in Southern Mythmaking.* New York: Knopf, 1970.

Gavins, Raymond. *The Perils and Prospects of Southern Black Leadership: Gordon Blaine Hancock, 1884–1970.* Durham, North Carolina: Duke University Press, 1977.

Gladney, Margaret Rose, ed. *How Am I To Be Heard: Letters of Lillian Smith.* Chapel Hill: University of North Carolina Press, 1993.

Godshalk, David F. "William J. Northen's Public and Personal Struggles against Lynching." In *Jumpin' Jim Crow: Civil War to Civil Rights,* edited by Jane Dailey, Glenda Elizabeth Gilmore, and Bryant Simon, 140–61. Princeton: Princeton University Press, 2000.

Goode, Richard C. "The Godly Insurrection in Limestone County: Social Gospel, Populism, and Southern Culture in the Late Nineteenth Century." *Religion and American Culture* 3 (Summer 1993): 155–70.

Goodwyn, Lawrence. *The Populist Moment: A Short History of the Agrarian Movement in America.* New York: Oxford University Press, 1979.

Gorrell, Donald K. *The Age of Social Responsibility: The Social Gospel in the Progressive Era, 1900–1920.* Macon, Georgia: Mercer University Press, 1988.

Green, James R. *Grass-Roots Socialism: Radical Movements in the Southwest, 1895–1943.* Baton Rouge: Louisiana State University Press, 1978.

Greenwood, Janette Thomas. *Bittersweet Legacy: The Black and White "Better Classes" in Charlotte, 1850–1910.* Chapel Hill: University of North Carolina Press, 1994.

Gregory, James Noble. *American Exodus: The Dust Bowl Migration and Okie Culture in California.* New York: Oxford University Press, 1989.

Gwaltney, Leslie Lee. *Forty of the Twentieth; or, The First Forty Years of the Twentieth Century.* Birmingham: Birmingham Printing Company, 1940.

Hall, Jacquelyn Dowd. *Revolt against Chivalry: Jessie Daniel Ames and the Women's Campaign against Lynching.* New York: Columbia University Press, 1979.

Hall, Jacquelyn Dowd, et al. *Like a Family: The Making of a Southern Cotton Mill World.* Chapel Hill: University of North Carolina Press, 1987.

Hall, Randal L. *William Louis Poteat: A Leader of the Progressive-Era South.* Lexington: University Press of Kentucky, 2000.

Hamilton, Charles Horace, and William Edward Garnett. *The Role of the Church in Rural Community Life in Virginia.* Blacksburg, Virginia: Virginia Agricultural Experiment Series, 1923.

Harlan, Louis R. *Booker T. Washington: The Making of a Black Leader, 1856–1901.* New York: Oxford University Press, 1972.

———. *Booker T. Washington: The Wizard of Tuskegee, 1901–1915.* New York: Oxford University Press, 1983.

Harper, Keith. *The Quality of Mercy: Southern Baptists and Social Christianity, 1890–1920.* Tuscaloosa: University of Alabama Press, 1996.

Hawkins, Merrill M., Jr. *Will Campbell: Radical Prophet of the South.* Macon, Georgia: Mercer University Press, 1997.

Haygood, Atticus G. *Our Brother in Black: His Freedom and His Future.* 1889. Reprint, Miami: Mnemosyne, 1969.

Horton, Myles. *The Long Haul: An Autobiography.* New York: Doubleday, 1990.

Jordan, Clarence. *The Substance of Faith and Other Cotton Patch Sermons.* Edited by Dallas Lee. New York: Association Press, 1972.

Kelly, Brian. *Race, Class, and Power in the Alabama Coalfields, 1908–1921.* Urbana: University of Illinois Press, 2001.

Kelsey, George D. *Social Ethics among Southern Baptists, 1917–1969.* Metuchen, New Jersey: Scarecrow Press, 1972.

Kester, Howard. *Revolt among the Sharecroppers.* Edited by Alex Lichtenstein. Knoxville: University of Tennessee Press, 1987.

K'Meyer, Tracy Elaine. *Interracialism and Christian Community in the Postwar South: The Story of Koinonia Farm.* Charlottesville: University Press of Virginia, 1997.

Knotts, Alice G. "'Bound by the Spirit, Found on the Journey': The Methodist Women's Campaign for Southern Civil Rights, 1940–1968." Ph.D. diss., Iliff School of Theology, 1989.

Lasch-Quinn, Elisabeth. *Black Neighbors: Race and the Limits of Reform in the American Settlement House Movement, 1890–1945.* Chapel Hill: University of North Carolina Press, 1993.

Link, William A. *The Paradox of Southern Progressivism, 1880–1930.* Chapel Hill: University of North Carolina Press, 1992.

Luker, Ralph. *The Social Gospel in Black and White: American Racial Reform, 1885–1912.* Chapel Hill: University of North Carolina Press, 1991.

———. *A Southern Tradition in Theology and Social Criticism, 1830–1930: The Religious Liberalism and Social Conservatism of James Warley Miles, William Porcher DuBose, and Edgar Gardner Murphy.* New York: Edwin Mellen Press, 1984.

Madison, James H. "Reformers and the Rural Church, 1900–1950." *Journal of American History* 73 (December 1986): 645–98.

Martin, Robert Francis. *Howard Kester and the Struggle for Social Justice in the South, 1904–1977.* Charlottesville: University Press of Virginia, 1991.

Mason, Lucy Randolph. *To Win These Rights: A Personal Story of the CIO in the South.* New York: Harper & Brothers, 1952.

McGlothlin, William J. *A Vital Ministry: The Pastor of Today in the Service of Man.* New York: Fleming H. Revell Co., 1913.

McKelway, Alexander J. "The Atlanta Riots: A Southern White Point of View." *Outlook* 86 (November 3, 1906): 557–62.

———. "The Awakening of the South against Child Labor." *Annals of the American Academy of Political and Social Science* 29 (January 1907): 9–18.

———. "Child Labor in the Southern Cotton Mills." *Annals of the American Academy of Political and Social Science* 27 (January–June 1906): 259–69.

Mebane, George Allen. *"The Negro Problem" As Seen and Discussed by Southern White Men in a Conference at Montgomery, Alabama.* New York: Alliance Publishing, 1900.

Meier, August. *Negro Thought in America, 1880–1915: Racial Ideologies in the Age of Booker T. Washington, 1880–1915.* Ann Arbor: University of Michigan Press, 1963.

Moore, Joanna P. *"In Christ's Stead": Autobiographical Sketches.* Chicago: Women's Baptist Home Mission Society, ca. 1902.

Morton, Nelle. *The Journey Is Home.* Boston: Beacon Press, 1985.

Murphy, Edgar Gardner. *The Basis of Ascendancy: A Discussion of Certain Principles of Public Policy Involved in the Development of the Southern States.* New York: Longmans, Green, and Co., 1909.

———. *Problems of the Present South: A Discussion of Certain of the Education, Industrial, and Political Issues in the Southern States.* New York: Macmillan Co., 1904.

Niebuhr, Reinhold. *Moral Man and Immoral Society: A Study in Ethics and Politics.* New York: C. Scribner's, 1932.

Patton, Randall Lee. "Southern Liberals and the Emergence of the New South, 1938–1950." Ph.D. diss., University of Georgia, 1990.

Pilkington, Charles Kirk. "The Trials of Brotherhood: The Founding of the Commission on Interracial Cooperation." *Georgia Historical Quarterly* 69 (1985): 55–80.

Primer, Ben. *Protestants and American Business Methods.* Ann Arbor: UMI Press, 1979.

Proctor, Henry Hugh. *Between Black and White: Autobiographical Sketches.* Freeport, New York: Books for Libraries Press, 1971.

———. *Up from the South.* Freeport, New York: Books for Libraries Press, 1971.

Pryor, Mark. *Faith, Grace, and Heresy: The Biography of the Rev. Charles M. Jones.* New York: Writer's Press, 2002.

Queen, Edward L., II. *In the South the Baptists Are the Center of Gravity: Southern Baptists and Social Change, 1930–1980.* Brooklyn, New York: Carlson, 1991.

Raper, Arthur F. *The Tragedy of Lynching.* Chapel Hill: University of North Carolina Press, 1933.

Rauschenbusch, Walter. *Christianity and the Social Crisis.* New York: Harper & Row, 1964.

Raybon, S. Paul. "Stick by the Old Paths: An Inquiry into the Southern Baptist Response to Populism." *American Baptist Quarterly* 11 (September 1992): 231–45.

Reed, Linda. *Simple Decency and Common Sense: The Southern Conference Movement, 1938–1963.* Bloomington: Indiana University Press, 1991.

Reich, Steven. "Soldiers of Democracy: Black Texans and the Fight for Citizenship, 1917–1921." *Journal of American History* 82 (March 1996): 1478–1504.

Rouse, Jacqueline Anne. *Lugenia Burns Hope: Black Southern Reformer.* Athens: University of Georgia Press, 1989.

Salmond, John A. "The Fellowship of Southern Churchmen and Interracial Change in the South." *North Carolina Historical Review* 69 (1992): 179–99.

———. *Miss Lucy of the CIO: The Life and Times of Lucy Randolph Mason, 1882–1959.* Athens: University of Georgia Press, 1988.

Scales, T. Laine. *All That Fits a Woman: Training Southern Baptist Women for Charity and Mission, 1907–1926.* Macon, Georgia: Mercer University Press, 2000.

Shepherd, Samuel C. *Avenues of Faith: Shaping the Urban Religious Culture of Richmond, Virginia, 1900–1929.* Tuscaloosa: University of Alabama Press, 2001.

Sledge, Robert Watson. "A History of the Methodist Episcopal Church, South, 1914–1939." Ph.D. diss., University of Texas at Austin, 1972.

Smith, Lillian. *Killers of the Dream*. New York: Norton, 1949.

Snecedor, James G. *Missionary Aspects of Our Negro Population*. Richmond, Virginia: L. D. Sullivan, 1906.

Sosna, Morton. *In Search of the Silent South: Southern Liberals and the Race Issue*. New York: Columbia University Press, 1977.

The Southern Society for the Promotion of the Study of Race Conditions and Problems in the South. *Race Problems of the South: Report of the Proceedings of the First Annual Conference*. Richmond, Virginia: B. F. Johnson, 1900.

Storey, John W. *Texas Baptist Leadership and Social Christianity, 1900–1980*. College Station: Texas A & M University Press, 1986.

Stricklin, David. *A Genealogy of Dissent: Southern Baptist Protest in the Twentieth Century*. Lexington: University Press of Kentucky, 1999.

Sullivan, Patricia. *Days of Hope: Race and Democracy in the New Deal Era*. Chapel Hill: University of North Carolina Press, 1996.

Thompson, James J. *Tried As by Fire: Southern Baptists and the Religious Controversies of the 1920s*. Macon, Georgia: Mercer University Press, 1982.

Valentine, Foy. *A Historical Study of Southern Baptists and Race Relations, 1917–1947*. New York: Arno Press, 1980.

Vinikas, Vincent. "Specters in the Past: The Saint Charles, Arkansas, Lynching of 1904 and the Limits of Historical Inquiry." *Journal of Southern History* 65 (1999): 535–64.

Watson, Larry Jerome. *Evangelical Protestants and the Prohibition Movement in Texas, 1887–1919*. College Station: Texas A & M University Press, 1993.

Weatherford, Willis Duke. *Interracial Cooperation: A Study of the Various Agencies Working in the Field of Social Welfare*. New York: Interracial Committee of the YMCA, 1920.

White, John E. "Prohibition: The New Task and Opportunity of the South." *South Atlantic Quarterly* 7 (April 1908): 130–42.

WOMEN AND RELIGION IN THE SOUTH

Allen, Catherine, B. *A Century to Celebrate: History of Woman's Missionary Union*. Birmingham: Woman's Missionary Union, 1987.

Berkeley, Kathleen C. "'Colored Ladies Also Contributed: Black Women's Activities from Benevolence to Social Welfare, 1865–1896." In *The Web of Southern Social Relations: Women, Family, and Education*, edited by Walter J. Fraser Jr., R. Frank Saunders Jr., and Jon L. Wakelyn. Athens: University of Georgia Press, 1985.

Bendroth, Margaret Lamberts. *Fundamentalism and Gender, 1875 to the Present*. New Haven: Yale University Press, 1993.

Bendroth, Margaret Lamberts, and Virginia Brereton, eds. *Women and Twentieth-Century Protestantism*. Urbana: University of Illinois Press, 2001.

Brereton, Virginia. *From Sin to Salvation: Stories of Women's Conversions, 1800 to the Present*. Bloomington: Indiana University Press, 1991.

Broughton, Virginia. *Twenty Years' Experience of a Missionary*. Chicago: Pony Press, 1907.

Burr, Virginia Ingraham, ed. *The Secret Eye: The Journal of Ella Gertrude Clanton Thomas, 1848–1889*. Chapel Hill: University of North Carolina Press, 1990.

Cobb, Reba, and Betty Pearce McGary, eds. *Folio*. Louisville: Center for Women in Ministry, 1984.

Dayton, Donald, ed. *Holiness Tracts Defending the Ministry of Women.* New York: Garland, 1985.

Deberg, Betty A. *Ungodly Women: Gender and the First Wave of American Fundamentalism.* Minneapolis: Fortress Press, 1990.

Douglas, Ann. *The Feminization of American Culture.* New York: Knopf, 1977.

Dunlap, Leslie Kathrin. "In the Name of the Home: Temperance Women and Southern Grass-Roots Politics, 1873–1933." Ph.D. diss., Northwestern University, 2001.

Faust, Drew Gilpin. *Mothers of Invention: Women of the Slaveholding South in the Civil War.* Chapel Hill: University of North Carolina Press, 1996.

Frederickson, Mary. " 'Each One Is Dependent on the Other': Southern Churchwomen, Racial Reform, and the Process of Transformation, 1880–1940." In *Visible Women: New Essays on American Activism,* edited by Nancy A. Hewitt and Suzanne Lebsock, 296–324. Urbana: University of Illinois Press, 1993.

———. "Shaping a New Society: Methodist Women and Industrial Reform in the South, 1880–1940." In *Women in New Worlds: Historical Perspectives on the Wesleyan Tradition.* Vol. 1, edited by Hilah F. Thomas and Rosemary Skinner Keller, 345–61. Nashville: Abingdon, 1981.

Friedman, Jean E. *The Enclosed Garden: Women and Community in the Evangelical South, 1830–1900.* Chapel Hill: University of North Carolina Press, 1985.

Gilmore, Glenda Elizabeth. *Gender and Jim Crow: Women and the Politics of White Supremacy in North Carolina, 1896–1920.* Chapel Hill: University of North Carolina Press, 1996.

Green, Elna L. *Southern Strategies: Southern Women and the Woman Suffrage Question.* Chapel Hill: University of North Carolina Press, 1997.

Green, Elna L., ed. *Before the New Deal: Social Welfare in the South, 1830–1930.* Athens: University of Georgia Press, 1999.

Hall, Jacquelyn Dowd. *Revolt against Chivalry: Jesse Daniel Ames and the Women's Campaign against Lynching.* New York: Columbia University Press, 1979.

Hammond, Lily Hardy. *In Black and White: An Interpretation of Southern Life.* Chicago: Fleming H. Revell, 1914.

———. *Southern Women and Racial Adjustment.* Lynchburg: J. P. Bell Company, 1917.

Hardesty, Nancy A. " 'The Best Temperance Organization in the Land': Southern Methodists and the W.C.T.U. in Georgia." *Methodist History* 28 (April 1990): 187–94.

Haskin, Sara. *Women and Missions in the Methodist Episcopal Church, South.* Nashville: Publishing House of the MECS, 1920.

Hassey, Janette. *No Time for Silence: Evangelical Women in Public Ministry Around the Turn of the Century.* Grand Rapids, Michigan: Academic Books, 1986.

Heck, Fannie E. S. *In Royal Service: The Mission Work of Southern Baptist Women.* Richmond: Educational Department, Foreign Mission Boards, Southern Baptist Convention, 1913.

Hobbs, June Hadden. *I Sing for I Cannot Be Silent: The Feminization of American Hymnody, 1870–1920.* Pittsburgh: University of Pittsburgh Press, 1997.

Hunter, Tera W. *To 'Joy My Freedom: Southern Black Women's Lives and Labors after the Civil War.* Cambridge, Massachusetts: Harvard University Press, 1997.

Keller, Rosemary Skinner, Louise L. Queen, and Hilah F. Thomas, eds. *Women in New Worlds: Historical Perspectives on the Wesleyan Tradition.* Nashville: Abingdon Press, 1982.

Knotts, Alice G. *Fellowship of Love: Methodist Women Changing American Racial Attitudes, 1920–1968*. Nashville: Kingswood Books, 1996.

LeGuin, Charles A., ed. *A Home-Concealed Woman: The Diaries of Magnolia Wynn LeGuin, 1901–1913*. Athens: University of Georgia Press, 1990.

Lumpkin, Katharine Du Pre. *The Making of a Southerner*. New York: Knopf, 1946.

MacDonnell, Mrs. R. W. *Belle Harris Bennett: Her Life Work*. 1928. Reprint, New York: Garland Publishing, 1987.

Martin, Patricia Summerlin. "Hidden Work: Baptist Women in Texas, 1880–1920." Ph.D. diss., Rice University, 1982.

McAfee, Sara Jane. *History of the Woman's Missionary Society in the Colored Methodist Episcopal Church*. Jackson, Mississippi: C.M.E. Publishing House, 1934.

McDowell, John Patrick. *The Social Gospel in the South: The Woman's Home Mission Movement in the Methodist Episcopal Church, South, 1886–1939*. Baton Rouge: Louisiana State University Press, 1982.

Newman, Harvey C. "The Role of Women in Atlanta's Churches, 1865–1906." *Atlanta Historical Quarterly* 24 (1980): 17–30.

Olson, Lynne. *Freedom's Daughters: The Unsung Heroines of the Civil Rights Movement from 1830 to 1970*. New York: Scribner, 2001.

Rice, Sarah. *He Included Me: The Autobiography of Sarah Rice*. Edited by Louise Westlin. Athens: University of Georgia Press, 1989.

Ruether, Rosemary Radford, and Rosemary S. Keller, eds. *Women and Religion in America*. Vol. 3, 1900–1968. New York: Harper & Row, 1986.

Salem, Dorothy C. *To Better Our World: Black Women in Organized Reform, 1890–1920*. Brooklyn, New York: Carlson, 1990.

Scott, Anne Firor. *Natural Allies: Women's Associations in American History*. Urbana: University of Illinois Press, 1991.

———. *The Southern Lady: From Pedestal to Politics*. Chicago: University of Chicago Press, 1970.

———. "Women, Religion, and Social Change in the South, 1830–1930." In *Religion and the Solid South*, edited by Samuel S. Hill, 92–121. Nashville: Abingdon Press, 1972.

Shadron, Virginia. "Out of Our Homes: The Woman's Rights Movement in the Methodist Episcopal Church, South, 1890–1918." M.A. thesis, Emory University, 1976.

Shankman, Arnold M. "Dorothy Tilly, Civil Rights and the Methodist Church." *Methodist History* 18 (January 1980): 95–108.

Sims, Anastatia. *The Power of Femininity in the New South: Women's Organizations and Politics in North Carolina, 1880–1930*. Columbia: University of South Carolina Press, 1997.

Sorrill, Bobbie. *Annie Armstrong: Dreamer in Action*. Nashville: Broadman Press, 1984.

Stevens, Thelma. *Legacy for the Future: The History of Christian Social Relations in the Women's Division of Christian Service, 1940–1968*. Cincinnati: Women's Division, Board of Global Ministries, United Methodist Church, 1976.

Thomas, Mary Martha. *The New Woman in Alabama: Social Reforms and Suffrage, 1890–1920*. Tuscaloosa: University of Alabama Press, 1992.

Turner, Elizabeth Hayes. *Women, Culture, and Community: Religion and Reform in Galveston, 1880–1920*. New York: Oxford University Press, 1997.

Woosley, Louisa. *Shall Woman Preach? or, The Question Answered.* Caneyville, Kentucky: Self-published, 1891.

FOLK RELIGION, MUSIC, AND WORSHIP TRADITIONS OF THE SOUTH

B. "Inside Southern Cabins, Georgia—no. 1." *Harper's Weekly*, November 13, 1880, 733–34.

B. "Inside Southern Cabins II—Georgia." *Harper's Weekly*, November 20, 1880, 749–50.

B. "Inside Southern Cabins III—Charleston, South Carolina." *Harper's Weekly*, November 27, 1880, 765–66.

Barton, William Eleazar. "Recent Negro Melodies." *New England Magazine*, February 1899, 707–19.

Blackwell, Lois S. *The Wings of the Dove: The Story of Gospel Music in America.* Norfolk, Virginia: The Donning Co., 1978.

Bliss, P. P., and Ira Sankey. *Gospel Hymns and Sacred Songs.* New York: Biglow and Main, 1875.

Boyd, Richard H., and William Posborough, eds. *The National Baptist Hymnal: Arranged for Use in Churches, Sunday Schools, and Young People's Societies.* 6th ed. Nashville: National Baptist Publishing Board, 1903.

Boyer, Clarence Horace. *How Sweet the Sound: The Golden Age of Gospel.* Washington, D.C.: Elliott & Clark, 1995.

Bragg, Rick. *All Over But the Shoutin'.* New York: Vintage Books, 1998.

Brewer, J. Mason, ed. *American Negro Folklore.* Chicago: Quadrangle Books, 1968.

Bruce, Dickson D. *And They All Sang Hallelujah: Plain-Folk Camp-Meeting Religion, 1800–1845.* Knoxville: University of Tennessee Press, 1974.

Campbell, Gavin James. "Music and the Making of a Jim Crow Culture." Ph.D. diss., University of North Carolina, Chapel Hill, 1999.

———. "'Old Can Be Used Instead of New': Shape-Note Music and the Crisis of Modernity in the New South, 1880–1920." *Journal of American Folklore* 110 (1997): 169–88.

Chireau, Yvonne. *Black Magic: Religion and the African American Conjuring Tradition.* Berkeley: University of California Press, 2003.

Cobb, Buell E. *The Sacred Harp: A Tradition and Its Music.* Athens: University of Georgia Press, 1978.

"Colored Revivals in Virginia." *Leslie's Illustrated Newspaper*, September 12, 1885, 54.

Coffin, Levi. *Unwritten History.* 1919. Reprint, New York: Negro Universities Press, 1968.

Comer, Carl. *Stars Fell on Alabama.* New York: The Literary Guild, 1934.

Cone, James H. *The Spirituals and the Blues: An Interpretation.* New York: Seabury Press, 1972.

Cooley, Rossa B. *School Acres: An Adventure in Rural Education.* 1930. Reprint, Westport, Connecticut: Greenwood Press, 1970.

Cusic, Donald. *The Sound of Light: A History of Gospel Music.* Bowling Green, Ohio: Bowling Green State University Popular Press, 1990.

Djedje, Jacquline Cogdell. *American Black Spiritual and Gospel Songs from Southeast Georgia: A Comparative Study.* Los Angeles: Center for Afro-American Studies, UCLA, 1978.

Dorgan, Howard. *The Airwaves of Zion: Radio and Religion in Appalachia.* Knoxville: University of Tennessee Press, 1993.

———. *Giving Glory to God in Appalachia: Worship Practices of Six Baptist Sub-Denominations.* Knoxville: University of Tennessee Press, 1987.

Dundes, Alan, ed. *Mother Wit from the Laughing Barrel: Readings in the Interpretation of Afro-American Folklore.* New York: Garland, 1973.

Ellington, Charles Linwood. "The Sacred Harp Tradition of the South: Its Origin and Evolution." Ph.D. diss., Florida, State University, 1969; also available Ann Arbor: University Microfilms, 1970.

Ellis, James B. *Blazing the Gospel Trail.* Plainfield, New Jersey: Logos International, 1976.

Epstein, Dena J. *Sinful Tunes and Spirituals: Black Folk Music to the Civil War.* Urbana: University of Illinois Press, 1977.

F., C. H. "Negro Worship and Music: Notes of a Foot Traveler—The Influences of a Black Parson's Sermon—the Remarkable Music of a Colored Congregation—Expression of Religious Sentiments of the Race." *New York Times,* February 25, 1877, 5.

"Fetish Follies." *American Missionary Magazine* 19, n.s. (January 1875): 17–18.

Fisher, Miles Mark. *Negro Slave Songs in the United States.* Ithaca: Cornell University Press, 1953.

Gage, Frances D. "Religious Exercises of the Negroes of the Sea Islands." *Independent,* January 15, 1863.

Giggie, John. "'When Jesus Handed Me a Ticket': Images of Railroad Travel and Spiritual Transformations among African Americans, 1865–1917." In *The Visual Cultures of American Religions,* edited by David Morgan and Salley Promey, 249–66. Berkeley: University of California Press, 2001.

Gillespie, Paul F., et al., eds. *Foxfire 7: Ministers and Church Members, Revivals and Baptisms, Shaped-Note and Gospel Singing, Faith Healing and Camp Meetings, Foot Washing, Snake Handling.* New York: Anchor Books, 1973.

Glenn, R. A., and Aldine Silliman Kieffer, eds. *New Melodies of Praise: A Collection of New Tunes and Hymns for the Sabbath School and Praise Meeting.* Dayton, Virginia: Ruebush, Kieffer, 1877.

Goldsmith, Peter David. *When I Rise Cryin' Holy: African-American Denominationalism on the Georgia Coast.* New York: AMS Press, 1989.

Goff, James R., Jr. *Close Harmony: A History of Southern Gospel.* Chapel Hill: University of North Carolina Press, 2002.

Guralnick, Peter. *Last Train to Memphis: The Rise of Elvis Presley.* Boston: Little, Brown, and Co., 1994.

Hale, Grace Elizabeth. *Making Whiteness: The Culture of Segregation in the South, 1890–1940.* New York: Pantheon, 1998.

Handy, William C. *Father of the Blues: An Autobiography.* Edited by Arna Bontemps. New York: MacMillan, 1941.

Harris, J. William. *Deep Souths: Delta, Piedmont, and Sea Island Society in the Age of Segregation.* Baltimore: Johns Hopkins University Press, 2001.

Harris, Michael W. *The Rise of Gospel Blues: The Music of Thomas Andrew Dorsey in the Urban Church.* New York: Oxford University Press, 1992.

Hatcher, William. *John Jasper, the Unmatched Negro Philosopher and Preacher.* New York: F. H. Revell, 1908.

Hood, Robert. "Ghosts and Spirits in Afro Cultures: Morrison and Wilson." *Anglican Theological Review* 73 (Summer 1991): 297–313.

Hurston, Zora Neale. *Dust Tracks on a Road: An Autobiography*. Philadelphia: Lippincott, 1941.

————. *Go Gator and Muddy the Water: Writings by Zora Neale Hurston from the Federal Writers' Project*. Edited by Pamela Bordelon. New York: W. W. Norton, 1999.

————. *The Sanctified Church*. Berkeley: Turtle Island, 1981.

Ingle, A. L. Bassett. "Religion in the South: A Negro Revival in Virginia." *Frank Leslie's Illustrated Newspaper*, August 9, 1873, 346–47.

"Inside Southern Cabins IV—Alabama, Agricultural Negroes." *Harper's Weekly*, December 24, 1880, 781–82.

Jackson, Bruce, ed. *The Negro and His Folklore in Nineteenth-Century Periodicals*. Austin: University of Texas Press, 1967.

Jackson, George Pullen, ed. *White and Negro Spirituals*. New York: Augustin, 1943.

————. *White Spirituals in the Southern Uplands*. 1933. Reprint, New York: Dover Publications, 1965.

Jackson, Irene. *More Than Dancing: Essays on Afro-American Music and Musicians*. Westport, Connecticut: Greenwood Press, 1985.

Jackson, Jerma. *Singing in My Soul: African American Gospel Music in a Secular Age*. Chapel Hill: University of North Carolina Press, 2004.

Jackson, Mahalia. *Movin' on Up*. New York: Hawthorn Books, 1966.

Johnson, Charles S. *Shadow of the Plantation*. Chicago: University of Chicago Press, 1934.

Johnson, Clifton H., ed. *God Struck Me Dead: Religious Conversion Experiences and Autobiographies of Ex-Slaves*. Philadelphia: Pilgrim Press, 1969.

Joyner, Charles W. *Shared Traditions: Southern History and Folk Culture*. Urbana: University of Illinois Press, 1999.

Kempton, Arthur. *Boogaloo: The Quintessence of American Popular Music*. New York: Pantheon Books, 2003.

Kilham, Elizabeth. "Sketches in Color." *Putnam's Monthly* 5 (March 1870): 304–11.

Lambert, Byron Cecil. *The Rise of the Anti-Mission Baptists: Sources and Leaders, 1800–1840*. New York: Arno Press, 1980.

Lawton, Samuel Miller. *The Religious Life of South Carolina Coastal and Sea Island Negroes*. Nashville: George Peabody College for Teachers, 1939.

Levine, Lawrence. *Black Culture and Black Consciousness: Afro-American Folk Thought from Slavery to Freedom*. New York: Oxford University Press, 1977.

Lomax, Alan. *The Land Where the Blues Began*. New York: New Press, 2002.

Lornell, Kip. *Happy in the Service of the Lord: Afro-American Gospel Quartets in Memphis*. Urbana: University of Illinois Press, 1995.

Malone, Bill C. *Country Music, U.S.A.* Austin: University of Texas Press, 1985.

————. *Singing Cowboys and Musical Mountaineers: Southern Culture and the Roots of Country Music*. Athens: University of Georgia Press, 1993.

————. *Southern Music, American Music*. Lexington: University Press of Kentucky, 1979.

Marshall, Howard Wight. "'Keep on the Sunny Side of Life': Pattern and Religious Expression in Bluegrass Gospel Music." *New York Folklore Quarterly* 30 (1974): 3–43.

McCauley, Deborah Vansau. *Appalachian Mountain Religion: A History*. Urbana: University of Illinois Press, 1995.

Mitchell, Henry H. *Black Belief: Folk Beliefs of Blacks in America and West Africa.* New York: Harper & Row, 1975.

Montell, William Lynwood. *Singing the Glory Down: Amateur Music in South Central Kentucky, 1900–1990.* Lexington: University Press of Kentucky, 1991.

National Baptist Convention Sunday School Board. *Gospel Pearls.* Nashville: National Baptist Convention, 1921.

"Negro Dances in Arkansas." *Journal of American Folklore* 1 (April–June 1888): 83.

Odum, Howard W., and Guy B. Johnson. "Religious Folk Songs of the Southern Negro." *American Journal of Religious Psychology and Education* 3 (July 1909): 265–365.

Oliver, Paul. *Songsters and Saints: Vocal Traditions on Race Records.* New York: Cambridge University Press, 1984.

Ownby, Ted. *Subduing Satan: Religion, Recreation, and Manhood in the Rural South, 1865–1920.* Chapel Hill: University of North Carolina Press, 1990.

Palmer, Robert. *Deep Blues.* New York: Penguin, 1977.

Parrish, Lydia A. *Slave Songs of the Georgia Sea Islands.* New York: Creative Age Press, 1942.

Patterson, Beverly Bush. *The Sound of the Dove: Singing in Appalachian Primitive Baptist Churches.* Urbana: University of Illinois Press, 1995.

Peacock, James L., and Ruel W. Tyson. *Pilgrims of Paradox: Calvinism and Experience among the Primitive Baptists of the Blue Ridge.* Washington: Smithsonian Institution Press, 1989.

Pinkston, Alfred Adolphus. "Lined Hymns, Spirituals, and the Associated Lifestyle of Rural Black People in the United States." Ph.D. diss., University of Miami, 1975.

Pitts, Walter. *Old Ship of Zion: The Afro-Baptist Ritual in the African Diaspora.* New York: Oxford University Press, 1993.

Powdermaker, Hortense. *After Freedom: A Cultural Study in the Deep South.* New York: Viking, 1939.

Rawick, George P., ed. *The American Slave: A Composite Autobiography.* 41 vols. Westport, Connecticut: Greenwood Press, 1972–79.

Reagon, Bernice Johnson. *If You Don't Go, Don't Hinder Me: The African American Sacred Song Tradition.* Lincoln: University of Nebraska Press, 2001.

——, ed. *We'll Understand It Better By and By: Pioneering African American Gospel Composers.* Washington, D.C.: Smithsonian Institution Press, 1992.

Ricks, George Robinson. "Some Aspects of the Religious Music of the United States Negro: An Ethnomusiological Study with Special Emphasis on the Gospel Tradition." Ph.D. diss., Northwestern University, 1960.

Robinson, T. L. "The Colored People in the United States: In the South." *Leisure Hour* 38 (1889): 54–59.

Rosenbaum, Art. *Shout Because You're Free: The African-American Ring Shout Tradition in Coastal Georgia.* Athens: University of Georgia Press, 1998.

Rosenberg, Bruce A. *The Art of the American Folk Preacher.* New York: Oxford University Press, 1970.

Shapiro, Henry D. *Appalachia on Our Mind: The Southern Mountains and Mountaineers in American Consciousness, 1870–1920.* Chapel Hill: University of North Carolina Press, 1978.

Siegfried, W. D. *A Winter in the South, and Work Among the Freedmen.* Newark: n.p., 1870.

Sizer, Sandra S. *Gospel Hymns and Social Religion: The Rhetoric of Nineteenth-Century Revivalism*. Philadelphia: Temple University Press, 1978.

Snyder, Howard. "Plantation Pictures II: The Ordination of Charlie." *Atlantic Monthly* 127 (March 1921): 338–42.

———. "A Plantation Revival Service." *Yale Review* 10, n.s. (October 1920): 168–80.

Sobel, Mechal. *Trabelin' On: The Slave Journey to an Afro-Baptist Faith*. Westport, Connecticut: Greenwood Press, 1979.

Spencer, Jon Michael. *Black Hymnody: A Hymnological History of the African-American Church*. Knoxville: University of Tennessee Press, 1992.

———. *Blues and Evil*. Knoxville: University of Tennessee Press, 1993.

———. *Protest and Praise: The Sacred Music of Black Religion*. Minneapolis: Fortress Press, 1990.

Stowe, Harriet Beecher. "A Negro Prayer-Meeting—Letter from Florida." Pts. 1 and 2. *Christian Watchman and Reflector*, April 18, 1867, 1; May 9, 1867, 1.

Stuckey, Sterling. *Slave Culture: Nationalist Theory and the Foundations of Black America*. New York: Oxford University Press, 1987.

Terrill, Thomas E., and Jerrold Hirsch, eds. *Such as Us: Southern Voices of the Thirties*. Chapel Hill: University of North Carolina Press, 1978.

Titon, Jeff Todd. *Powerhouse for God: Speech, Chant, and Song in an Appalachian Baptist Church*. Austin: University of Texas Press, 1998.

Towne, Laura M. *Letters and Diary of Laura M. Towne: Written from the Sea Islands of South Carolina, 1862–1884*. Edited by Rupert Sargent Holland. Cambridge: Riverside Press, 1912.

Tullos, Allen. *Habits of Industry: White Culture and the Transformation of the Carolina Piedmont*. Chapel Hill: University of North Carolina Press, 1989.

Walker, Sheila S. *Ceremonial Spirit Possession in Africa and Afro-America: Forms, Meanings, and Functional Significance for Individuals and Social Groups*. Leiden: Brill, 1972.

Walker, Wyatt T. *"Somebody's Calling My Name": Black Sacred Music and Social Change*. Valley Forge, Pennsylvania: Judson Press, 1979.

Waterbury, M. *Seven Years among the Freedmen*. 3rd ed. Chicago: T. B. Arnold, 1893.

Waters, Donald J., ed. *Strange Ways and Sweet Dreams: Afro-American Folklore from the Hampton Institute*. Boston: G. K. Hall, 1983.

Wayman, Lilli B. Chace. "Colored Churches and Schools in the South." *New England Magazine* 3, n.s. (February 1891): 785–96.

White, B. F., and E. J. King, eds. *The Sacred Harp*. Facsimile of 3rd ed., 1859. Reprint, Nashville: Broadman Press, 1968.

White, Charley. *No Quittin' Sense*. Austin: University of Texas Press, 1969.

Wilson, Charles Reagan. *Judgment and Grace in Dixie: Southern Faiths from Faulkner to Elvis*. Athens: University of Georgia Press, 1995.

———. "William Faulkner and the Southern Religious Culture." In *Faulkner and Religion*, edited by Doreen Fowler and Ann Abadie, 21–43. Jackson: University Press of Mississippi, 1991.

Wilson, Charles Reagan, and William Ferris, eds. *Encyclopedia of Southern Culture*. Chapel Hill: University of North Carolina Press, 1989.

Winston, Celia M. "Genuine Negro Melodies—Weird Hymnology of the Colored People of the South." *New York Times*, August 8, 1887, 6.

Wolfe, Michael C. *The Abundant Life Prevails: Religious Traditions of Saint Helena Island.* Waco, Texas: Baylor University Press, 2000.

Wyatt-Brown, Bertram. "The Anti-Mission Movement in the Jacksonian South: A Study in Regional Folk Culture." *Journal of Southern History* 36 (November 1970): 501–29.

Yoder, Don. "Toward a Definition of Folk Religion." *Western Folklore Quarterly* 33 (1974): 2–15.

Young, Alan. *Woke Me up This Morning: Black Gospel Singers and the Gospel Life.* Jackson: University Press of Mississippi, 1997.

HOLINESS-PENTECOSTALISM IN THE SOUTH

Alexander, David. "Bishop King: The Early Years." *Legacy* 3 (Winter 1996–97): 1–3.

Anderson, Robert M. *Vision of the Disinherited: The Making of American Pentecostalism.* Rev. ed. New York: Oxford University Press, 1999.

Angelou, Maya. *I Know Why the Caged Bird Sings.* New York: Random House, 1969.

Apostolic Overcoming Holy Church of God. *Discipline and Doctrine of the Apostolic Overcoming Church of God.* Birmingham: Church Publishing House, 1972.

Barfoot, Charles H., and Gerald T. Sheppard. "Prophetic Vs. Priestly Religion: The Changing Role of Women Clergy in Classical Pentecostal Churches." *Review of Religious Research* 22 (September 1980): 2–17.

Benson, John T. *A History 1898–1915 of the Pentecostal Mission, Inc. Nashville, Tennessee.* Nashville: Trevecca Press, 1977.

Best, Felton O. "Loosing the Women: African-American Women and Leadership in the Pentecostal Church, 1890–Present." Unpublished paper in Society for Pentecostal Studies Papers, Flower Pentecostal Heritage Center, Assemblies of God Archives, Springfield, Mo.

Blumhofer, Edith L. *Aimee Semple McPherson: Everybody's Sister.* Grand Rapids, Michigan: Eerdmans, 1993.

———. "The 'Overcoming' Life: A Study in the Origins of Pentecostalism." In *Reckoning with the Past: Historical Essays on American Evangelicalism from the Institute for the Study of American Evangelicals,* edited by D. G. Hart, 289–305. Grand Rapids: Baker Books, 1995.

———. *"Pentecost in My Soul": Exploration in the Meaning of Pentecostal Experience in the Early Assemblies of God.* Springfield, Missouri: Gospel Publishing House, 1989.

———. *Restoring the Faith: The Assemblies of God, Pentecostalism, and American Culture.* Urbana: University of Illinois Press, 1993.

Boland, J. M. *The Problem of Methodism: Being a Review of the Residue Theory of Regeneration and the Second Change Theory of Sanctification; and the Philosophy of Christian Perfection.* Nashville: Publishing House of the Methodist Episcopal Church, South, 1888.

Brasher, John Lakin. *Glimpses: Some Personal Glimpses of Holiness Preachers Whom I Have Known, and with Whom I Have Labored in Evangelism, Who Have Answered to Their Names in the Roll Call of the Skies.* Cincinnati: Revivalist Press, 1954.

Brasher, John Lawrence. *The Sanctified South: John Lakin Brasher and the Holiness Movement.* Urbana: University of Illinois Press, 1994.

Britton, Francis M. *Pentecostal Truth*. Royston, Georgia: Publishing House of the Pentecostal Holiness Church, 1919.

Butler, Anthea. "A Peculiar Synergy: Matriarchy and the Church of God in Christ." Ph.D. diss., Vanderbilt University, 2001.

Cagle, Mary Lee. *Life and Work of Mary Lee Cagle: An Autobiography*. Kansas City, Missouri: Nazarene Publishing House, 1928.

Campbell, Joseph E. *The Pentecostal Holiness Church, 1898–1948: Its Background and History*. Franklin Springs, Georgia: Publishing House of the Pentecostal Holiness Church, 1951.

Carradine, Beverly. *Sanctification*. Nashville: Publishing House of the Methodist Episcopal Church, South, 1891.

Church of God. *The Book of Doctrines, 1903–1970: Issued in the Interest of the Church of God*. Huntsville, Alabama: Church of God Publishing House, 1970.

Church of God Publishing House. *Book of Minutes: A Compiled History of the Work of the General Assemblies of the Church of God*. Cleveland: Church of God Publishing House, 1922.

Clark, William A. "Sanctification in Negro Religion." *Social Forces* 15 (October 1936): 544–51.

Clemmons, Ithiel C. *Bishop C. H. Mason and the Roots of the Church of God in Christ*. Bakersfield, Calif.: Pneuma Publishing, 1996.

Conkin, Paul. "Evangelicals, Fugitives, and Hillbillies: Tennessee's Impact on American National Culture." In *Tennessee History: The Land, the People, and the Culture*, edited by Carroll Van West, 287–322. Knoxville: University of Tennessee Press, 1998.

Conn, Charles W., ed. *The Evangel Reader: Selections from the Church of God, Evangel, 1910–1958*. Cleveland, Tennessee: Pathway Press, 1958.

———. *Like a Mighty Army Moves the Church of God, 1886–1955*. Cleveland: Church of God Publishing House, 1955.

The Constitution Government and General Decree Book of the Church of the Living God, the Pillar and Ground of the Truth, Inc. Chattanooga: The New and Living Way Publishing Co., n.d.

Crews, Mickey. *The Church of God: A Social History*. Knoxville: University of Tennessee Press, 1990.

Cross, James A., ed. *Healing in the Church*. Cleveland, Tennessee: Pathway Press, 1962.

Dayton, Donald W., ed. *Holiness Tracts Defending the Ministry of Women*. New York: Garland, 1985.

Discipline of the Fire Baptized Holiness Church of God of the Americas. Atlanta: Church Publishing House, by the Fuller Press, 1962.

Drake, Finis Jennings. *The Truth about Sin and Sanctification*. Bristol, Tennessee: Self-published, 1946.

Eason, James H. *Sanctification vs. Fanaticism*. Nashville: National Baptist Publishing Board, 1899.

Frodsham, Stanley Howard. *"With Signs Following": The Story of the Latter-Day Pentecostal Revival*. Springfield, Missouri: Gospel Publishing House, 1926.

Godbey, William Baxter. *Autobiography*. Cincinnati: God's Revivalist Office, 1909.

———. *Baptism of the Holy Ghost*. Greensboro, North Carolina: Apostolic Messenger Office, 1910.

Goff, Florence. *Fifty Years on the Battlefield for God: Being a Sketch of the Life of Rev. J. A. Hodges, Coupled with Some of the Lord's Dealings with H. H. Goff and Wife, Evangelists of the Cape Fear Conference of the Free Will Baptist Church*. Falcon, North Carolina: Copy in Pentecostal Holiness Church Archives, n.d.

Goff, James R., Jr. *Fields White unto Harvest: Charles F. Parham and the Missionary Origins of Pentecostalism*. Fayetteville: University of Arkansas Press, 1988.

Gohr, Glenn. "William Jethro Walthall and the Holiness Baptist Churches of Southwestern Arkansas." *Assemblies of God Heritage* (Fall 1992): 15–20.

———. "William Jethro Walthall and the Holiness Baptist Churches of Southwestern Arkansas United with the Assemblies of God." *Assemblies of God Heritage* (Winter 1992–93): 16–19, 30.

Goss, Howard A. *The Winds of God: The Story of Early Pentecostal Days (1901–1914) in the Life of Howard A. Goss*. New York: Comet Press Books, 1958.

Harrell, David Edwin, Jr. *Oral Roberts: An American Life*. Bloomington: Indiana University Press, 1985.

———. *White Sects and Black Men in the Recent South*. Nashville: Vanderbilt University Press, 1971.

Haynes, B. F. *Tempest-Tossed on Methodist Seas; or, A Sketch of My Life*. Louisville: Pentecostal Publishing Company, 1921.

History and Formative Years of the Church of God in Christ with Excerpts from the Life and Works of Its Founder—Bishop C. H. Mason. Memphis: Church of God in Christ Publishing House, 1969.

Holmes, N. J. *The Baptism by the Spirit, the Baptism by Christ, and Other Topics*. Greenville, South Carolina: Holmes Bible College, 1952.

———. *Life Sketches and Sermons*. Royston, Georgia: Press of the Pentecostal Holiness Church, 1920.

Hunter, Harold. "Spirit-Baptism and the 1896 Revival in Cherokee County, North Carolina." *Pneuma: The Journal of the Society for Pentecostal Studies* 5 (Fall 1983): 1–17.

Ingersol, Robert Stanley. "Burden of Dissent: Mary Lee Cagle and the Southern Holiness Movement." Ph.D., Duke University, 1989.

Jacobs, Claude F., and Andrew J. Kaslow. *The Spiritual Churches of New Orleans: Origins, Beliefs, and Rituals of an African-American Religion*. Knoxville: University of Tennessee Press, 1991.

Jernigan, C. B. *Entire Sanctification*. Kansas City: Nazarene Publishing House, n.d.

———. *Pioneer Days of the Holiness Movement in the Southwest*. Kansas City, Missouri: Pentecostal Nazarene Publishing House, 1919.

Jones, Charles Edwin. *Black Holiness: A Guide to the Study of Black Participation in Wesleyan Perfectionist and Glossolalic Pentecostal Movements*. Metuchen, New Jersey: American Theological Library Association and Scarecrow Press, 1987.

———. "Perfectionist Persuasion: A Social Profile of the National Holiness Movement within American Methodism, 1876–1930." Ph.D. diss., University of Wisconsin, 1968.

Jones, Charles Price. *The Work of the Holy Spirit in the Churches*. Jackson, Mississippi: n.p., 1896.

Kossie, Karen Lynell. "The Move Is On: African American Pentecostal-Charismatics in the Southwest." Ph.D. diss., Rice University, 1998.

Lawless, Elaine J. *God's Peculiar People: Women's Voices and Folk Tradition in a Pentecostal Church.* Lexington: University Press of Kentucky, 1988.

Lovett, Leonard. "Perspective on the Black Origins of the Contemporary Pentecostal Movement." *Journal of the Interdenominational Theological Center* 1 (Fall 1973): 36–49.

MacRobert, Ian. *The Black Roots and White Racism of Early Pentecostalism in the USA.* New York: St. Martin's Press, 1988.

Mason, E. W. *The Man . . . Charles Harrison Mason.* Published by the Author Elsie W. Mason, 1979.

Mason, Elsie, ed. *From the Beginning of Bishop C. H. Mason and the Early Pioneers of the Church of God in Christ.* Memphis: Church of God in Christ, 1991.

Mason, Mary. *The History and Life Work of Bishop C. H. Mason.* N.p., 1924.

McCulloch, George. *The Holiness Movement in Texas.* Ennis, Texas: J. H. Padgett, n.d.

McHelhany, Gary D. "Fire in the Pines: A History of the Assemblies of God in Mississippi, 1900–1936." M.A. thesis, Mississippi State University, 1992.

Michael, David. *Telling the Story: Black Pentecostals in the Church of God.* Cleveland, Tennessee: Pathway Press, 2000.

Nelson, Doug. "For Such a Time as This: The Story of Bishop William J. Seymour and the Azusa Street Revival, A Search for Pentecostal/Charismatic Roots." Ph.D. diss., University of Birmingham, England, 1981.

Noble, E. Myron. *History of the Apostolic Faith Church of God of Washington, D.C.* Self-published, n.d.

Phillips, William Thomas. *Excerpts from the Life of the Right Rev. W. T. Phillips and Fundamentals of the Apostolic Overcoming Holy Church of God.* Mobile, Alabama: A. O. H. Publishing House, 1967.

Robins, Roger Glenn. "Plainfolk Modernist: The Radical Holiness World of A. J. Tomlinson." Ph.D. diss., Duke University, 1999.

Robinson, Bud. *Sunshine and Smiles: Life Story, FlashLights, Sayings and Sermons.* Chicago: The Christian Witness Company, 1903.

Roebuck, David G. "Limiting Liberty: The Church of God and Women Ministers, 1886–1996." Ph.D. diss., Vanderbilt University, 1997.

Sanders, Cheryl. *Saints in Exile: The Holiness Pentecostal Experience in African American Religion and Culture.* New York: Oxford University Press, 1996.

Seaman, Ann Rowe. *Swaggart: The Unauthorized Biography of an American Evangelist.* New York: Continuum, 1999.

Seymour, W. J. *The Doctrines and Discipline of the Azusa Street Apostolic Faith Mission of Los Angeles, Cal. 1915.* N.p., n.d.

Stephens, Randall. "'There is Magic in Print': The Holiness-Pentecostal Press and the Origins of Southern Pentecostalism." *Journal of Southern Religion* 3 (2002), online at ‹http://jsr.as.wvu.edu/2002/Stephens.htm›.

Synan, Vinson. *The Holiness-Pentecostal Tradition: Charismatic Movements in the Twentieth Century.* Grand Rapids, Michigan: Eerdmans, 1997.

———. *OldTime Power: A Centennial History of the International Pentecostal Holiness Church.* Franklin Springs, Georgia: LifeSprings Resources, 1998.

Taylor, George F. *The Spirit and the Bride: A Scriptural Presentation of the Operations, Manifestation, Gifts and Fruit of the Holy Spirit in His Relation to the Bride, with Special Reference to the 'Latter Rain' Revival*. Dunn, North Carolina: Falcon Press, 1917.

Tomlinson, Ambrose J. *Diary of A. J. Tomlinson*. 3 vols. Queen's Village, New York: Church of God, World Headquarters, 1949–55.

———. *Historical Annual Addresses*. Compiled by Perry E. Gillum. 3 vols. Cleveland, Tennessee: White Wing Publishing House and Press, 1970–72.

———. *The Last Great Conflict*. 1913. Reprint, New York: Garland, 1985.

Trexler, Jeffrey. "From Chaos to Order: G. F. Taylor and the Evolution of Southern Pentecostalism." Unpublished paper. In Society for Pentecostal Studies Papers, Flower Pentecostal Heritage Center, Assemblies of God Archives, Springfield, Mo.

Turley, Briane Keith. *"A Wheel within a Wheel": Southern Methodism and the Georgia Holiness Association*. Macon, Georgia: Mercer University Press, 1999.

Turner, William Clair, Jr., "The United Holy Church of America: A Study in Black Holiness and Pentecostalism." Ph.D. diss., Duke University, 1984.

Wacker, Grant. *Heaven Below: Early Pentecostals and American Culture*. Cambridge, Massachusetts: Harvard University Press, 2001.

Warner, Wayne, ed. *Touched by Fire: Eyewitness Accounts of the Early- Twentieth-Century Pentecostal Revival*. Plainfield, New Jersey: Logos Press, 1978.

Wood, Dillard L., and William H. Preskit. *Baptized with Fire: A History of the Pentecostal Fire-Baptized Holiness Church*. Franklin Springs, Georgia: Advocate Press, 1982.

Woods, Daniel Glenn. "Living in the Presence of God: Enthusiasm, Authority, and Negotiation in the Practice of Pentecostal Holiness." Ph.D. diss., University of Mississippi, 1997.

Woodworth-Etter. Maria B. *Marvels and Miracles: God Wrought in the Ministry for Forty-Five Years*. Self-published, 1922.

———. *Signs and Wonders; God Wrought in the Ministry of Forty Years*. Bartlesville, Oklahoma: Oak Tree Publications, 1916.

AFRICAN AMERICAN RELIGION AND CULTURE IN THE SOUTH

Andrews, William L., ed. *Sisters of the Spirit: Three Black Women's Autobiographies of the Nineteenth Century*. Bloomington: Indiana University Press, 1986.

Baer, Hans A., and Merrill Singer. *African-American Religion in the Twentieth Century: Varieties of Protest and Accommodation*. Knoxville: University of Tennessee Press, 1992.

Bay, Nina. *The White Image in the Black Mind: African-American Ideas about White People, 1830–1925*. New York: Oxford University Press, 2000.

Beary, Michael J. *Black Bishop: Edward T. Demby and the Struggle for Racial Equality in the Episcopal Church*. Urbana: University of Illinois Press, 2001.

Billingsley, Andrew. *Mighty Like a River: The Black Church and Social Reform*. New York: Oxford University Press, 1999.

Camp, Elias Morris. *Sermons, Addresses, and Reminiscences and Important Correspondence*. Nashville: National Baptist Publishing Board, 1901.

Chafe, William, et al., eds. *Remembering Jim Crow: African Americans Tell about Life in the Segregated South*. New York: New Press, 2001.

Chestnut, J. L., and Julia Cass. *Black in Selma: The Uncommon Life of J. L. Chestnut, Jr.* New York: Farrar, Strauss, and Giroux, 1990.

Clinton, George. *Christianity under the Searchlight.* Nashville: National Baptist Publishing Board, 1909.

Cone, James H. *Black Power and Black Theology.* New York: Seabury Press, 1969.

Cornelius, Janet Duitsman. *Slave Missions and the Black Church in the Antebellum South.* Columbia: University of South Carolina Press, 1999.

Creel, Margaret Washington. *A Peculiar People: Slave Religion and Community-Culture among the Gullahs.* New York: New York University Press, 1988.

Davis, Allison, et al. *Deep South: A Social Anthropological Study of Caste and Class.* Chicago: University of Chicago Press, 1941.

Dixie, Quinton. *This Far by Faith: Stories from the African-American Religious Experience.* New York: Morrow, 2002.

Du Bois, W. E. B. *The Negro Church.* Atlanta: Atlanta University Press, 1903.

———. *Souls of Black Folk.* 1903. Reprint, New York: Bantam Books, 1989.

Faduma, Orishatukeh. "The Defects of the Negro Church." In *The American Negro Academy.* Occasional Papers No. 10. 1904. Reprint, New York: Arno Press, 1969.

Felton, Ralph A. *These My Brethren: A Study of 570 Negro Churches and 1542 Negro Homes in the Rural South.* Madison, New Jersey: Drew Theological Seminary, Department of the Rural Church, 1951.

Frazier, E. Franklin. *The Negro Church in America.* New York: Schocken Books, 1964.

Frederickson, George M. *The Black Image in the White Mind: The Debate on Afro-American Character and Destiny, 1817–1914.* New York: Harper & Row, 1971.

Frey, Sylvia R., and Betty Wood. *Come Shouting to Zion: African American Protestantism in the American South and British Caribbean to 1830.* Chapel Hill: University of North Carolina Press, 1998.

Gaines, Kevin Kelly. *Uplifting the Race: Black Leadership, Politics, and Culture in the Twentieth Century.* Chapel Hill: University of North Carolina Press, 1996.

Genovese, Eugene D. *Roll, Jordan, Roll: The World the Slaves Made.* New York: Pantheon, 1974.

Giggie, John. "God's Long Journey: African-Americans, Religion, and History in the Mississippi Delta, 1875–1915." Ph.D. diss., Princeton University, 1997.

Griggs, Sutton. *The Hindered Hand; or, The Reign of the Repressionist.* Nashville: Orion, 1905.

———. *Imperium in Imperio.* 1889. Reprint, Miami: Mnemosyne, 1969.

Hall, Robert L. "The Gospel According to Radicalism: African Methodism Comes to Tallahassee After the Civil War." *Apalachee: The Publication of the Tallahassee Historical Society* 8 (1978): 69–81. Reprinted in Donald G. Nieman, *Church and Community Among Black Southerners, 1865–1900.* New York: Garland, 1994.

Hamilton, Charles Horace, and John M. Ellison. *The Negro Church in Rural Virginia.* Blacksburg, Virginia: Virginia Agricultural Experiment Series, 1930.

Harris, Frederick C. *Something Within: Religion in African-American Political Activism.* New York: Oxford University Press, 1999.

Herskovits, Melville J. *The Myth of the Negro Past.* New York: Harper & Brothers, 1941.

Higginbotham, Evelyn Brooks. *Righteous Discontent: The Women's Movement in the Black Baptist Church, 1880–1920.* Cambridge, Massachusetts: Harvard University Press, 1993.

Hine, Darlene Clark, Wilma King, and Linda Reed, eds. *"We Specialize in the Wholly Impossible": A Reader in Black Women's History*. Brooklyn, New York: Carlson, 1995.

Johnson, James Weldon. *God's Trombones: Seven Negro Sermons in Verse*. New York: Viking Press, 1927.

Johnson, W. B. *Sparks from My Anvil: Sermons and Addresses*. Lynchburg, Virginia: n.p., 1899.

Jordan, Lewis G. *Negro Baptist History, U.S.A., 1750–1930*. Nashville: National Baptist Publishing Board, 1930.

Jordan, Winthrop D. *White over Black: American Attitudes toward the Negro, 1550–1812*. Chapel Hill: University of North Carolina Press, 1968.

Kelley, Robin D. G. "'We Are Not What We Seem': Rethinking Black Working-Class Opposition in the Jim Crow South." *Journal of American History* 80 (June 1993): 75–112.

Lakey, Othal Hawthorne. *The Rise of "Colored Methodism": A Study of the Backgrounds and Beginnings of the Christian Methodist Episcopal Church*. Dallas: Crescendo Publishers, 1972.

Lamon, Lester C. *Black Tennesseans, 1900–1930*. Knoxville: University of Tennessee Press, 1977.

Lewis, David Levering. *W. E. B. Du Bois: Biography of a Race, 1868–1919*. New York: H. Holt Press, 1993.

Lincoln, C. Eric, and Lawrence H. Mamiya. *The Black Church in the African-American Experience*. Durham: Duke University Press, 1990.

Litwack, Leon F. *Been in the Storm So Long: The Aftermath of Slavery*. New York: Knopf, 1979.

———. *Trouble in Mind: Black Southerners in the Age of Jim Crow*. New York: Knopf, 1998.

Love, Emmanuel K. *History of the First African Baptist Church, from Its Organization, January 20th, 1788, to July 1st, 1888: Including the Centennial Celebration, Addresses, Sermons, etc.* Savannah: Morning News Print, 1888.

Lovett, Bobby L. *A Black Man's Dream: The First Hundred Years—Richard and Henry Boyd and the National Baptist Publishing Board*. Jacksonville, Florida: Mega Corporation, 1993.

Maffly-Kipp, Laurie F. "Mapping the World, Mapping the Race: The Negro Race History, 1874–1915." *Church History* 64 (December 1995): 610–26.

Marrs, Elijah P. *Life and History of the Reverend Elijah P. Marrs*. Louisville: Bradley and Gilbert, 1885.

Mays, Benjamin Elijah. *Born to Rebel*. New York: Scribner, 1971.

———. *The Negro's God, as Reflected in His Literature*. Boston: Chapman and Grimes, 1938.

Mays, Benjamin Elijah, and Joseph W. Nicholson. *The Negro's Church*. New York: Institute of Social and Religious Research, 1933.

Meier, August. *Negro Thought in America, 1880–1915: Racial Ideologies in the Age of Booker T. Washington*. Ann Arbor: University of Michigan Press, 1963.

Morris, Robert C. *Reading, 'Riting, and Reconstruction: The Education of Freedmen in the South, 1861–1900*. Chicago: University of Chicago Press, 1981.

Morris, E. C. *Sermons, Addresses and Reminiscences and Important Correspondence.* Nashville: National Baptist Publishing Board, 1901.

Paris, Peter J. *The Social Teachings of the Black Churches.* Philadelphia: Fortress Press, 1985.

Parrish, C. H. *Golden Jubilee of the General Association of Colored Baptists in Kentucky: The Story of Fifty Years' Work from 1865–1915.* Louisville: Mayes Print, 1915.

Payne, Daniel Alexander. *Recollection of Seventy Years.* 1888. Reprint, New York: Arno Press, 1968.

Pipes, William Harrison. *Say Amen, Brother! Old-Time Negro Preaching: A Study in American Frustration.* 1951. Reprint, New York: Negro Universities Press, 1970.

Raboteau, Albert J. *Slave Religion: The "Invisible Institution" in the Antebellum South.* New York: Oxford University Press, 1978.

Raboteau, Albert, et al. "Retelling Carter Woodson's Story: Archival Sources for Afro-American Church History." *Journal of American History* 77 (1990): 183–99.

Redkey, Edwin S. *Black Exodus: Black Nationalist and Back-to-Africa Movements, 1890–1910.* New Haven: Yale University Press, 1969.

Reid, Ira De A. *The Negro Baptist Ministry: An Analysis of Its Profession, Preparation and Practices: Report of Survey Conducted by the Joint Survey Commission of the Baptist Inter-Convention Committee.* Philadelphia: H & L Advertising Co., 1951.

Richardson, Harry Van Buren. *Dark Glory: A Picture of the Church Among Negroes in the Rural South.* New York: Friendship Press, 1947.

Sernett, Milton C. *Black Religion and American Evangelicalism: White Protestants, Plantation Missions, and the Flowering of Negro Christianity in America, 1787–1865.* Metuchen, New Jersey: Scarecrow Press, 1975.

Sernett, Milton, ed. *Afro-American Religious History: A Documentary Witness.* 2nd ed. Durham: Duke University Press, 1999.

Simms, James M. *The First Colored Baptist Church in North America.* Philadelphia: Lippincott, 1888.

Smith, Theophus H. *Conjuring Culture: Biblical Formations of Black America.* New York: Oxford University Press, 1994.

Taulbert, Clifton L. *Once upon a Time When We Were Colored.* Tulsa: Council Oaks Books, 1989.

Thompson, Patrick H. *The History of Negro Baptists in Mississippi.* Jackson, Mississippi: R. W. Bailey Print, 1898.

Trawick, A. M., ed. *The New Voice in Race Adjustments: Addresses and Reports Presented at the Negro Christian Student Conference, Atlanta, Georgia, May 14–18, 1914.* New York: Student Volunteer Movement, 1914.

Tucker, David M. *Black Pastors and Leaders: Memphis, 1819–1972.* Memphis: Memphis State University Press, 1975.

Walker, Charles T. *The Negro Problem: Its Scriptural Solution. Address Delivered at Tabernacle Baptist Church, Augusta, Sunday June 4, 1893.* Augusta: Self-published, 1893.

Washington, James Melvin. *Frustrated Fellowship: The Black Baptist Quest for Social Power.* Macon, Georgia: Mercer University Press, 1986.

Wheeler, Edward L. *Uplifting the Race: The Black Minister in the New South, 1865–1902.* Lanham, Maryland: University Press of America, 1986.

Whitted, J. A. *A History of the Negro Baptists of North Carolina.* Raleigh: Edwards & Broughton, 1908.

Williams, Gilbert Anthony. *The Christian Recorder, Newspaper of the African Methodist Episcopal Church: History of a Forum for Ideas, 1854–1902.* Jefferson, North Carolina: McFarland & Company, 1996.

Williams, Walter L. *Black Americans and the Evangelization of Africa, 1877–1900.* Madison: University of Wisconsin Press, 1982.

Williamson, Joel. *After Slavery: The Negro in South Carolina during Reconstruction, 1861–1877.* Chapel Hill: University of North Carolina Press, 1965.

Wills, David W., and Richard Newman, eds. *Black Apostles at Home and Abroad: Afro-Americans and the Christian Mission from the Revolution to Reconstruction.* Boston: G. K. Hall, 1982.

Wilmore, Gayraud. *Black Religion and Black Radicalism: An Interpretation of the Religious History of the Afro-American People.* Maryknoll, New York: Orbis Books, 1983.

Woodson, Carter G. *The History of the Negro Church.* Washington, D.C.: Associated Publishers, 1921.

Works Progress Administration. *The Negro in Virginia.* 1940. Reprint, New York: Arno Press, 1969.

RELIGION AND THE CIVIL RIGHTS MOVEMENT

Abernathy, Ralph. *And the Walls Came Tumbling Down: An Autobiography.* New York: Harper & Row, 1989.

Alvis, Joel L., Jr. *Religion and Race: Southern Presbyterians, 1946–1983.* Tuscaloosa: University of Alabama Press, 1994.

Baldwin, Lewis V. *There Is a Balm in Gilead: The Cultural Roots of Martin Luther King, Jr.* Minneapolis: Fortress Press, 1991.

Bass, S. Jonathan. *Blessed Are the Peacemakers: Martin Luther King, Jr., Eight White Religious Leaders, and the "Letter from Birmingham Jail."* Baton Rouge: Louisiana State University Press, 2001.

Bauman, Mark K., and Berkley Kalin. *The Quiet Voices: Southern Rabbis and Black Civil Rights, 1880s to 1990s.* Tuscaloosa: University of Alabama Press, 1997.

Braden, Anne. *The Wall Between.* New York: Monthly Review Press, 1958.

Branch, Taylor. *Parting the Waters: America in the King Years, 1954–1963.* New York: Simon & Schuster, 1988.

Brooks, Jennifer. " 'Winning the Peace': Georgia Veterans and the Struggle to Define the Political Legacy of World War II." *Journal of Southern History* 66 (August 2000): 563–604.

Burns, Stewart, ed. *Daybreak of Freedom: The Montgomery Bus Boycott.* Chapel Hill: University of North Carolina Press, 1997.

Campbell, Will D. *Race and the Renewal of the Church.* Philadelphia: Westminster Press, 1962.

Carawan, Guy, and Candie Carawan, eds. *Sing for Freedom: The Story of the Civil Rights Movement through Its Songs.* Bethlehem, Pennsylvania: Sing Out Publications, 1992.

Carson, Clayborne. *In Struggle: SNCC and the Black Awakening of the 1960s.* Cambridge, Massachusetts: Harvard University Press, 1981.

Chafe, William H. *Civilities and Civil Rights: Greensboro, North Carolina, and the Black Struggle for Freedom.* New York: Oxford University Press, 1980.

Chappell, David L. *Inside Agitators: White Southerners and the Civil Rights Movement.* Baltimore: Johns Hopkins University Press, 1994.

———. *A Stone of Hope: Prophetic Religion and the Death of Jim Crow.* Chapel Hill: University of North Carolina Press, 2003.

Collins, Donald E. *When the Church Bell Rang Racist: The Methodist Church and the Civil Rights Movement in Alabama.* Macon, Georgia: Mercer University Press, 1998.

Crawford, Vicki. "Race, Class, Gender, and Culture: Black Women's Activism in the Mississippi Civil Rights Movement." *Journal of Mississippi History* 58 (Spring 1996): 1–21.

Crawford, Vicki L., Jacqueline Anne Rouse, and Barbara Woods, eds. *Women in the Civil Rights Movement: Trailblazers and Torchbearers, 1941–1965. Black Women in United States History,* edited by Darlene Clark Hine, 16. Brooklyn, New York: Carlson, 1990.

Curry, Constance, et al., eds. *Deep in Our Hearts: Nine White Women in the Freedom Movement.* Athens: University of Georgia Press, 2000.

Daniel, Pete. *Lost Revolutions: The South in the 1950s.* Chapel Hill: University of North Carolina Press, 2000.

Dittmer, John. *Local People: The Struggle for Civil Rights in Mississippi.* Urbana: University of Illinois Press, 1994.

Eagles, Charles W. "The Closing of Mississippi Society: Will Campbell, *The $64,000 Question,* and Religious Emphasis Week at the University of Mississippi." *Journal of Southern History* 67 (May 2001): 331–72.

Ehle, John. *The Free Men.* New York: Harper & Row, 1965.

Emerson, Michael O., and Houston Smith. *Divided by Faith: Evangelical Religion and the Problem of Race in America.* New York: Oxford University Press, 2000.

Eskew, Glenn T. *But for Birmingham: The Local and National Movements in the Civil Rights Struggle.* Chapel Hill: University of North Carolina Press, 1997.

Fairclough, Adam. "'Being in the Field of Education and Also Being a Negro . . . Seems . . . Tragic': Black Teachers in the Jim Crow South." *Journal of American History* 87 (June 2000): 65–91.

———. *Race and Democracy: The Civil Rights Struggle in Louisiana, 1915–1972.* Athens: University of Georgia Press, 1995.

Farmer, James. *Lay Bare the Heart: An Autobiography of the Civil Rights Movement.* New York: New American Library, 1985.

Findlay, James F. *Church People in the Struggle: The National Council of Churches and the Black Freedom Movement.* New York: Oxford University Press, 1993.

Friedland, Michael B. *Lift up Your Voice Like a Trumpet: White Clergy and the Civil Rights and Antiwar Movements, 1954–1973.* Chapel Hill: University of North Carolina Press, 1998.

Garrow, David J. *Bearing the Cross: Martin Luther King, Jr., and the Southern Christian Leadership Conference.* New York: Morrow, 1986.

Goldfield, David R. *Black, White and Southern: Race Relations and Southern Culture, 1940 to the Present.* Baton Rouge: Louisiana State University Press, 1990.

Graetz, Robert S. *A White Preacher's Memoir: The Montgomery Bus Boycott.* Montgomery: Black Belt Press, 1998.

Greenberg, Cheryl Lynn, ed. *A Circle of Trust: Remembering SNCC.* New Brunswick: Rutgers University Press, 1998.

Hays, Brooks. *A Southern Moderate Speaks.* Chapel Hill: University of North Carolina Press, 1959.

Henry, Aaron, and Constance Curry. *Aaron Henry: The Fire Ever Burning.* Jackson: University Press of Mississippi, 2000.

Hobson, Fred C. *But Now I See: The White Southern Racial Conversion Narrative.* Baton Rouge: Louisiana State University Press, 1998.

Holmes, Thomas J. *Ashes for Breakfast.* Valley Forge, Pennsylvania: Judson Press, 1969.

King, Mary. *Freedom Song: A Personal Story of the 1960s Civil Rights Movement.* New York: Morrow, 1987.

Lee, Chana Kai. *For Freedom's Sake: The Life of Fannie Lou Hamer.* Urbana: University of Illinois Press, 1999.

Lewis, John. *Walking with the Wind: A Memoir of the Movement.* New York: Simon and Shuster, 1998.

Lochbaum, Julie Magruder. "The Word Made Flesh: The Desegregation Leadership of the Rev. J. A. DeLaine." Ph.D. diss., University of South Carolina, 1993.

Luker, Ralph. *"The Man Who Started Freedom": The Vernon Johns Papers Project.* Ongoing, information available at ‹http://www.ralphluker.com/vjohns/index.html›.

Manis, Andrew Michael. *A Fire You Can't Put Out: The Civil Rights Life of Birmingham's Reverend Fred Shuttlesworth.* Tuscaloosa: University of Alabama Press, 1999.

———. *Southern Civil Religions in Conflict: Black and White Baptists and Civil Rights, 1947–1957.* Athens: University of Georgia Press, 1987.

Marsh, Charles. *God's Long Summer: Stories of Faith and Civil Rights.* Princeton: Princeton University Press, 1997.

Maston, T. B. *The Bible and Race.* Nashville: Broadman, 1959.

McWhorter, Diane. *Carry Me Home: Birmingham, Alabama: The Climactic Battle of the Civil Rights Revolution.* New York: Simon & Schuster, 2001.

Morris, Aldon. *The Origins of the Civil Rights Movement: Black Communities Organizing for Change.* New York: Free Press, 1984.

Newman, Mark. "The Baptist State Convention of North Carolina and Desegregation, 1945–1980." *North Carolina History Review* 75 (January 1998): 1–28.

———. *Getting Right with God: Southern Baptists and Desegregation, 1945–1995.* Tuscaloosa: University of Alabama Press, 2001.

———. "Getting Right with God: Southern Baptists and Race Relations, 1945–1980." Ph.D. diss., University of Mississippi, 1993.

Parsons, Sarah Mitchell. *From Southern Wrongs to Civil Rights: The Memoir of a White Civil Rights Activist.* Tuscaloosa: University of Alabama Press, 2000.

Patton, Sarah Boyle. *The Desegregated Heart: A Virginian's Stand in Time of Transition.* New York: Morrow, 1962.

Payne, Charles M. *I've Got the Light of Freedom: The Organizing Tradition and the Mississippi Freedom Struggle.* Berkeley: University of California Press, 1995.

Raines, Howell, ed. *My Soul Is Rested: The Story of the Civil Rights Movement in the Deep South.* New York: Penguin Books, 1977.

Ransby, Barbara. *Ella Baker and the Black Freedom Movement: A Radical Democratic Vision*. Chapel Hill: University of North Carolina Press, 2002.

Robinson, Jo Ann Gibson. *The Montgomery Bus Boycott and the Women Who Started It: The Memoir of Jo Ann Gibson Robinson*. Edited by David Garrow. Knoxville: University of Tennessee Press, 1987.

Sanger, Kerran. *"When the Spirit Says Sing!" The Role of Freedom Songs in the Civil Rights Movement*. New York: Garland Press, 1995.

Shattuck, Gardiner H. *Episcopalians and Race: Civil War to Civil Rights*. Lexington: University Press of Kentucky, 2000.

Tilson, Everett. *Segregation and the Bible*. Nashville: Abingdon, 1961.

Tyson, Timothy B. "Dynamite and 'The Silent South': A Story from the Second Reconstruction in South Carolina." In *Jumpin' Jim Crow: Southern Politics from Civil War to Civil Rights*, edited by Jane Dailey, Glenda Elizabeth Gilmore, and Bryant Simon, 275–97. Princeton: Princeton University Press, 2000.

———. *Radio Free Dixie: Robert F. Williams and the Roots of Black Power*. Chapel Hill: University of North Carolina Press, 1998.

Valentine, Foy Dan. "A Historical Study of Southern Baptists and Race Relations, 1917–1947." Th.D. diss., Southwestern Baptist Theological Seminary, 1949.

Washington, James Melvin, ed. *A Testament of Hope: The Essential Writings and Speeches of Martin Luther King, Jr.* San Francisco: Harper San Francisco, 1991.

Watters, Pat. *Down to Now: Reflections on the Southern Civil Rights Movement*. New York: Pantheon, 1971.

Young, Andrew. *An Easy Burden: The Civil Rights Movement and the Transformation of America*. New York: HarperCollins, 1996.

Youth of the Rural Organizing and Cultural Center. *Minds Stayed on Freedom: The Civil Rights Struggle in the Rural South, an Oral History*. Boulder, Colorado: Westview Press, 1991.

RELIGION, RACE, AND THE RIGHT

Ammerman, Nancy Tatom. *Baptist Battles: Social Change and Religious Conflict in the Southern Baptist Convention*. New Brunswick: Rutgers University Press, 1990.

———. *Southern Baptists Observed: Multiple Perspectives on a Changing Denomination*. Knoxville: University of Tennessee Press, 1993.

Barkun, Michael. *Religion and the Racist Right: The Origins of the Christian Identity Movement*. Chapel Hill: University of North Carolina Press, 1994.

Brattain, Michelle. *The Politics of Whiteness: Race, Workers, and Culture in the Modern South*. Princeton: Princeton University Press, 2001.

Carpenter, Joel A. *Revive Us Again: The Reawakening of American Fundamentalism*. New York: Oxford University Press, 1997.

Carter, Dan T. *The Politics of Rage: George Wallace, the Origins of the New Conservatism, and the Transformation of American Politics*. New York: Simon & Schuster, 1995.

Caucasian [William Campbell]. *Anthropology for the People: A Refutation of the Theory of the Adamic Origin of All Races*. Richmond, Virginia: Everett Wadley Co., 1891.

Chappell, David. "The Divided Mind of Southern Segregationists." *Georgia Historical Quarterly* 82 (Spring 1998): 45–72.

————. "Religious Ideas of the Segregationists." *Journal of American Studies* 32 (August 1998): 237–62.

Citizens' Council of North Carolina. *Is Segregation Un-Christian*. Greenwood, Mississippi: Citizens' Council Educational Fund, n.d.

Crespino, Joseph. "The Christian Conscience of Jim Crow: White Protestant Ministers and the Mississippi Citizens Councils, 1954–1964." *Mississippi Folklife* 31 (Fall 1998): 30–44.

Daniel, Carey. *God the Original Segregationist and Seven Other Segregation Sermons*. N.p., n.d.

Dixon, Thomas. *The Clansman: An Historical Romance of the Ku Klux Klan*. New York: Doubleday, Page and Co., 1905.

————. *The Leopard's Spots: A Romance of the White Man's Burden, 1865–1900*. New York: Doubleday, Page and Co., 1903.

Feldman, Glenn. *Politics, Society, and the Klan in Alabama, 1915–1949*. Tuscaloosa: University of Alabama Press, 1999.

Gillespie, G. T. *A Christian View on Segregation*. Greenwood, Mississippi: Educational Fund of the Citizens' Councils, 1954.

Glass, William R. *Strangers in Zion: Fundamentalists in the South, 1900–1950*. Macon, Georgia: Mercer University Press, 2001.

Hankins, Barry. *God's Rascal: J. Frank Norris and the Beginnings of Southern Fundamentalism*. Lexington: University Press of Kentucky, 1996.

————. *Uneasy in Babylon: Conservative Baptists and American Culture*. Tuscaloosa: University of Alabama Press, 2002.

Larson, Edward J. *Summer for the Gods: The Scopes Trial and America's Continuing Debate over Science and Religion*. New York: Basic Books, 1997.

MacLean, Nancy. *Behind the Mask of Chivalry: The Making of the Second Ku Klux Klan*. New York: Oxford University Press, 1994.

————. "The Leo Frank Case Reconsidered: Gender and Sexual Politics in the Making of Reactionary Populism." *Journal of American History* 78 (1991): 917–48.

Marsden, George M. *Fundamentalism and American Culture: The Shaping of Twentieth-Century Evangelicalism, 1870–1925*. New York: Oxford University Press, 1980.

Martin, William. *With God on Our Side: The Rise of the Religious Right in America*. New York: Broadway Books, 1996.

Morgan, David T. *The New Crusades, the New Holy Land: Conflict in the Southern Baptist Convention, 1969–1991*. Tuscaloosa: University of Alabama Press, 1996.

Nelson, D. M. *Conflicting Views on Segregation*. Greenwood, Mississippi: Education Fund of the Citizens' Councils, 1954.

Newby, I. A. *Jim Crow's Defense: Anti-Negro Thought in America, 1900–1930*. Baton Rouge: Louisiana State University Press, 1965.

Rosenberg, Ellen M. *The Southern Baptists: A Subculture in Transition*. Knoxville: University of Tennessee Press, 1989.

Sandeen, Ernest R. *The Roots of Fundamentalism: British and American Millenarianism, 1800–1930*. Chicago: University of Chicago Press, 1970.

Schmidt, Jean Miller. *Souls or the Social Order: The Two-Party System in American Protestantism*. Brooklyn, New York: Carlson, 1991.

Shurden, Walter B., and Randy Shepley, eds. *Going for the Jugular: A Documentary History of the SBC Holy War*. Macon, Georgia: Mercer University Press, 1996.

Silver, James W. "Mississippi: The Closed Society." *Journal of Southern History* 30 (February 1964): 3–34.

Smith, Oran P. *The Rise of Baptist Republicanism*. New York: New York University Press, 1997.

Tull, James E. *A History of Southern Baptist Landmarkism in the Light of Historical Baptist Ecclesiology*. 1960. Reprint, New York: Arno Press, 1980.

Vigil, Thomas Peter. *Ham and Japheth: The Mythic World of Whites in the Antebellum South*. Metuchen, New Jersey: Scarecrow Press and American Theological Library Association, 1978.

Weber, Timothy P. *Living in the Shadow of the Second Coming: American Premillennialism, 1875–1925*. New York: Oxford University Press, 1979.

Wilcox, Clyde. *God's Warriors: The Christian Right in Twentieth-Century America*. Baltimore: Johns Hopkins University Press, 1992.

MUSICAL CDS

American Primitive, Vol. I: Raw Pre-War Gospel, 1926–1936. Revenant Records.

Anthology of American Folk Music. Edited by Harry Smith. Revenant Records.

The Best of Bluegrass: Preachin', Prayin', Singin'. Polygram Records.

The Carter Family, 1927–1934. 5 CDs. JSP Records.

The Complete Blind Willie Johnson. 2 CDs. Sony Records.

Dranes, Arizona *Complete Recorded Works in Chronological Order, 1926–29*. Document Records.

The Essential Gospel Sampler. Columbia Records.

Gates, J. M. *Complete Recorded Works*. Vols. 1–3. Document Records.

The Gospel Ship: Baptist Hymns and White Spirituals. New World Records.

The Gospel Tradition: Roots & Branches. Vol. 1. Sony Records.

Graves, Blind Roosevelt, *Complete Recorded Works*. Document Records.

The Half Ain't Never Been Told. 2 CDs. Yazoo Records.

How Can I Keep From Singing. 2 CDs. Yazoo Records.

Jackson, Mahalia. *Gospels, Spirituals, and Hymns*. Sony.

Jubilation, Vol. I (Black Gospel). Rhino Records.

Jubilation, Vol. II (More Black Gospel). Rhino Records.

McGee, F. W. *Complete Recorded Works, Vol. 1*. Document Records.

Negro Religious Field Recordings. 2 CDs. Document Records, DOCD 5629.

Philips, Washington. *Complete Recorded Works*. Yazoo Records.

Preachers and Congregations, 1927–1938, vols. 1–3. Document Records.

Precious Lord: The Great Gospel Songs of Thomas A. Dorsey. Sony.

Roots 'n Blues: The Retrospective, 1925–1950. 4 CDs. Columbia Records (Sony).

Sacred Harp Singing. Rounder Select Records.

Sam Cooke with the Soul Stirrers. Specialty Records.

Sing for Freedom: The Story of the Civil Rights Movement through Its Songs. Smithsonian Folkways Records. CD SF 40032.

The Social Harp: Early American Shape-Note Songs. Rounder Records.

Southern Journey. Edited by Alan Lomax. 15 CD Series. Rounder/Folkway Records.
Stanley Brothers: 16 Greatest Gospel Hits. Hollywood Records.
Tharpe, Rosetta. *Complete Recorded Works.* Vols. 1–3. Document Records.
Wade in the Water. 4 vols. Smithsonian Folkways Series.
Voices of the Freedom Movement: Black American Freedom Songs, 1960–1966. Smithsonian Folkways.

Index

AMA. *See* American Missionary Association

"Amazing Grace," 185

A.M.E. Church Review, 149

American Baptist Free Mission Society, 33, 149

American Baptist Home Mission Society, 35, 91

American Dilemma (Myrdal), 241

American Missionary Association (AMA), 30–31, 186–87

American Religious Identification Survey (ARIS), 254

Ames, Jesse Daniel, 84

Ames Methodist Episcopal Church (New Orleans, La.), 15

Antebellum era, 8, 16, 111–12

Anthology of American Folk Music, 162

Anthropology for the People ("Caucasian"), 43

Anti-Saloon League (ASL), 55

Apostolic Faith, 131, 135

Apostolic Faith Church of God (Washington, D.C.), 89–90

Apostolic Faith Mission, 130

Appalachian mountain religion, 120

Appomattox, 6

"Are You Afraid to Die," 156

Armstrong, Annie, 73–74

Army Life in a Black Regiment (Higginson), 116

Ashes for Breakfast (Holmes), 244

Ashley, Samuel Stanford, 36

Assemblies of God, 134, 136, 145, 167

Association of Methodist Ministers and Laymen (Alabama), 237

Association of Southern Women for the Prevention of Lynching, 84–85

At Ease in Zion (Spain), 252

Atlanta Baptist Institute, 10

Atlanta Constitution, 89, 169, 242

Atlanta Methodist Advocate, 26

Atlanta riot, 11, 60

Atlantic Monthly, 63

Augusta, Ga., 11–12

Augusta Institute, 10, 32

Azusa Street revival (Los Angeles), 130–34

"Baby What I Say," 167

Bailey, Josiah, 52, 55

Baker, Ella, 49, 91–92, 185

Baptist Bible Union, 224

Baptists. *See* Segregation; Southern Baptist Convention; Theological racism; Women

Barnett, Ross, 231

Bartleman, William, 132

Bartlett, Eugene, 155

Basis of Ascendancy, The (Murphy), 66

Baxter, Jesse R., 154

Bennett, Belle, 76, 192

Bethel AME Church (Atlanta, Ga.), 72

Bethel Baptist Church (Birmingham, Ala.), 185

Bethlehem houses, 76, 85. *See also* Methodist Episcopal Church, South; Women

Bethune, Mary McLeod, 71, 93

Bible: African American interpretations of, 43–46; literal view of, 247; perceived support for slavery in, 1, 44; progressive views of, 47–49; racist interpretations of, 42–44, 220–21, 234–35; perceived support for civil rights activism in, 186–88, 192, 194–95, 198–99, 214–15; used to oppose Reconstruction, 38–39

Biblical Recorder, 51, 55, 63

Bilbo, Theodore, 90–91, 238

Biracial churches, 6–26

Biracial cooperation, 70, 74–77, 79, 84–89

Biracial worship, 107, 110–16. *See also* Worship practices

Birmingham, Ala.: civil rights movement in, 174–75, 185–87

Birth of a Nation, The (Griffith), 52

Black, Sam, 196

Blackwell, Unita, 196

Blackwood Brothers, 157

Bluegrass, 156

Blue Jay Singers, 165

Blues, 158–63; and Christianity, 159–60; and gospel, 163; Mississippi Delta,

Church of Christ (Holiness), U.S.A., 144

Church of God (Cleveland, Tenn.), 139–42

Church of God in Christ (COGIC), 143–44, 147, 167

Church of God of Prophecy (Cleveland, Tenn.), 141

Church of the Good Shepherd (Montgomery, Ala.), 66

Church of the Living God (Mississippi/Arkansas Delta), 142, 147

Church of the Living God, the Pillar and Ground of Truth, 142, 147

Church of the Nazarene, 153

Church Woman, 200

Civil rights movement: in Albany, Ga., 174; biracial cooperation in, 185, 192, 209; in Birmingham, Ala., 174–75, 185–87; children in, 175; divisions in black community about, 181–82; grassroots organizing in, 184, 196; in Greenwood, Miss., 196; in Jackson, Miss., 173; jailing of activists, 173, 189, 197; lack of African American church support of, 170–71, 176, 190, 196; in Mississippi, 190–99; in Montgomery, Ala., 172, 177–82; Montgomery bus boycott, 177–78; music of, 171–75; NAACP involvement in, 176, 191, 193; nonviolence in, 183, 186, 188, 204, 206; opposition from religious communities, 193; political aims of, 171; religious influences on, 169, 175, 192, 197, 199; religious leaders' resistance to, 170, 177; SNCC involvement in, 190–96; in South Carolina, 176; violence in, 170, 173, 177, 185, 190, 193–94; in Virginia, 189

Clansman, The (Dixon), 52

Clark, Septima, 49, 170

Cleveland, M. C., 180

Click, J. F., 51

Clinton African Methodist Episcopal Zion Chapel (Charlotte, N.C.), 56

Coal mine operators, 61

Coffin, Levi, 149

Cold Mountain (Frazier), 153

Cold War, 90, 95, 234. *See also* Communism

Collection of Songs for Religious Meetings, A, 151

Collins, Donald, 237

Collins Chapel (Memphis, Tenn.), 46

Colored Citizen's Monthly, 12

Colored Farmers' Alliance, 52

Colored Fire-Baptized Holiness Association, 128

Colored Methodist Episcopal Church (CME), 8, 39–41, 45

Colored Woman's Christian Temperance Union, 56

Columbia Bible College, 225

Columbia Records, 154, 161

"Come, Lord Jesus, Abide with Me," 164

Comer, Donald, 229

Comer, Laura, 21

Commission on Interracial Cooperation (CIC), 64, 67, 78–79, 227

Committee on Farm Security, 75

Communism: perceived association with integration, 95–96, 230, 232, 234, 235, 242

Communist Party, 94

Community Church of Chapel Hill, 96

Confederacy, 27, 49–50, 53, 60

Congregationalism, 31, 66

Congregationalist Convention of the South, 187

Congress of Industrial Organizations (CIO), 81

Congress of Racial Equality (CORE), 173

Conjure, 120–23. *See also* Supernaturalism; Worship practices

Connor, Theophilus Eugene ("Bull"), 93, 174

Contemporary South: changing demographics of, 253; identity, 253; politics in, 255–56; racism in, 253; religious affiliation in, 253–54; Republican Party in, 256

Conversion, 119, 123–24, 138. *See also* Worship practices

Coody, Archibald Stimson, IV, 238

Populism, 49–50; as basis for Reconstruction politics, 33–38; as basis for
Redemptionist politics, 38–45; in contemporary South, 251–56; criticisms of,
47; Populist use of, 49–53; in post–
Civil War South, 19–29; progressive
interpretations of, 78–84; progressive
women's views on, 55–56, 67–77, 84–
89, 199–206; radical interpretations of,
93–106; relationship with conservative
resurgence, 218–20; relationship with
labor organizing, 81–84; relationship
with proslavery, 42–44, 220–21; SNCC's
use of, 191–99; theology, 115; worship,
114
Evans, Eli, 114
Evers, Medgar, 176
Ewing, Quincey, 78
Ex-slaves. *See* Freedpeople

Fair Employment Practices Commission,
90
Family: SBC view on, 247
Farmer, James, 186
Farmers' Alliance. *See* Populism
Farrow, Lucy, 131–32
Faubus, Orval, 236
Federal Council of Churches, 66
Fellowship of Reconciliation (FOR), 97,
101, 183
Fellowship of Southern Churchmen
(FSC), 93, 100–103, 215
Fellowship of the Concerned, 87
Feminist theology, 74, 101
Fire-baptism, 136
Fire-Baptized Holiness Association, 128–
29
Fire-Baptized Holiness Church, 128, 136,
137
First African Baptist Church (Savannah,
Ga.), 90
First African Baptist Church (Tuscaloosa,
Ala.), 187–88
First Baptist Colored Church (Charlotte,
N.C.), 57
First Colored Baptist Church, 18

First Congregational Church (Atlanta,
Ga.), 59
Fisk University, 59
Flatt, Lester, 156
Folk traditions, religious, 114–20
Foster, Sarah Jane, 118
Fowler, Wallace, 154
Frazier, Charles, 153
Frazier, Garrison, 35
Freedmen's Aid Society, 31
Freedmen's Bureau, 35
Freedmen's Standard, 36
Freedom Rides, 1, 95, 173
Freedom songs, 1, 127, 166, 168, 171–75
Freedom Summer of 1964, 4, 193–94
Freedpeople: citizenship of, 9; conjure
practices of, 120–23; education of, 10,
30–33; evangelizing to, 8–9, 28–31; in-
dependent churches established by,
17–18; leadership of, 18; politics of, 33–
37; sacred music of, 148–52; views on
war and emancipation, 5–6; violence
against, 37, 39–42; worship practices
of, 114–20, 123–25
Freeman, Douglas Southall, 82
Free Will Baptists, 50
Friendship Baptist Church (Atlanta, Ga.),
18, 72
"From Auction Block to Glory," 164
Fuller, Erasmus Q., 26
Fuller, William. E., 128–29
Fundamentalism, 128, 222–24
Fundamentals of Methodism, The
(Mouzon), 224

Gaines, W. J., 107
Galloway, Charles B., 64
Gammon Theological Seminary, 105
Gandhi, Mahatma, 183
Gardner, Charles Spurgeon, 54
Garner, S. C., 61
Garvey, Marcus, 98
Gate City Free Kindergarten Association,
71
Gates, Rev. J. M., 155, 161
Gaye, Marvin, 142

Gender relations: Progressive Era views on, 67–77; SBC view on, 247

General Conference of the Methodist Episcopal Church, South. *See* Methodist Episcopal Church, South

General Missionary Baptist Convention, 191

Georgia Baptist, 11

Georgia Equal Rights and Educational Association, 10, 26

Georgia Equal Rights League, 11

Gideon's Band, 30

Gilbert, Ralph Mark, 90

Gillespie, C. T., 231, 237

Girardeau, John Lafayette, 28

Goings, George, 155

Gold, Elder E. P., 52

Golden Gate Quartet, 158

Goodman, Andrew, 193

Goodrich, Frances, 113

Gospel, 149–68; African American, 151, 155, 158, 163; and blues, 163; crossing racial lines, 162; groups, 156–58; musicians, 151, 157; professional, 155–58; publishing of, 150–51, 154, 155; quartets, 154, 158, 165–66; on radio, 154, 157–58; recording of, 154, 158, 162–64; schools, 154; singing, 150–55, 156; songwriters, 151; white, 149, 155, 157, 162

Gospel Pearls, 151, 164

Goss, Howard A., 133–34

Grace Church (Charlotte, N.C.), 57

Graetz, Robert S., 180

Graham, Frank Porter, 93, 95

"Great Speckled Bird," 142, 167

Green, Al, 167

Greenwood, Miss.: civil rights movement in, 196, 199

Griffith, D. W., 52

Gwaltney, Leslie, 228

Hadley, Elder J. J., 162

"Hallelujah, I'm A-Traveling," 175

Hamer, Fannie Lou, 197–98

Hammond, Lily, 77

Hampton, Wade, 36, 40

Hampton Institute, 121

Hancock, Gordon Blaine, 49, 61

Handy, W. C., 158–59

Harkeness, Ga., 74

Harmony Baptist Church (Augusta, Ga.), 11

Harper's, 79

Harris, Elizabeth Johnson, 113

Harris, R. H., 153

Harrison, Otis, 192

Hartzell, Joseph C., 15, 56

Harvey, Claire Collins, 202

Harvey, W. J., 151

Hatcher, William E., 112

Haven, Gilbert, 12

Hawthorne, J. B., 69

Hayes, R. B., 129

Haygood, Atticus, 63

Heard, William H., 36

Heck, Fannie E. S., 73

"He'll Understand It Better By and By," 151

Helm, Lucinda, 76

Henderson, Morris, 18

Henry, Aaron, 187

Herskovits, Melville, 150

"He Set Me Free," 157

Higginbotham, Evelyn Brooks, 70

Higginson, Thomas Wentworth, 116

Highlander Folk School, 85, 104, 177

Highway QCs, 166

Hill, Samuel S., Jr., 220

Hinton, James, 91

Hitler, Adolph, 90

Holiness: African Americans in, 142–44; racial interchange in, 129–30; revivals, 142; theology of, 127–28. *See also* Pentecostalism

Holloway, P. T., 78

Holmes, James Henry, 17

Holmes, Thomas J., 244

Holmes County, Miss.: white supremacist violence in, 195

Holsey, Lucius, 13

Holt, W. B., 146

Holy rollers, 141, 146

Palmer, Benjamin Morgan, 42

Palmer, Phoebe, 127

Parham, Charles Fox, 128, 131, 133

Paris, John, 36–37

Parker, Lucille Fisher, 176

Parks, Rosa, 177

Parrish, Lydia, 115

Parsons, James Arthur, 90

Paternalism, 16, 63–66, 79

Patriarchy: conservative Christian support of, 247–48

Patterson, Dorothy, 219, 248

Patterson, Paige, 246–47

Patting Juba, 116

Patton, Charley, 162

Payne, Charles, 170

Payne, Daniel Alexander, 41, 117, 149

Pentecostal Holiness Advocate, 137

Pentecostal Holiness Church (PHC), 134, 136–38

Pentecostalism, 126–48; African Americans in, 142–48; compared to fundamentalism, 110, 128; distinction from Holiness, 131; faith healers, 109, 129; Holy Spirit in, 128, 140; music of, 146, 148, 155–57, 165, 167; origins of, 126–27; politics in, 89–90; racial interchange in, 127–30; revivals, 130–34; second blessing, 127, 139; speaking in tongues in, 127, 131–32, 137–38, 140–42; theology of, 127–28; white denominations of, 141; women in, 147–48

Pentecostal music. *See* Music, Pentecostal; Worship practices, Pentecostal

"People Get Ready," 16

Persons, Carrie Booker, 151

Pierce, George F., 14

Pitt, Robert H., 82

"Please See My Grave Is Kept Clean," 162

Plessy v. Ferguson, 15

Polygeny, 43, 221

Poole, Lorena, 176

Popular music: religious roots of, 146, 158, 166

Populism, 49–53

Poteat, William Louis, 53–54

Powdermaker, Hortense, 122

"Prayer of Death," 162

"Preachin' the Blues," 159

"Precious Lord, Take My Hand," 163

Presbyterian Church of the United States, 20–21, 24, 28–29, 42, 58–59, 94–97, 212–13, 225–27

Presbyterian Standard, 58

Presley, Elvis, 158, 167

Pressler, Paul, 246–47

Pritchett, Carl, 236

Pritchett, Laurie, 174

Proctor, Henry Hugh, 59–60

Progressive Democratic Party, 91

Progressive Era, 54–66

Progressive Farmer, 52

Progressivism, southern Christian: African American, 48, 57–62; during Reconstruction, 54; goals of, 47–48, 53; paternalistic, 63–66, 79; racial divisions of, 55, 57, 56–57, 59–60, 62; support of prohibition, 55–56; violence in response to, 60, 61; women's, 55, 67–77

Prohibition, 55–56

Prophetic Religion, 100–101

Protestant Episcopal Church of Kentucky, 33

Providence, 38–39

Pruden, James Wesley, 236

Puckett, Newbell Niles, 122

Quakers, 50, 97

Rabun, Joseph, 236

Race purity, 43–44

Racial interchange: defined, 3

Racism: theology of, 41–44, 171, 192, 229–34

Radical, 36

Radicalism: among African Americans, 33–37, 89–92; Christian, 77–84, 92–106; during Reconstruction, 33–37; as expressed in civil rights movement, 203–

Vaughan's Family Visitor, 154

"Victory in Jesus," 155

Violence: against African American educators, 32, 37; Atlanta riot, 60–62; church bombings and burning, 170, 177, 185, 193–94; lynching, 44, 62, 84, 92, 98; segregationist defense of, 238; toward civil rights activists, 185, 190, 193–94

Visions in religious practice, 114, 120, 125

Voice of Missions, 10

Voter registration, 193, 196, 198

Wacker, Grant, 127

Waddell, Arthur, 6

Walker, Maggie Lena, 71

Walker, William ("Singing Billy"), 153

Wallace, Henry, 95, 106, 203

Warmoth, Henry Clay, 15

Washington, Booker T., 31

Washington, Jesse, 62

Washington, Margaret Murray, 59, 71

Watson, Thomas, 52

Watters, Pat, 172

Watts, Isaac, 151

The Way, 143

Weatherford, Willis D., 66–67

"We Shall Overcome," 105, 175

Wesley, John, 127

Wesley Community houses, 76

West, Don, 97, 104

Wheat Street Baptist Church (Atlanta, Ga.), 18, 72, 106

"When the Train Comes Along," 161

Whipple, George, 31

White, Benjamin Franklin, 153

White, Bernice, 123

White, Charley, 125, 147

White, John E., 56, 115

White, Walter, 62, 78

White, William Jefferson, 10, 18, 34

White Citizens' Council, 180, 232, 233, 237

White supremacy, 39–44, 48, 62–63; defined, 2. *See also* Racism; Theological racism

Whole Truth, 146

Willard, Frances, 69

Williams, Aubrey, 93

Williams, Claude, 97

Williams, Elbert, 90

Williams, Hank, 156

Williams, Smallwood, 90

Wilmington Daily Journal, 40

Wilmington massacre, 58

Wilson, Norvell Winsboro, 20

Winkler, E[dwin] T., 78

Woman's Christian Temperance Union (WCTU), 55

Woman's Convention, Auxiliary to the National Baptist Convention, 70–71, 74

Woman's Missionary Council, 76

Woman's Missionary Union, Auxiliary to the Southern Baptist Convention (WMU), 72–75, 248

Woman's Society of Christian Service, 86, 177, 240

Women: activism of, 70–75, 84–88; biracial cooperation of, 70, 74–77; church leadership of, 147–48; as church mothers, 125–26; civil rights activism of, 199–206; evangelical, 84–89; Methodist, 75–77, 84–88; in ministerial roles, 68–69; missionary societies of, 67–68, 70–77; in Pentecostalism, 147–48; prohibition activism of, 55–56, 68; Protestant, 67, 70; SBC views of, 219, 248; supportive of segregation, 243–44; Southern Baptist, 72–74; suffrage activism of, 69–70

Women's Committee of the Commission on Interracial Cooperation, 84

Women's Political Council (Montgomery, Ala.), 178–79

Worker, 75

Working Men's Club, 60

"Working on a Building," 156

Workmen's Chronicle, 61

World War II: energizing black activism, 90; intensifying racial conflicts, 92–93; introduction of music during, 158

Worship practices: African roots of, 117, 120–21, 125; condemnation of, 114–15, 119–20; conjure, 120–23; dancing, 118;